5G Radio Access Networks: Centralized RAN, Cloud-RAN, and Virtualization of Small Cells

5G Radio Access Networks: Centralized RAN, Cloud-RAN, and Virtualization of Small Cells

By

Hrishikesh Venkatarman and Ramona Trestian

CRC Press
Taylor & Francis Group
Boca Raton London New York

CRC Press is an imprint of the
Taylor & Francis Group, an **informa** business

CRC Press
Taylor & Francis Group
6000 Broken Sound Parkway NW, Suite 300
Boca Raton, FL 33487-2742

First issued in paperback 2020

© 2017 by Taylor & Francis Group, LLC
CRC Press is an imprint of Taylor & Francis Group, an Informa business

No claim to original U.S. Government works

ISBN 13: 978-0-367-57386-7 (pbk)
ISBN 13: 978-1-4987-4710-3 (hbk)

Library of Congress Cataloging-in-Publication Data

Names: Venkataraman, Hrishikesh, author. | Trestian, Ramona, 1983- author.
Title: 5G radio access networks : centralized RAN, cloud-RAN, and
virtualization of small cells / Hrishikesh Venkataraman and Ramona Trestian.
Description: Boca Raton : Taylor & Francis, CRC Press, 2017. | Includes
bibliographical references and index.
Identifiers: LCCN 2016039396| ISBN 9781498747103 (hardback : alk. paper) |
ISBN 9781315230870 (electronic)
Subjects: LCSH: Wireless LANs. | Cell phone systems. | Cloud computing.
Classification: LCC TK5105.78 .V46 2017 | DDC 621.3845/6--dc23
LC record available at https://lccn.loc.gov/2016039396

Visit the Taylor & Francis Web site at
http://www.taylorandfrancis.com

and the CRC Press Web site at
http://www.crcpress.com

Contents

Preface

In the ever-evolving telecommunication industry, smart mobile computing devices have become increasingly affordable and powerful, leading to a significant growth in the number of advanced mobile users and their bandwidth demands. According to Cisco, high-end devices such as smartphones, iPhones, netbooks, and laptops will account for 24.3 EB per month of data traffic by 2019. In order to achieve this, alternate solutions are required wherein traditional base stations can be replaced by more generic, simple, and small-sized nodes that can carry out minimal tasks such as radiofrequency operations, while moving other computationally intensive tasks such as resource allocation, baseband processing, and so on to a centralized location. In this context, a centralized or cloud radio access network (C-RAN) offers many advantages over a traditional radio access network and the architectural design and techniques offered by C-RAN make it a strong candidate to be incorporated into the 5G wireless network standard. C-RAN would enable joint scheduling and processing between multiple cells, which would eventually enable a collaborative radio environment. Notably, C-RAN would enable a seamless integration between multiple operators and a multiproduct vendor design. On similar lines, small cells have also been looked at, for moving the computation from the user terminal/device to the network; either to the small cell node itself or to the core network. In this regard, the functionality of small cells resembles that offered by the C-RAN. In fact, with the rapid development of network function virtualization (NFV) in the telecommunication world, communication service providers and product vendors have been looking to offer virtualized small cells.

Organization of the Book

Being at a very nascent stage, C-RAN and virtualized small cell technology poses several major research challenges. This book aims to provide a deeper insight into the next generation of RAN architecture; especially in the presence of virtualization and the cloud environment. The book will present a survey of the coexistence of software-defined networking (SDN), C-RAN, and small cell solutions proposed in the literature at different levels, for example, physical characteristics, open access, dynamic resource allocation, technology neutrality, coverage obligations, the minimization of interference problems, and so on.

The book is structured into two main sections. The first section on 5G RAN Architectures and Applications, describes the current challenges in the radio access network environment, which leads to the next generation of wireless networks. It includes important chapters written by researchers from prestigious laboratories in China, the Czech Republic, Germany, Spain, and the United Kingdom, which each present what is currently state of the art in the area of next-generation 5G networks, including possible architectures and solutions, performance evaluation and interference mitigation, resource allocation management, energy efficiency and cloud computing, and so on. The 5G RAN Architectures and Applications section consists of five chapters. The following offers a brief description of each of the chapters in this section:

Chapter 1 discusses a new kind of user-centric network architecture for the next generation of mobile systems (5G), referred to as a Frameless Network Architecture (FNA). The proposed FNA decomposes the functionality of the traditional base station into a centralized processing entity (CPE) and an antenna element (AE), such that the CPE will maintain the networking, implement the signal processing, handle the control plane and user place, manage the radio resources, and construct on-demand user-centric serving sets.

Chapter 2 identifies the need for a distributed architecture in 5G networks for efficient computation management in mobile edge computing. Importantly, it introduces two options for newly distributed deployments of the management unit. The chapter also discusses the integration of the proposed solution into 5G mobile networks based on C-RAN. Through an analysis and simulations of the proposed architectures, we prove that both signaling delay and signaling load could be significantly reduced compared with centralized solutions.

Chapter 3 provides a comprehensive survey of the latest developments and the use of nonorthogonal multiple access (NOMA) schemes for next-generation 5G networks. The survey first provides a comparison between orthogonal multiple access schemes and NOMA schemes, identifying the advantages and disadvantages of each of the technologies. The solutions offered by NOMA schemes for the uplink and downlink transmissions are discussed with an emphasis on the NOMA-based solutions for downlink transmissions.

Chapter 4 looks into the performance evaluation of a NOMA-based mechanism used within the wireless downlink cloud radio access network (WD-CRAN) environment. The mechanism makes use of successive interference cancellation (SIC) receivers in order to enhance the reception and to lay multiple base stations over each other in the power domain.

Chapter 5 begins with a detailed background and terminologies to set a common understanding of cloud computing, toward a flexible networking future. The chapter will detail future network clouds and the need for efficient frameworks for cloud management and control. Furthermore, the chapter will outline OpenStack in order to offer the reader the tools for experimenting.

The second section, entitled 5G RAN Virtualization Solutions, presents various solutions proposed by world-known researchers in different areas of software-defined networks and virtualization. It includes important chapters written by researchers from prestigious laboratories in Belgium, Germany, Greece, India, Italy, and the United Kingdom, presenting results in the areas of software-defined networks, mobility management, the Internet of things (IoT), sensor applications, and so on. The 5G RAN virtualization solutions section consists of six chapters; the following offers a brief description of each of these.

Chapter 6 discusses two enabling technologies for C-RAN that allow decoupling beyond baseband and radio, that is, SDN and NFV. Importantly, the pros and cons of these enabling technologies are thoroughly discussed.

Chapter 7 begins with an introduction on the need for SDN. The new SDN paradigm is then briefly explained and compared with traditional networks. Furthermore, following a bottom-up approach, an in-depth overview of SDN architecture is provided.

Chapter 8 is a detailed chapter that provides a comprehensive yet practical walkthrough for managing the mobility of next-generation wireless networks with SDN.

Chapter 9 provides a detailed description of self-x network management, beginning with autonomic and cognitive networking and then goes on to describe in detail the proposed next-generation self-configurable and self-optimized framework.

Chapter 10 discusses different distributed data aggregation mechanisms and compression techniques for the 5G virtual RAN IoT-based sensor applications. It shows the mechanism for combining a centralized C-RAN architecture for the mobile cloud and a cluster head–based architecture for the wireless sensor network. Also, it demonstrates the importance of their approach in two application domains—the *distributed aggregation of temperature measurements* and *distributed video coding of visual data* obtained with wireless visual sensors.

Chapter 11 explains the 5G C-RAN uplink cross-layer optimization mechanism to support massive traffic in sensor network services. Importantly, the chapter investigates and studies the planning difficulties and restrictions that are related to interference, throughput, accessibility, and uplink connectivity, proposing solutions and rules to be followed. Furthermore, it explains why C-RAN planners should fulfill the proposed recommendations when optimizing the 5G IoT's network performance.

The prospective audiences for this book are mainly undergraduate students, postgraduate students, and researchers who are interested in learning more about the latest developments in the areas of mobile and wireless communications. It also targets industry professionals who are working or are interested in this area, providing them with a reference to the latest efforts that advance the research further by addressing some of the shortcomings of the existing solutions.

The editors wish you a pleasant reading.

Hrishikesh Venkataraman
Indian Institute of Information Technology, India

Ramona Trestian
Middlesex University, United Kingdom

MATLAB® is a registered trademark of The MathWorks, Inc. For product information, please contact:

The MathWorks, Inc.
3 Apple Hill Drive
Natick, MA 01760-2098 USA
Tel: 508 647 7000
Fax: 508-647-7001
E-mail: info@mathworks.com
Web: www.mathworks.com

Acknowledgments

5G Radio Access Networks: Centralized RAN, Cloud-RAN, and Virtualization of Small Cells would not exist without the efforts of many people whose names may not appear on the cover of the book. However, their hard work, cooperation, friendship, and understanding were very important to the preparation and production of the book. The editors would like to sincerely thank the entire team at CRC Press for their support and help in the publication of this book. As in general, the work associated with the chapter review is underestimated and forgotten, the editors would like to thank the team of reviewers for the generous commitment of time and effort that they have put into the reviewing process and for providing their expertise to ensure a high-quality review process. Last but not least, the editors would like to thank their families for their continuous support along the way.

In particular, Hrishikesh Venkataraman would like to thank both of his parents for instilling a confidence in learning new topics and the ability to produce the learning in proper form to an audience. Also, he would like to thank his wife and his mother-in-law for their patience and dedication to other aspects of personal life while writing the chapters and editing this book. Importantly, he would like to thank his institution for their support for allowing him to focus on his research and allowing him to write/edit the book.

Furthermore, Ramona Trestian would like to thank her wonderful and loving parents, Maria and Vasile, for their unconditional love and care and for being an immense source of inspiration throughout her life. Her special gratitude goes toward her husband Kumar, for his immense love and continual patience and support, both of which were essential to this project, as well as toward her little bundle of joy, Noah Anthony, for making her life worth living.

Editors

Hrishikesh Venkataraman completed his M.Tech at the Indian Institute of Technology, Kanpur, from 2002 to 2004 and his PhD at Jacobs University, Bremen, Germany, from 2004 to 2007. He was a recipient of the Indo-German DAAD scholarship from 2003 to 2004 and was awarded an Irish national research fellowship from 2008 to 2010. From 2008 to 2013, he was a research fellow, and subsequently, principal investigator (PI) with the Irish national research center, the RINCE Institute, at Dublin City University, Ireland. During this period, he also served as project manager for two research projects at RINCE, funded by Everseen Limited and Ericsson Research, Ireland. In 2013, Dr. Venkataraman returned to India and worked as a technical architect in the Chief Technology Office of Network Technology Unit of Tech Mahindra for two years. Here, he was involved in developing algorithms, building solutions, and made a contribution to ETSI-based consortium in the area of virtualization.

From May 2015 onwards, Dr. Venkataraman has been a professor at Indian Institute of Information Technology, Chittoor, Sricity, leading the vehicular and wireless communication research theme. He is the institute nodal officer for national knowledge networks and also serves as the faculty-in-charge for networks, servers, and information systems. Furthermore, he has filed 2 patents, has more than 50 international publications in different journals of IEEE, ACM, and Springer, and international conferences, including 2 best paper awards; and served as editor of *Transactions on Emerging Telecommunication Technologies*; for 5 years, from April 2011–2016. Also, he has edited two books published by CRC Press and Springer.

Ramona Trestian received her BEng degree in telecommunications from the Electronics, Telecommunications, and Technology of Information Department, Technical University of Cluj-Napoca, Romania in 2007, and her PhD degree from the School of Electronic Engineering, Dublin City University, Dublin, Ireland in 2012 for her research in adaptive multimedia systems and network selection mechanisms. She worked with IBM Research, Dublin as an IBM/IRCSET exascale postdoctoral researcher, from December 2011 to August 2013. She is currently a senior lecturer with the Design Engineering and Mathematics Department, School of Science and Technology, Middlesex University, London, UK. She has published in prestigious international conferences and journals and has edited two books. Her research interests include mobile and wireless communications, multimedia streaming, handover and network selection strategies, and software-defined networks. She is a reviewer for international journals and conferences and a member of the IEEE Young Professionals, IEEE Communications Society, and IEEE Broadcast Technology Society.

Contributors

Giuseppe Araniti is an assistant professor of telecommunications at the University Mediterranea of Reggio Calabria, Italy. From the same university he received his Laureate (2000) and his PhD degree (2004) in electronic engineering. His major area of research includes personal communications systems, enhanced wireless and satellite systems, traffic and radio resource management, multicast and broadcast services, device-to-device and machine-type communications over 4G/5G cellular networks.

Zdenek Becvar received his MSc and PhD in telecommunication engineering from the Czech Technical University in Prague, Czech Republic, in 2005 and 2010, respectively. From 2006 to 2007, he joined Sitronics R&D center in Prague focusing on speech quality in voice-over IP (VoIP). Furthermore, he was involved in the research activities of the Vodafone R&D center at Czech Technical University in Prague in 2009. He was an intern at the Budapest Polytechnic, Hungary (2007), CEA-Leti, France (2013), and EURECOM, France (2016). Now, he is an associate professor at the Department of Telecommunication Engineering, Czech Technical University in Prague, Czech Republic. He has participated in several European and national research projects focused on mobile networks. In 2013, he became a representative of the Czech Technical University in Prague in ETSI and 3GPP standardization organizations. He is a member of more than 15 program committees at international conferences or workshops and he has published 3 book chapters and more than 60 conference or journal papers. He acts as a reviewer for many prestigious journals including journals published by IEEE, Wiley, Elsevier, and Springer. He works on the development of solutions for future mobile networks (5G and beyond) with a special focus on the optimization of radio resource management and mobility support, self-optimization, the architecture of radio access networks, and small cells.

Namadev Bhuvanasundaram received his MSc degree in telecommunications engineering from Middlesex University, London, UK, in 2012 and his BEng in electrical, electronics, and communications engineering from Pondicherry University, Puducherry, India, in 2009. His research interests include mobile and wireless communications, multiple-input multiple-output systems, and multiple access technologies for next-generation networks.

Massimo Condoluci is currently a postdoctoral research associate at the Center for Telecommunications Research, Department of Informatics, King's College London, UK. He received his MSc degree in telecommunications engineering and his PhD in information technology in 2011 and 2016, respectively, from the University Mediterranea of Reggio Calabria, Italy. His main current research interests include softwarization, virtualization, mobility management, and group-oriented and machine-type communications over 5G systems.

Xuan Thuy Dang received his diploma in computer sciences from the Technical University, Berlin, Germany, in 2013. Since then, he has been a research associate at the German-Turkish Advanced Research Centre for information communication technology and a PhD candidate in the future mobile network at DAI-Labor/TU-Berlin. His main research interests include (1) software-defined networking, (2) cloud computing, (3) service-aware agile networks, (4) mobile ad hoc, delay-tolerant, and information-centric networking.

Nikos Deligiannis is an assistant professor with the Electronics and Informatics Department at Vrije Universiteit Brussel (VUB) and principal investigator in data science at the iMinds Institute in Belgium. He is also the codirector of the VUB-Duke-UCL joint lab on big data, together with M. Rodrigues (University College London, UK) and R. Calderbank (Duke University, USA) and the vice director of the Master of Applied Computer Science program at Vrije Universiteit Brussel.

He received a diploma in electrical and computer engineering from the University of Patras, Greece, in 2006, and his PhD in applied sciences (awarded with highest honors and congratulations from the jury) from Vrije Universiteit Brussel, Belgium, in 2012. His research interests include big data mining, processing and analysis, compressed sensing, Internet of things networking, and distributed processing. Professor Deligiannis has authored over 75 journal and conference publications, book chapters, and he holds one US patent (promoted by BAFTA, UK). He was the recipient of the 2011 ACM/IEEE International Conference on Distributed Smart Cameras Best Paper Award and the 2013 Scientific Prize, IBM, Belgium. Professor Deligiannis is a member of the IEEE. From July to September 2013, Professor Deligiannis was the external advisor to the Greek prime minister's cabinet, responsible for consultation on the integration of the Internet of things and big data technologies in the Greek public sector. From October 2013 to February 2015, he was a senior researcher at the Department of Electronic and Electrical Engineering at University College London, UK, and a technical consultant on big visual data technologies at the British Academy of Film and Television Arts (BAFTA), UK. Professor Deligiannis has been consulting companies and startups operating in the area of big data analytics for smart cities.

Manzoor Ahmed Khan received his PhD degree in computer science from the Technical University, Berlin, Germany, in December 2011. Since 2011, he has served as a senior researcher and the vice director of the Competence Center, Network and Mobility at DAI-Labor. He has served in the deployment and optimization departments of a major mobile operator in Pakistan. His main research interests include (i) software-defined networking; (ii) cloud computing; (iii) learning in agent-based autonomic networking; (iv) experimental research focusing on various use cases of long-term evolution (LTE), network virtualization, 5G vision, and LTE protocols and operations; (v) user-centric network selection, resource allocation, and the quality of experience (QoE) in future wireless networks and in distributed cloud computing systems. He received a gold medal and a silver medal for securing highest marks (first position) in his batch for his master's and bachelor's degrees, respectively. He was also the recipient of several best paper awards. Dr. Khan is the author of several scientific publications including conference papers, journal articles, and book chapters.

Joanna Kusznier received her diploma in economics from Humboldt University in Berlin, Germany, in 2013. Her main research interests include cloud computing, autonomous learning, and robotics.

Jiaxiang Liu is currently pursuing his master's degree at the Beijing University of Posts and Telecommunications, China. His current research interests include cache-enabled networks and software-defined networks for 5G.

Felicia Lobillo received an MSc degree in telecommunication engineering from the University of Seville in 1998. She has been involved in system integration projects for telecommunication operators for more than 12 years, which have provided her with a deep knowledge of business support systems in the telecommunications sector and how to implement technology solutions to meet business requirements. She participated in European research and development projects for 4 years in the scope of future networks, dealing with cutting-edge technologies including small cells, the cloud, big data or SDN, and NFV for 5G. During this time, she acquired an overview of the main technology trends that will drive the IT and telecommunication market in the near future. In November 2015, she joined the Business Intelligence and Analytics team in Atos Iberia, where she is focused on developing business opportunities for Atos around big data and analytics.

Spyridon Louvros is assistant professor in the Computer & Informatics Engineering Department, Supreme Technological & Educational Institute of Western Greece in Patras, Greece. He has offered, for more than 10 years, R&D consultancy and training services in Teledrom *aktiebolag* (AB), an official subcontractor for Ericsson AB. He is also one of the founders of Mobile Cloud and Network Services (MCNS), Cyprus, a telecommunication and cloud services company offering expertise services in big data analysis and models as well as mobile network planning and optimizing. He graduated from the Physics Department, University of Crete, with a specialization (minor field) in applied physics, microelectronics, and lasers. He engaged in postgraduate studies (MSc) in the United Kingdom, Department of Electronic System Design, RF Design & Telecommunications Section of Aviation Electronics, School of Aeronautics & Aerospace Engineering, the University of Cranfield, UK. During his studies, he was awarded a 2-year full scholarship from the Alexandros Onassis Foundation for Postgraduate Studies in Western Europe due to academic excellence. In 2004, he received his PhD diploma from the Signal Processing Laboratory, Section of Electronics & Information Technology, Physics Department, University of Patras, Greece. Dr. Louvros has worked as microwave planning and optimizing engineer in Siemens TELE S.A., and a senior switching engineer in Vodafon Hellas S.A. for the Network Operational & Maintenance Department. He joined Cosmote Cellular Technologies S.A. as a section manager for network statistics and a quality assurance engineer. Dr. Louvros is well experienced in statistical analysis and key performance indicators (KPIs) for live networks and has offered consultancy services in several projects aimed at developing real-time monitoring solutions and expert data–based systems for automatic problem solving. He has participated in national and international research projects and his research interests focus on wireless communications, mobile network and big data analysis and performance, mobile network capacity planning and dimensioning, applied algebraic topology in telecommunication networks, 5G technologies with emphasis on C-RAN and wireless optical communication technologies (LiFi). He holds 75 papers for international conferences and journals, as well as 12 book chapters in international publication, his papers have been cited (more than 100 citations) by international researchers, and he is an active reviewer for international journals. He is a member of the IEEE Society, Hellenic IEEE Communications Chapter, Physics Hellenic Union.

Pavel Mach received his MSc and PhD degrees in telecommunication engineering from the Czech Technical University in Prague, Czech Republic, in 2006 and 2010, respectively.

During his study, he joined research groups at Sintronics and Vodafone R&D centers focusing on wireless mobile technologies. He is a member of more than 15 program committees of international conferences. He has published more than 50 papers in international journals and conferences. He has been actively involved in several national and international projects. He participated in several projects founded by the European Commission. His research interests include cognitive radio, device-to-device communication, and mobile edge computing. He is dealing with aspects relating to radio resource management, such as mobility management, radio resource allocation, and power control in emerging wireless technologies.

Toktam Mahmoodi is currently a lecturer in telecommunications at the Department of Informatics, King's College London. She was a visiting research scientist with F5 Networks, in San Jose, CA, in 2013, a postdoctoral research associate in the intelligent systems and networks research group at the Electrical and Electronic Engineering Department of Imperial College during 2010 and 2011, and a Mobile Virtual Center of Excellence researcher from 2006 to 2009. She worked on European FP7 and EPSRC projects aiming to push the boundaries of next-generation mobile communications forward. She also worked in the mobile and personal communications industry, from 2002 to 2006, and in an R&D team on developing digital enhanced cordless telecommunication standards for wireless local loop applications. She has a BSc degree in electrical engineering from Sharif University of Technology, Iran, and a PhD degree in telecommunications from King's College London, UK.

Huan X. Nguyen received his BSc degree at the Hanoi University of Science and Technology (Vietnam) in 2000. He then pursued his PhD at the University of New South Wales (Australia) during 2003–2006. He has since worked in various posts for several universities in the UK. He is currently a senior lecturer at the School of Science and Technology, Middlesex University (London, UK). His research interests include physical layer security, energy harvesting, multiple-input multiple-output techniques, network coding, relay communication, cognitive radio, and multicarrier systems. Dr Nguyen is a senior member of the IEEE. He is currently serving as editor of the *KSII Transactions on Internet and Information Systems*.

Ngozi Ogbonna received her MSc degree in telecommunications engineering from Middlesex University, London, UK, in 2014 and her BEng from Federal University of Technology Owerri, Nigeria, in 2011. She is currently working as a research and development officer for Concept Nova, Lagos, Nigeria. Her research interests include mobile and wireless communications, cloud radio access networks, and the Internet of things.

Miguel A. Puente received his MSc in telecommunications engineering from the Universidad Politécnica de Madrid (UPM) in 2012. In this period, he also completed an information technology masters' degree at the University of Stuttgart (2010–2012). Since 2012, he has been with Atos Research & Innovation (Spain), where he is involved in European research projects addressing 5G, LTE, cloud computing, mobile cloud/edge computing, QoE/QoS optimization and recursive Internet among other topics. Particularly within the European project TROPIC, he has worked on architectural enhancements of LTE mobile networks to cope with computationally enabled base stations for mobile cloud computing, and cloud orchestration and virtual infrastructure management for mobile edge computing. Since 2014, he has been a PhD candidate at UPM.

Matej Rohlik received his MSc and PhD degrees from the Czech Technical University in Prague, Czech Republic, in 2008 and 2012, respectively. His research addresses cybersecurity topics with a focus on the security of the next-generation mobile networks and sensor networks. From 2008 to 2015, he was actively involved in international FP7 projects funded by the European Commission (such as FREEDOM and TROPIC), national projects (funded by the Ministry of the Interior of the Czech Republic and the National Security Authority of the Czech Republic), and contributed to 3rd generation partnership project standardization. From 2014 to 2015, he coordinated the International Telecommunication Union Center of Excellence for Cybersecurity at the Colorado Technical University. He is an innovative, diligent, and highly organized cybersecurity expert with more than 10 years of professional experience in the design, implementation, and management of top-notch, compliant, and cost-effective solutions for global clients spread across the Asia-Pacific, Europe, Middle East, and Africa, and American regions. He has been awarded with internationally recognized certifications, such as the Certified Information Systems Security Professional, Cisco Certified Network Professional, Cisco Certified Design Professional, Cisco Certified Network Associate, and the Security and Cisco Cyber Security Specialist certificates.

Purav Shah is a senior lecturer in the School of Science and Technology at Middlesex University, London. He received his PhD in communication and electronics engineering from the University of Plymouth, UK, in 2008. He worked as an associate research fellow at the University of Exeter on the EU-FP6 PROTEM project on scanning probe-based memories from 2008 to 2010. His work included read channel design, noise modeling, and signal processing for probe storage. His research interests are broadly in the field of the performance evaluation of wireless sensor networks (protocols, routing, and energy efficiency), the Internet of things, and M2M solutions, system modeling of heterogeneous wireless networks, and intelligent transportation systems. He is an active member of the IEEE and a reviewer of the *IET Electronics Letters*, *IEEE Transactions on Circuits and Systems for Video Coding*, *KSII Transactions on Internet and Information Systems*, *MDPI Sensors and International Journal on Communication Systems*, Wiley, and *Computer Networks*, Elsevier.

Bolagala Sravya is an undergraduate honors student of computer science at the Indian Institute of Information Technology, focusing on information security and networking. She is in the top 5% of the students in her institute and will be graduating in July 2017.

Zhao Sun is currently pursuing his PhD degree in Beijing University of Posts and Telecommunications, China. He has 5 years of research experience in the area of mobile communication. His current research interests mainly include mobility management in heterogeneous networks and evolved network architecture for 5G.

Tomas Vanek received his MSc and PhD in telecommunication engineering from the Czech Technical University in Prague, Czech Republic, in 2000 and 2008, respectively. He has participated in several European and national research projects focused on security and mobile networks. In 2013, he was an intern at Universidad de Costa Rica. He is currently an assistant professor at the Department of Telecommunication Engineering, Czech Technical University in Prague, Czech Republic. He has published more than 20 conference or journal papers. Since 2014, he has been working as an ICT security consultant in a privately held company with a focus on public key infrastructure systems and authentication processes. He participates in the development of security solutions for next-generation mobile networks and IoT networks with a special focus on the security of over-the-air update processes.

Quoc-Tuan Vien received his BSc (Hons) degree from Ho Chi Minh City University of Technology, Vietnam, in 2005; his MSc degree from Kyung Hee University, South Korea, in 2009; and his PhD degree from Glasgow Caledonian University, UK, in 2012, all in telecommunications. From 2005 to 2007, he was with Fujikura Fiber Optics Vietnam Company, Binh Duong, Vietnam, as a production system engineer. From 2010 to 2012, he worked as a research and teaching assistant with the School of Engineering and Built Environment, Glasgow Caledonian University. In spring 2013, he worked as a postdoctoral research assistant with the School of Science and Technology, Nottingham Trent University, Nottingham, UK. He is currently a lecturer in computing and communications engineering with the School of Science and Technology, Middlesex University, London, UK. His research interests include multiple-input-multiple-output, space–time coding, network coding, physical layer security, cross-layer design and optimization, relay networks, cognitive radio networks, heterogeneous networks, and cloud radio access networks. Dr. Vien is a senior member of the IEEE, a member of the Institution of Engineering and Technology, and a fellow of the Higher Education Authority. He is an author of a book, a leading author of 38 papers, and a coauthor of 19 papers published at major conferences and Institute for Scientific Information journals. He is an editor of the *International Journal of Big Data Security Intelligence* since 2015, an associate editor of the *International Journal of Computing and Digital Systems* since 2015, a technical symposium co-chair for the IEEE International Conference on Emerging Technologies and Innovative Business for the Transformation of Societies (EmergiTech 2016) and the International Conference on Recent Advances in Signal Processing, Telecommunications and Computing (SigTelCom 2017), a session chair of the IEEE VTC Spring Conference in 2016, the IEEEWCNC and ISWCS Conferences in 2015, and the IEEE VTC Fall Conference in 2014, and a technical program committee member and reviewer of more than 50 conferences and journals since 2011.

Michal Vondra received his BSc degree in electronics and telecommunication engineering and his MSc degree in telecommunication engineering and radioelectronics from Czech Technical University in Prague, in 2008 and 2010, respectively. In 2015, he received his PhD degree in telecommunication engineering from the Czech Technical University in Prague. His thesis, the "Allocation of Resources in Network with Small Cells," earned the Dean's Award for prestigious dissertation thesis. Since 2010, he has continuously participated in FP7 projects founded by the European Commission (FREEDOM, TROPIC) and also in several national projects. From January to June 2014, he was an intern at the Performance Engineering Laboratory at University College Dublin, Ireland, where he cooperated on project TRAFFIC. Currently, he is a visiting researcher at Wireless@KTH where he is cooperating on the Instruments to Remove Confiscated Asset Recovery Obstacles project. He has published more than 15 conference papers, journal papers, and book chapters. His research interests include mobility management in wireless networks and vehicular ad hoc networks, intelligent transportation systems, and direct air-to-ground communication.

Xiaodong Xu received his PhD degrees from Beijing University of Posts and Telecommunications (BUPT), China, in 2007. He is currently an associate professor at BUPT. From January 2014 to January 2015, he worked as a guest researcher at Chalmers University of Technology, Sweden. His research interests cover radio access network architecture, radio resource management, wireless network virtualization, and interference management.

5G RAN ARCHITECTURES AND APPLICATIONS

Chapter 1

Frameless Network Architecture for User-Centric 5G Radio Access Networks

Xiaodong Xu, Zhao Sun, and Jiaxiang Liu

Contents

The system capacity for future mobile communication needs to be increased to fulfill the emerging requirements of mobile services and innumerable applications. For a long time, the cellular network topology and networking strategies have been regarded as the most promising way to provide the required capacity increase. However, with the emerging densification of cell deployments, the traditional cellular structure limits resource efficiency, and the coordination between different types of base stations is more complicated and entails heavy cost.

Consequently, this chapter discusses a new kind of user-centric network architecture for the 5th generation mobile system (5G), known as *frameless network architecture* (FNA). As there have been several studies on the network architectural evolution required for 5G, we first make a general introduction about current work.

For FNA, by decomposing the traditional Base Station (BS) into a Centralized Processing Entity (CPE) and Antenna Element (AE), the Radio Access Network (RAN) of FNA consists of two new network elements. The function of the CPE is to maintain the networking, implement the signal processing, handle the Control Plane (CP) and User Plane (UP), manage the radio resources including the connected AEs, and construct an on-demand user-centric serving set for specific users. The AEs are selected to construct a serving set for the specific user according to its quality of service (QoS) requirement.

Based on FNA, each user is always focused as being the coverage center of the serving AE set, which means that the cell boundary or the traditional cellular structure will no longer exist. The CP and UP are separated based on the FNA. The designated controlling AE implements the function of the CPE, which is handling and maintaining the control plane. The Data-AEs maintain their own User Plane under the control of Controlling-AEs.

In addition, based on FNA, the Control Plane and User Plane adaptation strategy is discussed in this chapter to improve the system Energy Efficiency (EE). A three-step system EE optimization with constraints on the CP/UP adaptation is given. We optimize the system EE via CP and UP construction and adaptation while guaranteeing the user QoS. The system-level simulation results show that, with constraints on the QoS of the users, the system EE performances are improved.

Finally, in order to further improve resource efficiency, especially the AE usage efficiency in the coordination-based user-centric RAN, we discuss the routing strategy in FNA. Based on the decoupling of CP and UP, the network virtualization is explored through Software Defined Network (SDN) approaches. We virtualize the wireless resources into a shared Resource Pool. In the User Plane, we use the *flow* to support different service slices. There can be multiple coordinated flows selected to meet the requirement of central user–specific QoS. In the Control Plane, we maintain an access route table to support the flow-selecting strategy. By choosing a flexible and appropriate routing strategy, we can prevent performance degradation due to the randomness and variance of mobile channels. Through this approach, relatively more stable services can be provided to users and the resource efficiency can be improved. On the aspect of routing algorithms, with reference to the wireless mesh network routing algorithms, we define a utility function–based routing selection algorithm, which achieves better performance.

Those highlighted aspects discussed in this chapter within FNA depict the way forward for the user-centric RAN of the 5G evolution. It is believed that, with the breakthroughs of the fundamental cellular network architecture, the future mobile network will surely have new performance improvements.

1.1 Related Works

Currently, mobile Internet applications and versatile mobile services are affecting every aspect of our daily life. Specifically, the dramatic increase in data traffic poses a great challenge to the network capacity and forces the mobile operators to make revolutionary changes. Besides expanding the spectrum and improving radio transmission, the mobile network architecture is considered as another potential way of further increasing the capacity of the 5G system [1,2].

Along with the evolutionary efforts for the 5G system, the cellular network topology and modeling are faced with urgent requirements for further evolution. The traditional hexagonal grid cellular network topology is believed not to be suited to centralized processing but rather to distributed deployments of RAN architecture [1], featuring as multi-tier Heterogeneous Networks (HetNet), ultra-dense small cells, and user-centric service-providing environments. The evolved network architecture should accommodate the separation of the central control entity and a large amount of distributed remote antenna elements. The BS and user association should also be evolved for on-demand service provision for users with specific QoS requirements, which are typical user-centric requirements. Moreover, an accurate depiction of the network topology modeling needs to be found for future network deployments, which will provide the operators with instructions for future network planning and optimization.

Focusing on the aforementioned requirements, there has been some research on OpenRAN, Soft Cell, and C-RAN [3–5]. The authors of [3] propose a software-defined RAN architecture, which is implemented through virtualization. For the Soft Cell concept proposed in [4], the transparent sets of BSs are provided for users. Based on the baseband pool, China Mobile Research Institute proposes C-RAN with features such as a centralized baseband unit, coordination, and cloud computing [5]. In order to solve the key challenges with regard to the way forward for C-RAN, much attention has been paid to evolved network architectures and promising key technologies [6–10]. To overcome the disadvantages of C-RANs with fronthaul constraints, heterogeneous cloud radio access networks (H-CRANs) have been proposed in [6] as a cost-effective potential solution to alleviate intertier interference and improve cooperative processing gains in HetNets in combination with cloud computing. While in [7], a fog computing–based radio access network (F-RAN) is presented, which can take full advantage of local radio signal processing, cooperative radio resource management, and the distributed storing capabilities in edge devices. These features could effectively decrease the heavy burden on fronthaul and avoid large-scale radio signal processing in the centralized baseband unit pool. In addition, some key technologies for C-RAN and H-CRAN have been proposed, including remote radio head (RRH) association strategies, inter-tier interference cancellation, and the performance optimization of a constrained fronthaul. In [8], the single nearest and N-nearest RRH association strategies are presented. Closed-form expressions for the ergodic capacity of the proposed RRH association strategies are also derived. Lately, in [9], a contract-based interference coordination framework is proposed to mitigate the inter-tier interference between RRHs and macro BSs in H-CRANs. A hybrid coordinated multipoint transmission scheme is designed for the downlink scenario of C-RAN in [10], which fulfills flexible tradeoffs between cooperation gains and fronthaul constraints.

1.2 FNA for User-Centric Radio Access Networks

Apart from the promising evolved RAN architecture mentioned in Section 1.1, the FNA was proposed lately as an evolved user-centric architecture for the radio access network of 5G, which aims to provide a set of concepts and principles to guide the development of the centralized processing network architecture and the topology for RAN evolution [11–13]. The evolved implementation scenario of FNA is shown in Figure 1.1, including the Core Network (CN), RAN deployments, and serving User Equipment (UE).

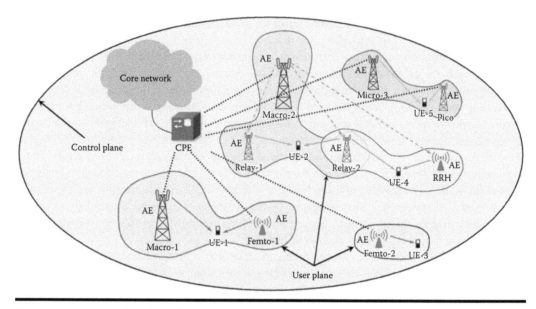

Figure 1.1   FNA with typical deployment scenarios.

The RAN of FNA consists of two main network elements. By decomposing the traditional BS into CPE and AE, FNA develops in an evolved manner. The main functions of the CPE are to maintain networking strategy, implement the signal processing, handle the CP and UP, manage all of the radio resources including the connected AEs, cope with the mobility management, and construct the on-demand user-centric service-providing environments. The CPE can be located with a macro BS or any other kinds of BSs that have the required processing ability, by which the CPE mainly functions as a logical node.

The AE is responsible for the radio signal transmission/reception. The backhaul links between the CPE and AE could be the optical fiber, wireless backhaul, wired connections, or other kinds of links. The capacity and latency features for different types of backhaul links are different, which will also be included in the consideration of resource allocations.

The AEs are selected to construct a serving set for the specific user according to its QoS requirement, which also forms the UP for the above user. The serving set may contain one or several AEs. The AE can also be a single antenna or an antenna array. According to the different transmission power limitations of their radio frequency (RF) abilities, the AEs are classified into several types that have different coverage abilities, such as the Macro AE, Micro AE, Pico AE, Femto AE, RRH AE, and so on. The AE in the serving set can also be different types, with coordination techniques supported between AEs and CPEs to provide a more flexible construction of the serving set for the specific users.

As shown in Figure 1.1, there are Macro, Pico, Femto, Relay and RRH AEs that are deployed as an underlay Scenario. UE-1 is served with a coordinated transmission mode with AEs Macro-1 and Femto-1 as the corresponding serving set according to the UE-1 QoS requirement. UE-2 is served by AEs Macro-2, Relay-1, and Relay-2. Femto-2 serves the UE-3 as the only corresponding AE. The AE Relay-2 in the serving set for UE-4 is the common node for the serving set of UE-2. For the UE-5, the AEs Micro-3 and Pico AE construct the serving set. The coordinated transmission scheme can be joint processing schemes based on the CoMP [14,15] or enhanced coordinated transmission schemes with precoding techniques applied in the transmission nodes.

The coverage area for the serving set of each UE will be amorphous because of the dynamically adaptive updated serving-set construction.

In FNA, the coordinated transmission is managed by one CPE with an arbitrary deployment of AEs within the coverage area. Similar to the phantom cells [16,17], the CP and UP are separated based on the FNA. The designated Controlling-AE implements the function of the CPE, which is handling and maintaining the Control Plane. The Data-AEs maintain their own User Plane under the control of Controlling-AEs. The Data-AEs distributed within the coverage area of a Controlling-AE are supposed to be managed by the Controlling-AE through the CPE.

According to the FNA deployments, network topology modeling will be the most fundamental research topic. For the network topology modeling, the traditional single-tier hexagonal grid network deployment model has been implemented for a long time. But with increasing deployments of HetNet and small cells, the multi-tier and ultra-dense HetNet topology cannot be depicted by the traditional hexagonal grids. The actual locations of the small cell BSs inside the future network will be more randomized, especially when the femtocells are randomly deployed in the network and the user can also have the ability to determine the ON/OFF state of their femtocells. The stochastic geometry method with the Poisson point process (PPP) model has been proposed for the aforementioned network topology [18,19], which provides good tractability for multi-tier HetNet and ultra-dense small cell deployments. The system outage capacity, mobility management, and interference management can be analyzed with closed-form solutions for many scenarios, which provide valuable theoretical instructions for the actual network planning and performance analyses.

But with more and more research focused on the PPP model, there are also some limitations found with the PPP model and the most important problem lies in the random features of the PPP. There is not a state of complete independency for the intratier and even intertier BS deployments in the actual network, which are the typical characters of field network planning and optimization. The PPP model is conservative because it deploys the BSs arbitrarily close to each other, which limits its suitability for the actual network. Recently, another model, Ginibre point process (GPP) has been proposed for depicting the multitier ultra-dense HetNet deployment topology with supporting the repulsion for deploying the BSs [20], which will be a promising tool for network topology modeling. Although the research about the GPP model is just beginning, the key challenges for RAN evolution in terms of its network topology and modeling are believed to have more breakthroughs based on deeper research about the FNA topology and Stochastic Geometry approaches. Further theoretical support will also be expected to be achieved for the centralized processing but distributed deployment architecture of 5G user-centric networks.

1.3 Energy-Efficient Control Plane and User Plane Adaptation

As described in Section 1.1, CP/UP separation and adaption is one of the most significant features of FNA. In this section, we will give the CP/UP adaptation scheme for improving the system EE performance in the downlink scenario of the FNA networks. A three-step EE optimization process is designed as follows.

1.3.1 CP Construction and Adaptation with Voronoi Diagram

As depicted in Section 1.1, there is a master–slave relationship between the controlling AE and the data AE. To quantify the relationship, we focus on a simplified scenario that includes a single Controlling-AE and multiple related Data-AEs. For notational simplicity, the controlling AE is denoted as AE_0 while the data AEs are denoted as AEi ($i=1$, ..., N). We denote P_i as the maximum transmission power of the ith AE, p_c, p_0 as the allocated transmission power for the CP and UP of the controlling AE, which satisfy the constraints that $p_c \leq P_0$, $p_0 \leq P_0$. For the Data-AE, the constraints should be $p_i \leq P_i$ ($i=1$, ..., N), where p_i denotes the allocated transmission power of the ith data AE for the UP. Since the CP transmits the necessary signaling for the UP, additional coverage constraints should be made for the UP. That is, the whole coverage of all the UPs constructed by the data AEs should not surpass the coverage of the CP. Then, this constraint can be transformed as the coverage radius of data AE:

$$d_i + r_i \leq r_0 \tag{1.1}$$

where:

d_i is the distance between the controlling AE and ith data AE
r_i is the coverage radius of the ith data AE
r_0 is the coverage radius of the controlling AE

The coverage radius of the ith data AE r_i is actually determined by its transmission power p_i, while the coverage radius of the controlling AE r_0 is determined by its CP transmission power p_c. Then, Equation 1.1 can be further transformed into a power constraint of the ith data AE:

$$p_i \leq p_c - P(d_i), i \in \{1, ..., N\} \tag{1.2}$$

where $P(d_i)$ is the power attenuation from the ith data AE to the controlling AE. The power constraint just given still guarantees that the coverage of the UPs doesn't surpass the CP coverage, which will be used in the UP construction step of Section 1.3.2.

In order to formulate the constraints mentioned in the preceding paragraphs, a basic signal propagation model capturing pathloss as well as shadowing is defined as [21]

$$P_{rx} = K \left(\frac{r}{r_0} \right)^{-\alpha} \cdot \varphi \cdot P_{tx} \tag{1.3}$$

where:

P_{rx} is the receiving power
P_{tx} is the transmission power
r is the propagation distance
α is the pathloss exponent

The random variable φ is used to model slow-fading effects and commonly follows a log-normal distribution. K is set to the free-space path gain at distance r_0 with the assumption of omnidirectional antennas. Here, the coverage is defined as the maximum coverage range, which satisfies the UE's minimum required received power P_{min}. The effect of shadowing will be averaged out for the network planning of the CP's construction and adaptation. The coverage radius can be expressed as $r_i = r_0 \sqrt[\alpha]{K P_i / P_{min}}$.

In order to achieve EE optimization for CP/UP adaptation, the first step aims at constructing a seamless deployment of the CP with minimum transmission power. The Voronoi diagram, a geometric structure in computational geometry, divides the space into a number of regions consisting of all the points closer to a specific site than to any other. As energy consumption is proportional to distance, the Voronoi diagram also defines regions where less energy consumption is required. In order to achieve better EE in the CP's construction and adaptation, we construct a Voronoi coverage area for the Controlling-AEs. The Data-AEs located within the Voronoi coverage area are controlled by the corresponding Controlling-AE.

The CP construction can be well represented by Figure 1.2, in which a Voronoi tessellation is created by the deployment of Controlling-AEs. Assuming that C represents the set of n controlling AEs in 2D Euclidean space, $d_E(c_i, x)$ denotes the Euclidean distance between the ith controlling AE and a position x. Therefore, the Voronoi coverage of the ith controlling AE is defined as

$$Vor(c_i) = \left\{ x \in R^2 \parallel \forall j \neq i, d_E\left(c_j, x\right) \right\} \tag{1.4}$$

In order to further adapt the transmission power of a controlling AE with an updated AE deployment or coverage area, the Voronoi coverage can be redefined based on the path loss between the controlling AE and point x. Let $\alpha(c_i, x)_t$ be the path loss between the ith controlling AE and the position x at time slot t, the Voronoi coverage will be revised as

$$Vor(c_i)_t = \left\{ x \in R^2 \parallel \forall j \neq i, \alpha\left(c_i, x\right)_t < \alpha\left(c_j, x\right)_t \right\} \tag{1.5}$$

Then, the whole CP can be formed in the expression as $U_{1 \leq i < n} Vor(c_i)$. This definition makes any position in the Voronoi coverage area closer to its Voronoi Controlling-AE than any others, which yields less power consumption. As a consequence, the required transmission power for the controlling AE is minimized. The simulation evaluation of the proposed CP construction and adaptation can be found in Section 1.3.4.

1.3.2 User-Centric UP Construction with Joint AE and Subchannel Allocation

The initial deployment of the UP should be constructed right after the CP construction and each user should be allocated available system resources with the user's QoS requirement. Based

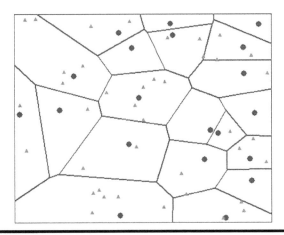

Figure 1.2 Voronoi tessellation of the CP construction. (Spots represent the locations of the controlling AEs and triangles are data AEs.)

on FNA, AE is released as a new dimensional radio resource for allocation and scheduling. By jointly allocating the AE and subchannel resources, the on-demand user-centric UP is constructed with the user's QoS requirements. The AE's transmission powers are allocated equally in this step. Moreover, the transmission power will be further adjusted based on Game theory in the third step.

1.3.2.1 Joint Resource Allocation Model for UP Construction

Considering a network with two types of Data-AEs, i.e., the Macro AE and Small cell AE, each AE has the same bandwidth and is divided into M subchannels. We set P_i as the maximum transmission power of the ith data AE. Meanwhile, K users are randomly distributed in the coverage area of the FNA, including K_1 users with guaranteed bit rate (GBR) service and K_2 users with non-GBR service. The space division multiple access scenario is considered, in which each subchannel of an AE can only be allocated to one user.

In order to quantify the different QoS requirements of users, the utility theory in economics is introduced to describe the characteristics of service by mapping the data rate to the user satisfaction level [22]. According to the user service QoS constraints, the utility functions of the GBR and non-GBR service are verified as the S-shaped function and convex function correspondingly [22,23]. Based on the conclusions in [24], the utility function that satisfies both types of services is obtained as Equation 1.6.

$$U(r) = \frac{E}{A + Be^{-C(r-d)}} + D \tag{1.6}$$

where:

r	is the data rate allocated to the user
R	is the total resource of the system
C	mainly influences the slope of the curve
A, B, D, E	mainly effect the range of the utility value
d	is the inflection point of the utility function, which indicates the user requirement of the resource

By setting different parameter values, the utility function can present different characteristics, both the S-shaped function and the convex function. The utility functions of the GBR service $U_{real}(r)$ and non-GBR service $U_{non\,real}(r)$ are obtained from Equation 1.6 [24].

The *system utility* is defined as the linear weighted sum of all users' utility values. In Equation 1.7, λ represents the priority of GBR service and μ represent the priority of non-GBR service. These two weights are constrained by $\lambda, \mu \in [0,1]$ and $\lambda + \mu = 1$.

$$U_{System} = \lambda \sum_{k=1}^{K_1} U_{real}(r_k) + \mu \sum_{k=K_1+1}^{K_1+K_2} U_{non-real}(r_k) \tag{1.7}$$

The system utility can be further extended to include more types of service. Since the utility value represents the satisfaction level of the user, the system utility indeed represents all users' satisfaction levels, which can provide a better reflection of system performance than throughput.

1.3.2.2 Genetic Algorithm–Based Centralized Resource Allocation

As described above, in the FNA, AE will be allocated as a new dimension of radio resource. Consequently, in the UP construction process, users with different QoS requirements are allocated with AEs and subchannels jointly. Such a multidimensional resource allocation problem can be solved by using the resource pooling–based centralized radio resources management (RRM) scheme [11]. This scheme is processed by the CPE to manage all of the available resources uniformly. Since the optimization problem of the centralized resource allocation has a large and complex search space, the genetic algorithm (GA) is implemented to obtain near-optimal solutions with a relatively fast convergence speed.

Based on the GA, a chromosome, which is a two-dimension-integer matrix, is used to represent the potential resource allocation solution. Each row of the matrix represents the resource allocation strategy for the specific user. Moreover, each row can be further divided into several parts. Each part lists the allocated elements of a particular dimension of resources. In particular, the chromosome G in the following GA process is given by

$$G = \begin{cases} a_{1,1}, a_{1,2}, \cdots, a_{1,N_a}; b_{1,1}, b_{1,2}, \cdots, b_{1,N_s}; \\ \qquad \cdots \cdots \\ a_{K_1,1}, a_{K_1,2}, \cdots, a_{K_1,N_a}; b_{K_1,1}, b_{K_1,2}, \cdots, b_{K_1,N_s}; \\ a_{K_1+1,1}, a_{K_1+1,2}, \cdots, a_{K_1+1,N_a}; b_{K_1+1,1}, b_{K_1+1,2}, \cdots, b_{K_1+1,N_s}; \\ \qquad \cdots \cdots \\ a_{K_1+K_2,1}, a_{K_1+K_2,2}, \cdots, a_{K_1+K_2,N_a}; b_{K_1+K_2,1}, b_{K_1+K_2,2}, \cdots, b_{K_1+K_2,N_s}; \end{cases} \tag{1.8}$$

where the first K_1 rows represent the resource allocation strategies of the K_1 users with GBR service, and the remaining K_2 rows represent the resource allocation strategies of the users with the non-GBR services. Each row is further divided into two parts. The first part containing N_a integers indicates the allocated AEs, while the second part containing N_s integers lists the allocated subchannels. The initial population, which includes N_p chromosomes, is generated by a random process.

In order to evaluate the chromosomes, fitness function needs to be constructed by the system utility function mentioned above. The larger the fitness value, the better the solution. Thus, the optimized objective is to maximize the fitness value, that is, to maximize the system utility. Since the utility value represents the satisfaction level of the user, the proposed algorithm tends to meet the requirements of two types of services simultaneously under the three constraints in the user-centric UP construction process. Specifically, we assume that at most N_a out of N AEs and N_s out of M subchannels can be allocated to the user k. In addition to AE and subchannel limitations, we also apply the constraint derived from Equation 1.2 in the power limitation, where we choose the minimum value between the two power constraints P_i (maximum transmission power limitation) and $p_c - P(d_i)$. By using such constraints, we are able to guarantee that the coverage of UPs will not surpass the CP coverage.

$$\max F = \max U_{system} = \max\left[\lambda\sum_{k=1}^{K_1} U_{real}(r_k) + \mu\sum_{k=K_1+1}^{K_1+K_2} U_{non-real}(r_k)\right] \tag{1.9}$$

s.t.

$$|A_k| \leq N_a, A_k \subseteq \{0,1,2,\ldots,N\}, \forall k$$

$$|S_k| \leq N_s, A_k \subseteq \{0,1,2,\ldots,M\}, \forall k$$

$$p_i \leq \min\{P_i, p_c - P(d_i)\}, i \in \{1,2,\ldots,N\}$$

The chromosomes will be passed to the next generation through a four-step breeding process including selection, crossover, mutation, and modification.

First of all, a pair of parent individuals is selected based on so-called roulette wheel selection, such that the higher the fitness, the greater the opportunity for the individual to be selected. The possibility of chromosome G_i being selected is

$$p(G_i) = \frac{F(G_i)}{\sum_{k=1}^{N_p} F(G_k)} \tag{1.10}$$

where $F(G_i)$ is the value of the fitness function of chromosome G_i. Note that the selected chromosomes are still in the population, and as a result it is entirely likely that a chromosome is selected more than once.

Then, two children are generated by combining their parent's genes. In particular, a crossover point is first chosen randomly at a certain column of the two given chromosomes. Next, in order to form the first offspring, all the row vectors before the crossover point of the first matrix will combine with the row vectors after the crossover point of the second matrix. The second offspring is generated in the opposite way. Herein, the crossover process is illustrated.

Assume that we have two selected parent individuals, A and B, as follows:

$$A = \begin{cases} a_{1,1}, a_{1,2}, \cdots, a_{1,N_a}; b_{1,1}, b_{1,2}, \cdots, b_{1,N_s}; \\ \cdots\cdots \\ a_{K_1,1}, a_{K_1,2}, \cdots, a_{K_1,N_a}; b_{K_1,1}, b_{K_1,2}, \cdots, b_{K_1,N_s}; \\ a_{K_1+1,1}, a_{K_1+1,2}, \cdots, a_{K_1+1,N_a}; b_{K_1+1,1}, b_{K_1+1,2}, \cdots, b_{K_1+1,N_s}; \\ \cdots\cdots \\ a_{K_1+K_2,1}, a_{K_1+K_2,2}, \cdots, a_{K_1+K_2,N_a}; b_{K_1+K_2,1}, b_{K_1+K_2,2}, \cdots, b_{K_1+K_2,N_s}; \end{cases} \tag{1.11}$$

$$B = \begin{cases} a'_{1,1}, a'_{1,2}, \cdots, a'_{1,N_a} ; b'_{1,1}, b'_{1,2}, \cdots, b'_{1,N_s} ; \\[4pt] \cdots\cdots \\[4pt] a'_{K_1,1}, a'_{K_1,2}, \cdots, a'_{K_1,N_a} ; b'_{K_1,1}, b'_{K_1,2}, \cdots, b'_{K_1,N_s} ; \\[4pt] a'_{K_1+1,1}, a'_{K_1+1,2}, \cdots, a'_{K_1+1,N_a} ; b'_{K_1+1,1}, b'_{K_1+1,2}, \cdots, b'_{K_1+1,N_s} ; \\[4pt] \cdots\cdots \\[4pt] a'_{K_1+K_2,1}, a'_{K_1+K_2,2}, \cdots, a'_{K_1+K_2,N_a} ; b'_{K_1+K_2,1}, b'_{K_1+K_2,2}, \cdots, b'_{K_1+K_2,N_s} ; \end{cases} \tag{1.12}$$

The crossover point can be chosen randomly. Suppose that the crossover point is located between $b_{1,1}$ and $b_{1,2}$. Then the two children chromosomes C and D can be expressed as

$$C = \begin{cases} a_{1,1}, a_{1,2}, \cdots, a_{1,N_a} ; b_{1,1}, b'_{1,2}, \cdots, b'_{1,N_s} ; \\[4pt] \cdots\cdots \\[4pt] a_{K_1,1}, a_{K_1,2}, \cdots, a_{K_1,N_a} ; b_{K_1,1}, b'_{K_1,2}, \cdots, b'_{K_1,N_s} ; \\[4pt] a_{K_1+1,1}, a_{K_1+1,2}, \cdots, a_{K_1+1,N_a} ; b'_{K_1+1,1}, b_{K_1+1,2}, \cdots, b'_{K_1+1,N_s} ; \\[4pt] \cdots\cdots \\[4pt] a_{K_1+K_2,1}, a_{K_1+K_2,2}, \cdots, a_{K_1+K_2,N_a} ; b_{K_1+K_2,1}, b_{K_1+K_2,2}, \cdots, b'_{K_1+K_2,N_s} ; \end{cases} \tag{1.13}$$

$$D = \begin{cases} a'_{1,1}, a'_{1,2}, \cdots, a'_{1,N_a} ; b'_{1,1}, b_{1,2}, \cdots, b_{1,N_s} ; \\[4pt] \cdots\cdots \\[4pt] a'_{K_1,1}, a'_{K_1,2}, \cdots, a'_{K_1,N_a} ; b'_{K_1,1}, b_{K_1,2}, \cdots, b_{K_1,N_s} ; \\[4pt] a'_{K_1+1,1}, a'_{K_1+1,2}, \cdots, a'_{K_1+1,N_a} ; b'_{K_1+1,1}, b_{K_1+1,2}, \cdots, b_{K_1+1,N_s} ; \\[4pt] \cdots\cdots \\[4pt] a'_{K_1+K_2,1}, a'_{K_1+K_2,2}, \cdots, a'_{K_1+K_2,N_a} ; b'_{K_1+K_2,1}, b_{K_1+K_2,2}, \cdots, b'_{K_1+K_2,N_s} ; \end{cases} \tag{1.14}$$

In this way, the offspring are expected to provide better chromosomes with their parents' partial characteristics.

Moreover, in order to avoid converging to local optimized solution, all of the children will go through the mutation operation after the crossover process. Besides, since the individuals generated by crossover and mutation may no longer satisfy the system constraints, some modification should be made.

Finally, in order to prevent good solutions from being lost in the breeding process and to ensure the convergence of the algorithm, we take the two best solutions (named *elites*) from the parent generation and direct them into the child generation. Meanwhile, all other parents will be replaced by the offspring generation. The new generation will replace the original generation and these procedures are repeated for a total of N_g times. The whole population will evolve from generation to generation and gradually converge to the optimized solution. When the algorithm is terminated, the centralized resource allocation solution is based on the best individual G_{best} among the current population.

In the second step of EE optimization, the UP can be constructed with equal transmission power allocation mentioned above based on the optimized solution of GA scheme. Moreover, the UP adaptation via power adjustment scheme will be implemented in Section 1.3.3 according to the UP construction parameters to further optimize the EE performance. The simulation evaluation of the proposed user-centric UP construction scheme can be found in Section 1.3.4.

1.3.3 UP Adaptation with Game Theory–Based Power Adjustment

For the purpose of maximizing the system EE [25], Game theory could be further implemented as a power adjustment strategy for the UP adaptation based on CP and UP construction mentioned above. This is a noncooperative game model in which the pricing function is used to achieve the optimized system EE for the Data-AEs. Here, *penalty* is defined as the excessive power consumption from Macro Data-AEs, which yield severe interferences. The existence and uniqueness of the Nash equilibrium for the proposed game model is also verified.

1.3.3.1 Game Theory Model for the UP Adaptation

As we have assumed thus far, the FNA network consists of N_1 macro Data-AEs and N_2 small cell Data-AEs. One Data-AEs is able to serve several users within its coverage area. It is assumed that there is only one scheduled active user in each serving set during each signaling slot. Let $k \in \{1, 2, ..., N\}$ denote the scheduled user k. According to the results of G_{best} and $p_i \in \{1, 2, ..., N\}$ derived in the UP construction step, the received signal-to-interference-plus-noise-ratio (SINR) on subchannel m for the scheduled user k can be expressed as

$$\gamma_k^m = \frac{\sum_{i \in A_k^m} p_i \left| h_{i,k}^m \right|^2}{\sum_{j \in \bar{A}_k^m} p_j \left| h_{j,k}^m \right|^2 + n_k^m} \tag{1.15}$$

where $\gamma_k \geq \gamma_k^m$ and $p_k = \sum_{i \in A_k^m} p_i$ is the aggregate SINR and transmission power of the scheduled user k, respectively. Considering the user k's QoS requirement, its received SINR has the constraint as $\gamma_k \geq \gamma_k^{threshold}$. But the threshold $\gamma_k^{threshold}$ for the GBR service and non-GBR service are different.

1.3.3.2 UP Adaption Based on Game Theory

The UP adaption focuses on the transmission power of serving set Data-AEs. Based on the Game theory, we propose a power adjustment scheme for the system EE optimization from the perspective of Data-AEs. Each data AE within the serving set will choose a reasonable transmission power to maximize its own utility of EE performance, which is a typical noncooperative N-player game problem. Let $G = [N, \{p_k\}, \{u_k(p_k, \gamma_k | \mathbf{p_{-k}})\}]$ denote the noncooperative power adjustment game with pricing (NPGP), where

- $N = \{1, 2, \ldots, N\}$ is the index of the serving set Data-AE.
- $\{p_k\} = \{p_k | p_k | \in [0, p_{max}]\}$ is the transmission power of serving set Data-AEs for user k and $p_{max} > 0$ is the maximum power constraint of the corresponding Data-AEs.

Let $\{u_k(p_k, \gamma_k | \mathbf{p_{-k}})$ denote the utility of the scheduled user k, where γ_k and p_k is the aggregated SINR and transmission power of the user k, respectively; $\mathbf{p_{-k}}$ is the vector of transmission power of all serving set Data-AEs other than the serving set Data-AEs for user k.

Considering the Energy Efficiency measured in bit/joule [26], the utility function of the serving set Data-AEs for user k is defined as

$$u_k(p_k, \gamma_k | \mathbf{p_{-k}}) = a_k \frac{f(\gamma_k)}{p_k} - b_k p_k \tag{1.16}$$

where:

$a_k(f(\gamma_k)/p_k)$ denotes the EE of the user k
$b_k p_k$ denotes the linear pricing for the user k
a_k and b_k are positive factors

$f(\gamma_k)$ is defined as

$$f(\gamma_k) = 1 - e^{\frac{-\gamma_k}{2}} \tag{1.17}$$

which means that the revenue of the user k will increase slowly as γ_k increases [27].

The pricing $b_k p_k$ will ensure that the serving set data AEs for the user k could be penalized when they cause serious interference to other users with more transmission powers.

Finally, the EE optimization problem for UP adaption is formulated as the game model:

$$\max_{0 \leq p_k \leq p_{max}} u_k(p_k, \gamma_k | \mathbf{p_{-k}}), \forall k = 1, 2, \ldots, N \tag{1.18}$$

1.3.3.3 Nash Equilibrium for the Power Adjustment Game

The Nash equilibrium is a steady state that offers a predictable outcome for a game, where data AEs compete with selfish actions through self-optimization and converge to a point that no Data-AEs wish to deviate unilaterally. For the proposed game model (Equation 1.18), the Nash equilibrium is defined as follows.

Definition 1:

Suppose $p_k^*, \forall k = 1, 2, \ldots, N$ is a solution for Equation 1.18. Hence, the point $\mathbf{p}^*$ is a Nash equilibrium for the proposed noncooperative game if for any $\mathbf{p}$, the following conditions are satisfied:

$$u_k(p^*_k, \gamma^*_k | \mathbf{p}^*_{-k}) \geq u_k(p_k, \gamma_k | \mathbf{p}_{-k}), \forall k = 1, 2, \ldots, N \tag{1.19}$$

The proposed game model with pricing in this chapter is a supermodular game [28]. The existence and uniqueness of the Nash equilibrium will be verified as follows.

1. *Existence of Nash Equilibrium*

   Theorem 1:

   The set of Nash equilibria of a supermodular game is nonempty. Furthermore, the Nash set has a largest element and a smallest element.

   A proof of the theorem can be found in [29]. Let E denote the set of Nash equilibria. Let $\mathbf{p}_S$ and $\mathbf{p}_L$ denote the smallest and the largest elements of E, respectively. The theorem states that all of the equilibria $\mathbf{p} \in E$ are located such that $\mathbf{p}_S < \mathbf{p} < \mathbf{p}_L$.

   We introduce a totally asynchronous algorithm that generates a sequence of powers that converges to the smallest Nash equilibrium $\mathbf{p}_S$. Suppose that the serving set data AEs for user k update their power at time instances given by the set $T = \{t_{k1}, t_{k2}, t_{k3}, \ldots\}$, where $t_{k0} < t_{k(l+1)}$ and for $t_{k0} = 0$ all k. Define $T = \{\tau_1, \tau_2, \tau_3, \ldots\}$ as the set of update instances $T_1 \cup T_2 \ldots \cup T_N$ sorted in increasing order. Assume that there are no two time instances in set T that are exactly the same. The algorithm for finding the Nash equilibrium is designed as follows.

   Algorithm 1:

   Let us consider the proposed noncooperative power adjustment game with pricing as given in Equation 1.21. We will generate a sequence of transmission powers:

   Set the initial power vector at time $t = 0$: $\mathbf{p} = \mathbf{p}(0)$. Also let $l = 1$.

   For all l such that $\tau_1 \in T$

   For all serving set data AEs for the user k such that $\tau_1 \in T_k$

   1. Given $\mathbf{p}(\tau_{l-1})$, compute $p^*_k = \arg \max_{p_k \in p_k} u_k(p_k, \gamma_k | \mathbf{p}_{-k})$
   2. If $\gamma^*_k \geq \gamma^{threshold}_k$

      Then $p_k(t_1) = \min(p^*_k, p_{\max})$.

      else

      Remove user k in this iteration and continue the algorithm in the next iteration [30].

      end For.

      end For.

   Theorem 2:

   The proposed Algorithm 1 converges to a Nash equilibrium of the NPGP. Furthermore, it is the smallest equilibrium $\mathbf{p}_S$, in the set of Nash equilibria.

   The proof can be found in [31], which implies that the Nash equilibrium in the proposed NPGP exists and can be reached from either the top or the bottom of the strategy space with Algorithm 1. Since we do not know if there is a unique equilibrium, we compare the equilibrium in the Nash set E to determine if there exists a single equilibrium that dominates all other equilibria. Indeed, we can show that $\mathbf{p}_S$ is the best equilibrium in the set E.

2. *Uniqueness of Nash Equilibrium*

   Theorem 3:

   If $x, y \in E$ are two Nash equilibria in NPGP and $x \geq y$, then $u_k(x) \leq u_k(y)$ for all k.

Proof:

Notice that, for fixed p_k, the utility $u_k = a_k \dfrac{f(\gamma_k)}{p_k} - b_k p_k$ decreases with increasing $\mathbf{p}_{-k}$ for all k. Therefore, since $\mathbf{x}_{-k} \geq \mathbf{y}_{-k}$, we have

$$u_k(x_k, \mathbf{x}_{-k}) \leq u_k(x_k, \mathbf{y}_{-k}) \tag{1.20}$$

Also, by definition of the Nash equilibrium and since $\mathbf{y}$ is a Nash equilibrium of NPGP, we have

$$u_k(x_k, \mathbf{y}_{-k}) \leq u_k(y_k, \mathbf{y}_{-k}) \tag{1.21}$$

From Equations 1.20 and 1.21, then

$$u_k(\mathbf{x}) \leq u_k(\mathbf{y}) \tag{1.22}$$

According to Theorem 3, we know that smaller Nash equilibrium leads to higher utilities for all users. Since $\mathbf{p}_S < \mathbf{p}$ for all $\mathbf{p} \in E$, we conclude that for all $\mathbf{p} \in E$,

$$u_k(\mathbf{p}_S) \geq u_k(\mathbf{p}) \qquad \text{for all } k \tag{1.23}$$

This result implies that, in case the NPGP has Nash equilibria, the one that yields the highest utilities is the Nash equilibrium with the minimum total transmission powers.

In conclusion, the existence and the uniqueness of the Nash equilibrium for the proposed NPGP have been proved. It means that the transmission power of the serving set data AEs at the Nash equilibrium are regarded as a reasonable solution for the EE improvement of the UP adaption scheme. The simulation evaluation of the proposed UP adaption scheme can be found in Section 1.3.4.

1.3.4 Simulation Results and Analyses

In this section, the system level simulations are conducted to evaluate the proposed CP and UP adaptation scheme.

1.3.4.1 Simulation Environment

The simulation scenario is based on the deployment scenario of the FNA, the heterogeneous coverage environment is set up, which contains different types of AEs connected with one centralized CPE. There are 9 macro AEs and 72 small cell AEs generated in a 2×2 km square coverage area. In the coverage of each macro AE, small cell AEs are randomly distributed as several clusters. The CPE constructs and maintains the CP by choosing controlling AEs to guarantee the signaling requirements in the coverage area. In addition, the CPE also constructs and updates the user-centric UP by allocating Data-AEs to make up the coordinated serving set to fulfill the user's QoS requirements. More detailed simulation settings including the system and GA parameters for joint resource allocation are listed in Table 1.1.

Table 1.1 Simulation Setting

System Parameter	
Number of macro AEs	9
Number of small cell AEs	72 (Each macro AE has two clusters with four small AEs.)
Number of subchannels	20
Maximum power of macro AE	46 dBm
Maximum power of small cell AE	30 dBm
Carrier frequency	2 GHz
Bandwidth	10 MHz
Path loss model	$PL = 128.1 + 37.6\log_{10}d, d(\text{km})$
Shadowing standard deviation	8 dB
Shadowing correlation distance	50 m
Fast fading	Rayleigh fading
Noise density	−174 dBm/Hz
Maximal size of the serving set N_a	3
Maximal size of the subchannel set N_S	3
GA Parameters	
Population size N_p	500
Number of generations N_g	200
Mutation rate p_m	0.001

1.3.4.2 Simulation Results

1.3.4.2.1 CP Construction and Adaptation with Voronoi Diagram

In this section, the EE performance of the proposed CP construction and adaptation scheme and traditional CP construction scheme is revealed in Figure 1.3. Compared with the traditional CP construction scheme, which is the baseline scheme, the system gain of our scheme is significant. The simulation results are collected in the generated coverage area, choosing different numbers of controlling AEs.

Figure 1.3 shows the EE performance versus different numbers of controlling AEs selected for the CP construction. As the number of controlling AEs in the generated coverage area increases, the EE performances of both schemes experience a decline. This is because the inter-site distance between Controlling-AEs can improve the energy consumption. However, the Voronoi Diagram based CP construction and adaptation scheme still outperforms the traditional scheme.

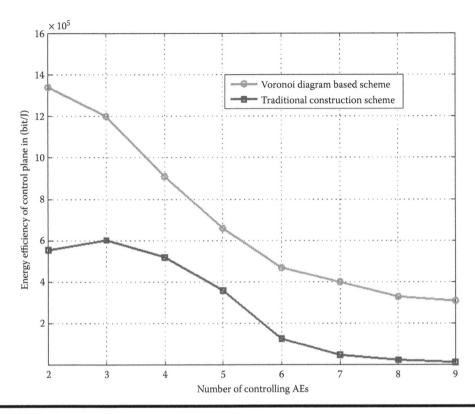

Figure 1.3   **Energy Efficiency of the CP construction and adaptation.**

1.3.4.2.2 User-Centric UP Construction with GA-Based Joint AE and Subchannel Allocation

During the simulations, two algorithms are used as comparisons. One is the path loss–based AE selection for the user-centric serving set construction and randomized subchannel set allocation (abbreviated to *PL-Random*). The other compared algorithm is the path loss–based user-centric serving set construction and maximum SINR subchannel set allocation (abbreviated to *PL-MaxSINR*). The simulation results of the system utility and the system throughput are plotted in Figures 1.4 and 1.5, respectively.

As shown in Figure 1.4, the performance of the proposed UP construction scheme is shown in terms of the system utility value versus the number of users. It is observed that the GA-based scheme achieves the highest system utility value, PL-MaxSINR ranks second, and PL-Random has the lowest performance. Note that the performance gap between GA and other algorithms becomes larger as the number of users increases. This is mainly because when the resources are not sufficient, the advantages of allocating resources effectively based on different user QoS requirements in optimized resource management is more obvious, which improves the system utility further.

In Figure 1.5, we can observe that the PL-MaxSINR algorithm, which pursues maximal throughput, ranks first as expected. The GA-based scheme ranks second and also achieves relatively high system throughput. This confirms that the GA-based scheme can achieve a better balance between user satisfaction and system throughput. In other words, it can provide better resource utilization, with just slightly worse system throughput.

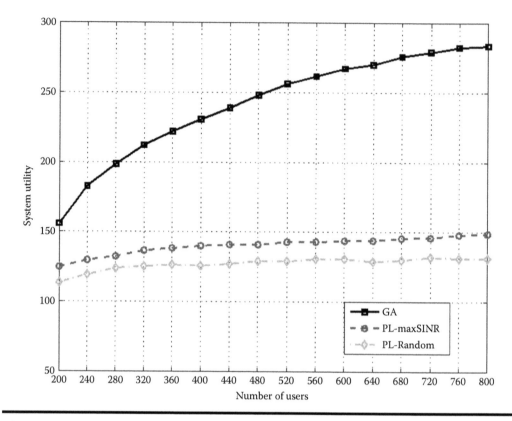

Figure 1.4 System utility of the user-centric UP construction.

1.3.4.2.3 UP Adaptation with Game Theory–Based Power Adjustment

Let $\eta = K_1/K_2$ denote the ratio of users with GBR service to users with non-GBR service, where K_1 and K_2 denote the number of GBR service users and non-GBR service users, respectively. We use the Equal Transmission Power Allocation (EPA) derived in the second step with GA based UP construction [31] as the comparison algorithms. The EPA scheme, which employs the non-cooperative game model but with a different utility and pricing function design compared with our proposed scheme, is chosen as the performance baseline. The system EE performance of the Data-AEs at the Nash equilibrium solution (abbreviate to *NPGP* scheme) versus the ratio η is evaluated in Figure 1.6.

As shown in Figure 1.6, we can observe that the average system EE performance of NPGP is better than that achieved by the EPA schemes. The system EE at the Nash equilibrium solution of the proposed NPGP is much better than that of the EPA at each value of η, which proves the performance improvements of the UP adaptation scheme.

1.4 Routing Strategy in OpenFlow-Enabled FNA Evolution

In order to further improve the resource efficiency, especially the AE usage efficiency, we discuss the routing strategy in the densely deployed RAN of FNA in this section. Firstly, we

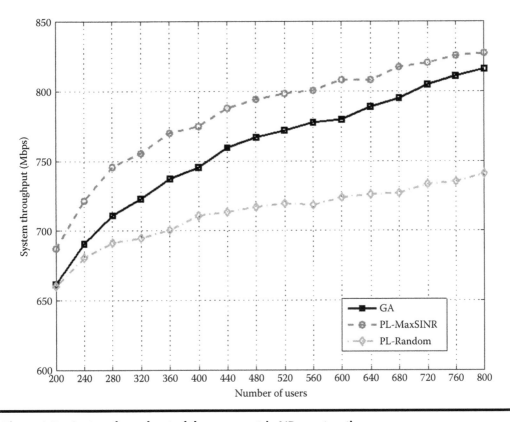

Figure 1.5   System throughput of the user-centric UP construction.

introduce the framework of OpenFlow-enabled FNA evolution, which decouples CP from UP, and explore network virtualization through Software-Defined Network approaches. Second, the concept of *flow*, which has the ability to support different kinds of service slices, is proposed to adapt the RAN environment. From the perspective of routing, which is critical for computer networks, we maintain an access route table to support the flow-selecting strategy in the Control Plane. Finally, the simulation results are provided to demonstrate the advantages of the proposed strategy.

1.4.1 OpenFlow-Enabled FNA Evolution

In order to have an overall perspective of network conditions and improve the performance of FNA in the aspects of efficiency and feasibility, the OpenFlow protocol is embedded in FNA to help decouple the CP and UP, which is inspired by SDN. In the User Plane, we use CPE to execute the centralized managing strategy. With an enhanced ability to manage radio resources, CPE can virtualize the wireless resources, such as spectrum, time-slot, and AE, into a shared resource pool. Furthermore, a flow-selecting strategy, which is generated in the Control Plane, can be conducted to support an on-demand user-centric service through CPEs. In the Control Plane, the OpenFlow controller has a whole view of the resource pool and can make global schedules to meet the exact QoS of different services. The OpenFlow-based FNA evolution is shown in Figure 1.7. The detailed architecture can be found in [12].

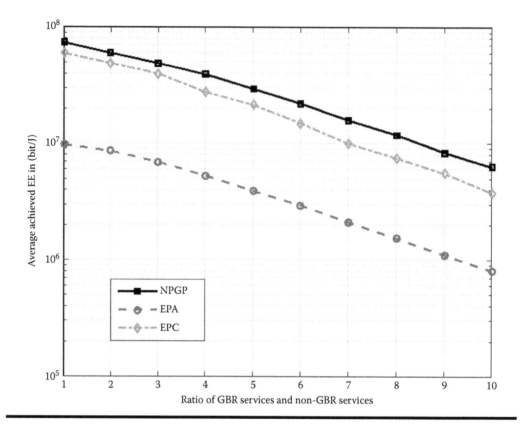

Figure 1.6   Average achieved system EE at the Nash equilibrium.

The OpenFlow controller exchanges information with CPEs through the OpenFlow protocol. On the one hand, CPE sends resource conditions and user mobility information to the OpenFlow controller. On the other hand, the OpenFlow controller maintains the resource pool database to map the real-time wireless resources into virtual ones and make strategies to instruct CPEs to schedule flows for supporting different service slices. With better adaption between slices and flows, the OpenFlow-enabled FNA evolution can perform better in the aspect of service ability and resource efficiency.

1.4.2 Flow Definition and Routing Strategy

In order to support different service slices, we define the concept of *flow*, which means the data flow supported by wireless resources, including the AE, as a kind of resource. In the User Plane, the CPE can dynamically schedule flows with the help of a flow-selecting strategy managed by the OpenFlow controller at the time that the wireless resources' condition changes. In this way, FNA can provide a more stable support to guarantee user-centric service requirements.

There can be multiple coordinated flows to serve one user at the same time. In the Control Plane, the OpenFlow controller maintains an access route table to instruct a flow-selecting strategy.

In order to conduct the routing selection strategy's design, the routing technology is referred from the wireless mesh network, which is self-organized. Its routing protocols can be

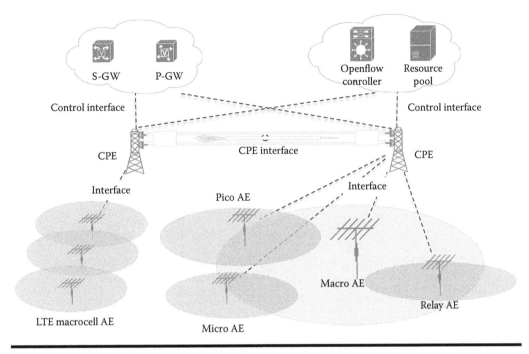

Figure 1.7   OpenFlow-based system architecture.

divided into table-driven protocols, which update the network topology by periodic broad-cast information, and on-demand-driven protocols, which only update the route table when the destination node is not accessible. How to improve the reliability of connect links is a critical problem in a wireless environment. In [32], the author proposes an algorithm called *associativity-based long-lived routing* (ABR), but it just measures the reliability of wireless links by way of statistical methods while we can deal with the problem better with the technology in the mobile network.

In this section, we define a utility based routing selection algorithm, which takes link capacity, user satisfaction, and CPE load into account. The first two parts have been considered in Equation 1.6 and the last part is measured by the load factor. The load factor is defined as follows:

$$L_k = \frac{\sum_{j \in JK} \beta_j p_j}{\sum p_j} \tag{1.24}$$

where:

β_j is the power consumption percent of CPE which supports the jth flow

p_j is the power consumption of the jth flow

$j \in JK$ is the flow set serving for the kth user

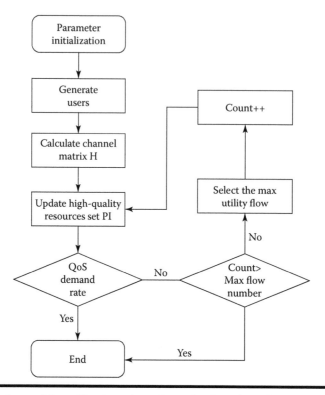

Figure 1.8   Flowchart of the utility-based routing selection algorithm.

The final utility function in the OpenFlow controller can be defined as the linear weighted sum of Equations 1.6 and 1.24. The final utility function is shown as follows:

$$U_k = \alpha U(r) - (1 - \alpha)L_k \tag{1.25}$$

with the restriction of $0 < \alpha < 1$ and $0 < \beta_j < 1$. The first part of Equation 1.25 reflects the gain achieved by the scheduled resources of flows to satisfy the specific QoS rate of users, while the second part reflects the cost that is needed by the CPE. The utility-based routing selection algorithm can be described as follows:

At first, UE measures its wireless environment and obtains the condition of the available resources such as the wireless channels, bandwidth, AEs, and so on. Then, it will choose the wireless links whose reference signal received power (RSRP) and reference signal received quality (RSRQ) are both better than the thresholds as the alternative resource set, and sends messages to the CPE. The CPE gathers resource information and helps the OpenFlow controller to form an access route table to find the flow set with the maximum system utility for the specific users' QoS requirements. Finally, the OpenFlow controller instructs the CPE to realize the flow-selecting strategy by the OpenFlow protocol. Details of the utility-based routing selection algorithm are shown as a flowchart in Figure 1.8.

1.4.3 Simulation Results

In this section, we use the same simulation settings that are shown in Table 1.1 to evaluate the performance of the utility-based routing selection algorithm. The compared algorithms are a random routing-selection algorithm, which selects flows randomly, and the MaxSINR routing selection algorithm, which selects the maximum SINR flows to support service.

Figure 1.9 shows the system throughput versus different numbers of users. We can find out that as the user number increases, the system throughput of the utility-based routing selection algorithm and MaxSINR routing selection algorithm improves at first and tends to be at the same level later while the throughput of the random routing selection algorithm has seen little change. When the number of users is suitable, the utility-based routing selection algorithm achieves the highest system throughput. This is mainly because the utility-based routing selection algorithm emphasizes the cooperation between flows to achieve global efficiency optimization for the resource pool, while the MaxSINR routing selection algorithm only selects resources with the highest quality to provide service.

Figure 1.10 shows the system utility value versus the number of users. It is obvious that the utility-based routing selection algorithm achieves the highest system utility value. When the number of users grows, the proposed utility-based routing selection algorithm shows the biggest advantages, compared with the other two algorithms.

Figure 1.11 shows the average user rate versus the number of users. We can find out that even though the MaxSINR routing selection algorithm chooses the highest SINR link to serve users, its average user rate is lower than that of the proposed utility-based routing selection algorithm. This is because the utility-based routing selection algorithm takes the users' demands, resource conditions, and AE's load-condition into consideration, which can result in better decisions for exerting the maximum utility of the resource pool.

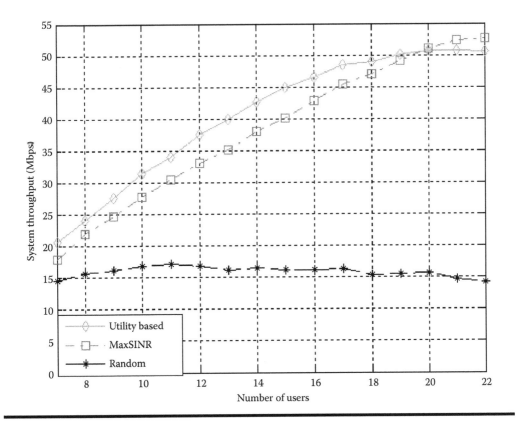

Figure 1.9 System throughput of routing selection algorithms.

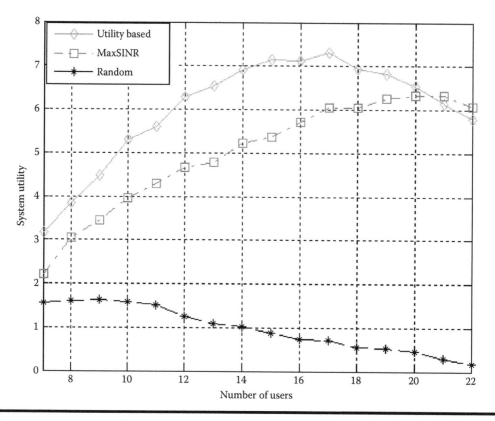

Figure 1.10   System utility of routing selection algorithms.

1.5 Summary

In this chapter, FNA is introduced as one potential solution for user-centric radio network architecture for the future 5G system, in which AEs are selected dynamically to construct the serving set for a specific user according to its QoS. Based on the FNA, a CP/UP construction and adaptation strategy is proposed that can guarantee the specific user QoS as well as optimize the system Energy Efficiency. In addition, in order to further improve resource efficiency, especially the AE usage efficiency, this chapter introduces the OpenFlow-enabled FNA evolution, which establishes the utility-based routing selection algorithm through an access route table maintained to instruct the flow-selecting strategy. Simulation results show the performance gain of the above strategies, which depicts the way forward for the 5G user-centric RAN.

For further research on FNA and the corresponding networking strategies, network modeling with stochastic geometry, mobility management, and interference control needs to be designed within the FNA architecture. For the modeling of user-centric networks, the correlation of intra-tier and inter-tier dependence should be included in the PPP model for more real dense network deployments. In terms of mobility management, the user-centric handover policy needs to be considered within the amorphous coverage features. The interference control for an ultradense network is still one of the key challenges for the evolved architecture. The combination of interference cancelation in the physical layer and interference coordination in the network layer needs to be jointly researched.

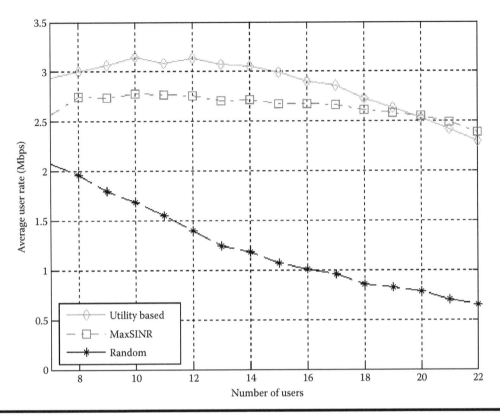

Figure 1.11   Average user rate of routing selection algorithms.

References

1. J. G. Andrews, Seven ways that HetNets are a cellular paradigm shift, *Communications Magazine*, IEEE, Vol. 51, No. 3, pp. 136–144, 2013.
2. L. Hanzo, H. Haas, S. Imre, D. O'Brien, M. Rupp, L. Gyongyosi, Wireless myths, realities, and futures: From 3G/4G to optical and quantum wireless, *Proceedings IEEE*, Vol. 100, pp. 1853–1888, 2012.
3. M. Yang, Y. Li, D. Jin, OpenRAN: A software-defined RAN architecture via virtualization. *ACM SIGCOMM*, pp. 549–550, 2013.
4. X. Jin, L. E. Li, L. Vanbever, J. Rexford, Softcell: Scalable and flexible cellular core network architecture, ACM Conference on Emerging Networking Experiments and Technologies, Santa Barbara, CA, 2013.
5. China Mobile Research Institute, C-RAN, The road towards green RAN, White Paper, v3.0, 2013.
6. M. Peng, Y. Li, J. Jiang, J. Li, C. Wang, Heterogeneous cloud radio access networks: A new perspective for enhancing spectral and energy efficiencies, *IEEE Wireless Communications*, Vol. 21, No. 6, pp. 126–135, December 2014.
7. H. Xiang, M. Peng, Y. Cheng, H. Chen, Joint mode selection and resource allocation for downlink fog radio access networks supported D2D, *QSHINE*, pp. 177–182, August 2015.
8. M. Peng, S. Yan, Poor, H.V., Ergodic capacity analysis of remote radio head associations in cloud radio access networks, *Wireless Communications Letters, IEEE*, Vol. 3, No. 4, pp. 365–368, August 2014.
9. M. Peng, X Xie, Q. Hu, J. Zhang, Poor, H.V., Contract-based interference coordination in heterogeneous cloud radio access networks, *Selected Areas in Communications, IEEE*, Vol. 33, No. 6, pp. 1140–1153, June 2015.

10. J. Li, M. Peng, A. Cheng, Y. Yu, C. Wang, Resource allocation optimization for delay-sensitive traffic in fronthaul constrained cloud radio access networks, *Systems Journal, IEEE*, 1–12, November 2014.

11. X. Xu, D. Wang, X. Tao, T. Svensson, Resource pooling for frameless network architecture with adaptive resource allocation, *Science China Information Sciences*, Vol. 56, No. 12, pp. 83–94, 2013.

12. X. Xu, H. Zhang, X. Dai, Y. Hou, X. Tao, P. Zhang, SDN based next generation mobile network with service slicing and trials, *China Communications*, Vol. 11, No. 2, pp. 65–77, 2014.

13. X. Xu, X. Dai, Y. Liu, R. Gao, X. Tao, Energy efficiency optimization-oriented control plane and user plane adaptation with a frameless network architecture for 5G, *EURASIP Journal on Wireless Communication and Networking*, Vol. 159, 2015.

14. S. Fu, B. Wu, H. Wen, Transmission scheduling and game theoretical power allocation for interference coordination in CoMP, *IEEE Transactions on Wireless Communications*, January 2014, Vol. 13, No. 1, pp. 112–123.

15. X. Zhang, Y. Sun, X. Chen, S. Zhou, J. Wang, Distributed power allocation for coordinated multi-point transmissions in distributed antenna systems, *IEEE Transactions on Wireless Communications*, Vol. 12, No. 5, pp. 2281–2291, February 2013.

16. H. Ishii, Y. Kishiyama, H. Takahashi, A novel architecture for LTE-B C-plane/U-planesplit and phantom cell concept, IEEE Globecom Workshops, 2012, pp. 624–630.

17. H. Lokhandwala, V. Sathya, B. R. Tamma, Phantom cell realization in LTE and its performance analysis, *IEEE ANTS*, 2014, pp. 1–6.

18. M. Haenggi, J. G. Andrews, F. Baccelli, O. Dousse, Stochastic geometry and random graphs for the analysis and design of wireless networks, *IEEE Journal on Selected Areas in Communications*, Vol. 27, No. 7, pp. 1029–1046, 2009.

19. X. Lin, R. Ganti, P. Fleming, and J. Andrews, Towards understanding the fundamentals of mobility in cellular networks, *IEEE Transactions on Wireless Communication*, Vol. 12, No. 4, pp. 1686–1698, April 2013.

20. N. Deng, W. Zhou, and M. Haenggi, The Ginibre point process as a model for wireless networks with repulsion, *IEEE Transactions on Wireless Communication*, Vol. 14, No. 1, pp. 107–121, January 2015.

21. A. Goldsmith, *Wireless Communications*, Cambridge: Cambridge University Press, 2005.

22. C. Liu, L. Shi, B. Liu, Utility-based bandwidth allocation for triple-play services, ECUMN, 2007.

23. Z. Niu, L. Wang, X. Duan, Utility-based radio resource optimization for multimedia DS-CDMA systems, *ACTA ELECTRONICA SINICA*, Vol. 32, No. 10, pp. 1594–1599, 2004.

24. L. Chen, W. Chen, Utility based resource allocation in wireless networks, *China Academic Journal*, Vol. 6, No. 10, pp. 3600–3606, 2009.

25. Y. Cai et al, A joint game-theoretic interference coordination approach in uplink multi-cell OFDMA networks, *Wireless Personal Communications*, Vol. 80, No. 3, pp. 1203–1215, February 2015.

26. Y. S. Soh, T. Q. S. Quek, M. Kountouris, Energy efficient heterogeneous cellular networks, *IEEE Journal on Selected Areas in Communications*, Vol. 31, No. 5, pp. 840–850, 2013.

27. C. U. Saraydar, N. B. Mandayam, D. J. Goodman, Efficient power control via pricing in wireless data networks, *IEEE Transactions on Communications*, Vol. 50, No. 2, pp. 291–303, 2002.

28. D. M. Topkis, Equilibrium points in nonzero-sum n-person submodular games, *SIAM Journal of Control and Optimization*, Vol. 17, No. 6, pp. 773–787, 1979.

29. D. M. Topkis, *Supermodularity and Complementarity*, Princeton, NJ: Princeton University Press, 1998.

30. M. Andersin, Z. Rosberg, J. Zander, Gradual removals in cellular PCS with constrained power control and noise. *Wireless Network*, Vol. 2, No. 1, pp. 27–43, 1996.

31. Y. Ma, T. Lv, Y. Lu, Efficient power control in heterogeneous femto-macro cell networks, *IEEE Wireless Communication and Network Conference*, pp. 2515–2519, 2013.

32. C. K. Toh, *Ad Hoc Mobile Wireless Networks: Protocols and Systems*, Upper Saddle River, NJ: Prentice Hall, 2001.

Chapter 2

Distributed Architecture of 5G Mobile Networks for Efficient Computation Management in Mobile Edge Computing

Zdenek Becvar, Matej Rohlik, Pavel Mach, Michal Vondra, Tomas Vanek, Miguel A. Puente, and Felicia Lobillo

Contents

2.1 Introduction

The evolution of mobile networks toward 5G consists in providing new services to users and continuous improvement of quality of service (QoS) [1]. However, new services are often limited by the capabilities of user equipment (UE). UE, represented by smartphones, tablets, and so on, has limited computing power constrained by the device's central processing unit (CPU). Besides the limited computational power, these devices also suffer from a short battery life. The battery could be depleted in a short time by services and applications that have high computational requirements. Examples of such applications are speech/video/image processing, augmented/virtual reality, or games.

A suitable option for extending battery life is to offload computationally demanding applications from the UE to a cloud [2] by means of the mobile cloud computing (MCC) concept. However, exploitation of a conventional MCC introduces an additional communication delay, that is, an increased time of data delivery from the UE to the cloud and back. Hence, such an approach is not suitable for real-time or delay-sensitive applications. To minimize communication delay caused by remote computation, the cloud capabilities can be incorporated at the edge of a mobile network. The edge of a mobile network can be understood as a part of the network composed of small cell base stations (SCeNBs) that are expected to be deployed massively in the near future [3,4]. Therefore, integration of the MCC capabilities into the SCeNBs is seen as an interesting option for 5G mobile networks to improve QoS for applications that are both computationally demanding and delay sensitive [5]. The idea of computation distributed over the edge of a mobile network is represented by a small cell cloud (SCC) concept, which refers to a cluster of interconnected computationally enhanced SCeNBs (SCeNBces) [6]. The SCC can be understood as part of the mobile edge computing (MEC) concept, which exploits virtualized computing resources distributed at the edge of mobile networks, including all types of base stations (eNBs), not only for the computation of users' tasks but also for the optimization of radio access network performance [7]. The SCC and MEC methods are based on the enhancement of base stations by additional computing capabilities that can be pooled together and exploited by the UE. The SCC and MEC enable the offloading of computation from the UE to the (SC)eNBs in the proximity of users in order to accelerate computation and/or save the energy of the UE. Note that the problem of accelerated computation persists even with the advancement of CPUs in UE. The reason is that in parallel with more powerful CPUs, we can expect also the development of more computationally demanding applications. So we can assume that the ratio between required computing power and the power of the piece of equipment's CPU will not change substantially. Moreover, the offloading itself is also profitable for UE in terms of battery consumption as it prolongs battery life since computation is done at the SCeNBs.

The enhancement of the (SC)eNBs toward the SCC or MEC consists of the inclusion of a new general purpose processor(s) and additional memory as described in [8]. Such extension introduces a new generation of cloud-enabled SCeNB (SCeNBce). It is assumed that the general purpose processor is representative of a common CPU used in conventional computers or servers. Hence, the computing power of the SCeNBces is similar to that of common computers or servers. If, in addition to these features, the SCeNBs are enhanced with storage capabilities, those can be exploited for offloading backhaul by caching content, which can be potentially further exploited by other users in the same area [9]. Finally, the distributed computation at the edge of mobile networks is interesting for mobile network operators or service providers, since it allows for the design of innovative and attractive services for their customers [10].

The SCC is an evolutionary step beyond the concept of cloudlets, which enable efficient convergence of cloud and wireless communication [11]. The cloudlets are part of a three-tier hierarchy that operates at the intermediary layer between a mobile device and a cloud [12]. Compared with the cloudlets, the SCC integrates both computation and communication aspects into a single concept toward 5G [13]. By merging these two formerly independent areas, the SCC enables joint optimization of both communication and computing resources. Nevertheless, smooth implementation of the SCC into the future mobile networks is conditioned by modifications of mobile network architecture, since a conventional architecture of the mobile network is not designed to handle computation aspects, such as the management of virtual machines (VMs) or allocation of computing resources.

The major challenge of the SCC is the design and deployment of a new control entity, which should be able to coordinate the computation depending on the radio channel, backhaul conditions, required computing power, and status of the SCeNBces (e.g., computational load of the VMs) [14]. Such a control entity, denoted as a *small cell cloud manager* (SCM), should be tightly integrated into the mobile network architecture [15]. From the operator's point of view, the simplest and the easiest option to begin with is to merge the SCM with an existing node in the network, for example, a mobility management entity in the core network, a baseband unit (BBU) in C-RAN, or a femtocell gateway, if available (see [6]). To prevent negative aspects of strict mobile network timings or the overloading of existing hardware, the SCM is implemented as additional hardware dedicated to computing management. Another feasible option is to use the SCM as a new standalone entity [6].

Since the SCM is a completely new entity in the network dedicated solely to the control plane, its deployment inevitably introduces additional overhead due to the extra signaling required to manage SCeNBces (handling users' data and forwarding control plane) in the SCC. The additional signaling increases backhaul load, which can become critical; especially, if the SCC incorporates Home eNBs (HeNBs) that could be connected via a low bit rate connection such as a digital subscriber line (DSL). The other important aspect that has to be taken into account when the SCM is deployed is the signaling delay. The reason for this is that the signaling delay plays an important role in the satisfaction of users with provided services and it is also critical in joint optimization of radio communication and computational resources.

In this chapter, we introduce two new options for the distributed deployment of the SCM in order to minimize the signaling load related to SCC management and signaling delay. The first option, denoted as a *hierarchical SCM*, exploits control at two levels: distributed local management and remote centralized management. The second option, denoted as a *virtual SCM*, consists of the deployment of the SCM entirely at the SCeNBces, sharing a dedicated part of computational capacity designated for the processing of users' tasks. Furthermore, we propose a protocol enabling the exchange of the required management information among all involved entities. Subsequently, we analyze the signaling overhead needed to handle a new computation request. Based on this analysis, we compare both proposed options with the state-of-the-art centralized deployment of the SCM in terms of signaling delay and load introduced by the computation management.

The rest of this chapter is organized as follows. In Section 2.2, we provide an overview of 4G mobile network architecture and a potential centralized solution for the management of the SCC. In Section 2.3, we outline novel approaches for the decentralized management of the SCC and its integration into 5G mobile networks based on C-RAN. Section 2.4 defines a protocol for the SCC management in the developed architecture. Afterward, in Section 2.5, we analyze the proposed signaling messages along with additional overhead introduced at other layers of the open systems interconnection (OSI) model. Scenarios used for evaluation and simulation results are presented in Section 2.6. The last section summarizes the chapter, provides major conclusions, and discusses possible future work.

2.2 Toward an Architecture of Future Mobile Networks

To incorporate the SCC concept into the mobile networks, the SCM is required to be integrated in the existing infrastructure to enable the management of computational resources over the SCeNBces and benefit from network status knowledge. Therefore, we briefly introduce the architecture of the 4G mobile networks in this chapter. Furthermore, we describe basic principles related to C-RAN architecture. We also provide an overview of state-of-the-art centralized SCM deployment for future mobile networks toward 5G.

2.2.1 Architecture of 4G Mobile Networks

The architecture of LTE-A mobile networks [16] is composed of an access part, denoted as an *evolved universal terrestrial radio access network* (E-UTRAN) and an *evolved packet core* (EPC) as shown in Figure 2.1. The E-UTRAN is basically composed of the eNBs, the SCeNBs, and the UE. The E-UTRAN is responsible for scheduling and allocating radio resources, mobility control, the encryption of radio data transmission, and for enabling connectivity to the EPC. The EPC is composed of a mobility management entity (MME), a serving gateway (S-GW), and a packet gateway (P-GW). The MME controls and manages all signaling between the UE and the EPC. The S-GW routes and forwards all IP packets among the pieces of user equipment and other IP-based networks (such as the Internet). Finally, the P-GW is responsible for actions related to the QoS and flow management toward other networks.

2.2.2 Architecture of Mobile Networks Based on C-RAN

The evolution of mobile networks and the requirements of users have resulted in a need to improve the efficiency of control functionality, cost, capacity, and energy consumption. This then gives rise to the need for the cloud RAN (C-RAN), that is, the radio access network controlled in a centralized manner where control resources are implemented in a cloud. C-RAN, introduced by China Mobile Research [17], assumes a splitting of the control and communication part of eNBs

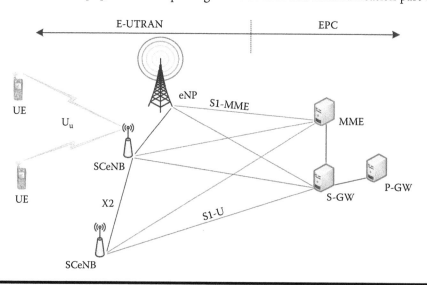

Figure 2.1   Architecture of LTE-A mobile network.

into a centralized BBU and distributed radio remote heads (RRH) [18] as shown in Figure 2.2. Depending on the level of centralization, the RRH can be either implemented as a simple transmitter/receiver with no baseband processing so that a full baseband I/Q signal (i.e., signal represented by changes in the amplitude and phase of a sin wave, see [19] for more details) is transmitted between the BBU and the RRH (full centralization), or the RRH can handle baseband processing in order to lower the load of the link between the BBU and RRH (partial centralization). In both cases, upper layer functionalities are handled by the BBU. Nevertheless, transmission of the raw I/Q representation of a signal is not very efficient and it requires huge bitrates to deliver data between RRH and the BBU (see [20] for more details).

Besides the cost and energy efficiency of C-RAN, it has been shown that C-RAN can also significantly improve the performance of promising technologies, increasing the network coverage and capacity; such as with coordinated multipoint (CoMP) [21,22], multiple-input multiple-output (MIMO) [23], or non-orthogonal multiple access [24] technologies. The performance gain reported in these papers indicates that C-RAN can significantly contribute to the evolution of mobile networks toward 5G and can help to meet requirements on 5G mobile networks.

Further evolution of the C-RAN is represented by a RAN as a service (RaaS) [25], which also enables the splitting of the functionalities of upper layers between the BBU and RRH. This assumes that the RRH is equipped with virtualized resources to handle required control and management procedures. Due to the virtualization of resources, the control functionalities can be shared among neighboring base stations.

2.2.3 Architecture Encompassing SCC with Centralized Management

Exploiting the virtualized resources deployed in base stations (RRH or SCeNBs), we can smoothly evolve the network architecture to support the SCC. The architecture of mobile networks with SCC has to incorporate virtualized computing resources integrated into the SCeNBces and a new entity in order to control and maintain the cloud interoperability and to interact with the E-UTRAN and the EPC. This entity, denoted as the SCM, coordinates the available computing

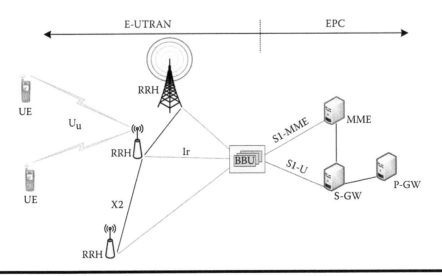

Figure 2.2   Architecture of C-RAN.

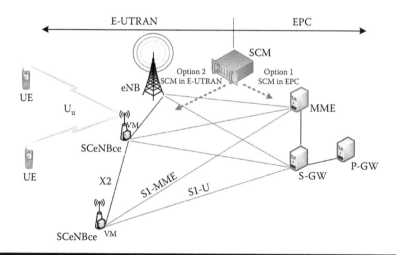

Figure 2.3   Integration of the centralized SCM into a mobile network.

resources with respect to the radio channel and backhaul conditions [14]. The SCM also allocates computing resources for the processing of users' applications over the SCeNBces. These computing resources are virtualized by means of the VMs. The efficient deployment of the SCM is supposed to minimize supplementary protocol data overhead, implementation complexity, impact on current LTE-A, cost of deployment, and operation and maintenance [6].

In [6], several options for the centralized SCM (C-SCM) placement and interconnection with existing LTE-A architecture have been introduced as shown in Figure 2.3. The first option (in Figure 2.3 denoted as Option 1) is to place the SCM directly in the EPC, since it is under the supervision of a mobile operator. The advantage of this approach consists of the possibility to exploit the computing power of all SCeNBces connected to the network. However, as the majority of the signaling required for offloading management is originating from the SCeNBs [6], this solution requires the exchange of all signaling through the EPC. Consequently, it overloads the backhaul links. The second option (Option 2) is to deploy the SCM closer to the user. In other words, the SCM is located within the radio access network close to the SCeNBce (e.g., the SCM can be collocated with a gateway or router close to the SCeNBs or could be implemented as a standalone unit). A disadvantage of this solution is a constrained computing power of subordinated SCeNBces, as only the SCeNBces topologically underlying the SCM can be clustered and their computing power can be virtually merged. On the other hand, the SCM closer to the users significantly reduces signaling overhead between the network edge (E-UTRAN) and the EPC. Obviously, both of the aforementioned options (and their minor modifications as presented in [6]) introduce some drawbacks, which limit the exploitability and deployment of the SCC.

2.3 Proposed Architecture with Distributed Management of Computation in SCC

In order to minimize the drawbacks related to the centralized SCM for the control of computation in the future mobile networks with the SCC, we propose two new architectural options in this section: a hierarchical SCM (H-SCM) and a virtual hierarchical SCM (VH-SCM). Both of these proposed options utilize decentralization of the SCM to minimize signaling delay and signaling load at the interface between the E-UTRAN and the EPC. We also indicate the synergy of the proposed distributed and virtualized concept of computational control with C-RAN architecture.

2.3.1 Hierarchical SCM

The fundamental idea of the H-SCM concept is to physically split the SCM into two parts: into a local SCM (L-SCM) and a remote SCM (R-SCM) (see Figure 2.4). The L-SCM is located close to the SCeNBces. Due to a need for proximity between the L-SCM and the SCeNBces, the L-SCM is assumed to coordinate several SCeNBces in its vicinity (the number of the SCeNBs basically depends on their density in L-SCM vicinity). Consequently, the L-SCM can only handle computing requests of relatively low complexity. Note that the SCeNBces are assumed to be similar in their computing power to common personal computers [8,26]. Hence, the low computing demand is understood as a demand, which can be handled by several SCeNBces. Still, the computing power of several SCeNBces is much higher than the computing capabilities of present or future smartphones. Note that even with evolution of CPUs in smartphones, also CPUs for SCeNBces will evolve. As a result, the computing power of several SCeNBces will be much higher than that of smartphones or similar mobile devices, which are, moreover, limited by battery capacity. The L-SCM allows for low signaling delay if the requested computational power can be offered by nearby SCeNBces, because the tasks can be handled in proximity to the UE. In the case that the L-SCM is not able to serve additional UE demands due to the unavailability of computing resources from underlying SCeNBces, the R-SCM takes responsibility over the UE's requests. The R-SCM follows a principle of the centralized SCM (in exactly the same way that was described in Section 2.2), since it is located in the EPC and it is able to exploit the computing power of all SCeNBces connected to the EPC.

The request for computational offloading generated by an application running on the UE is processed as follows. In the first step, a decision on whether to offload an application to the cloud or not is performed. For this decision, conventional offloading decision algorithms, as described, for example, in [27–29], can be exploited. If the result of the offloading decision is positive, the L-SCM evaluates if its subordinate SCeNBces can handle the given task. The subordinate SCeNBces of the L-SCM are

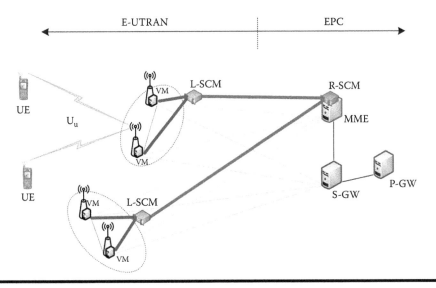

Figure 2.4 Deployment of the L-SCM and R-SCM for hierarchical SCM.

those SCeNBces that are managed by the same L-SCM as the SCeNBce to which the UE requesting computational offloading is connected. The subordinate SCeNBces then create a cluster of computing resources managed by the L-SCM. If the computation power of the subordinate SCeNBces within the cluster is sufficient, the L-SCM selects and assigns one or more SCeNBces to participate in the offloading job. On the other hand, if not enough resources are available to handle the request at the moment, the duty is forwarded to the R-SCM, which distributes the computation among L-SCMs and their subordinated SCeNBces according to the availability of resources. To evaluate the computing capabilities of the subordinated SCeNBces, information on the network status must be continuously collected in either a reactive or a proactive manner (see details in [30]). Note that the R-SCM can also act as an entity that balances the computational load among the L-SCMs to ensure service availability across the whole network. For example, the R-SCM can instruct the L-SCM to forward delay-tolerant tasks to another L-SCM to balance the computational load among them and to ensure the availability of computing resources for delay-sensitive tasks in clusters of the L-SCMs.

For the L-SCM deployment, we distinguish between a residential scenario and a corporate scenario.

- ◾ *L-SCM in residential scenario*: The residential scenario assumes that the SCeNBces are spread among close houses or flats. Still, the L-SCM needs to be deployed (from a topological point of view) as close to the end user as possible in order to minimize the signaling delay and load. Physically, the L-SCM can be located in a specific separate location. The management requires a dedicated interface at the SCeNBces to enable communication with the L-SCM. The dedicated interface, intended for the exchange of signals only, can be implemented using a fixed connection (wired or fiber) or over-the-air (OTA) communication [31].

  As a disadvantage of the H-SCM approach with L-SCM located in the residential scenario, we should mention a relatively high cost, which is associated with the implementation of the new infrastructure interconnecting all participating entities. However, by leveraging the OTA interface, the costs can be lowered. Nevertheless, the cost of the deployment of a high amount of L-SCM (each for a relatively small region) remains.

- ◾ *L-SCM in corporate scenarios*: The complexity of the H-SCM is substantially reduced in corporate scenarios where we assume SCeNBces that are interconnected through a local infrastructure by means of LAN. This enables a low delay because the L-SCM and all potentially computing SCeNBces are relatively close to each other (within the premises of a company) and interconnected with a high-quality backhaul. Also for this scenario, the overall cost of the SCMs in the whole network might be high, as we need to deploy a high number of the L-SCMs, each managing relatively small area.

2.3.2 Virtual Hierarchical SCM

Potential limitation of the H-SCM consists of a relatively high cost of the L-SCM's deployment. To reduce the high cost of the H-SCM, we introduce a virtual hierarchical SCM, denoted by VH-SCM, which virtualizes the role of the L-SCM directly into the SCeNBces. As a result, the entire L-SCM's functionality is a logical function distributed among the VMs of the participating SCeNBces (see Figure 2.5).

This *virtualized L-SCM* is denoted as VL-SCM. The advantage of this solution is that there is no need for installing new hardware, as the VL-SCM is just a piece of code running on the virtualized resources of the particular SCeNBce(s). The resources of the VL-SCM's functionality are allocated within the resources normally dedicated to the computation of the offloaded applications by users (as shown in Figure 2.6). This can be seen as a potential drawback for this solution,

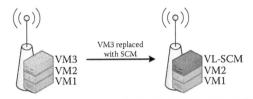

Figure 2.5   Allocation of resources for SCM.

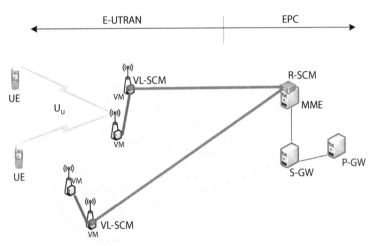

Figure 2.6   Virtualization of the L-SCM in SCeNBce for virtual hierarchical SCM.

as a lower processing power remains for the users' computation. Nevertheless, this impact can be minimized by the selection of a proper SCeNBce within a cluster with enough computational resources to serve as the VL-SCM or by circulating and sharing the role of the VL-SCM between all participating SCeNBces according to their current computational load.

Note that the VL-SCM can also act independently without the R-SCM. In this case, the processing capacity is limited only to the sum of the capacities of the local SCeNBces.

If the VL-SCM is allocated to a SCeNB owned by a user, there is a risk of unexpected turn-off (e.g., in case of a femtocell base station) or the malfunction of the SCeNBce hosting the VL-SCM. To avoid this risk, one of the SCeNBces is elected as the VL-SCM while another cell is selected as a secondary VL-SCM, that is, it represents a backup. Any communication from the SCeNBce to the VL-SCM uses a specific multicast address as its destination address. If a failure of the VL-SCM occurs (i.e., status information of the VL-SCM is not updated during a hold-down timer), the backup VL-SCM takes over the primary function and a new backup VL-SCM is selected. Specific values of all timing procedures (timers) are subject to future analysis, since they depend on network topology, the total number of SCeNBces, and other aspects.

The proposed hierarchical deployment of the SCM enables easy integration of the SCC into 5G mobile networks based on C-RAN. To integrate the proposed VH-SCM into the mobile network architecture based on the C-RAN concept, the functionalities of the R-SCM should be located in the BBU while the functionalities of the VL-SCM should be located in the RRH. As our distributed solution enables dynamic shifting of the control functions between the R-SCM and the VL-SCMs, the solution is also suitable for an RaaS extension of the C-RAN. In such a case, the control procedures of the upper layers can be dynamically moved from the BBU (in our case, represented by the R-SCM) to the RRH (in our case, the VL-SCM) and vice versa. In other words, the control functionalities of the R-SCM, which are conventionally located in a centralized way, as for the BBU, can be shifted closer to the users, that is, to the RRH, which takes over the functionalities of the VL-SCM.

2.4 Small Cell Cloud Management Protocol (ScCMP)

The architectural options proposed in the previous section require an interaction between the VL-SCM and the R-SCM in order to manage the distribution of tasks. In this section, we describe a new small cell cloud management protocol (ScCMP). Note that despite our use of the notation of VL-SCM, the ScCMP can be used also for communication between the L-SCM and the R-SCM in the hierarchical control without virtualized local SCM.

The ScCMP is an extension of Z-protocol (see [32]), which is intended only for communication between the SCM and the SCeNBces [33] and does not cover communication between the VL-SCM and the R-SCM. In order to enable third parties to develop their applications compatible with the cloud-based offloading architecture, an appropriate application programming interface (API) must be defined [34]. Therefore, ScCMP is a comprehensive protocol for end-to-end communication among all devices involved in the offloading process, that is, the UE, the SCeNBces, and all types of the SCMs.

During the whole management process, the UE communicates via radio interface only with its serving SCeNBce. The serving SCeNBce forwards the management messages to the SCM only if the UE is approved to use the cloud services. The system design does not allow the UE to communicate with the SCM directly to provide a preventive measurement against a Distributed Denial of Service (DDoS) to protect the SCM, which could be otherwise easily targeted by malicious UE. The entire process of the small cell cloud management is divided into three phases (Figure 2.7):

■ Authorization and allocation of cloud resources
■ Offloading
■ System cleanup

Note that the format of the messages, which is discussed in Sections 2.4.1 through 2.4.3, is considered as a "general concept" for further reference. Moreover, notice that some messages are periodic in nature. It means that these messages provide a keep-alive mechanism in order to ensure that all interested communication parties are available during the whole offloading and computing process.

2.4.1 Authorization Process and Allocation of Cloud Resources

We consider that the UE follows the authentication and key agreement scheme known as the IMS AKA [35] in order to establish both the encryption keys and integrity mechanisms. Therefore, the UE has set its PDP context and it is assigned with the IP address [36]. Once the UE is authorized to the network for common communication purposes and allowed to access the mobile network, it is allowed to demand mobile edge computing services using a *cloud service request* message. This message comprises the UE's identification and port numbers (e.g., IP address). Consequently, this message is encapsulated within a *cloud service allocation request*, where the previous information from the UE is supplemented with the identification of the SCeNBce, the SCM, and the communication ports. Then, the message is forwarded by the SCeNBce to the SCM expecting to receive a {*YES|NO*} response in order to accept or reject any offloading requests from the UE.

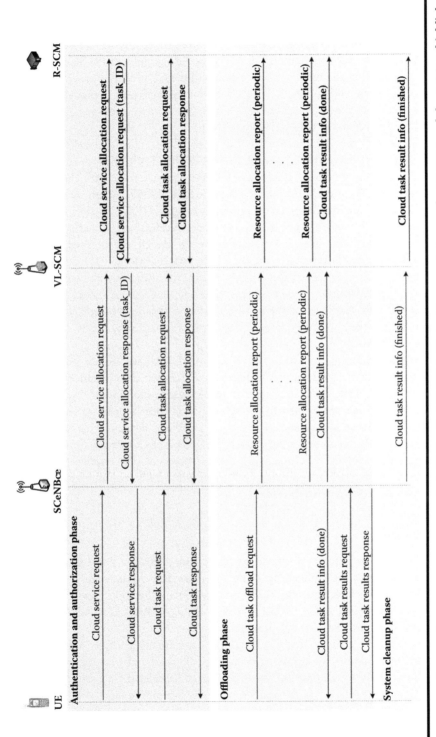

Figure 2.7 Exchange of management messages in ScCMP with VH-SCM. (Note: Messages between the VL-SCM and the R-SCM [highlighted by bold] are transmitted only if the VL-SCM cannot provide requested resources and the task must be handled by the R-SCM.)

Two processes can be distinguished: the connection of individual SCeNBces to the SCM and the connection of UE to those SCeNBces.

The connection of the SCeNBces comprises *CONNECT* and *RECONNECT* messages of the Z-protocol. The CONNECT message is sent the first time the SCeNBce connects to the SCM and carries the data for the connection on the SCeNBce side along with the SCeNBce's resource data, such as the local CPU and memory. The response to the CONNECT message is the ID that the SCM assigns to the SCeNBce. The RECONNECT message is sent in case the SCeNBce has already been connected to the SCM and the connection has to be reestablished. This message carries the SCeNBce ID assigned to the SCeNBce in the past.

The connection of the UE comprises the *CONNECT_UE*, *RECONNECT_UE*, and *UE_CONNECTED* messages of the Z-protocol. The CONNECT_UE message carries information regarding the UE connection (port, etc.) and the user (SCeNBce owner, guest, etc.). The system responds to this message with the allocated UE ID and VM ID. The RECONNECT_UE message is sent when the UE has already been connected, carrying the previously assigned UE ID. The UE_CONNECTED message is sent by the SCM when the UE connection process has finalized, including the deployment of the corresponding virtual machines. This message conveys to the UE the information regarding the connection with its virtual machines, that is, the IP address, port, and so on.

The UE is either allowed or denied the ability to utilize the available cloud services depending on the results of this authorization process. The response on a cloud service allocation request from the SCM to the SCeNBce (carried in a *cloud service allocation response* message) corresponds to the *RESPONSE* message of the Z-protocol, and this message is forwarded by the SCeNBce to the UE as a *cloud service response*.

If cloud resources can be granted to the UE (i.e., the UE is allowed to use cloud services), the SCeNBce is assigned a dedicated identifier (called a *Task_ID*), which is included in cloud service allocation response. The Task_ID is used later to recognize the individual tasks of a single UE. Then, the UE sends a *cloud task request* to the serving SCeNBce in order to allocate particular resources at the SCeNBce(s) for the task. The serving SCeNBce forwards this request as a *cloud task allocation request*, which comprises the CONNECT_UE, RECONNECT_UE, as well as the *MONITOR* and *UE_CONNECTED* messages of the Z-protocol. The response messages (cloud service allocation response) are then aligned with the Z-protocol, based on which the SCeNBce assigns the appropriate resources for the task.

2.4.2 Offloading

After the allocation of resources, an offloading phase can start. The offloading phase is initiated when the UE begins task offloading using the *cloud task offload request* message, which is forwarded by the SCeNBce to the SCM as a resource allocation report that comprises *OFFLOADING_DECISION*, *REQ_OFFLOADING*, *REQ_PARALLELIZATION*, and *END_PARALLELIZATION* messages of the Z-protocol.

In the Z-protocol, the *OFFLOADING_DECISION* message is sent from the UE so that the SCM can decide what parts of the computation can be offloaded and what parts should be computed in the UE. The information carried by this message includes the necessary information to make the offloading decision, such as the description of the computing tasks, time and energy constraints, and so on. Once the UE knows what computing tasks are to be offloaded, it offloads the tasks sending a REQ_OFFLOADING message including the necessary processes' descriptions and data along with the number of VMs requested for a possible parallelization of the computing tasks. When the parallelization is feasible, the executing VM sends a REQ_PARALLELIZATION message to the SCM asking for additional VMs. Then, the SCM assigns available VMs to the parallelization tasks, which are freed by means of the END_PARALLELIZATION message sent from the executing VM.

Once the offloaded computation is completed, the UE as well as the SCMs are informed about the successful task resolution using the *cloud task result info* message. Since this message is sent by the SCeNBce to the UE, it is not covered by the Z-protocol. Once suitable for the UE, it pools the SCeNBces for the offloading results using a *cloud task result request* message. The results are delivered using the *cloud task result response* message.

2.4.3 System Cleanup

Successful delivery of results to the UE is followed by the system cleanup phase. In this phase, the SCeNBce informs the VL-SCM and the R-SCM that the offloaded task in the cloud has been completed via a cloud task result info message including the flag *Finished*. This ensures that the system resources are released and all SCMs are informed about it. As a result, released resources can be used for another request.

2.5 Analysis of Signaling between SCM and SCeNBce

The proposed deployment of the SCM aims to minimize the signaling delay and to reduce the signaling load of individual communication links. Thus, in this section, we provide an analysis of the signaling for the existing centralized SCM (using so-called Z-protocol, see [33]) and for new deployments of the SCM using proposed ScCMP.

Basically, the Z-protocol messages are differentiated based on the communication flow direction (from/to SCeNBce to/from SCM). The messages taken over from [33] are presented in Table 2.1 along with the size of each message. Note that message flow and exchange rules are also presented in [33]). An average size of a typical Z-protocol message exchange including all headers is approximately 40B plus contextual information for the offloading decision (included in OFFLOADING DECISION and REQ_OFFLOADING messages) as can be seen from Table 2.1.

In the case of the proposed H-SCM and VH-SCM, the role of the R-SCM is to handle resource management in case the resources underlying the VL-SCM are not sufficient for users. Therefore, available memory, CPU, and all computation status information must be exchanged. This information is stored in the SCM, structuring the data in tables as follows:

- *SC table*: ID, Internet Protocol version 4 (IPv4) address, port number, status, owner_ID, CPUs, memory, disk (*10B*). This table contains static SCeNBce data and status information. It also contains dynamic information regarding the utilization of physical resources, that is, the CPU and memory.
- *VM table*: Table_ID, IPv4, SC_ID, type, state, virtual CUPs (VCPUs), memory, disk, priority, "2ary_Assigned" (secondary assigned), 2ary_Assigned_to_ID (*10B*). This table contains the information related to the VMs including the connection information, virtual resources utilization, hosting SCeNBce, type of VM, and so on.
- *User table*: User ID, Name, VM_ID, status (*36B*). This table contains the information regarding the user (i.e., UE) mainly including the information about the associated VMs and user status.

Table 2.1 Management Messages for Communication between SCeNBce and SCM

Message	Size
SCeNB → SCM	
CONNECT	12B
RECONNECT	6B
CONNECT_UE	3B
DISCONNECT_UE	2B
MONITOR	3B
UE_CONNECTED	4B
OFFLOADING_DECISSION	>100B
REQ_OFFLOADING	>100B
REQ_PARALELIZATION	2B
END_PARALLELIZATION	2B
SCM → SCeNB	
PING	5B
MONITOR	3B

Source: Calvanese-Strinati E. et al., Deliverable D4.2 of FP7project TROPIC funded by European Commission, 2014.

◼ *Parallelization table*: Required time and number of unattended VMs (*4B*). This is a dynamic table that is intended to contain the status of the parallelization processes at runtime. It logs the available VMs for parallelization, which of them are currently in use, and so on.

Based on the aforementioned content, the amount of information needed to be exchanged is 60B (10 + 10 + 36 + 4B) in order to successfully synchronize the SCM context information. Since each SCM has to be addressed for the message exchange, two additional bytes are required (occupying two ID field protocol headers) making the size of the complete signaling message exchange equal to 62B.

We assume IPv4-based scenarios incorporating a network address translation (NAT) mechanism applied at the LAN perimeter. The NAT mechanism is considered as it is assumed in all real-world scenarios. Furthermore, we also consider architecture that includes IP security (IPsec) traffic flow to utilize an appropriate NAT traversal (NAT-T) mechanism in order to successfully pass through the NAT.

Since the communication is based on the well-known TCP/IP and related protocols, the header sizes (and related trailer sizes, where applicable) are assumed to be of a size presented in Table 2.2.

The overhead (*H*) in the particular network parts, as depicted in Figure 2.8, is defined by the following equations:

Table 2.2 Protocol Header Size

Protocol	Header Size [B] (Incl. Trailer Size Where Applicable)
TCP	20
IPv4	20
ESP (IP protocol 50)	24
UDP (port 4500 for NAT-T)	8
Eth (Ethernet)	26

$$H_{\text{LAN}} = H_{\text{TCP}} + H_{\text{IPv4}} + H_{\text{Eth}}$$

$$H_{\text{LAN\_IPsec}} = H_{\text{TCP}} + H_{\text{IPv4}} + H_{\text{ESP}} + H_{\text{IPv4}} + H_{\text{Eth}}$$

$$H_{\text{INT\_IPsec}} = H_{\text{TCP}} + H_{\text{IPv4}} + H_{\text{ESP}} + H_{\text{IPv4}} + H_{\text{Eth}}$$

$$H_{\text{LAN\_IPsec\_NAT-T}} = H_{\text{TCP}} + H_{\text{IPv4}} + H_{\text{ESP}} + H_{\text{UDP}} + H_{\text{IPv4}} + H_{\text{Eth}}$$

$$H_{\text{INT\_IPsec}} = H_{\text{TCP}} + H_{\text{IPv4}} + H_{\text{ESP}} + H_{\text{UDP}} + H_{\text{IPv4}} + H_{\text{Eth}}$$

$$H_{\text{EPC}} = H_{\text{TCP}} + H_{\text{IPv4}} + H_{\text{Eth}}$$

where the bottom index after H denotes the overhead of a related part of the protocol stack as presented in Table 2.2.

We consider four scenarios according to a practical aspect of SCM deployment (see Figure 2.8). The first scenario is a centralized approach (denoted as C-SCM), which assumes that the SCeNBce is assigned a publicly accessible IP address. The second scenario represents the C-SCM with NAT-T, the third scenario corresponds to the proposed H-SCM with NAT, and the last scenario is the VH-SCM with NAT. Note that all scenarios except the first one consider the SCeNBces to be hidden behind a device (e.g., a router) that implements a sort of NAT mechanism. In order to enable the SCeNBce to communicate outside of the (private) LAN, it is necessary to utilize the NAT-T feature, which establishes and maintains IP-based connections through gateways that implement NAT. In our case, the IPsec tunnel is utilized in order to connect the SCeNBce to the SCM.

Notice that Z-protocol communication in the latter scenario is internal. This means that the data do not flow across the network, but are exchanged only in the memory (RAM) of the SCeNBce.

This analysis of the overhead is transformed into the overall amount of signaling overhead per offloading task and into the delay of signaling in mobile networks enhanced with the SCC. Both are presented in the following section.

2.6 Performance Analysis

In this section, we exploit an analysis from the previous section to evaluate the signaling delay and relative signaling overhead. We compare both proposed architectures (H-SCM and VH-SCM)

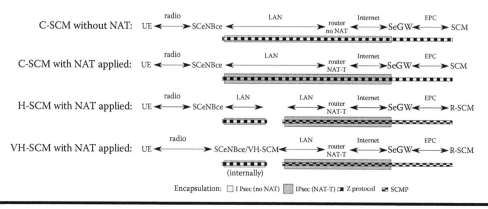

Figure 2.8 **Encapsulation of signaling protocol for different architectural options: (a) central-ized SCM without NAT, (b) centralized SCM with NAT-T, (c) hierarchical SCM with NAT-T, (d) virtual hierarchical SCM with NAT-T.**

with centralized SCC management with and without the NAT defined in [6]. To enable a performance comparison of all four options illustrated in Figure 2.8, we also present a scenario and system parameters for the performance evaluation in this section.

2.6.1 Scenario and Parameters for Performance Evaluation

For the simulation, we considered two scenarios: a corporate and a residential scenario. To that end, we define two types of backhaul connection: a high-speed fiber-optic connection and an asymmetric digital subscriber line (ADSL). The fiber optic represents a local area network with a 100 Mbps bitrate, as could be used in a corporate scenario. On the other hand, the ADSL represents a residential scenario, assuming the maximum asymmetric link bitrate of 8 Mbps and 1 Mbps in downlink and uplink, respectively.

We assume that 30 pieces of UE and two SCeNBces are deployed in the simulated area for both, corporate as well as residential scenarios.

As discussed earlier, some control messages are periodic in nature in order to ensure that all communication parties are available during the whole offloading and computing process. For that purpose, Z-protocol uses periodic updates that are sent between the SCeNBce and SCM (L-SCM or VL-SCM) every 15 s. The ScCMP synchronizes up-to-date statuses and keeps sessions alive between the L-SCM (VL-SCM) and R-SCM. Periodic updates of the ScCMP are not as "life threatening" as those of the Z-protocol, since they synchronize the current status between SCMs in the respective hierarchy (local and remote SCMs) in case the VL-SCM is not able to provide adequate computing resources. For that reason, the timer value is set to be four times higher compared with the value of the Z-protocol. However, there is no universal value for both timers. Similar to dynamic routing protocols [37,38], the timer values depend on the physical network topology. Optimization of these values is beyond the scope of this chapter and we leave it for further research and testing in real networks.

Initial conditions, which are set up for the analysis, can be found in Table 2.3. During the simulation, we assume the normal operation of computation without any unexpected problems such as memory or disk resource depletion.

Table 2.3 Simulation Parameters

Parameter	Value
Number of UE devices	30
Number of SCeNBces	2
Average number of requests per single UE device within simulation	1
Simulation time	6000 s
Z-protocol periodic updates due in every (keep-alive)	15 s
ScCMP periodic updates due in every (keep-alive)	60 s
EPC symmetric bitrate	100 Mbps
LAN symmetric bitrate	100 Mbps
ADSL downlink bitrate	8 Mbps
ADSL uplink bitrate	1 Mbps
Fiber symmetric bitrate	100 Mbps

2.6.2 Performance Evaluation

In this section, we provide simulation results and their discussion to show efficiency of the proposed distributed architectures for selected scenarios (residential and corporate). We compare both H-SCM and VH-SCM with the state-of-the-art centralized approach. For benchmarking purposes, we also consider a centralized solution without network address translation (in figures denoted as C-SCM no NAT). As discussed earlier, we assume that NAT is considered for all compared architectures (i.e., for the C-SCM, the H-SCM, and the VH-SCM as depicted in Figure 2.8), since it is in line with real-world deployments.

2.6.2.1 Signaling Overhead

The proposed architectures require signaling to coordinate the work of the VL-SCM and the R-SCM. This subsection deals with the signaling overhead required for the management of the offloaded computing. As we collect all signaling messages, the result contains the average signaling overhead of offloading processes.

As shown in Figure 2.9, the cumulative overhead generated by management message exchange for offloading a single task in architecture with conventional C-SCM is roughly 8.3 kb (no NAT) and 8.5 kb (NAT), respectively. This overhead is composed of protocols as shown in Table 2.2. As can be seen, there is no significant increase in overhead due to NAT (roughly 0.2 kb). An extension of the architecture toward the H-SCM or the VH-SCM can reduce the signaling overhead roughly to 5.7 kb and 5.4 kb compared with the C-SCM (i.e., by 34% and 37%, respectively). This reduction is a result of the fact that the appropriate part of the messages does not need to be transmitted from the SCeNBce to the VL-SCM across the network, since the VL-SCM is hosted in the virtualized resources of the SCeNBce. In other words, the proposed approaches decrease the total number and size of the exchanged messages, which are necessary for properly working offloading

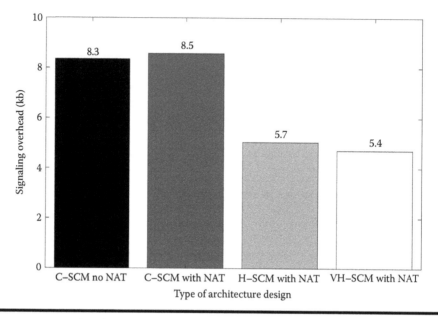

Figure 2.9   Average signaling overhead of an average offloading request.

and signaling mechanisms (i.e., authorization phase, offloading phase, and system cleanup phase messages as shown in Section 2.3). In the case of the C-SCM, these messages would be delivered across the respective network segments. Note that the amount of the overhead is independent on the backhaul technology (fiber optic and ADSL).

2.6.2.2 Signaling Delay

Besides signaling overhead, it is also important to minimize the delay of the signaling procedures required to successfully offload computational tasks to the cloud. Therefore, we also examine the delay of signaling. Since the delay is strongly dependent on the backhaul type, we distinguish optical fiber (for the corporate scenario) and ADSL (for the residential scenario) connections between the SCeNBces and the core network.

The simulation results show that the hierarchical designs are far more efficient in terms of signaling delay when compared with conventional C-SCM (see Figures 2.10 and 2.11). The conventional C-SCM with NAT results in a delay of roughly 20.2 and 1.3 ms for ADSL and optical fiber, respectively. We can see that NAT increases signaling delay by roughly 5% and 7% for ADSL and optical fiber, respectively. Nevertheless, both proposed solutions (H-SCM and VH-SCM) lead to a reduction of signaling delay to roughly 8.6 ms and 0.6 ms for ADSL and optical fiber, respectively. This represents a reduction of the end-to-end signaling delay of both proposed solutions by approximately 60%. This shortening in transmission delay is caused by avoiding the transmission of signaling from the SCeNBces to the centralized SCM. It can also be seen that slightly lower delay is achieved by the VH-SCM because there is no delay for transmission signaling from the SCeNBce to the L-SCM and back. Nevertheless, difference between both approaches can be considered as negligible since it is lower than 0.03 ms.

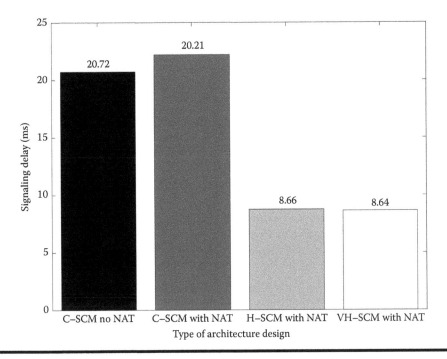

Figure 2.10 **Average transmission signaling delay of an average cloud service request in a residential scenario (ADSL).**

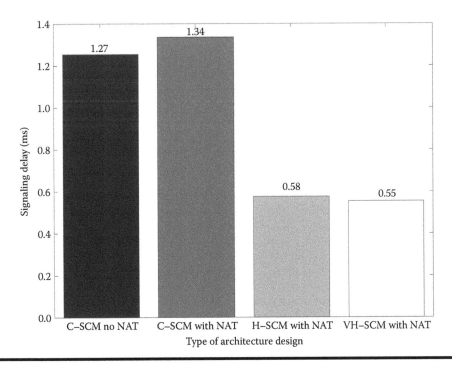

Figure 2.11 **Average transmission signaling delay of an average cloud service request in corporate scenario (optical fiber).**

2.7 Conclusions

This chapter addresses architecture for 5G mobile networks enabling cloud computing at the edge of a mobile network and it's merging with C-RAN. We have proposed two distributed options for the deployment of SCM management and the control of the allocation of computing resources with respect to radio and backhaul status in mobile edge computing. The proposed solution is based on the distributed virtualization of resources for network control. The first option exploits a hierarchical splitting of functionalities of the cloud management entity between local (distributed) and remote (centralized) SCM units. The second approach further virtualizes control features of the local SCM in the base stations. This architecture can be efficiently merged with the C-RAN concept by the inclusion of cloud control functionalities by the BBU or by their splitting among the BBU and the RRH.

Both proposed solutions reduce the amount of signaling overhead (by more than 34%) and lower the signaling delay (by approximately 60%). A drawback of proposed hierarchical solutions is a higher implementation cost. This drawback is, however, mitigated by the virtualization of the local SCM.

Still, several challenges need to be solved to make a use of the proposed solution feasible in 5G mobile networks. The key issue is the allocation and splitting of the control functionalities between the BBU and the RRH. Then, in case of distribution of a part of the control functionalities over small cells or femtocells, a backup solution for the case of a failure of such a node must be developed and security of access to processed data must be ensured. Another challenge is to efficiently share virtualized resources for control functionalities and for offloaded applications, having in mind strict requirements on network reliability, stability, and security while improving the quality of services for users offloading their applications to the edge of the mobile network.

Acknowledgment

This work has been performed in the framework of the FP7 project TROPIC IST-318784 STP, which is funded by the European Community. The authors would like to acknowledge the contributions of their colleagues from the TROPIC Consortium (http://www.ict-tropic.eu).

References

1. J. G. Andrews, S. Buzzi, W. Choi, S. V. Hanly, A. Lozano, A. C. K. Soong, J. C. Zhang, What will 5G be?, *IEEE Journal on Selected Areas in Communications*, Vol. 32, No. 6, pp. 1065–1082, June 2014.
2. M.V. Barbera, S. Kosta, A. Mei, J. Stefa, To offload or not to offload? The bandwidth and energy costs of mobile cloud computing, IEEE INFOCOM 2013, April 2013.
3. N. Bhushan et al., Network densification: The dominant theme for wireless evolution into 5G, *IEEE Communications Magazine*, Vol. 52, No. 2, pp. 82–89, February 2014.
4. Nokia Solutions and Networks, Nokia outdoor 3G/LTE small cells deployment strategy: The race to the pole, White Paper, 2014.
5. S. Barbarossa, S. Sardellitti, P. Di Lorenzo, Computation offloading for mobile cloud computing based on wide cross-layer optimization, Future network and mobile summit (FuNeMS2013), IEEE, July 2013.
6. F. Lobillo, Z. Becvar, M.A. Puente, P. Mach, F. Lo Presti, F. Gambetti, E. Calvanese Strinati, An architecture for mobile computation offloading on cloud-enabled LTE small cells, IEEE WCNC workshops 2014, April 2014.

7. Huawei, IBM, Intel, Nokia Networks, NTT DOCOMO, Vodafone, Mobile-edge computing, Mobile-edge computing: Introductory technical white paper, available at https://portal.etsi.org/Portals/0/TBpages/MEC/Docs/Mobile-edge_Computing_-_Introductory_Technical_White_Paper_V1%2018-09-14.pdf, September 2014.
8. M.A. Puente, Z. Becvar, M. Rohlik, F. Lobillo, E. Calvanese-Strinati, A seamless integration of computationally-enhanced base stations into mobile networks towards 5G, IEEE VTC Spring Workshop on 5G Architecture, 2015.
9. Nokia Siemens Networks, Liquid net: Nokia Siemens networks intelligent base stations, White Paper, 2012.
10. T. Nakamura, S. Nagata, A. Benjebbour, Y. Kishiyama, T. Hai, S. Xiaodong, Y. Ning, L. Nan, Trends in small cell enhancements in LTE advanced, *IEEE Communications Magazine*, Vol. 51, No. 2, pp. 98–105, February 2013.
11. M. Satyanarayanan, P. Bahl, R. Cáceres, N. Davies, The case for VM-based cloudlets in mobile computing, *IEEE Pervasive Computing*, Vol. 8, No. 4, pp. 14–23, October 2009.
12. S. Simanta, G.A. Lewis, E. Morris, H. Kiryong Ha, M. Satyanarayanan, A reference architecture for mobile code offload in hostile environments, IEEE/IFIP WICSA and ECSA, August 2012.
13. O. Muñoz, A. Pascual-Iserte, J. Vidal, Joint allocation of radio and computational resources in wireless application offloading, Future network and mobile summit (FuNeMS 2013), Lisbon, Portugal, July 2013.
14. V. Di Valerio, F. Lo Presti, Optimal virtual machines allocation in mobile femto-cloud computing: An MDP approach, IEEE WCNC workshops, April 2014.
15. Radio Access and Spectrum, FP7 Future Networks Cluster, 5G radio network architecture, White Paper, 2013.
16. 3GPP TS 36.300 v 12.5.0, Technical specification group radio access network, evolved universal terrestrial radio access (E-UTRA) and evolved universal terrestrial radio access network (E-UTRAN), overall description, Stage 2 (Release 12), March 2015.
17. China Mobile Research, C-RAN international workshop, C-RAN international workshop, April 2010.
18. China Mobile Research, C-RAN: The road towards green RAN, White Paper, version 2.5, October 2011.
19. National Instruments, What is I/Q data?, tutorial, March 2016, available at http://www.ni.com/tutorial/4805/en/.
20. A. Checko, H.L. Christiansen, Y. Yan, L. Scolari, G. Kardaras, M.S. Berger, L. Dittmann, Cloud RAN for mobile networks: A technology overview, *IEEE Communications Surveys and Tutorials*, Vol. 17, No. 1, pp. 405–426, November 2015.
21. Y. Huiyu, Z. Naizheng, Y. Yuyu, P. Skov, Performance evaluation of coordinated multipoint reception in CRAN under LTE-advanced uplink, EAI, CHINACOM, 2012.
22. L. Li, J. Liu, K. Xiong, P. Butovitsch, Field test of uplink CoMP joint processing with C-RAN testbed, EAI, CHINACOM, 2012.
23. A. Liu, V.K.N. Lau, Joint power and antenna selection optimization for energy-efficient large distributed MIMO networks, IEEE ICCS, 2012.
24. Q.T. Vien, N. Ogbonna, H.X. Nguyen, R. Trestian, P. Shah, Non-orthogonal multiple access for wireless downlink in cloud radio access networks, European wireless, 2015.
25. D. Sabella, P. Rost, Y. Sheng, E. Pateromichelakis, U. Salim, P. Guitton-Ouhamou, M. Di Girolamo, G. Giuliani, RAN as a service: Challenges of designing a flexible RAN architecture in a cloud-based heterogeneous mobile network, Future Network and Mobile Summit, 2013.
26. Z. Becvar, et al., Distributed computing, storage and radio resource allocation over cooperative femtocells: Scenarios and requirements, deliverable D2.1 of FP7 project TROPIC funded by European Commission, July 2013.
27. J. Oueis, E. Calvanese-Strinati, S. Barbarossa, Multi-parameter decision algorithm for mobile computation offloading, IEEE WCNC, 2014.
28. O. Munoz, A. Pascual Iserte, J. Vidal, M. Molina, Energy-latency trade-off for multiuser wireless computation offloading, IEEE WCNC workshops, 2014.

29. O. Munoz, A. Pascual-Iserte, J. Vidal, Optimization of radio and computational resources for energy efficiency in latency-constrained application offloading, *IEEE Transactions on Vehicular Technology*, Vol. 64, No. 10, pp. 4738–4755, October 2015.
30. M.A. Puente, et al., Distributed cloud services, deliverable D5.2 of FP7project TROPIC funded by European Commission, June 2014.
31. C. Yang, et al., Over-the-air signaling in cellular communication systems, *IEEE Wireless Communications Magazine*, Vol. 21, No. 4, pp. 102–129, 2014.
32. M. Goldhamer, Offloading mobile applications to base stations, U.S. 20140287754 A1, U.S. patent, 2014.
33. E. Calvanese Strinati et al., Adaptation of virtual infrastructure manager and implemented interfaces, Deliverable D4.2 of FP7project TROPIC funded by the European Commission, February 2014.
34. M. Rohlik, T. Vanek, Securing offloading process within small cell cloud-based mobile networks, IEEE Globecom workshops, Austin, TX, 2014.
35. J.K. Tsay et al., A vulnerability in the UMTS and LTE authentication and key agreement protocols, *Computer Network Security*, Springer, Berlin, 2012.
36. 3GPP TS 33.203 3G security; Access security for IP-based services, Rel. 13, version 13.0.0, September 2015.
37. F. Zhao, P. Zhu, M. Wang, B. Wang, Optimizing network configurations based on potential profit loss, *ACIS International Conference on Software Engineering, Artificial Intelligence, Networking, and Parallel/Distributed Computing (SNPD 2007)*, IEEE, pp. 327–332, July 2007.
38. D. Kiwior, E.G. Idhaw, S.V. Pizzi, Quality of service (QoS) sensitivity for the OSPF protocol in the airborne networking environment, *IEEE Military Communications Conference (MILCOM 2005)*, pp. 2366–2372, October 2005.

Chapter 3

Non-Orthogonal Multiple Access Schemes for Next-Generation 5G Networks: A Survey

Namadev Bhuvanasundaram, Huan X. Nguyen, Ramona Trestian, and Quoc-Tuan Vien

Contents

3.1 Introduction

The rapid advances in both mobile and wireless communication technologies and the high-end mobile devices have led to an increase in the number of users and their quality of service expectations. This in turn has led to an exponential increase in the amount of traffic that the network operators need to accommodate within their networks. According to Cisco [1], by 2020 the global IP network will carry 6.4 EB of Internet traffic per day and 21 GB per capita. Therefore, in order to cope with this explosion of broadband data traffic, the network operators will make use of various new solutions and technologies to be integrated in the next generation of mobile networks, for example, 5G networks to increase their network capacity. Some of the promising solutions include the deployment of a complex structure of heterogeneous small cell networks (HetNets) [2] enabling the dynamic cooperation of different radio access technologies (RATs), Wi-Fi, and femtocell opportunistic offloading techniques of the mobile traffic; techniques such as multiple-input multiple-output (MIMO) [3] or massive MIMO [4], that allow for numerous antennas to simultaneously serve a number of users in the same time-frequency resource; cloud radio access networks (C-RAN) [5], which offers a centralized, cooperative, clean, and cloud computing architecture for 5G radio access networks; software-defined networks (SDN) [6]; and network function virtualization (NFV) that could help the mobile operators to reduce their capital expenditure (CAPEX) intensity by transferring their hardware-based network to software- and cloud based solutions.

However, some of the solutions might result in high costs and an increase in intercell interference levels. In this context, another promising solution is increasing the spectral efficiency in next-generation 5G networks by using advanced receivers with interference cancellation or advanced coding and modulation solutions such as non-orthogonal multiple access (NOMA) techniques [12].

Therefore, this book chapter will present a survey on the latest developments on NOMA techniques for next-generation 5G networks. The chapter is organized as follows: Section 3.2 presents a comparison between orthogonal multiple access (OMA) schemes and NOMA. Section 3.3 introduces the system model for NOMA. Section 3.4 presents various solutions for using NOMA in the uplink, whereas Section 3.5 discusses the use of NOMA for downlink. Several types of NOMA proposed in the literature are addressed in Section 3.6, and Section 3.7 concludes the chapter.

3.2 OMA versus NOMA

3.2.1 Orthogonal Multiple Access

With the exponential growth in mobile broadband traffic attention has been put on the development of different access technologies in order to enable the anytime anywhere connectivity and satisfy the users' increasing demands. These multiple access schemes are a key feature of the mobile wireless communications systems that enable different users to gain access to the network simultaneously. Therefore, researchers have been focusing on the design of the multiple access schemes. Starting with the frequency division multiple access (FDMA) scheme [7], which was used in 1G technology and is based on the analog frequency modulation. Whereas the 2G systems employed FDMA in combination with time division multiple access scheme (TDMA) [8] to enable multiple access. TDMA makes use of time multiplexing and is based on the digital modulation. However, starting with the 3G systems a new multiple access scheme was employed, such as code division multiple access (CDMA) [9]. CDMA makes use of the orthogonality of a spreading sequence to enable the access of an increased number of users to the cellular system. Because of the existing problems on spectrum resources scarcity, the new 4G systems introduced the use of orthogonal frequency division multiple access (OFDMA) [10]. OFDMA is based on orthogonal frequency division multiplexing (OFDM) and makes use of many orthogonal closed spaced carriers improving the spectral efficiency and enabling an increased number of users connections.

Some of the advantages of OFDM and OFDMA used in the 4G systems could be identified as follows:

- Intercell interference is eliminated by ensuring orthogonality between subcarriers.
- Compatibility with MIMO systems by employing the fast Fourier transform.
- Interference within the cell is avoided by using a cyclic prefix.
- The transmission power could be adjusted based on the users' bit rates.
- Frequency diversity is achieved by spreading the carriers across the available spectrum.
- Robust against intersymbol interference (ISI) and multipath distortion.

However, the main disadvantages of OFDM and OFDMA are as follows:

- The peak-to-average rower ratio (PAPR) is relatively high due to parallel transmission of modulated symbols.
- The limited spectral efficiency due to the cyclic prefix.
- Highly sensitive to frequency offsets and phase noise.
- Proper synchronization between transmitter and receiver is a must for better performance.

These disadvantages prevent OMA schemes from being immediately used in 5G systems and a new type of multiple access scheme needs to be developed to provide higher spectral efficiency and the increased capability and capacity of the system.

3.2.2 Non-Orthogonal Multiple Access

Some of the access techniques that are promising to become 5G standard candidates are the non-orthogonal access schemes, such as NOMA [11].

NOMA is defined as an intercell multiuser multiplexing scheme that proposes the use of an additional domain, that is, the power domain, which has not been utilized in the previous 2G, 3G, and even 4G wireless systems [12]. At the transmitter side, the user's data is multiplexed on the power domain, which means less power allocated for the user equipment (UE) located near the base station (BS) and more power allocation for far (cell-edge) users. NOMA supports simultaneous connections, which is suitable to address the challenges related to massive user connectivity. User multiplexing on NOMA is performed without relying on the knowledge of the transmitter of the instantaneous channel state information (CSI) of each user. Successive interference cancellation (SIC) [13] is employed at near users, which also has a good enough channel to decode the far users' data first and cancel out the interference. Studies have shown that NOMA enhances the reception, capacity, and cell-edge user (CEU) throughput performance [11,14–18]. Moreover, NOMA uses superposition coding (SC) [19] for downlink transmission, where all the users' data is combined together and then transmitted.

Liu et al. [20], presents a short survey on NOMA, which illustrates the functionality of basic NOMA with SIC when two user are considered in order to provide a better understanding of

	3G	3.9/4G	Future radio access
User multiplexing	Nonorthogonal (CDMA)	Orthogonal (OFDMA)	Nonorthogonal with SIC (NOMA)
Signal waveform	Single carrier	OFDM	OFDM
Link adaptation	Fast TPC	AMC	AMC + Power allocation
Representation	Nonorthogonal assisted by power control 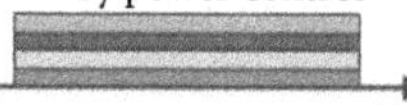	Orthogonal between users 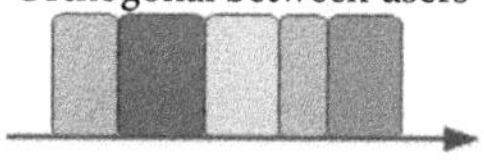	Superposition and power allocation 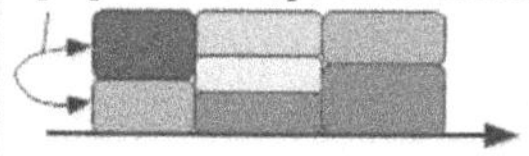

Figure 3.1 Comparison of cellular multiple access schemes for 3G, 3.9G/4G, and future radio access networks.

NOMA along with the expression of capacity of both users. The authors also discuss the link-level and system-level evaluation of NOMA in relation to SIC. Finally, a discussion on how NOMA can be used for multiple access relay channel schemes is provided.

Some of the main features of NOMA are listed as follows [12]:

- NOMA introduces controllable interferences to realize overloading at the cost of a slightly increased receiver complexity, which results in higher spectral efficiency and massive connectivity.
- The power domain is used for modulation processing and user multiplexing in NOMA.
- NOMA increases the system capacity and coverage and supports mass user connectivity.
- NOMA promises robust performance in practical wide-area deployments despite mobility or CSI feedback latency.
- NOMA retains the advantages of OFDMA and filter bank multicarrier (FBMC), because basic carrier waveforms in NOMA can still be generalized from OFDMA or FBMC.
- NOMA necessitates a careful design to schedule the right partners to share the same resource block for performance optimization.

A comparison between the multiple access schemes for 3G, 3.9/4G, and the future radio access for 2020s as seen by Saito et al. [11] is illustrated in Figure 3.1.

3.3 NOMA System Model

In this section, we formulate the system model for NOMA in downlink and uplink cellular networks.

Figure 3.2 represents an example of the basic functionality of NOMA when SIC is employed at the receiver. The example scenario consists of one BS and two UE devices, where UE_1 is located near the BS and UE_2 is located far from the BS in downlink transmission. The far user is also referred to as the *cell-edge user*.

In this scenario, the piece of UE near the BS decodes the CEU data first and then decodes its corresponding user data, whereas the CEU decodes only its corresponding data by considering the near user's data as noise. SC is used at the transmitted side to combine all user symbols together.

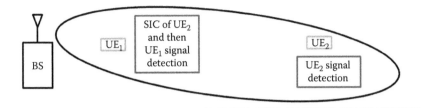

Figure 3.2   Basic NOMA employed with SIC at the receiver.

Therefore, the received signal y at the ith UE for the downlink transmission is given as

$$y_i = h_i X + n_i \tag{3.1}$$

where:

h_i represents the channel between the BS and the ith user with $i \in \{1, 2, ..., M\}$

n_i is the additive white Gaussian noise (AWGN) of the ith user

$X = \sum_{i=1}^{M} x_i$ is the SC data transmitted from the BS to the UE devices where x_i is the transmitted data signal for the ith user and M is the total number of users in the system

However, in case of uplink transmission, the received signal Y at the BS can be formulated as

$$Y = \sum_{i=1}^{M} H_i z_i + N \tag{3.2}$$

where:

z_i is the signal transmitted from ith ($i \in \{1, 2, ..., M\}$) piece of UE to the corresponding serving BS

N is the AWGN at the BS

H_i is the channel from the ith piece of UE ($i\{1, 2, ..., M\}$) to the BS

M represents the total number of UE devices present in the system. At the BS receiver side, all the UE devices' data is combined together

3.4 NOMA for Uplink Transmission

The authors in [21] propose a NOMA scheme for uplink transmission for OFDM systems, which removes the resource allocation exclusively and allows more than one user to share the same subcarrier without any coding/spreading redundancy. To control the receiver complexity in the uplink, the number of users in each subcarrier is limited to a specific number, which is considered as the upper limit as shown in Figure 3.3. The spectral efficiency of the NOMA technique is higher than the current OMA and the receiver complexity is lower when compared with the conventional unconstrained NOMA scheme. The authors propose new subcarrier and power allocation algorithms for the new NOMA scheme. At the receiver side, the optimum multiuser detection is implemented to separate the users' data. The results show that the system-level performance of the proposed NOMA scheme improves the spectral efficiency and fairness compared with the OMA scheme.

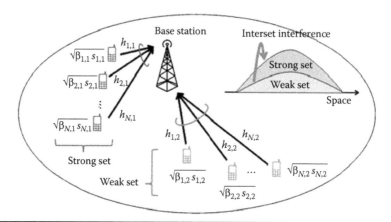

Figure 3.3 Uplink NOMA system.

In [22], the authors investigate the system-level throughput performance of the NOMA with minimum mean squared error-based liner filtering followed by the successive interference canceller (MMSE-SIC) for the cellular uplink transmissions. NOMA with MMSE-SIC can achieve the multiuser capacity region in the multiple access channel (MAC), which should be beneficial to enhance the total user throughput and CEU throughput simultaneously compared with the OMA. The multiplexing of multiple users within the same frequency block may increase the intercell interference in the context of the cellular uplink transmissions. The aim is to mitigate the intercell interference increase due to non-orthogonal user multiplexing. Therefore, the authors employ the proportional fair–based (PF-based) scheduling scheme to achieve the trade-off between the total user throughput and the CEU throughput. SIC is employed at the BS side which reduces the signaling overhead introduced by the NOMA. The results show that the proposed transmission power control significantly enhances the system-level throughput performance compared with OMA.

In the case of single carrier non-orthogonal multiple access (SC-NOMA), an evolved node B (eNB) with an iterative interference cancellation receiver is employed. This is capable of allocating overlapped spectra to multiple intra-cell UE exceeding the number of receiver antennas. A novel frequency-domain (FD) scheduling based on the expected value of cell throughput for the SC-NOMA is proposed in [23]. Firstly, the eNB selects a candidate subband (SB) for a piece of UE by using the metric, which is the signal-to-noise ratio (SNR) after turbo equalization. Then, the expected cell throughput is calculated by both the candidate SB to a piece of UE and all the previously allocated SBs. When the expected cell throughput increases in comparison with the throughput received before assigning the candidate SB, then the eNB allocates the candidate SB to the piece of UE. The proposed method increases the throughput performance of the FD based scheduling in the SC-NOMA system compared with the SB criterion-based scheduling.

For an uplink multiantenna environment, Endo et al. [22] considered a non-orthogonal access in multiple cells. The users assumed are present within the same cell and are orthogonally allocated in terms of a resource block. In [24], a set selection algorithm and optimal power control scheme is proposed for maximizing the sum capacity of uplink with multiantenna NOMA. The proposed uplink NOMA (UL-NOMA) system shares the space resources to improve the sum capacity. The set selection algorithm is used to reduce the interference and the interset interference that is caused by a set selection algorithm, is mitigated by using the orthogonality between users' channels. The optimal power control is used to maximize the sum capacity of the system. The numerical results show that the proposed set selection algorithm and power control can improve the sum capacity of UL-NOMA system over that of the conventional OMA system.

3.5 NOMA for Downlink Transmissions

3.5.1 System-Level Performance of NOMA

In [15], the authors first discuss the working principle and benefits of NOMA over OMA, by comparing their corresponding sum rates and exploiting the channel gain difference among users of both NOMA and OMA. Secondly, they discuss practical considerations regarding NOMA, such as signaling overhead, multiuser power allocation, SIC error propagation, performance in high mobility scenarios and a combination of MIMO systems. They apply random beamforming (BF) to transform the MIMO channel into a single-input multiple-output (SIMO) channel and for interbeam and intrabeam interference mitigation they employ a SIC and interference rejection combining (IRC) scheme at the receiver side. The results show that the system-level performance of NOMA is 30% higher when compared with OMA.

A system-level evaluation of NOMA is performed in [11], and the performance of the proposed system is compared with the OFDMA scheme. NOMA with SIC improves the capacity of the system and the CEU throughput performance based on wideband channel quality information (CQI). The transmitter side (BS) does not need to rely on the frequency-selective CQI to improve the system performance. The authors discuss applying NOMA to MIMO using SIC and IRC at the UE side in order to achieve further capacity gain.

The outage performance and ergodic capacity of NOMA is studied in [25], and the achieved performance is compared with the OMA techniques. Furthermore in [14], to clarify the potential gains of NOMA over OFDMA, they consider some key link adaptation functionalities of long-term evolution (LTE) radio interfaces such as adaptive modulation and coding (AMC), hybrid automatic repeat request (HARQ), time/frequency-domain scheduling, and outer loop link adaptation (OLLA), in addition to NOMA functionalities such as multiuser power allocation. Channel gain order is used to determine the order of UE devices for data deduction. The UE devices located near the transmitter will have high channel gain and less power is required for data transmission. CEUs will have low channel gain and require more transmission power for data to be received at the UE side. The simulation results show that the overall cell throughput, CEU throughput, and the degree of proportional fairness of NOMA are all superior to that of OMA.

3.5.2 Cloud Radio Access Network (C-RAN)

C-RAN has recently been proposed to connect all the BSs via a cloud, as shown in Figure 3.4. In the C-RAN environment, the network services are provided in a cloud for the respective BSs to connect and supply services to the mobile users. The proposed system model in [26] uses NOMA for downlink in C-RAN with respect to the distance between the BS and the cloud-based central station along with their corresponding channel quality.

The authors show that the proposed NOMA-based C-RAN system model achieves a sum rate of up to eight times more than the case when the conventional OFDMA is employed.

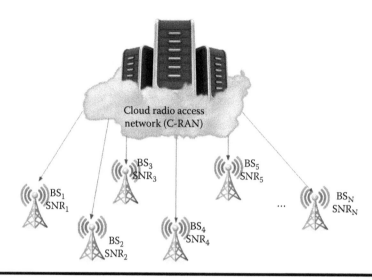

Figure 3.4 System model of downlink C-RAN.

3.5.3 Multiuser Beamforming System

The authors in [27] propose a new clustering algorithm to minimize the intercluster and interuser interference and effective power allocation scheme that maximizes the sum capacity while guaranteeing the weak users' capacity. The proposed clustering algorithm selects two users that have high correlation and a large channel gain difference in each cluster. Based on the clustering algorithm, the power will be allocated for both the users, so that these users will be supported by a single BF vector. A comparative study of the proposed clustering algorithm with other existing models such as exhaustive search and random selection is presented. The results show that the proposed NOMA-BF sum capacity is greater than the conventional BF system model.

The proposed BF method in [28] uses NOMA with zero forcing (ZF) precoding for multiple users exceeding the degree of freedom at the BS antenna. The achievable rate is 1.5–3.0 times better when compared with the case where ZF precoding alone is used. By introducing maximum ratio combining (MRC) at the UE device's side, the authors were able to improve the achievable rate at low SNR values. The proposed system model has been studied under two- and four-user case scenarios to show its efficiency.

3.5.4 Relay Channel

Figure 3.5 illustrates a multiple access relay channel, which consists of M sources (e.g., $S_1, S_2, ..., S_M$) transmitting data to a destination node (e.g., D) via a relay node (e.g., $R_1, R_2, ..., R_L$) [29]. A new power adaptive network coding (PANC) strategy for a NOMA relay channel (MARC) is proposed in [30]. To achieve full diversity gain, the authors use the proposed PANC, in which the relay decides which power level should be applied to each network coded symbol based on the received signals. In order to achieve high coding gain, they optimize the power adaptation factor at the relay to minimize the symbol pair error rate (SPER) at the destination by considering the relation between the Euclidean distance of the received constellation and SPER. The simulation results show that the proposed PANC scheme with power adaptation factor optimizations and

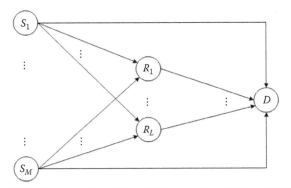

Figure 3.5   A multiple access multiple relay channel: example.

power scaling factor design achieves full diversity and higher coding gains compared with other network coding schemes from the literature.

In [31], Mohamad et al. discuss the relay channel problem from an information theoretical perspective. The scenario of multiple independent sources that wish to transmit to one destination via multiple relays is considered. Each relay is half duplex and implements the selective decode and forward (SDF) strategy and cooperates with other relays. The authors compared the individual and common outage event for the relay assisted cooperative communication issue non-orthogonal MARC (NOMAMRC). The simulation results illustrate that the NOMAMRC always gets a better performance than the no cooperation case even under the noisy slow fading source-to-relay links, which is a quite perfectly desirable feature.

Kim et al. [32] propose a cooperative relaying system (CRS) using NOMA. The achievable average rate of the proposed solution is analyzed assuming independent Rayleigh fading channels and also its asymptotic expression is provided using a high SNR approximation. A suboptimal power allocation scheme for two data signals transmitted by the source is also proposed. The results show that the proposed CRS using NOMA can achieve more spectral efficiency than the conventional CRS when the SNR is high and the average channel power of the source-to-relay link is better than those of the source-to-destination and relay-to-destination links.

3.5.5 Cooperative NOMA

Choi et al. in [33] use cooperative NOMA to analyze the performance of the system when three pieces of UE within the cell are considered; such as one CEU and two UE devices. The scenario consists of two BSs in different cells that cooperate with each other to serve the CEU along with the users within each cell. Here, the rate of these three users are compared under three different conditions, such as (1) when both BSs transmit data to the CEU under cooperation, (2) when only one BS serves the CEU, and (3) when the CEU selects the BS from which it wants to receive data based on dynamic cell selection. Individual rates and the sum rate of the three users within these scenarios are compared with respect to the distance between the piece of UE and BSs and with increasing SNR values. The simulation results under the cooperative NOMA provide the CEU with a reasonable transmission rate without degrading the rates to near users and increase the spectral efficiency.

Investigation of the CEU sum rate was carried out in [34]. In the conventional NOMA systems, the performance of the system model considers the near and far users. Since the near users

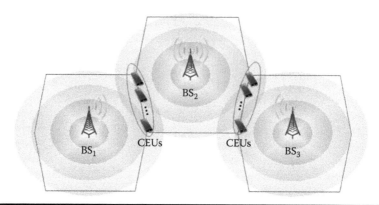

Figure 3.6   Cooperative NOMA with inter-user and intra-cell interference among cell-edge users.

require less power for data transmission its interference on the CEU is significantly less and is considered as noise. The authors consider a special case to analyze the effect of interference on the CEU. The effect of intra- and intercell interference on the CEU is considered under a cooperative scenario as illustrated in Figure 3.6. The proposed system model employs interference cancellation techniques such as SIC and random BF at the receivers' and transmitters' sides. The sum rate of the proposed system is compared with the conventional cooperative system, which does not employ any interference cancellation techniques at the transceivers' sides. If the number of users increases the receiver complexity also increases. The results show that the overall throughput of the proposed system outperforms the conventional system model.

Ding et al. in [35] propose a cooperative transmission scheme in order to fully exploit prior information available in NOMA system. In the conventional NOMA system the users with better channel conditions decodes the information of other users in order to cancel the interference. In the proposed system model, the users with better channel conditions are used as relay to improve the reliability for the users with poor connections to the BS. The outage probability and diversity order achieved by the analyzed and analytical results demonstrate that the proposed cooperative NOMA can achieve the maximum diversity gain for all users. In order to reduce the system complexity the authors make use of user pairing, with channel gains whose absolute squares of the channel coefficients are more distinctive, rather grouping users with high channel gain.

In the conventional NOMA scheme, the user who is near to the BS cancels the far user's signal and then detects the desired signal. But the far user considers the near user's signal as noise and decodes its desired signal. In [36], a joint detection and decoding scheme for the far user in a NOMA downlink is proposed and its constellation-constrained capacity (CCC) is evaluated through numerical analysis. The proposed scheme allows user pairing with a difference in the propagation losses of less than 8 dB. In this way, the number of user pairs in the NOMA system increases, leading to the achievement of a larger total capacity.

3.5.6 Frequency Reuse for Downlink NOMA

In [37], Lan et al. focus on improving the cell edge throughput by reducing the interference from the cell-interior users. This is done by the allocation of more transmission power for the CEU and by allocating wider bandwidths to cell-interior users. A novel fractional frequency reuse (FFR) scheme is used to reduce the significant interference at the cell-edge zone due to large reuse factor. Unlike the conventional FFR the proposed FFR allocates different levels of transmission power to the users. Numerical results show that the proposed FFR scheme achieves good improvement in CEU throughput and cell average throughput, by using more transmission for CEU for better prevention against intercell interference and expanding the bandwidth for cell-interior users.

3.5.7 NOMA with Single-User MIMO

The combination of NOMA with open-loop and closed-loop single-user MIMO (SU-MIMO) is investigated in [38]. The purpose is to investigate the performance gain of NOMA combined with SU-MIMO with respect to OMA for both open-loop and closed-loop cases. The results show that the performance gain of NOMA for open-loop and closed-loop SU-MIMO is 23% for cell average throughput and 33% for CEU throughput compared with the OMA system. The authors discuss the key issues involved in the combinations such as the scheduling algorithm, SIC order determination, transmission power assignment, and feedback design.

In [39], the impact on rank optimization on the performance of NOMA with SU-MIMO in downlink is discussed. Enhancements of rank selection and feedback were considered in the LTE Release 8 framework. The authors propose rank optimization methods at the transmitter side. A geometry-based rank adjustment method is studied first and enhanced feedback method for rank adjustment methods at the transmitter side is discussed in the later part. From the simulation results, the performance gain of NOMA improves with proposed rank adjustment methods when compared with the OMA system.

3.5.8 Receiver Complexity

Different receiver designs are studied in [40] and their performance is evaluated and compared by using link-level simulations. A new transmission and receiving scheme is proposed for downlink NOMA. In order to achieve Gray mapping of the superposed signal of different users, joint modulation is applied at the transmitter side. At the receiver side a simple log-likelihood ratio (LLR) calculation method is used to directly decode the desired signal without SIC processing and to reduce the complexity at the receiver side. From the analysis, codeword-level SIC achieves almost the same performance as ideal SIC, while the interference of the CEU cannot be perfectly cancelled in all cases for symbol-level SIC.

In the proposed receiver scheme, the desired signal of the cell center user can be directly detected without detecting the signal of the CEU and SIC processing. Its performance is evaluated and compared with other SIC receivers. The proposed receiver achieves much better performance than symbol-level SIC with the advantage of having no need for SIC processing. The codeword-level SIC and the proposed receiver can work for a large range of power allocation ratios, while the symbol-level SIC is sensitive to the power allocation ratio assigned to CEUs. When high-order modulation is applied for cell center users, even larger power allocation ratio should be allocated to CEUs.

3.6 Types of Non-Orthogonal Access Schemes

A comparative study on three different types of NOMA schemes is presented in [41] with respect to their uplink bit error rate performance. The authors discuss three multiple access schemes that are seen as possible 5G standard candidates; such as sparse code multiple access (SCMA), multiuser shared multiple access (MUSA), and pattern division multiple access (PDMA).

SCMA tries to further improve the spectrum efficiency by considering the spatial and code domain. SCMA was proposed by Huawei, and is a frequency-domain NOMA technique that makes use of the sparse codebook to improve the spectrum efficiency by code domain multiple access.

MUSA was proposed by Zhongxing Telecommunication Equipment Corporation (ZTE) and is a 5G multiple access scheme that makes use of a spreading sequences, which can be non-orthogonal, and advanced SIC receivers. The user data is first spread by using the spreading sequence and then all the users' data is combined and transmitted. At the receiver side, the advanced SIC-based receiver will demodulate and retrieve the data of each user.

PDMA was proposed by Datang and is a novel NOMA scheme based on the joint design of SIC-amenable pattern at the transmitter's side and low-complexity quasi-ML SIC detection at the receiver's side. Non-orthogonal characteristic patterns in different domains, like power, space, or code domains are used to distinguish between the users at the transmitter side. By using the SIC amendable detection at the receiver side, the multiple users could get equivalent diversity degree.

The performance of SCMA in terms of bit error rate is good compared with MUSA and PDMA. This is because of its near-optimal design of sparse codewords together with a near-optimal message passing algorithm receiver. The authors identify areas that need to be optimized in the future in order to achieve better system performance for NOMA such as, sparse codebooks for SCMA, low-correlation spreading sequences for MUSA, and non-orthogonal patterns for PDMA.

Another type of NOMA, the interleave division multiple access (IDMA), is a type of NOMA technique. IDMA can improve the system efficiency by giving access to a large number of stations. IDMA utilizes different interleaver patterns, which are used to distinguish between users. In [42], IDMA is studied under higher-order quadrature amplitude modulation (QAM) systems with low complexity detection at the receiver side. The authors provide simplified logarithm likelihood ratios (LLR) computation to reduce the complexity in QAM modulation. The drawback of the system is that the number of user it can serve is slightly less when compared with the conventional system. The proposed QAM-based IDMA system achieves 25% less complexity compared with the previous works which is in the context of superposition coded modulation (SCM) based IDMA, where multiple layers of BPSK or QPSK modulated symbols are transmitted.

3.7 Conclusions

Currently, there is an increasing amount of research done in the area of multiple access technologies coming from the academia as well as the industry in order to find potential candidates for the next-generation 5G standard. This chapter presents a survey on the most recent developments in terms of multiple access technologies for 5G networks, with the emphasis on NOMA schemes in different areas in both uplink and downlink scenarios in terms of scheduling, system-level performance, relaying, cooperative scenarios, receiver complexity, and so on. The aim is find the best multiple access technology that could address the current limitations of 4G systems. In this context, some of the promising multiple access technologies have been discussed.

The new proposed access technologies introduce the use of new domains, for example NOMA is based on the power domain multiplexing and it has been shown to eliminate the near-far effect and to improve the spectral efficiency in the uplink and the throughput in the downlink. However, the complexity of the receiver makes it difficult for implementation. Other access technologies introduce new ways of distinguishing between multiple users, such as SCMA or PDMA. SCMA has shown improvements in spectral efficiency, uplink system capacity, and downlink cell throughput and coverage gain. However, it presents increased interference between users and implementation complexity of the code design. PDMA also shows improvements in uplink system capacity and downlink spectral efficiency at the cost of increasing interference between users and the complexity of achieving the design and optimization pattern. MUSA makes use of SC and symbol expansion technology to achieve low block error rates, and to accommodate mass users at an improved spectral efficiency. However, the interference between users is still increasing and the implementation complexity of the spread symbols' design represents a challenge.

It has been seen that by employing NOMA schemes improvements in terms of spectral efficiency and system capacity are obtained. However, several drawbacks still remain in terms of interference problems and the increased implementation complexity that need to be addressed by the future multiple access 5G standard.

References

1. Cisco visual networking index: Forecast and methodology, 2015–2020 White Paper, Cisco. (Online). Available: http://cisco.com/c/en/us/solutionscollateral/service-provider/ip-ngn-ip-next-generation-network/white_paper_c11-481360.html. (Accessed: 10-Jun-2016.)
2. I. Hwang, B. Song, and S. Soliman, A holistic view on hyper-dense heterogeneous and small cell networks, *IEEE Communications Magazine*, Vol. 51, No. 6, pp. 2027, 2013.
3. D. Gesbert, M. Kountouris, R. W. H. Jr, C. B. Chae, and T. Salzer, Shifting the MIMO paradigm, *IEEE Signal Processing Magazine*, Vol. 24, No. 5, pp. 36–46, 2007.
4. J. Hoydis, S. ten Brink, and M. Debbah, Massive MIMO: How many antennas do we need?, *49th Annual Allerton Conference on Communication, Control, and Computing, Proceedings*, pp. 545–550, 2011.
5. Y. Lin, L. Shao, Z. Zhu, Q. Wang, and R. K. Sabhikhi, Wireless network cloud: Architecture and system requirements, *IBM Journal of Research and Development*, Vol. 54, No. 1, pp. 4:14:12, 2010.
6. H. H. Cho, C. F. Lai, T. K. Shih, and H. C. Chao, Integration of SDR and SDN for 5G, *IEEE Access*, Vol. 2, pp. 1196–1204, 2014.
7. G. L. Lui, FDMA system performance with synchronization errors, *MILCOM 96, IEEE Military Communications Conference, Proceedings*, Vol. 3, pp. 811–818, 1996.
8. K. Raith and J. Uddenfeldt, Capacity of digital cellular TDMA systems, *IEEE Transactions on Vehicular Technology*, Vol. 40, No. 2, pp. 323–332, 1991.
9. D. G. Jeong, I. G. Kim, and D. Kim, Capacity analysis of spectrally overlaid multiband CDMA mobile networks, *IEEE Transactions on Vehicular Technology*, Vol. 47, No. 3, pp. 798–807, 1998.
10. X. Zhang and B. Li, Network-coding-aware dynamic subcarrier assignment in OFDMA-based wireless networks, *IEEE Transactions on Vehicular Technology*, Vol. 60, No. 9, pp. 4609–4619, 2011.
11. Y. Saito, Y. Kishiyama, A. Benjebbour, T. Nakamura, A. Li, and K. Higuchi, Non-orthogonal multiple access (NOMA) for cellular future radio access, *IEEE Vehicular Technology Conference, Proceedings*, 2013.
12. F. L. Luo, ZTE communication, 5G wireless: Technology, standard and practice, *ZTE Communication*, pp. 20–27, 2015.
13. N. I. Miridakis, D. D. Vergados, A survey on the successive interference cancellation performance for single-antenna and multiple-antenna OFDM systems, *Communication Surveys & Tutorials, IEEE*, Vol. 15, No. 1, pp. 312, 335, 2013.
14. Y. Saito, A. Benjebbour, Y. Kishiyama, and T. Nakamura, System-level performance evaluation of downlink non-orthogonal multiple access (NOMA), *IEEE International Symposium on Personal Indoor Mobile and Radio Communication PIMRC, Proceedings,* Vol. 2, pp. 611–615, 2013.

15. A. Benjebbour, Y. Saito, Y. Kishiyama, A. Li, A. Harada, and T. Nakamura, Concept and practical considerations of non-orthogonal multiple access (NOMA) for future radio access, *ISPACS, Symposium on Intelligent Signal Processing Communication Systems, Proceedings*, pp. 770–774, 2013.

16. H. Osada, M. Inamori, and Y. Sanada, Non-orthogonal access scheme over multiple channels with iterative interference cancellation and fractional sampling in MIMO-OFDM receiver, *IEEE VTC 2013-Fall, Proceedings*, Las Vegas, NV, pp. 15, September 2013.

17. H. Osada, M. Inamori, and Y. Sanada, Non-orthogonal access scheme over multiple channels with iterative interference cancellation and fractional sampling in OFDM receiver, *Vehicular Technology Conference (VTC Spring), 2012 IEEE 75th, Proceedings*, pp. 15, 2012.

18. N. Otao, Y. Kishiyama, and K. Higuchi, Performance of non-orthogonal access with SIC in cellular downlink using proportional fair-based resource allocation, *ISWCS 2012, Proceedings*, Paris, France, pp. 476–480, 2012.

19. S. Vanka, S. Srinivasa, Z. Gong, P. Vizi, K. Stamatiou, and M. Haenggi, Superposition coding strategies: Design and experimental evaluation, *IEEE Transmission and Wireless Communication.*, Vol. 11, No. 7, pp. 2628–2639, 2012.

20. Q. Liu, B. Hui, and K. Chang, A survey on non-orthogonal multiple access schemes, *Korea Institute of Communication and Science Conference, Proceedings,* pp. 98–101, 2014.

21. M. Al-Imari, P. Xiao, M. A. Imran, and R. Tafazolli, Uplink non-orthogonal multiple access for 5G wireless networks, *11th International Symposium on Wireless Communications Systems (ISWCS), Proceedings*, pp. 781, 785, 26–29 August 2014.

22. Y. Endo, Y. Kishiyama, and K. Higuchi, Uplink non-orthogonal access with MMSE-SIC in the presence of inter-cell interference, *International Symposium on Wireless Communication Systems, Proceedings*, pp. 261–265, 2012.

23. J. Goto, O. Nakamura, K. Yokomakura, Y. Hamaguchi, S. Ibi, S. Sampei, A frequency domain scheduling for uplink single carrier non-orthogonal multiple access with iterative interference cancellation, *Vehicular Technology Conference (VTC Fall), IEEE 80th, Proceedings,* pp. 1–5, September 2014.

24. B. Kim, W. Chung, S. Lim, S. Suh, J. Kwun, S. Choi, D. Hong, Uplink NOMA with multi-antenna, *IEEE 81st Vehicular Technology Conference (VTC Spring), Proceedings*, pp. 1–5, 11–14 May, 2015.

25. A. Benjebbovu, A. Li, Y. Saito, Y. Kishiyama, A. Harada, and T. Nakamura, System-level performance of downlink NOMA for future LTE enhancements, *2013 IEEE Globecom Work, GC Workshops 2013, Proceedings*, No. 1, pp. 66–70, 2013.

26. Q. Vien, N. Ogbonna, H. X. Nguyen, R. Trestian, and P. Shah, Non-orthogonal multiple access for wireless downlink in cloud radio access networks, *IEEE 21th European Wireless Conference, Proceedings*, pp. 1–6, 20–22 May 2015.

27. B. Kimy, S. Lim, H. Kim, S. Suh, J. Kwun, S. Choi, C. Lee, S. Lee, and D. Hong, Non-orthogonal multiple access in a downlink multiuser beamforming system, *IEEE Military Communication Conference, MILCOM, No. 2012, Proceedings*, pp. 1278–1283, 2013.

28. N. Keita, K. Nishimori, S. Sasaki, and H. Makino, Spatial multiplexing for multiple users exceeding degree of freedom by successive interference cancellation and zero forcing, In *2014 IEEE International Workshop on Electromagnetics (iWEM), Proceedings,* pp. 94–95, 2014.

29. G. Kramer and A. J. van Wijngaarden, On the white Gaussian multiple access relay channel, *IEEE ISIT Sorrento, Proceedings*, June 2000.

30. S. Wei, J. Li, and W. Chen, Network coded power adaptation scheme in non-orthogonal multiple-access relay channels, *International Conference on Communication, Proceedings*, pp. 4831–4836, 2014.

31. A. Mohamad, and R. Visoz, Outage achievable rate analysis for the non-orthogonal multiple access multiple relay channel, *IEEE WCNCW, Proceedings*, pp. 160–165, April 2013.

32. J. Kim, I. LEE, Capacity analysis of cooperative relaying systems using non-orthogonal multiple access, *IEEE Communication Letters*, No. 99, pp. 1–1, 2015.

33. J. Choi, Non-orthogonal multiple access in downlink coordinated two-point systems, in *IEEE Communication Letters*, Vol. 18, No. 2, pp. 313–316, 2014.

34. N. Bhuvanasundaram, H. X. Nguyen, R. Trestian and Q. T. Vien, Sum-rate analysis of cell edge users under cooperative NOMA, *8th IFIP Wireless and Mobile Networking Conference (WMNC), Proceedings,* pp. 239–244, 2015.

35. Z. Din, M. Peng, H.V. Poor, Cooperative non-orthogonal multiple access in 5G systems, in *IEEE Communication Letters*, Vol. 19, No. 8, pp. 1462–1465, 2015.
36. T. Yazaki, Y. Sanada, Effect of joint detection and decoding in non-orthogonal multiple access, *IEEE International Symposium on Intelligent Signal Processing and Communication Systems (ISPACS)*, *Proceedings*, pp. 245–250, 1–4 December, 2014.
37. Y. Lan, A. Benjebbour, L. Anxin, A. Harada, Efficient and dynamic fractional frequency reuse for downlink non-orthogonal multiple access, *IEEE 79th Vehicular Technology Conference (VTC Spring)*, *Proceedings*, pp. 1–5, 18–21 May, 2014.
38. X. Chen, A. Benjebboui, Y. Lan, L. Anxin, J. Huiling, Evaluations of downlink non-orthogonal multiple access (NOMA) combined with SU-MIMO, *IEEE 25th Annual International Symposium on Personal, Indoor, and Mobile Radio Communication (PIMRC)*, *Proceedings*, pp. 1887–1891, 2–5 September, 2014.
39. X. Chen, A. Benjebboui, Y. Lan, L. Anxin, J. Huiling, Impact of rank optimization on downlink non-orthogonal multiple access (NOMA) with SU-MIMO, *IEEE International Conference on Communication Systems (ICCS)*, *Proceedings*, pp. 233–237, 19–21 November, 2014.
40. C. Yan, A. Harada, A. Benjebbour, Y. Lan, L. Anxin, H. Jiang, Receiver design for downlink non-orthogonal multiple access (NOMA), *IEEE 81st Vehicular Technology Conference (VTC Spring)*, *Proceedings*, pp. 1–6, 11–14 May, 2015.
41. B. Wang, K. Wang, Z. Lu, T. Xie, J. Quan, Comparison study of non-orthogonal multiple access schemes for 5G, *Broadband Multimedia Systems and Broadcasting (BMSB), IEEE International Symposium, Proceedings*, pp. 1–5, 17–19 June, 2015.
42. T. T. T. Nguyen, L. Lanante, Y. Nagao, H. Ochi, Low complexity higher order QAM modulation for IDMA system, *IEEE Wireless Communication and Networking Conference Works (WCNCW)*, *Proceedings*, pp. 113–118, 9–12 March, 2015.

Chapter 4

Performance Evaluation of NOMA under Wireless Downlink Cloud Radio Access Networks Environments

Quoc-Tuan Vien, Ngozi Ogbonna, Huan X. Nguyen, Ramona Trestian, and Purav Shah

Contents

4.1 Introduction

The current telecommunications environment is facing a data storm with Cisco predicting that by 2020 the number of Internet protocol (IP)-connected devices will reach three times the global population, generating up to 25GB of IP traffic per capita [1]. In this context, the network operators are facing different challenges on how to meet the required coverage and capacity of their networks, how to deal with interferences, and how to manage the increased complexity and deal with higher capital expenditure (CAPEX) and operating expenditure (OPEX). To this extent, in order to cope with all these issues, the next generation of wireless systems could make use of various new solutions and technologies, such as software-defined networks (SDNs) and network function virtualization (NFV), which help the network operators to reduce their CAPEX intensity by transferring their hardware-based network to software- and cloud-based solutions; Wi-Fi and femtocell opportunistic offloading techniques for mobile traffic; cloud radio access networks (C-RANs), which offer a centralized, cooperative, clean (green), and cloud computing architecture for radio access networks (RANs); and higher spectral efficiency by using advanced receivers with interference cancellation or advanced coding and modulation solutions such as the non-orthogonal multiple access (NOMA) technique.

This chapter explores the use of multiple access techniques for C-RANs, which have been recently proposed to connect all base stations (BSs) via a cloud [2]. Thus, by making use of cloud computing at a central station (CS), the C-RAN could manage the interference and handover at the cell-edge mobile users and could also reduce the load at the BSs for lower energy consumption [2–4].

One of the promising multiple access schemes for future radio access technologies is NOMA [5]. NOMA is an access scheme that lays multiple users over each other in the power domain. It assigns different power allocation to users depending on their distance to the BS. By making use of a successive interference cancellation (SIC) receiver, NOMA shows to enhance the reception, capacity, and cell-edge user throughput performance [5–10].

In this chapter, we will investigate the use of NOMA in the wireless downlink C-RAN (WD-CRAN) environment. A NOMA scheme is used to allocate the power at the BSs based on their relative distance to the cloud-based CS [11]. An SIC mechanism is designed at the cloud-based CS to lay multiple BSs over each other in the power domain. The achieved throughput through the use of NOMA is expressly analyzed and compared with the one obtained if conventional orthogonal frequency division multiple access (OFDMA) is used within a WD-CRAN environment. The derived expression is used to show the effectiveness of NOMA over OFDMA and also to evaluate the impact of the BS positioning and propagation environment on the throughput performance.

Finally, numerical results are provided showing a significant improvement in the sum data rate that could be achieved with the proposed NOMA over the OFDMA scheme.

4.2 Technical Background

Nowadays, there is a very competitive environment for mobile operators with each operator trying to offer the best services to retain their customers and increase their revenue. However, the cost of setting up a RAN, maintaining it, and upgrading it is getting more expensive and the revenue generated from customers is not increasing at the same rate as the costs. In order to maintain a balance, mobile operators have been seeking a solution that could help them reduce their cost of operation without a reduction in the quality of service (QoS) that they provide for their customer. The RAN is the key component of the network that helps by supplying constant and high QoS to the customers. Thus, in order to enable cost savings for network providers and still provide high QoS, there has to be an improvement in the existing RAN.

4.2.1 Traditional Radio Access Network

The RAN consists of the BS technology, the air interface, and the mobile user equipment (UE) within a cellular network. The traditional radio access network (TRAN) is the RAN that has been in use since the inception of cellular technology. It comprises the BS that makes the connections to sector antennas. These antennas cover a small region depending on their capacity and can handle the reception and transmission of information within this small coverage region only. With TRAN, the obtainable capacity is subject to interference and this reduces the spectrum capacity to a large extent. BSs in the network are also built on a specific proprietary platform that makes it difficult to integrate any changes. However, several challenges within TRAN could be identified as follows [2]:

- As network operators *increase the number of BSs* to expand the coverage area of their network, there is also an increase in the required power for the BSs. This in turn leads to a much higher OPEX and leaves a great undesirable impact on the environment. In order to resolve this, the number of BSs has to be reduced. However, by doing this within TRAN it will lead to a reduction in coverage and a corresponding drop in the QoS. There is, therefore, the need for a better RAN infrastructure that would centralize all the BSs in order to better maximize resources and reduce the power challenge of TRAN.
- A rapid increase in RAN's *cost of operation*. The rate at which customers are consuming mobile data is increasing exponentially and network operators need to enhance their capacity to enable them to serve their customers. However, network operators face the challenge of the high cost involved in upgrading the traditional BS as the returns from the customers are not high enough to cover this cost. It has be shown that about 80% of the mobile operator's CAPEX is spent on RAN. This brings up a need for a RAN infrastructure that will cost less but still achieve high QoS.
- Mobile operators have to work with *incompatible platforms* due to propriety hardware and software, especially if the providers are purchasing systems from different vendors. This prevents flexibility in case there is a need for network upgrade.
- TRAN cannot support the *interference management* that will be required for heterogeneous network environments such as next-generation 5G networks.
- Within TRAN, a BS's processing capabilities are accessible only by the users that are active within its coverage area. This results in some BSs remaining idle in some areas at different times and in other areas some BSs being overloaded. Since the BS has to provide coverage at all times, an idle BS will consume the same power as an overloaded BS leading to a waste of energy. Since BSs are designed to handle more traffic during the peak period, there is a waste of the processing capacity of the BS during less busy periods. Therefore, there is a need for a system that allows for the sharing of processing capabilities between different coverage regions.

4.2.2 Cloud-Radio Access Network

In order to solve the challenges of the TRAN, a possible solution is C-RAN, which integrates centralized processing, a cloud-based radio access network, and cooperative radio. C-RAN naturally evolved from the distributed form of the base transceiver station (BTS), comprising the remote radio head (RRH) and the baseband unit (BBU). With a focus on the full centralization option, where the BTS functions and the baseband is located in the BBU, the architecture of C-RAN was proposed as illustrated in Figure 4.1 [2].

By using this proposed architecture for C-RAN, it was observed that a system upgrade and maintenance is easier and different standards could be supported using this network with good capabilities for resource sharing [2]. Several advantages of using C-RAN over the TRAN could be identified as follows [2]:

■ C-RAN improves energy efficiency by reducing the number of essential BS sites due to its centralized processing capabilities. This in turn leads to a reduced number of sites management and resources needed thereby saving cost.
■ The cooperative radio technology helps to reduce the interference level between the RRH and the mobile UE. It makes use of lower transmission power small cells that require less energy to operate without reducing the required QoS.
■ C-RAN reduces the waste of resources due to its centralized nature. With lower power consumption, resources are used more efficiently by the BSs. If a BS in a remote area is idle and its services are not needed, the BS could be put into a lower power consumption state or turned off to preserve energy.

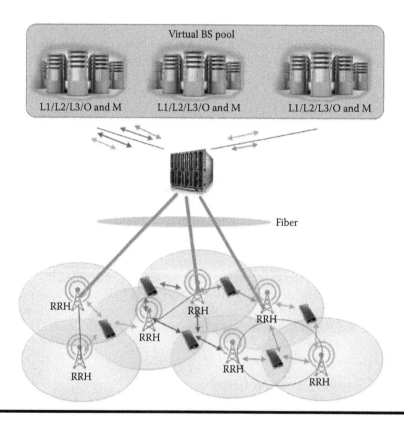

Figure 4.1   Centralized form of C-RAN architecture.

■ C-RAN uses a centralized operation and management system as all the BBUs and support equipment are in a centralized location. This brings savings in terms of cost that would have been spent on separate BS sites for maintenance.

■ In the C-RAN infrastructure, remote BSs can work with other BSs to share data traffic, signaling, and channel information in the network. If a BS in a busy area is overloaded, it is able to offload its users to another BS in a less busy area through the cloud. There can also be a smart offload mechanism from an operator's core network.

Apart from the immediate advantages and benefits brought by the C-RAN architecture several challenges could be identified as follows [2]:

■ There is an existing challenge with the effective distribution of services to BSs at the cloud-edge.

■ The optical fiber that exists between the RRHs and the BBUs carries a large amount of data in real time. The advanced networks, such as long-term evolution (LTE), require wideband, which is not easy to obtain as the bandwidth restriction of the optical is 10GB with strict latency and jitter requirements.

■ C-RAN makes use of joint processing and therefore requires an algorithm with multipoint processing capabilities that could be used to reduce interference in the system. The algorithm should also be able to use specialized channel information and the cooperation of multiple antennas in different locations.

■ There is a need for a virtualization technology that would help to group the baseband processing units (BPU) into different virtual entities in the cloud. It should also be able to use real-time algorithms and efficiently allocate processing capacity in a dynamic load-balancing system.

4.2.3 Multiple Access Schemes

As this chapter explores the use of multiple access schemes within C-RAN, it becomes essential to look into what they really stand for and their relevance in C-RAN. Multiple access schemes are access methods that allow different users to gain access to a network at the same time. With the advancement of cellular technology, there has also been a corresponding development of different access schemes. Access schemes determine to a very great extent how the radio technology works. The main schemes that are in use starting from the ones that have been developed in the past to the most recent ones are the frequency division multiple access scheme (FDMA) [12], time division multiple access scheme (TDMA) [13], code division multiple access scheme (CDMA) [14], and orthogonal frequency division multiple access scheme (OFDMA) [15]. FDMA divides the available bandwidth into different frequency slots and a user is allocated a specific band for communication throughout the entire call. This scheme is mainly used in the analogue systems [12]. TDMA was developed as a result of the advent of digital systems. Here, digital data are split into time slots and sent as required. Each subscriber is given a different time slot in which they could receive or send data. The setback here is that only a specific number of users can access the system at a specific time [13]. CDMA involves allocating to each user a code in order to be able to gain access to the cellular system. The data is first multiplied by a chip code, which spreads the signal before it is being transmitted [14]. OFDMA is a form of digital modulation where a signal is split into different channels of narrowband signals operating at different frequencies [15]. It divides a modulating stream of high data rate into many other slowly modulated channels of narrowband signals, thereby making these channels less susceptible to the fading caused by selective frequency [15]. This is considered to be the best access scheme so far for advanced third generation cellular networks and for the fourth generation networks as it makes use of many closed spaced carriers and is based on FDMA. OFDMA allows different data rates to be used for uplinking while another is being used for the downlink section of the network [15].

It has been seen that orthogonal multiple access schemes have been very effective in achieving high throughput for services of the packet domain with a simple receiver design. However, there is still room to achieve better spectrum efficiency and to be able to do that, there is a need to enhance the receiver design to be able to deal with the interference better.

One of the promising multiple access schemes to be used in future radio access technologies is NOMA especially in the downlink area. This is because it uses a SIC receiver as its basic receiver and this makes the network more robust. SIC applies a good level of resource management and fractional frequency to NOMA and this enhances the trade-off between the spectral efficiency of the system and the user fairness [9].

4.3 Literature Review

The C-RAN concept is widely investigated in the literature with different solutions trying to maximize the benefit introduced by C-RAN.

Sundaresan et al. [3] proposed the use of an expandable framework, referred to as *Fluidnet*, which is lightweight and could be used to get the maximum potential from C-RAN. The Fluidnet framework makes use of an intelligent controller in the BBU pool, which exploits the feedback received from the network to reconfigure the fronthaul. The fronthaul is reconfigured logically to apply different strategies of transmission to different parts of the network in order to be able to cater for a heterogeneous network environment that has varied user profiles (including static and mobile users) and different traffic load patterns. They made use of an algorithm that is able to maximize different traffic requirements on the RAN and at the same time improve the computational resource usage in the BBU pool. Fluidnet uses a two-step method where it first finds out the best configuration combination to support the system traffic based on user demands and distribution patterns. After that, it makes use of an effective algorithm to gather different configurations of many sectors in order to reduce the resources needed for computing without affecting the traffic. Moreover, it supports the coexistence of different standards and technologies especially from different network operators. The framework was tested using a prototype consisting of six (BBU, RRH) worldwide interoperability for microwave access (WiMAX) test beds for C-RAN using radio over fiber as the fronthaul. The results show a 50% improvement in traffic demand and reduced computational resource usage.

Ding et al. [4] proposed the use of random BSs that are spatially positioned in C-RAN. The authors studied different strategies using a scattered antenna array, and analyzed the impact they had on the quality of the signal reception. Two phases were conducted: (1) The analysis of the performance attained by a distributed beam forming, in which case there was a characterization of the BS selection order; (2) the analysis of the smallest number of BSs adequate enough to achieve a specific data rate. This was done by finding the density function considering a total of n highest order statistics.

Benjebbour et al. [6] proposed a NOMA scheme to be used in a downlink network for receiver enhancement. The scheme, would allow multiple users on the transmitter side to be multiplexed in the power domain. On the other hand, the signal separation for different users on the receiver side was done using a SIC receiver. The authors found this to be optimal in the sense that it achieves the maximum capacity region of the downlink section of the broadcast channel and this in turn outperforms its orthogonal counterpart. The authors also argue that NOMA could also be applied on the uplink part in which case, the SIC would be applied to the BSs.

The performance evaluation for the proposed NOMA was done in order to show the benefits of using the downlink NOMA in a cellular network and also the practicability of the NOMA concept in terms of frequency-domain scheduling and adaptive modulation and coding. The results obtained depicted that the throughput achieved using NOMA was more than 30% higher than that achieved using orthogonal multiple access schemes considering different configurations.

Osada et al. [8] investigated the use of non-orthogonal access scheme in a multiple channel system taking into consideration fractional sampling and interference cancellation in an OFDMA receiver. Using the proposed scheme, they transmitted non-orthogonally an imaging component in an adjacent channel. This imaging component was underlaid by a desired signal in order to accommodate it. The authors created a diversity factor through the use of fractional sampling and an iterative interference canceller in order to achieve their goal of realizing non-orthogonal access to multiple channels. However, the drawback of the proposed solution is that it can only accommodate non-orthogonal signals that have limited diversity gain.

Otao et al. [9] investigated the throughput achieved if NOMA is used together with a SIC in the downlink part of a cellular network with an assumption that all the resources are proportionally distributed. The authors consider the application of this concept in cellular systems higher than 4G networks. With the proposed technology, the same frequency was used by all the users with the use of multiuser scheduling. The proposed scheme allotted different power allocations to the users depending on their location in the cell that is whether they are at the cell edge or cell center. Simulation results show that a considerable level of system throughput enhancement was achieved by using NOMA with the SIC.

Saito et al. [10] focused on the use of NOMA for future cellular radio networks. The authors established that by using NOMA, many users would be able to make use of one frequency allocation as they will be superposed in the power domain and given different power allocations. However, OFDMA was still used as the basic signal waveform and based the NOMA on it. At the receiver side, they proposed the use of a SIC receiver as it would make the reception more robust according to them. The authors also suggested that NOMA could be extended using a NOMA/MIMO (multiple-input multiple-output) scheme that they proposed to cover multiple antenna technologies. The simulation results show that the proposed solution achieves a threefold efficiency through the use of NOMA.

Benjebbovu et al. [6] investigated the use of NOMA to enhance the LTE network using multiplexing in the power domain on the transmitter side and a SIC receiver on the receiver side. The authors proposed grouping the users and giving each user group a different power allocation depending on their distance from the BS. The research put good consideration into different design aspects of the LTE network, such as error propagation and frequency domain scheduling. The simulation results showed that NOMA provided a much higher gain both for mobile and static users and also for subband and wideband scenarios.

The field of NOMA and C-RAN is currently widely investigated as they might be considered as new technologies integrated in the next-generation 5G networks. Effort is put into looking at different ways in which NOMA could be used to achieve greater efficiency in different networks. However not many have ventured into the area of using the NOMA technology within the C-RAN environment.

To this extent, this chapter will investigate the performance of a NOMA-based solution [11] together with a SIC receiver aiming to achieve high efficiency within the UE. The concept is then applied to the C-RAN network in which case the BSs will replace the users and the cloud-based CS will then replace the BS from the instances previously mentioned.

4.4 System Model Design and Analysis

This section discusses the complete system model that is being proposed for C-RAN, it looks at different throughput achieved when either NOMA or OFDMA is being used. An adequate power allocation formula is modeled that could enhance fair power allocation for any number of BSs connected to the cloud by taking into consideration the total power available. A thorough analysis is also provided and some generalized equations are established.

4.4.1 System Model of Wireless Downlink C-RAN

Figure 4.2 illustrates the system model of a WD-CRAN under consideration within this research. It assumes the use of a cloud with multiple transmitters. A total number of N BSs are connected to the cloud, such as $\{BS_1, BS_2, BS_3, ..., BS_N\}$. The BSs are located at different distances to the cloud-based central access CS, such that the distance between BS_i, $i = 1,2, ..., N$ and CS is d_i, similar to real-life scenarios. There is a corresponding gain in terms of the signal-to-noise ratio (SNR) attained by these BSs depending on their proximity to the cloud-based CS. The closest BS having the highest SNR while the farthest BS has the lowest SNR. This parameter is used in efficient power allocation in order to be able to achieve maximum throughput from all of the BSs.

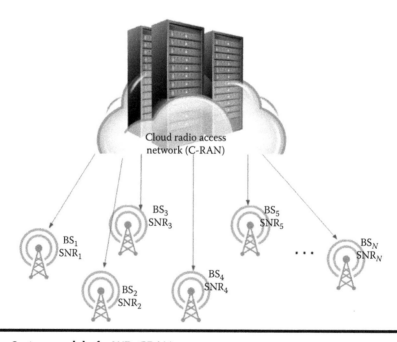

Figure 4.2   System model of a WD-CRAN.

4.4.2 Throughput Analysis of WD-CRAN

The overall system bandwidth is assumed to be constant as the main focus is on varied power allocation. The cloud-based CS transmits signals xi to base station BSi, $i = 1, 2, 3, ..., N$.

The total transmission power available in the WD-CRAN is given by

$$P_{\text{tot}} = \sum_{i=1}^{N} P_i \tag{4.1}$$

The signals sent by the cloud-based CS to the base stations $\{BSi\}$, $i = 1, 2, ..., N$ are superimposed to generate the following:

$$x = \sum_{i=1}^{N} \sqrt{P_i} x_i \tag{4.2}$$

This signal is sent taking into consideration the various distances from the BS to the cloud and allocating corresponding power resources to them. On the other hand, the received signal at BSi is given by

$$y_i = h_i x + n_i \tag{4.3}$$

where:
  h_i represents the complex channel coefficient that exists between the cloud-based CS and BS_i
  n_i denotes the power density of the Gaussian noise for BS_i

With the use of NOMA, SIC is carried out at the BSs in a certain order. The order is determined by channel gain, which is a function of the distance between the BSs and the cloud-based CS. Following the order, the BS with the highest channel gain is first decoded, after which the one with a lower channel gain than the first is decoded, and this goes on until the very last BS has been decoded. The channel gain is being normalized by the intercell and noise interference power $|h_i|^2/n_i$. Using this order of decoding, a BS can decode the signal of its previous BS and this can be used for interference cancellation.

The achievable throughput at BS_i connected to the cloud-based CS using the NOMA-based solution can be calculated as follows:

$$R_i^{(NOMA)} = \log_2 \left(1 + \frac{P_i \, |h_i|^2}{\sum_{k=1}^{i-1} P_k \, |h_i|^2 + n_i} \right) \tag{4.4}$$

Whereas, the achievable throughput at BS_i connected to the cloud-based CS using OFDMA principles can be calculated as follows:

$$R_i^{(OFDMA)} = \propto_i \log_2 \left(1 + \frac{P_i \, |h_i|^2}{\propto_i n_i} \right) \tag{4.5}$$

where:

α_i represents the normalized bandwidth assigned to BS_i where $\Sigma_{i=1}^{N}\alpha_i = 1$ and $0 < \alpha_i <$
$|h_i|^2/n_i$ represents the general system gain (SNR)
P_i represents the power allocated to BS_i

4.4.2.1 Throughput Comparison between NOMA and OFDMA

Figure 4.3 illustrates a comparison between OFDMA and NOMA for WD-CRAN in terms of power allocation. It can be noticed that by using NOMA with SIC approach, the power allocated to a BS is dependent on the power of the preceding BS having higher channel gain.

In order to compare the throughput achieved using NOMA with the one achieved using OFDMA for WD-CRAN, the following example scenario is considered: Assuming a C-RAN with 10 BSs $\{BS_1, BS_2,\ldots, BS_{10}\}$ and the user orthogonal multiplexing is combined with OFDMA, a total network bandwidth of 1 Hz is considered with each BS having an assigned bandwidth of 0.1 Hz. Moreover, assuming that the total available power is 100 W, then each BS gets the same power allocation of 10 W each. Given that the SNR for the links between the 10 BSs and the CS are {20 dB, 19.5 dB, 19 dB, 18.5 dB, 18 dB, 17.5 dB, 17 dB, 16.5 dB, 16 dB, 15.5 dB} with the SNRs distributed with respect to the distance from the BS to the cloud-based CS. That is, the least SNR being assigned to the farthest BS (e.g., BS_{10}), the highest SNR to the closest BS (e.g., BS_1), and so on.

Assuming proportional fairness, the data rates achieved at the 10 BSs using the OFDMA scheme by using Equation 4.5 are {1.33, 1.31, 1.29, 1.27, 1.26, 1.24, 1.22, 1.21, 1.19, 1.17} bits/sec/ Hz; giving a total data rate with OFDMA of 12.49 bits/sec/Hz.

Whereas by using NOMA, the power is allocated according to the distance of the BS to the cloud-based CS with the farthest BS receiving the highest power allocation and the closest BS receiving the lowest. The SNR of the 10 links between the BSs and the cloud-based CS is assumed to be the same as considered in the OFDMA scenario. Having the total network power of 100 W, the power allocated to the 10 BSs is done in the following way {0.28, 0.32, 0.54, 1.03, 1.95, 3.69, 6.98, 13.21, 24.99, 47.27} W.

Calculating the data rates at the 10 BSs when NOMA is employed and using Equation 4.4, the following data rates are achieved {4.86, 2.07, 0.92, 0.92, 0.92, 0.92, 0.92, 0.92, 0.92, 0.92} bits/ sec/Hz giving a total available data rate of 14.29 bits/sec/Hz.

We can notice from this example scenario, that the total data rate for OFDMA is 12.49 bits/sec/ Hz and that of NOMA is 14.29 bits/sec/Hz. This shows that NOMA is 14% more efficient when

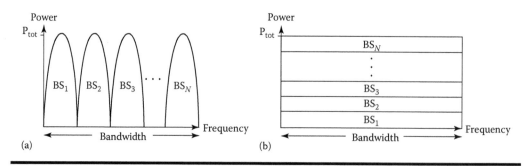

Figure 4.3   OFDMA (a) vs. NOMA (b) for WD-CRAN.

compared against OFDMA considering the 10 BSs scenario. Moreover, it can be anticipated that as the number of BSs under consideration increases, the efficiency of NOMA over OFDMA also increases.

4.4.3 Power Allocation for NOMA in WD-CRAN

In order for NOMA to work efficiently for BSs connected to a C-RAN, there has to be a fair method of power allocation. This method should be able to put into consideration the total power available for distribution to the BSs and the system gain of each BS, which is a function of the distance from the BS to the cloud-based CS. This is to ensure that the maximum throughput that can be achieved from a BS that is very close to the cloud is also achievable from a cloud-edge BS or a BS that is far from the cloud. In Figure 4.3 it can be noticed that the power allocated to a BS is dependent on the power of the preceding BS having higher channel gain.

Given the formula

$$E\left[|h_i|^2\right] = \frac{1}{d_i^{\vartheta_i}}$$

(4.6)

where:

d_i represents the distance from the BS_i to the cloud
ϑ_i represents the path-loss exponent (with average value of 3)
h_i represents the complex channel coefficient
$|h_i|$ is a function of the path-loss exponent and the distance between the BSi and the cloud-based CS

it is assumed that the distance between each BS and the cloud and the path-loss exponent are known. Thus, the total transmitted power is given by Equation 4.1. However, the power allocated to a BS is dependent on the power allocated to its preceding BS with a constant ζ. Therefore, denoting with τ the corresponding ratio of the power at BS_2 and the power at BS_1, we have the following:

$$\tau_1 = \frac{P_2}{P_1}$$

(4.7)

Similarly,

$$\tau_2 = \frac{P_3}{P_1 + P_2}$$

(4.8)

Thus, the power allocation at BS_3 can be given by

$$P_3 = \tau_2\left(P_1 + P_2\right)$$

$$= \tau_2\left(\tau_1 + 1\right)P_1$$

(4.9)

In general, let us denote

$$\tau_i = \frac{P_{i+1}}{\sum_{k=1}^{i} P_k}$$

(4.10)

where $i = 1, 2, ..., N-1$. By applying the recursive approach, we can obtain the power at BS_i, as

$$P_i = \tau_{i-1} \prod_{k=1}^{i-2} (\tau_k + 1) P_1 \qquad (4.11)$$

Knowing that the total power available in C-RAN (e.g., P_{tot}) for allocation is limited, there is a need to determine the power allocation based on the total power available to be shared. Assuming $\tau_1 = \tau_2 = ... = \tau_{N-1} = \tau$ from Equations 4.1, 4.7, and 4.11 we have

$$P_{tot} = P_1 + P_1 \tau \sum_{i=1}^{N-1} (\tau + 1)^{i-1}$$

$$= P_1 (\tau + 1)^{N-1} \qquad (4.12)$$

Therefore, the power allocated at BS_1 to BS_i, $i = 2, 3, ..., N$, can be given by

$$P_1 = \frac{P_{tot}}{(\tau + 1)^{N-1}} \qquad (4.13)$$

$$P_i = \frac{\tau P_{tot}}{(\tau + 1)^{N-i+1}} \qquad (4.14)$$

4.5 Simulation Environment and Results

This section presents the simulations carried out to show that NOMA is more efficient compared with OFDMA. To further the investigation of the effectiveness of NOMA over OFDMA, simulations were carried out using MATLAB [registered symbol] under different practical scenarios by varying the number of BSs, the channel quality, and the propagation path loss. The results obtained further solidify the theoretical proofs already established earlier.

4.5.1 Impact of the Number of BSs on Sum Rate

In this simulation scenario we investigate the impact of an increasing number of BSs on the sum rate. The achievable sum rate of NOMA and OFDMA is modeled as a function of the number of BSs. It is assumed that the total available power of the WD-CRAN is 100 W. The number of BSs considered ranges from 2 to 40 at intervals of 2. Channel gain was assumed to be within the range of 20 dB–0 dB with a decrement factor of –1/2 dB. The wireless propagation medium has a path-loss exponent of 3. The distance between the BSs and the cloud-based CS is assumed to be between 1 m and 80 m with an interval of 2 m. A unit bandwidth of 1 Hz was used in this simulation to ensure uniformity in both OFDMA and NOMA instances.

The results are illustrated in Figure 4.4. It can be seen that the proposed NOMA for WD-CRAN achieves better performance as compared with OFDMA. The throughput gain for NOMA is approximately eight times better than that of OFDMA in this scenario. It is worthy

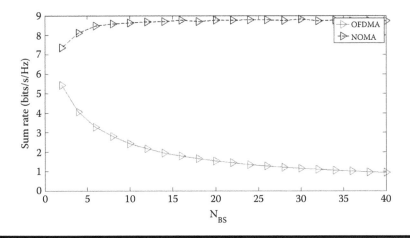

Figure 4.4   NOMA vs. OFDMA sum rate in WD-CRAN.

to note that when using NOMA, with the increase in the number of BSs, there is an increase in the total sum rate up to a certain level, which is the maximum achievable sum rate. By further increasing the number of BSs the same maximum rate will be maintained. For this particular scenario, NOMA achieves a maximum sum rate of 8.7 bits/sec/Hz. This implies that the total power available is sufficient to maintain a good efficiency for only a certain number of BSs. This information could be further used to determine the maximum number of BSs to be deployed in order to achieve the best efficiency and make the best use of the available power.

4.5.2 Impact of the Wireless Propagation Environment

In this simulation scenario we investigate the impact of the wireless propagation environment on the sum rate under an increasing number of BSs. This simulation considers the achievable sum rate of NOMA and OFDMA as a function of the number of BSs with respect to different propagation models. To do this, the simulation setup is kept the same, however, two path-loss models having path-loss exponents of 3 and 2.4 are considered in this scenario.

The results obtained are plotted in Figure 4.5, it can be seen that NOMA has a better performance gain of about eight times more than OFDMA. However, an extra efficiency of about 5% was experienced for the NOMA curve with the lower propagation model. This was because the medium with a path-loss factor of 2.4 had less interference and deterioration of signals as compared with a medium with a path-loss factor of 3. In other words, the higher the path-loss factor, the less the performance throughput achieved.

4.5.3 Impact of the Cloud-Edge BS

This simulation scenario studies the performance at cloud-edge BSs. The simulation considers the data rate at BS_N located far away from the cloud-based CS as a function of the number of BSs. The BSs are placed in such locations that the available power is not sufficient to accommodate them effectively. The simulation setup and parameters are kept the same as in the first scenario, however, the number of cloud-edge BSs is increased.

The obtained results are illustrated in Figure 4.6, which shows that it is unwise to keep increasing the number of BSs at the cloud edge, especially when the available power is not sufficient to

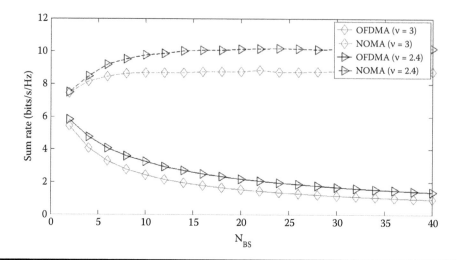

Figure 4.5 **NOMA vs. OFDMA sum rate in WD-CRAN under different wireless propagation environment.**

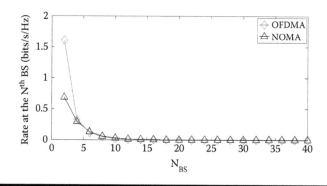

Figure 4.6 **NOMA vs. OFDMA rate in WD-CRAN at cloud-edge BS.**

maximally sustain the BS at the edge. In both NOMA and OFDMA cases, there was a reduction in performance as the number of BSs increased. It can also be observed that a higher data rate at the cloud-edge BS is achieved with the NOMA scheme over the OFDMA scheme.

4.5.4 Impact of the Channel Quality

In this simulation scenario, we look at the impact of the SNR of the BSs on the sum rate performance of WD-CRAN under NOMA and OFDMA. The same scenario setup and parameters are considered as for scenario one. However, the SNR values are varied and it is assumed that there are 10 BSs in the WD-CRAN, the path-loss exponent is set to 3, and the total available power is 100 W.

Figure 4.7 illustrates the results. It can be noticed that NOMA is about 44% more efficient than OFDMA. It is worthy of note that in both cases as the SNR increases, the throughput also increases up to a certain level. This is due to the fact that the closer the BSs are to the cloud, the better the quality of the signal received from the cloud-based CS. Moreover, it can be seen that the performance slope of the NOMA scheme is much steeper and extends to a longer length than the slope of OFDMA. This again validates the superiority of NOMA over OFDMA under all the SNR ranges.

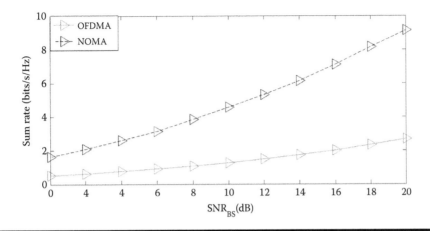

Figure 4.7   NOMA vs. OFDMA sum rate in WD-CRAN over BS SNR.

4.5.5 Impact of the Channel Quality versus Sum Rate under Different Propagation Models

This simulation scenario investigates the achievable sum rate of NOMA and OFDMA against the SNR under different propagation models. It is assumed that the total available power of the WD-CRAN is 100 W and the channel gain is considered to be within the range of 0 dB–20 dB with an increment factor of 2 dB. Different path-loss factors were considered ranging from 2 to 3.5 at intervals of 0.5. The distance between the BSs and the cloud was considered to be between 1 m and 80 m at intervals of 2 m.

The results are plotted in Figure 4.8. It can be seen that the lower the propagation model, the better the achieved throughput and the better the performance of NOMA over OFDMA. For the path loss of 3, there was a better efficiency of 44% with NOMA when compared with OFDMA. However, with reducing path loss, the performance of NOMA over OFDMA gets 5% better, resulting in an improvement in throughput. This gives NOMA a good edge over OFDMA.

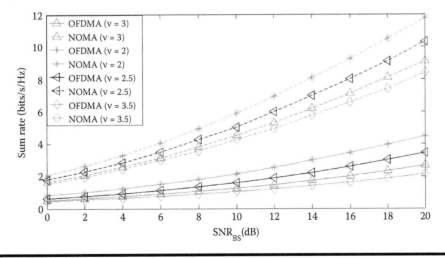

Figure 4.8   NOMA vs. OFDMA sum rate in WD-CRAN vs. BS SNR under different propagation environment.

4.6 Conclusions

In this chapter, the performance of an efficient NOMA-based scheme with SIC has been investigated for WD-CRAN. In order to facilitate the implementation of the NOMA-based scheme, a power allocation scheme was developed to allocate power to any number of BSs by taking into consideration the total power available within the WD-CRAN, the respective distances of the BSs from the cloud-based CS, as well as the channel quality.

An analytic evaluation was performed to compare the performance of NOMA with OFDMA. It was noticed that the sum rate of NOMA was about 14% higher than that of OFDMA and it was established that the efficiency improves as the number of BSs increases up to the maximum capacity that the total available power can accommodate.

Furthermore, the performance of the NOMA-based scheme was evaluated under various simulation scenarios. The simulation results show that NOMA is more efficient when compared with OFDMA. For example, NOMA is eight times more efficient than OFDMA in terms of sum rate under an increasing number of BSs. It was also established that a good efficiency cannot always be attained if the number of BSs increases more than the total available power can accommodate in both NOMA and OFDMA cases.

It was also established that the propagation environment has a significant impact on the performance of WD-CRAN, as NOMA under a lower propagation model had a better performance than NOMA under a higher propagation model. Also, NOMA under a certain propagation model had a much greater efficiency than OFDMA under the same propagation model. It was also established that it is unwise to keep increasing the number of BSs to support the cloud-edge when the total available power in the C-RAN is not sufficient to sustain the BSs at the edge.

When comparing the sum rate against the SNR of the BSs for both NOMA and OFDMA cases, it was noted that NOMA achieves about 44% more efficiency and it was established that the higher the SNR of the BSs, the more efficient NOMA is over OFDMA.

References

1. Cisco, Cisco visual networking index: forecast and methodology, 2015–2020 White Paper, http://cisco.com/c/en/us/solutions/collateral/service-provider/ip-ngn-ip-next-generation-network/white_paper_c11-481360.html. (Accessed: 8 June, 2016.)
2. China Mobile Labs, C-RAN: The road towards green RAN, White Paper, Ver. 3.0, Dec. 2013, http://labs.chinamobile.com/cran/wp-content/uploads/2014/06/20140613-C-RAN-WP-3.0.pdf. (Accessed: 8 June, 2016.)
3. K. Sundaresan, M. Y. Arslan, S. Singh, S. Rangarajan, and S. V. Krishnamurthy, Fluidnet: A flexible cloud-based radio access network for small cells, *ACM MobiCom 2013, Proceedings*, Miami, FL, pp. 99–110, September 2013.
4. Z. Ding and H. Poor, The use of spatially random base stations in cloud radio access networks, *IEEE Signal Processing Letters*, vol. 20, no. 11, pp. 1138–1141, November 2013.
5. Y. Saito, Y. Kishiyama, A. Benjebbour, T. Nakamura, A. Li, and K. Higuchi, Non-orthogonal multiple access (NOMA) for cellular future radio access, *IEEE VTC 2013-Spring, Proceedings*, Dresden, Germany, pp. 1–5, June 2013.
6. A. Benjebbour, Y. Saito, Y. Kishiyama, A. Li, A. Harada, and T. Nakamura, Concept and practical considerations of non-orthogonal multiple access (NOMA) for future radio access, *ISPACS 2013, Proceedings*, Okinawa, Japan, pp. 770–774, November 2013.

7. H. Osada, M. Inamori, and Y. Sanada, Non-orthogonal access scheme over multiple channels with iterative interference cancellation and fractional sampling in MIMO-OFDM receiver, *IEEE VTC 2013 Fall, Proceedings*, Las Vegas, NV, pp. 1–5, September 2013.

8. H. Osada, M. Inamori, and Y. Sanada, Non-orthogonal access scheme over multiple channels with iterative interference cancellation and fractional sampling in OFDM receiver, Vehicular Technology Conference (VTC Spring) 2012 IEEE 75th, Las Vegas, pp. 1–5, 2012.

9. N. Otao, Y. Kishiyama, and K. Higuchi, Performance of non-orthogonal access with SIC in cellular downlink using proportional fair-based resource allocation, *ISWCS 2012, Proceedings*, Paris, France, pp. 476–480, August 2012.

10. Y. Saito, A. Benjebbour, Y. Kishiyama, and T. Nakamura, System-level performance evaluation of downlink non-orthogonal multiple access (NOMA), *IEEE PIMRC 2013, Proceedings*, London, UK, pp. 611–615, September 2013.

11. Q. T. Vien, N. Ogbonna, H. X. Nguyen, R. Trestian, and P. Shah, Non-orthogonal multiple access for wireless downlink in cloud radio access networks, *European Wireless 2015; 21st European Wireless Conference, Proceedings*, Budapest, Hungary, pp. 1–6, 2015.

12. G. L. Lui, FDMA system performance with synchronization errors, *MILCOM'96 IEEE Military Communications Conference, Proceedings*, vol. 3, pp. 811–818, 1996.

13. K. Raith and J. Uddenfeldt, Capacity of digital cellular TDMA systems, *IEEE Transactions on Vehicular Technology*, Vol. 40, No. 2, pp. 323–332, 1991.

14. D. G. Jeong, I. G. Kim, and D. Kim, Capacity analysis of spectrally overlaid multiband CDMA mobile networks, *IEEE Transactions on Vehicular Technology*, Vol. 47, No. 3, pp. 798–807, 1998.

15. X. Zhang and B. Li, Network-coding-aware dynamic subcarrier assignment in OFDMA-based wireless networks, *IEEE Transactions on Vehicular Technology*, Vol. 60, No. 9, pp. 4609–4619, 2011.

Chapter 5

Cloud Computing: The Flexible Future

Joanna Kusznier, Xuan Thuy Dang, and Manzoor Ahmed Khan

Contents

5.1 Introduction

In traditional systems, computing has been based on bare-metal machines. These dictated constraints on capacity and computation, since it had to be available in a physical infrastructure. The systems were not flexible and were difficult to scale. The consumers needed in-house trained and skillful people for maintaining the structure. Furthermore, because of the static nature of hardware, supply had to be always higher than the inconstant hardware demand. This is not a cost-efficient approach since the supply does not follow the elastic demand, resulting in underused hardware. For example, an extra 1% need in capacity at any time instant *t*, meant the change for a new whole hard drive. Nowadays, software evolution outperforms hardware evolution. Although virtualization is not a new concept, it turns out to be the panacea to the demand and supply challenges of the modern digital world. It has given the possibility for a more cost-efficient approach to optimization. This layer of abstraction brought emancipation from the hardware, opening new ways of answering a growing demand for informatics that is, flexible allocation of resources on pay-as-you-go model.

This brings in the now commonly known "cloud computing" concept. It was originally designed as Internet-based calculation with shared resources provided to the users on demand. This essentially means freedom for the users: no physical infrastructural boundaries, evolving capacities, and enabling a more efficient mobility. Users are then released from the maintenance of software and hardware. With the exploding of cloud computing and with the passing of time, demand has grown and resulted in dozens of new vendors of cloud products. This has opened a new window of possibilities: a federation of clouds, also called a *cloud of clouds*. The term *federated clouds* describes the joining up and management of multiple cloud environments; that is, pooling all capacities and making it available as a massive pool of cloud resources to anyone who needs it. The federation of cloud resources allows a client to choose the most suitable vendor for each part of a company's infrastructure, in terms of flexibility, cost efficiency, and the availability of services, to meet a specific business or technological need within their organization.

In what follows next, we provide the background and basic terminologies for setting a common understanding in this study. Then, the focus will be on the clouds in the future networks and seeing the need for efficient frameworks for cloud management and control. We will finish with a walkthrough of OpenStack to offer the tools for experimentation before concluding.

5.2 Background and Basic Terminologies

It is imperative to understand the background and the terminologies related to cloud computing specifically when it comes to answering questions such as how cloud computing attained its current position in the IT market? Why has cloud computing substantially changed the way in which IT services are sold and bought? The overview of the background starts with a cloud computing definition before introducing federated clouds. Then, we offer basic knowledge on a cloud management framework before continuing further in the study.

5.2.1 Cloud Computing

Cloud computing has emerged as a technology to offer the opportunity to access IT services, infrastructural resources, or a deployment environment over a network. It has changed the entire computer industry: users have started to load one application instead of installing a suite of software. The application allows users to log into a web-based service that hosts all of the programs that they need. Remote machines owned by another company run everything from e-mail and word processing to complex data analysis programs [1].

It is based on the philosophy of "pay-as-you-go," offering the possibility to adjust to an elastic consumption and self-service basis; that is, the consumer rents the required amount of cloud services for the specific time and surrenders it when it is not needed. Figure 5.1 presents the contrast between the traditional evolution of the capacity and the cloud capacity [2]. It shows clearly that the cloud approach offers a better follow-up of the utilization needed by the users. It can offer an almost instant response to avoid the cost of overcapacity and the damage of being under capacity.

5.2.1.1 Definitions

There are many different definitions of cloud computing. The most referred to, the most current, and the most precise definition comes from the US National Institute of Standards and Technology (NIST), which reads as follows:

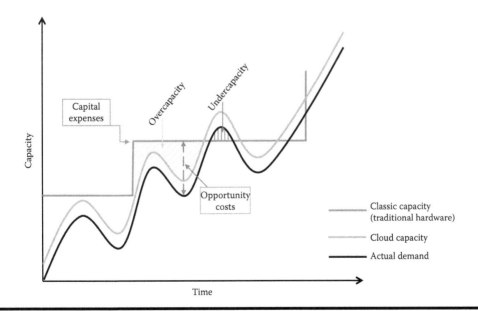

Figure 5.1 From classic capacity to cloud one: capacity vs. utilization curves.

Cloud computing is a model for enabling convenient, on-demand network access to a shared pool of configurable computing resources (e.g., networks, servers, storage, applications, and services) that can be rapidly provisioned and released with minimal management effort or service provider interaction

Yet, the other definition that is worthy our attention, is made by Foster. It covers the economic aspect, in terms of virtualization and scalability:

A large-scale distributed computing paradigm that is driven by economies of scale, in which a pool of abstracted, virtualized, dynamically-scalable, managed computing power, storage, platforms, and services are delivered on demand to external customers over the internet. [3]

Furthermore, Vaguero, after the examination of 22 different definitions of cloud computing proposed the following interpretation:

Clouds are a large pool of easily usable and accessible virtualized resources (such as hardware, development platforms and/or services). These resources can be dynamically re-configured to adjust to a variable load (scale), allowing also for an optimum resource utilization. This pool of resources is typically exploited by a pay-per-use model in which guarantees are offered by the Infrastructure Provider by means of customized SLAs [4].

5.2.1.2 Cloud Service Models

On an abstract level, the cloud computing may be categorized based on two criteria: (1) the type of services offered and (2) the location of the cloud computing services. Figure 5.2 pictorially depicts these categories. This section focuses on providing the details of an earlier category, whereas the latter is discussed in Section 5.2.1.3.

When we categorize cloud computing based on the type of service, we can distinguish three primary cloud-based service models: infrastructure as a service (IaaS), platform as a service (PaaS), and software as a service (SaaS). We explain these as follows:

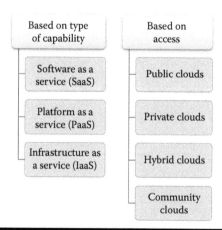

Figure 5.2   Figure depicting the two major categories of cloud computing.

- *IaaS—infrastructure as a service*: Provides hardware infrastructure available as a service and delivers virtualized computing resources over the Internet, for example, Amazon. It is a standardized, highly automated offering, where the hardware resources (storage, computation, power, interfaces) are owned and hosted by a service provider and offered to customers on demand. Customers are using a hypervisor (with a web-based graphical user interface, for example, web-based e-mail) that serves as an IT operations management console for the overall environment. The consumer does not manage or control the underlying cloud infrastructure including the network, servers, operating systems, storage, or even individual application capabilities, with the possible exception of limited user-specific application configuration settings (ref. NIST). The hypervisor makes it possible to consumers to be able to self-provide the infrastructure. There exist many IaaS frameworks, such as OpenStack, Eucalyptus, and the Ubuntu cloud infrastructures.
- *PaaS—platform as a service*: Provides the cloud customer with the ability to interface with a server-side hosted system of some sort through the use of web services (known as *application programming interfaces*, or APIs). The consumer of the PaaS will then leverage additional tools and libraries provided to them to create their own software offerings or augment the existing offering. The consumer does not manage or control the underlying cloud infrastructure, including the network, servers, operating systems, or storage, but has control over the deployed applications and possibly the application hosting environment configurations. (ref. NIST) Generally speaking, the most common mechanisms for this type of interface would be in the form of web services, usually either SOAP (simple object access protocol) or REST (representational state transfer) types. An example of a PaaS offering would be Google Analytics.
- *SaaS—software as a service*: Provides the cloud customer with a mobile or web-enabled interface to an application, such as a Salesforce system, that the user can access from any device that is internet enabled. Product offerings in the cloud space give the user the flexibility of leveraging a powerful application without the need to install or maintain/update that application on their own. The consumer does not manage or control the underlying cloud infrastructure but has control over operating systems, storage, deployed applications, and possibly limited control of select networking components (ref. NIST) In case of a computational need, they can also not use the local resources but the cloud one (which can be more powerful than the smartphone). It also offers new business model possibilities. Software is not bought "forever" but rather rented for the period needed.

The differences between IaaS, PaaS, and SaaS are presented in Figure 5.3. The figure demonstrates a side-by-side look at each offering by IaaS, PaaS, SaaS compared with the traditional model. In the traditional model, users had just the left-hand side of this diagram, requiring them to manage everything. The graph explains exactly how the cloud computing contributes to offloading the customers work. We can recognize that the SaaS is delivered over the web and designed for the end users, PaaS is the set of services and tools designed to make the coding and deployment of applications quicker and more efficient, and IaaS is the hardware and software that powers it all—storage, servers, operating systems, and networks. After getting a general view of how SaaS, IaaS, and PaaS interact with each other, in the following chapter we will turn our attention and examine in more detail the first layer of the stack—SaaS.

5.2.1.3 Deployment Types

The second classification of cloud computing may be realized based on the location of the cloud computing, that means based on the deployment of the cloud services in different deployment

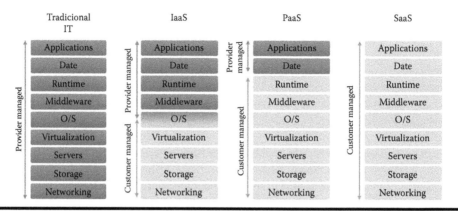

Figure 5.3 Figure identifying the stakeholders' management scopes over the different components of cloud computing. (From Harms, R and M. Yamartino, The economics of the cloud. Microsoft White Paper, Nov. 2015. Accessed: 2016-06-01.)

configurations. The deployment models exemplify the precise category of cloud environment and give us information about the purpose and the nature of the cloud. They are principally distinguished by access, size, and the proprietorship. A group of experts set up by the NIST categorized cloud architectures into four groups [6]:

- *Private clouds*: The cloud infrastructure is operated solely for an organization. It may be managed by the organization or a third party and may exist on premise or off premise. A private cloud gives the organization greater and more direct control over their data since it permits only the authorized users' access to the data.
- *Public clouds*: This is a type of cloud hosting in which the cloud infrastructure is made available to the general public or a large industry group and is owned by an organization selling cloud services. The customers do not have any control or distinguishability over the location of the infrastructure. Public cloud facilities may be availed of for free (e.g., Google) or in the form of the license policy, like a pay-per-user policy. The cost of the cloud usually is shared by all of the users; therefore, public clouds achieve their profit by economies of scale.
- *Hybrid clouds*: The cloud infrastructure is a composition of two or more clouds (private, community, or public) that remain as unique entities but are bound together by standardized or proprietary technology that enables data and application portability (e.g., cloud bursting for load balancing between clouds).
- *Community clouds*: The cloud infrastructure is shared by several organizations and supports a specific community that has shared concerns (e.g., mission, security requirements, policy, and compliance considerations). It may be managed by the organizations or by a third party and may exist on premise or off premise.

5.2.1.4 Generic Architecture of Cloud Computing

We believe that the future will witness a number of small entrants owing to the dynamic business models, which are enabled by the cloud-like services. This dictates that there may be a number of additional stakeholders than what we see today. In what follows next, we briefly discuss a few envisioned stakeholders of the cloud paradigm.

- *Cloud service provider*: It is an individual or organization that provides access to computing resources in a visualized environment. In simple words: a cloud service provider owns a cloud-based service.
- *Cloud service consumer*: It is a temporary run-time role taken by a workstation, laptop, mobile device, or cloud service running software or API, designed to interact with a cloud service by remotely accessing an IT resource.
- *Service broker*: It is an intermediary who performs value-added brokerage between a cloud service provider and cloud service consumer. A service broker can be a piece of software, an appliance, platform, or suit of technologies.

5.2.2 Federated Clouds: An Overview

In the beginning of the era of cloud computing, there were only a few large companies offering public cloud services. These companies dominated the cloud landscape. However, with the revolution of cloud vision, the situation evolved for example, a growing demand has resulted in dozens of new vendors of cloud products. This led to a window of potential solutions, of which the one new one that stood out was a federated cloud. *Federated clouds* describes the joining up and management of multiple public cloud environments, that is, the pooling together of resources, and makes it available as a massive pool of cloud resources to anyone who needs it. The federation of cloud resources allows a client to choose the most suitable vendor for each part of a company's infrastructure, in terms of flexibility, cost efficiency, and the availability of services, to meet a specific business or technological need within their organization [7].

5.2.2.1 Federated Clouds Relevant Terminologies

In view of the fact that federation of cloud services has just recently received attention and that it is still in a stage of development, many distinct terms have been used to define it; for example, *cloud federation*, *Intercloud*, and so on. Precise understandings of these terms simplify the current study and support future directions.

Goiri [8] explains the paradigm of the federation of the clouds:

> Different providers running services that have complementary resource requirements over time can mutually collaborate to share their respective resources in order to fulfill each one's demand. For instance, a provider could outsource resources to other providers when its workload cannot be attended with its local resources. In this way, the provider would obtain higher profit because it can attend more customers.

Reuven Cohen, founder and CEO of Enomaly Inc., explains the paradigm of federation of the clouds: [9]

> Cloud federation manages consistency and access controls when two or more independent geographically distinct clouds share either authentication, files, computing resources, command and control or access to storage resources.

From these definitions, we can state that the term *cloud federation* indicates the formation of a group of aggregated providers that are conjointly collaborating to allocate their resources in order to improve each other's services. The goal of the federated cloud is to allow providers to avoid the limitation of owning only a restricted amount of resources to fulfill their customers' requirements (and coming back to the classical model of capacity limitation). Since federated clouds offer a message of transmission and collaboration among clouds, they are an ideal solution to the overloaded

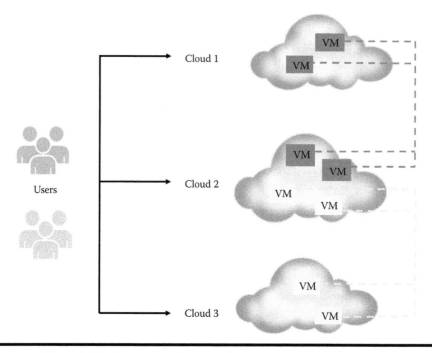

Figure 5.4   Federated clouds: an example scenario.

tasks in a single cloud; users need to transplant their cloud apps and, primarily, they are a better business model for cloud providers. Figure 5.4 presents an example of federated clouds.

In the literature, in relation to federated clouds, the term *Intercloud* can be found. It is imperative to understand this term, since it was a pioneering idea of the integration and aggregation of cloud services. The concept of Intercloud was introduced by Kevin Kelly in 2007 and became famous as the "cloud of clouds," an extension of the Internet "network of networks" on which it is based. One definition of a cloud federation can be deduced from Vint Cerf [10], who is recognized as one of "the fathers of the Internet," he defines the Intercloud in the following way:

> It's time to start working on Inter-cloud standards and protocols so your data doesn't get trapped in one of the problems with cloud computing… [and these standards and protocols] allow people to manage assets in multiple clouds, and for clouds to interact with each other.

The term *Intercloud* signifies a mesh of clouds that are unified, having on open standard protocol to provide cloud interoperability. The goal of the Intercloud is ubiquitously connecting everything together in a multiple-provider infrastructure, similar to the telephone system or Internet model [10].

There are some significant differences between the federated cloud and the Intercloud. The major one is that the Intercloud is based on future standards and open interfaces, whereas the federated cloud uses a provider version of the interfaces. Therefore, the federated cloud can be recognized as a prerequisite of the Intercloud. For the Intercloud vision, it is necessary that the clouds are federated and interoperative, so that everyone can have a unified understanding of how applications should be deployed. Thus interoperability of different cloud platforms can be achieved in the Intercloud, even without explicit referencing by user [10].

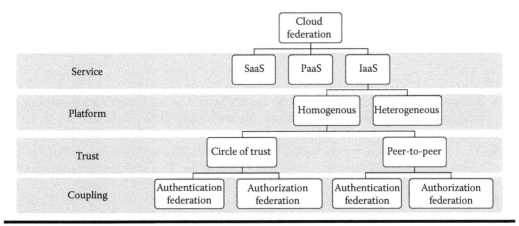

Figure 5.5   Figure depicting various characteristics of federated clouds. (From N. Pustchi et al., ***3rd International Workshop on Security in Cloud Computing, SCC@ASIACCS '15, Proceedings*** **Singapore, April 14, pp. 63–71, 2015.)**

Vint Cerf* has noted aptly, that in the current situation we do not have any standards in the cloud:

> We don't have any inter-cloud standards. The current cloud situation is similar to the lack of communication and familiarity among computer networks in 1973.

5.2.2.2 *Main Attributes of Federated Clouds*

Pustchi [11] has classified cloud federations into four types: service, platform, trust, and coupling. These are offered in a federation, which we pictorially present in Figure 5.5. The first type is relevant to cloud services, where the services are briefly discussed in Section 5.2.12. The second characteristic is a platform, which demonstrates that cloud federation deployment models can form heterogeneous or a homogeneous clouds. The third type concentrates on trust, that is, on trust relations among federating cloud members, and is divided into the circle-of-trust or the peer-to-peer categories. In the circle of trust, trust relationships are typically established by a set of agreements outlining the rights and obligations for each party. All cloud federation members have to agree on trusting if a new member is entering a cloud. In contradiction to the circle-of-trust, a peer-to-peer trust agreement, the trust is established between each two members. The last type of classification done by Pustchi [11] is coupling. It is about accessing services by users from trusted clouds and it is divided into authentication and authorization. The authentication federation is about instruments to authenticate users in clouds other than their initially authenticated cloud. In contrast, the authorization federation is about mechanisms to determine which authenticated users from trusted clouds have access to which resources in federated service providers.

According to Kurze [13], we can also classify the federation of the cloud based on how an organization expands their resources, namely: horizontally, vertically, and by hybridization. The terminology is driven by the service type. In the horizontal class, the Intercloud expands within the same type of service. In the vertical class, the multiple cloud providers expand along a variety

---

* Vint Cerf, Vice President and Chief Internet Evangelist, Google.

of services; that is, IaaS and PaaS. In the hybrid class, both a horizontal and vertical expansion can take place.

A cloud that can be considered as a federated cloud, should have the following characteristics [14]:

- *Multitude of players*: In order to ensure that the system does not develop a monopoly, the federated cloud system has to have at least one open-source cloud platform.
- *Heterogeneity of cloud platforms*: It is a necessity to avoid so-called cascading failures.
- *No vendor lock-in*: Customers applying cloud solutions do not have to tailor their applications to fit the models and interfaces of the cloud provider. That makes future relocation less costly and simpler.
- *Interoperability and portability*: This is significantly important for the protection of the user investments and also for the realization of computing as a utility. It allows for the movement of workloads and data between different providers.
- *Geographical distribution*: This is required to satisfy computing requirements of long tail regions and regulatory regimes.

It is important to understand the necessity of avoiding a monopoly in the standardization process for the federated clouds. If the Internet had been created with vendore lock-in, we would not have seen this type of development.

5.3 Mobile Cloud Computing Redefined with Future Mobile Networks

Cloud computing has proven its benefits, cost efficiency, and flexible operational models [15]. The pay-per-use model with its quick provision of huge computing resources enables an array of new applications to end users. Those applications, which used to require investment in expensive hardware and software are now provided on cloud-based platforms and shared between multiple users over the Internet; for example, video processing, data analysis and consolidation, media creation, storage and sharing, and so on. At the same time, mobile computing becomes more and more popular in our mobile work and lifestyles due to advances in production technologies. The use of increasingly capable mobile devices, that is, smart phones, tablets, netbooks, and so on, to access online data-processing tools forces businesses to take the bring our own device (BYOD) trend seriously and to change IT in order to securely integrate online services in business processes. The convergence of cloud computing and mobile computing is referred to as *mobile cloud computing* (MCC).

The MCC forum defines mobile cloud computing as an infrastructure where both the data storage and data processing happen outside of the mobile device. Mobile cloud applications move the computing power and data storage away from mobile phones and into the cloud, bringing applications and mobile computing not just to smartphone users but to a much broader range of mobile subscribers [16]. Although the definition focuses on the offloading of computing resources from mobile devices to the cloud, the communication aspect of MCC is implicitly understood. In the definition offered by Khan et al. [17], wireless access is shown as important factor in the realization of MCC, which is a service that allows resource-constrained mobile users to adaptively adjust processing and storage capabilities by transparently partitioning and offloading the computationally intensive and storage-demanding jobs on traditional cloud resources by providing ubiquitous wireless access. Network conditions and communication overhead should be considered in the realization of MCC in order to benefit mobile users.

In this section, we first provide a review of MMC with its solutions toward the improvement of mobile application responsiveness, local resource consumption, and utilization. We further analyze future challenges to MCC and the role of a flexible mobile network infrastructure in providing MCC services with a consistent quality of experience (QoE) to mobile users.

5.3.1 State of Mobile Cloud Computing

In recent years, there have been bodies of work produced for the realization of MCC. Most of those focus on various aspects when moving mobile applications from end-user devices to cloud platforms [18]. The ultimate goal is to resolve the trade-off between overcoming limitations of mobile devices and those of wireless networks, in order to guarantee the QoS of cloud applications for mobile users. Limitations of mobile devices result from their designs in terms of portability, that is, small form-factor, light weight. They are often equipped with small storage and low-power processors for the efficient use of limited battery life. This impedes computing-intensive applications and storing large amount of data on mobile devices. Limited visualization and human interfaces also affect the design of cloud-based mobile services. On the other hand, mobile network limitations are the main factors in the design of MCC solutions. The heterogeneity of access networks, for example, cellular, Wi-Fi, small cells, can impact service reliability in the case of user mobility. Network bandwidth and latency constitute restrictions on responsiveness and the level of cloud offloading. Network availability is a unique issue in MCC, in contrast to accessing cloud services from wire networks. Lack of coverage and congestion causes service disruptions, which require special designs to realize the consistency and reliability of MCC services. The design of services for MCC needs to take both device and network limitations into account, in order to realize end-to-end service access as depicted in Figure 5.6.

5.3.1.1 Mobile Cloud Computing Architecture

The MCC architecture in Figure 5.6 shows a service infrastructure in which mobile devices and cloud services are service end-points connected by mobile Internet. Mobile devices provide service access to users by connecting with cloud services over the Internet. End users must be provided with access to operators' radio networks with an Internet gateway. In that architecture, cloud services are separated by the heterogeneous and multiprovider mobile networks. Current mobile network technologies mainly aim at providing wireless alternatives to fixed networks. Their capacities are restricted by the respective radio technologies, for example, bandwidth, coverage, and so on. Moreover, due to a high cost of deployment, wireless coverage is often provided by multiple providers with their own infrastructures, users management, and business and operation support system (B/OSS). This results in a lack of interoperability and mobility between operator networks. While providing limited mobility, wireless networks are considered static constraints between cloud services and end users [19]. Consequently, MCC solutions mostly focus on the combination of the efficiency of mobile computing on mobile devices and the flexibility of cloud computing resources in data centers.

MCC technologies provide additional advantages to mobile computing by leveraging the benefits of cloud computing, for example, dynamic provisioning, scalability, multitenancy, and so on. Extended battery life is achieved by offloading computing-intensive processes to the cloud. Intelligent task scheduling and network selection can result in greater power saving. By enabling remote service execution, MCC can take the advantages of scalable storage and processing capacity

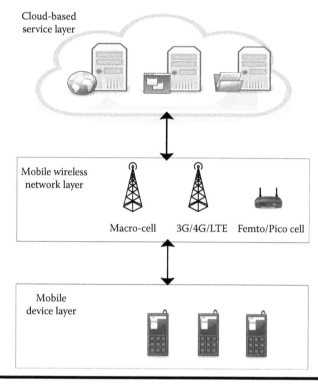

Figure 5.6 Mobile cloud computing architecture. (From H. Qi and A. Gani, *Digital Information and Communication Technology and its Applications (DICTAP), 2012 Second International Conference on*, pp. 195–202, IEEE, 2012.)

of the cloud for resource-demanding mobile applications. Reliability and security are guaranteed by centralized data silos and computing platforms. This centralization of data and processing logic also support the consistency and ease of service composition and access. Realizing MCC requires solutions for challenges inherent to limited computing and network capacity, as well as the dynamic characteristics of a wireless network environment. MCC solutions are detailed in the following section.

5.3.1.2 Challenges and Solution

Although a mobile network constitutes significant restrictions on MCC, cumbersome operator infrastructures, business models and current network technologies, among others, make the network an invariable factor in MCC solution design. Most approaches discussed here focus on overcoming the limitations of the communication network and mobile computing capacity of mobile devices.

5.3.1.2.1 Mobile Network Limitations and Approaches

5.3.1.2.1.1 Low Bandwidth   Low bandwidth is an inherited limitation of a wireless network. Despite advances of radio technologies through each network generation, the added capacity is outpaced by the even faster growing demand of data communication [20]. The authors in [21] propose a collaboration scheme among users based on game theory approach. In which each mobile device within close proximity downloads a part of a video's data and shares it with the other users. Similar approaches allow device-to-device communication based on the data storing, carrying, and forwarding feature of bundle protocol [22]. While such techniques eliminate the need for redundant data transfer from the cloud, they are very application-specific and require additional computing and storage resources on mobile devices.

5.3.1.2.1.2 User Mobility

Causes service disruptions due to either intermittent network connectivity or a change of access technology. While viable solutions can be based on mobile ad hoc networking and disruption-tolerant network technologies, the design of MCC services that can handle client disruption is an approach from a service perspective. Authors in [23] propose a generic service framework for cloud-based social markets. The framework enables mobile users both access to online auctioning platforms and trading resources on mobile ad hoc networks. An asynchronous communication model that separates a network session and service session is designed and prototypically implemented for Android platforms. The separation of services and networks, assuming an intermittent characteristic of communication, allows flexible MCC service design as opposed to wired network services.

5.3.1.2.1.3 Long End-to-End Latency

Results from long WAN distance between wireless clients and cloud computing platforms where services are hosted. Current wireless network architectures have identifiable bottlenecks, that is, wireless base stations, service gateways. Additional delays are caused by contention between an increasing number of mobile devices for limited bandwidths and mobile network capacities. One of the solutions proposed for WAN latency is cloudlet [24]. A cloudlet is a resource-rich computer or cluster of computers that is connected to the Internet and available in the vicinity of mobile devices. Virtual machines are created on cloudlet clusters to rapidly instantiate customized service software that is accessible by mobile devices over a local wireless network. This architecture reduces the distance from mobile client and cloud services. Using a cloudlet also simplifies the challenge of meeting the peak bandwidth demand of multiple users interactively generating and receiving media such as high-definition video and high-resolution images. Similar architecture for offloading to proximate clouds are proposed by MOMCC [25].

5.3.1.2.2 Mobile Computing Limitations and Approaches

5.3.1.2.3.1 Computation Offloading

Computation offloading is the most challenging problem for realizing the fundamental idea of MCC. Different approaches are proposed for the partial execution of a mobile application by other computing resources than the user's mobile device. Authors in [18] summarize application models of task offloading, which take into account performance criteria, that is, bandwidth utilization, scalability, and the external platform. Implementation of the approaches involves the selection of a platform, software abstraction, and a decision model, that is, performance, constraint, energy, or multiobjectivity.

CloneCloud [26] is an offloading approach to overcoming performance issues with mobile devices. It is based on and augmented execution technique that offloads parts of the application execution to the cloud. CloneCloud does not require conversion of applications for a cloud platform. A clone of the Android smart phone is placed on a remote cloud, whose state is synchronized with the real device. When an application process is offloaded, its state is transferred to the clone. The virtual machine (VM) creates a new process state and overlays the received information, followed by the execution of the clone. On completion of the execution, the process state of the clone's application is sent to the smartphone, where the process state is reintegrated into the smartphone's application.

MAUI [27] is another offloading approach that does not require code conversion for a cloud-platform, although hardware architecture of mobile devices and clouds are different. In the Mobile Assistance Using Infrastructure (MAUI) system, offloading a task is decided at method level instead of the whole application module. Each method is marked as local, that is, an I/O operation, or remote-able . The method and state are sent to the cloud for remote execution. Offloading the decision is based on the profiling of the communication cost, energy consumption cost, and network capacity.

5.3.1.2.3.2 Energy Constraint

Energy constraint is the main challenges of MCC application design. Computation offloading approaches aim to preserve power on mobile devices. However, offloading a decision depends very much on the estimation of a device's energy consumption. Moreover, offloading involves data transfer and network access that also increase power usage. There are solution approaches for an intelligent selection of less energy-consuming wireless technologies, for example, Wi-Fi over cellular [28]. The energy footprint of MCC applications may be recorded in order to decide if an application should be offloaded or executed locally.

5.3.1.2.3.3 Platform Heterogeneity

Among mobile devices and mobile platforms impedes the interoperability, portability, and data integrity of MCC applications. The diversity of mobile OS platforms and hardware requires the same application to be developed for each platform. Their interactions with the cloud platform require code conversion or data transformation. This has a great impact on providing consistent service for mobile users accessing services from a multicloud platform. Hardware abstraction and container technology provide one of the solutions for platform heterogeneity. Madhavapeddy et al. [29] propose a cloud OS called *Mirage*, based on virtualization technology. Mirage runs on top of a hypervisor to produce cross-platform applications that are portable to heterogeneous mobile devices and cloud servers. Applications are developed on a common operating system like Linux and then compiled into a kernel that is able to run directly on mobile devices and virtual clouds. Mirage provides an adaptation layer that links the microkernel to an application on top of the hypervisor. Mirage microkernel leverages Xen hypervisor to lessen the impact of the architectural heterogeneity of mobile devices and PCs on mobile applications. However, creating, maintaining, and destroying a virtual machine over a smartphone consumes local resources and shortens battery life.

The limitations due to a lack of flexibility and a low capacity of mobile networks prohibit many advantages of cloud computing for mobile computing. This results in complex solution approaches as discussed in the previous paragraphs, which require profound modifications to operation platforms and application frameworks. Though improved efficiency in many specific cases can be achieved, the approaches cannot be applied to widely deployed applications and a diversity of mobile platforms.

5.3.1.3 Future Requirements

The fast-growing mobile computing environment, with its exponential increase in number of devices and amount of mobile data traffic creates great demands for more efficiency in data center networks and especially in mobile networks. Several features of mobile computing can be observed [20]. First, the popularity of applications for creating and sharing high-quality videos using mobile devices has caused a sharp increase in mobile data traffic. Video services, for example, Internet TV, video on demand, and P2P become part of a mobile lifestyle and their users' participation within social networks. Consequently, increased data traffic in content delivery network requires more intelligent content replications and routing to improve delay and user experience. Secondly, the number of IP devices connected to the Internet will increase manyfold the world's population. New applications rely on connected devices to provide an improved quality of life, leveraging cloud capacity to analyze a vast amount of sensor and context data. These devices also contribute to the exploding of data traffic in the future Internet. Finally, mobile networks will constitute a greater part of the Internet. With an improved capacity and coverage of wireless networks, connecting new devices, that is, sensors, actuators, and home appliances, using wireless technologies provides a faster and more flexible solution for system integration. Wireless networks are becoming ubiquitous; price and speed is no longer a distinguishing factor between mobile network operators. Innovations are sought by operators to compensate for vanishing revenue from increased connected devices, while the costs for network expansion and operation are increasing.

5.3.2 Mobile Networking Approaches for MCC

Cloud computing has become a ubiquitous IT service infrastructure with blurred boundaries between public, private cloud, and Intercloud providers resulting from standardized cloud APIs [30]. Services are built with designs for utilizing dynamically scalable and parallel cloud resources. Cloud-based application can provide an unprecedented quality of experience to users. However, these advantages cannot be delivered to mobile users because of slow advances in mobile network technologies, which lag behind cloud computing development. This creates a perceivable experience gap for users between service access using wired and wireless networks. Mobile users expect constant service quality on mobile networks, regardless of the increasing number of network devices or competing data traffic given limited bandwidth. Consistent experience must also be provided while users are moving at high speed and through coverage areas of heterogeneous wireless technologies. The emergence of machine-type communication, that is, in e-health, smart grid, autonomous driving, and so on, is defining new requirements for real-time communication and access to unlimited cloud resources.

Researchers on mobile networks are exploring new paradigms and approaches in order to meet the demand of future MCC applications. The following section will discuss some important enabling technologies and their application in solving MCC challenges.

5.3.2.1 Mobile Cloud Network Enablers

1. *Software-defined networks* (*SDN*): The concept of separating the control and forwarding planes has triggered radical designs for future network infrastructures [31]. It is the enabler for the required flexibility and programmability of the many architectures proposed for 5G systems and beyond [32]. A future-proof, evolving system has to cope not only with the exponentially growing inherent requirements for latency, scalability, reliability, security, and so on, but also with the dynamics of future application services and user demands. This is an immense challenge for regulators, infrastructure providers, and operators to maintain a stable, adaptive infrastructure through cooperation while guaranteeing their conflicting objectives and competitiveness. SDN replaces traditional monolithic network components with programmable virtual network slices, which are essential for creating elastic networks. They are in turn required to realize the envisioned collation of heterogeneous, multiprovider

networks in order to meet the dynamic requirements of future applications. The combination of SDN, cloud computing, and network-virtualization technologies helps to create a logical structure on top of the base network. Applications services are provided on demand with virtual connectivity along with the required functionalities without any dependency on the underlying network infrastructure. SDN architecture and carrier-grade virtualization approaches provide multitenant networks, which make use of the total infrastructural capacity while guaranteeing performance, isolation, and security for individual services and network operators. Cloud computing infrastructure can be utilized for an on-demand, pay-per-use operation model in the provisioning of computing resources and network functions.

2. *Network function vitualization (NFV)* [33]: This benefits from SDN, which enables the creation of virtual network functionalities with elastic and scalable virtual resources. These functionalities, for example, mobility management, load balancing, deep packet inspection, and so on, are traditionally provided by specific hardware components, which have fixed capacities and are slow to scale. The centralization of programmable virtual network components allows for flexible management and the dynamic reconfiguration of the networks to adapt to changing demands. This greatly reduces expansion and the operation costs for operators, and decreases network provisioning time.

3. *Device-to-device (D2D) networking*: This has been considered in some of the aforementioned approaches to MCC. Recent advancements in low-power, high-bitrate wireless technologies, for example, IEEE 802.11p, dedicated short-range communications (DSRC), and bluetooth, enable more efficient device-to-device communication. This makes offloading cellular traffic to D2D networks a feasible option for mobile networks to support both mobile data and machine-type communication. Emerging applications, for example, autonomous driving and robotics, rely on low-delay communication between intelligent mobile objects. In such cases, local, direct communication between devices is more effective then routing over infrastructural networks. Self-organizing network (SON) techniques can be applied in the D2D domain for a fully adaptive network environment. For the full benefit of D2D to be unfolded, the controlling and management of D2D in accordance with mobile wireless infrastructure needs to be explored.

4. *Wireless fronthaul and backhaul*: Future wireless networks are characterized by an ultradense small cell environment. Classical network management schemes are difficult to implement in this novel architecture due to their compact and unplanned topologies. On the one hand, the dynamics of a dense network further increase the complexity, for example, an increased interference, mobility, and energy efficiency. Autonomous solutions are necessary for network reconfiguration to cope with those dynamics. It is crucial to sustain the manageability of small cell network architecture and ensure flexibility. On the other hand, the expansion of data traffic, the hard-to-reach locations of heterogeneous network (HetNet) access points (APs) (e.g., femtocells) and the need to provide cost-effective solutions require novel wireless backhaul/fronthaul networks. A wireless backhaul is cost-effective and flexible to deploy when compared with fiber backhaul solutions. Due to some physical constraints, wireless backhaul may be the only deployment option.

5. *Spectrum and interference management*: An elastic network infrastructure requires a flexible air interface and coordinated interference management algorithms to increase the spectral efficiency. A dense deployment of cells in the 5G environment brings frequent reuse of the spectrum and makes interference a more serious problem. In addition to that, coalition formations between operator networks and the wireless mesh network also require adaptive interference management algorithms that are able to readjust to the transmission of network

elements for novel topologies. For this reason, interference management of the proposed wireless mesh network has to be able to enhance the existing 5G interference management solutions. Advanced flexible air-interface techniques for wireless networks, for example, information architecture (IA), sparse code multiple access (SCMA), low-density signature (LDS) spreading and orthogonal frequency and code division multiplexing (OFCDM), among others, can improve spectrum efficiency. This is supported by coordination techniques to address the interference resulting from the dynamic collation of multiple network layers (e.g., adaptive coordinated multipoint [CoMP] clustering, providing dynamic channel information). Additionally, energy-efficient management of radio infrastructure can be realized with algorithms for the autonomous power setting of wireless base stations and joint power control in a cluster.

6. *Network as a service*: Enabling network-virtualization technologies turns monolithic network infrastructures into software-definable services. Network operators can realize new network efficiencies, reduce cost, and at the same time diversify service-offering models. Network infrastructure can be offered as fine granular services, for example, RAN as a service or network as a service. Communication networks can be seen as a composition of loosely coupled services, instead of ubiquitous resources with fixed and often high costs. This results in a new combined offering of applications and network services to MCC users. Mobile users are offered cost-effective mobile cloud services, which include on-demand access to their cloud applications, whose quality of delivered experience is guaranteed by mobile network operators.

5.3.2.2 Enabling Mobile Cloud Computing with 5G Radio Access Network Architecture

Emerging mobile applications are creating new challenges for future mobile networks. Novel architectures are required, especially in the RAN domain, in order to meet new requirements. One of those challenges is network capacity. The rise of IoT results in a vast number of devices to be connected by mobile networks. The produced data must be communicated across networks between devices and data services in clouds for mobile users. This also results in a massive number of connections and signals traffic in data networks. Other challenges emerge from a higher level of and the dynamics of service demands, for example, a higher grade of mobility, QoE, data rate, and low end-to-end (E2E) latency. With an increasing number of capable smart devices generating most of the future of data traffic [20], it is the defining feature of future networks to support users' mobility while maintaining large bandwidth and imperceivable delay. These requirements cannot be met by current network infrastructures due to both the monolithic design and high expansion costs of deployed technologies. This is evidenced by the lack of support for long envisioned applications; for example, network access on high-speed vehicles, vehicle-to-vehicle (V2V) communication, virtual reality (VR), among others. That said, current network-centered architectures are designed to route data traffic through a core network to the Internet. This makes them no longer suitable for future users and context-centered services, where most data are generated and consumed inside the boundary of network edges.

With the aim of a flatter and more flexible architecture, various designs for future 5G networks have some features in common, which eliminate the boundaries of current network segments, enable demand-attentive RAN, separate and softwarize control functions from forwarding elements and the virtualization of the elements, among other things. The fundament for such designs is provided by the aforementioned enabling technologies, for example, network densification,

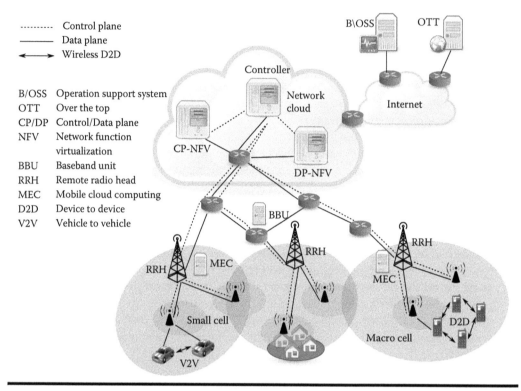

Figure 5.7 A vision of 5G mobile network architecture. (From P. K. Agyapong et al., *IEEE Communications Magazine*, Vol. 52 No.11, pp. 65–75, 2014.)

SDN, NFV, intelligent management, and so forth. In [32], the authors envision a future mobile network architecture, depicted in Figure 5.7.

The architecture features two logical layers: a RAN that provides minimal, low-level forwarding (L1/L2), and a network cloud that provides the functionalities of higher layers. In the network cloud, the core network functions, which are traditionally provided by special hardware elements, are implemented as software and hosted in data centers with carrier-grade virtualization infrastructures. This enables quick and flexible composition and autonomous up/down scaling of core network resources according to current demands; for example, the dynamic provisioning of mobility management, package inspections, and gateway functions for certain RAN edges. Enabled by SDN, this decoupling and shifting of control functions to a cloud infrastructure left simple forwarding functions on network elements, allowing their replacement by standardized forwarding switches network wide. In the RAN layer, a similar design can be applied to RAN elements up to radio interfaces with mobile devices. Control and signaling functions, which are currently coupled with wireless APs and base station controllers; for example, baseband units (BBUs) and radio network controllers (RNCs) can be softwarized and hosted in remote infrastructures. The remote radio heads (RRHs) or antennas, providing air interfaces for the transfer of data to/form mobile devices, are connected with the control functions by broadband wire/wireless backhaul. The radio interfaces can also be sliced using software-defined radio (SDR) techniques, for example, beamforming, spectrum, and interference management, among others. As the result, both computing and radio resources in the two layers can be dynamically allocated to meet current network conditions. Control functions in the network cloud can be migrated closer to the network edge, and assigned to the additional radio units in certain areas to cope with the demand peak for high data rate and low latency.

Another feature of the proposed architecture in [32] is the split of the control plane (CP) from the data plane (DP) for the independent provisioning of coverage and capacity in the RAN layer. Capacity in the RAN network is increased by the dense deployment of small cells in the current coverage of macro and metro cells. Small cell deployment provides more bandwidth and the number of connected devices and makes use of the unlicensed spectrum. Using smaller cells allows for the reuse of the radio spectrum multiple times. In such settings, macro cells provide wireless backhaul, serving control traffic to small cells. In contrast to macro cells, the small cells' deployment is more susceptible to fluctuating traffic demands, users' distribution, and mobility. However, the separation of the CP and DP in RAN and network programmability allow for the demand-attentive allocation of resources. Small cells can be grouped and controlled to enforce certain network policies; for example, QoE along users' trajectories. In the case of a low network load, selectively turning small cells off can guarantee energy-efficient operation and reduced costs for mobile network operators.

A simpler protocol stack is envisioned in the proposed architecture. In current LTE system architecture, multiple CP protocols exist in the core network to facilitate various system operations; for example, mobility management, session management, and security. Each protocol used between a few entities results in termination points and creates boundaries in CP, that is, access stratum (AS) protocols between UE and eNB for radio resource control, non-access stratum (NAS) protocols between eNB and MME for mobility management, between gateways and various information points for policy enforcement. In future networks, where the control functions are softwarized, network entities carry out simple forwarding, these protocols can be replaced by software APIs and the chaining of network functions. The communication between soft network elements is realized using a standardized east–west bound protocol in the same control hierarchy and a north–south bound protocol for different control layers and data planes. As this results in faster connection establishment, reduced control overhead and delay can be achieved. In addition, the standardized and lean protocol stack supports the incorporation of information-centered paradigms (ICN) and content-centered protocols, such as dynamic adaptive streaming over HTTP (DASH) or multipath transmission control protocol (TCP).

Network intelligence of future networks is more context aware and data driven. The centralization of CP functions in the cloud platform enables greater computing resources and complex algorithms to be applied. Network policies and control decisions are based on service-centered, network-centered, and user context information. For example, proactive mobility management approaches improve efficiency and handover delay, whereby mobility prediction results from complex learning algorithms over users' behavior, network utilization history, and service availability, among other things. Similarly, better performance can be realized for resource management, data offloading, routing, and service provisioning. Moreover, the centralization of network intelligence enables integration with over-the-top (OTT) services and B/OSS, allowing flexible and fast policy-driven, service-centered network operations. The application of a centralized network intelligence further benefits from emerging big data analytics and federated information systems.

D2D communication will be an important feature of future RAN networks. As discussed previously, data traffic in edge networks will account for half of the Internet traffic. It is essential to support D2D, and MTC communication in RAN, eliminating the inefficient routing of data through core networks. This also means that RAN architecture must take contradicting network requirements into account, for example, short living, high data-rate, dynamics of V2V communication and low data-rate, energy preserving, stationary IoT communication. Another challenge for the support of D2D is the impact of signaling and control protocols on E2E delays. The flexibility of the network cloud can be extended to RAN, that is, with mobile edge computing (MEC). Control functions and computing resources can be dynamically allocated at macro-cell access points or shared between mobile devices. However, this is only possible with the application of context awareness and application and network service integration, among other things, in RAN.

In summary, emerging mobile applications are creating new challenges for future mobile networks. Proposed future network architectures take advantage of advancements in cloud computing, network virtualization, and programmability, for example, SDN, NFV, MEC. These technologies enable flatter, simpler network layers, increased flexibility and capacity, intelligent network functions, and extend the Internet with M2M and V2V communications.

5.4 Main Cloud Management Frameworks: An Overview

Cloud management frameworks arose as an answer to the necessity of IaaS solutions to provide privacy and control over virtualized environments and to make the management of cloud computing easier and more efficient. Ultimately, cloud management frameworks can be used to set up different kinds of clouds: public clouds, private clouds, or a mix of them, that is, hybrid clouds, and at the end also the federated clouds. With the development of different open-source cloud management frameworks, the decision to choose the most suitable one becomes a challenging task. Therefore, in this section we will briefly describe, analyze, and compare some of them. Since nowadays the most popular and powerful cloud management platforms are OpenStack, CloudStack, Eucalyptus, and OpenNebula, we will concentrate on them. All of them are open-source software management platforms for IaaS that offer cloud orchestration architectures.

5.4.1 OpenNebula

OpenNebula is a project originated in the European academic world. It is an open-source cloud computing toolkit for managing heterogeneous distributed data center infrastructures. The OpenNebula platform manages a data center's virtual infrastructure to build private, public, and hybrid implementations of infrastructure as a service [34]. Its important characteristic is that OpenNebula does not have any specific infrastructural requirements; therefore, it is easier to fit in the existing environment. It is based on the idea of OpenNebula as a purely private cloud, in which users actually log into the head node to access cloud functions. This interface is a wrapper around an XML remote procedure call (XML-RPC) interface, which can also be used directly. Sempolinski [35] note that a front-end interface, such as the Elastic Compute Cloud (EC2), can be appended to this default configuration.

5.4.2 CloudStack

This is a young project that was launched in February 2012 by Citrix. It is a piece of open-source software designed to deploy and manage large networks of virtual machines, Infrastructure as a Service (IaaS), and cloud computing platforms. Basically, CloudStack has been invented for centralized management and massive scalability, that is, to facilitate the successful management of numerous geographically distributed servers from a single portal. CloudStack is running on hypervisors like the Kernel-based Virtual Machine (KVN), vSphere, XenServer, and now Hyper-V. The advantage of CloudStack is that its deployment is very smooth. It consists of only one VM running the

CloudStack management server and another that acts as the actual cloud infrastructure. It can be deployed on one physical host [36]. Unfortunately, since CloudStack is comparatively new, it is lacking a large community support base, and it is not backed as much by the industry. [34]

5.4.3 Eucalyptus

Eucalyptus is the acronym for Elastic Utility Computing Architecture for Linking Your Program To Useful System (see Figure 5.8). It is one of the longest standing open-source projects. It is a piece of open-source software that was developed by the University of California, Santa Barbara, for cloud computing to implement infrastructure as a service and released in May 2008. This software framework allows the building of Amazon Web Services (AWS) for compatible private and hybrid clouds. Eucalyptus provides an EC2-compatible cloud computing platform and S3- or Simple Storage Service–compatible cloud storage. Eucalyptus consists of five high-level components: Cloud Controller (CLC), Cluster Controller (CC), Storage Controller (SC), Node Controller

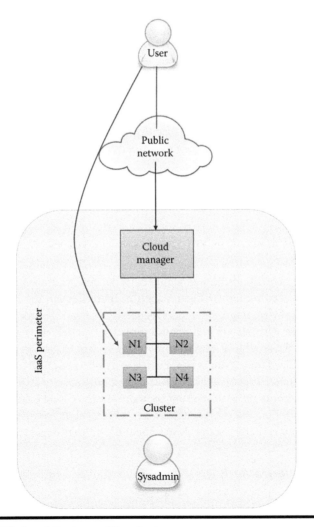

Figure 5.8   Simplified architecture of Eucalyptus.

(NC), and Walrus. The large advantage of this solution is that it integrates very well with Amazon. Although it gives users the ability to run and control entire virtual machine instances deployed across a variety physical resources [34], it still has a very strong separation from user space and administrator space, that is: root access is required for everything done by the administrator on the physical machines themselves and users are only allowed to access the system via a web interface or some type of front-end tools.

5.4.3.1 OpenStack

OpenStack is seen as the leader in cloud platform management. It was started as an open-source project in July 2010 by NASA and Rackspace Hosting Inc. and has attracted a huge number of well-known players (i.e., AT&T, HP, IBM) in a very short time. It has developed itself quickly through a half yearly release cycle. OpenStack is a cloud operating system that controls large pools of compute, storage, and networking resources throughout a data center, all managed through a dashboard that gives administrators control while empowering their users to provision resources through a web interface. OpenStack Code is freely available under the Apache 2.0 license. It supports most virtualization solutions: Elastic Sky X (ESX), Unified Modeling Language (UML), Xen, Hyper-V, Kernel-based Virtual Machine (KVM), Linux containers (LXC), Quick Emulator (QEMU), and XenServer [37].

5.4.4 Comparison of Different Cloud Management Frameworks

In this section, we will compare Eucalyptus, OpenStack, CloudStack, and OpenNebula to each other. All of these cloud management platforms provide infrastructure as a service (IaaS) to deliver a virtualization environment. In Table 5.1 we have listed the main characteristics of different cloud management frameworks.

Figure 5.9 and Table 5.1 summarize the comparison of different cloud management frameworks in terms of different evaluation criteria.

5.4.4.1 Architecture

One of the main differences between these four open-source platforms is their architecture. OpenStack follows fragmented, distributed architecture. It consists of three core software projects: compute, storage, and networking. (1) OpenStack Compute (Nova): the provision and management of large networks of virtual machines. (2) OpenStack Storage: object storage (Swift) and block storage (Cinder) for use with servers and applications. (3) OpenStack Networking: a pluggable, scalable, API-driven network with IP management [40]. CloudStack has monolithic architecture. It was designed for centralized management and massive scalability. Its purpose was to enable an effective management of numerous geographically distributed servers from a single portal. Eucalyptus architecture principally contains five important components: the Cloud Controller, Walrus, Cluster Controller, Node Controller, and Storage Controller. OpenNebula has classical cluster architecture. It consists of a front end and a set of cluster nodes to run the virtual machines (VMs).

5.4.4.2 Cloud Implementation

OpenStack and CloudStack are open-source platforms for the development of private and public clouds. Eucalyptus is only for the development of private clouds, and OpenNebula is a platform for deploying private, public, and hybrid clouds.

Table 5.1   Comparison of OpenStack, CloudStack, Eucalyptus, and OpenNebula

Attributes	OpenStack	CloudStack	Eucalyptus	OpenNebula
Cloud form	IaaS	IaaS	IaaS	IaaS
Source code	Fully open-source, Apache v2.0	Fully open-source, Apache v2.0	Fully open-source, GPL v3.0	Fully open-source, Apache v2.0
API ecosystem	OpenStack API	Amazon API	Amazon API	Amazon API
Architecture	Fragmented into lots of pieces	Monolithic controller, Datacenter model, not object storage.	Five main components, AWS clone	Classical cluster architecture
Installation	Difficult, many choices, not enough automation	Fewest parts to install, resource provisioning manager (RPM) needed	Nice RPM/DEB, still medium effort	Few packages to install and cursory configurations
Administration	Web user interface (UI), euca2ools, native command line interface (CLI)	Good web UI, a belated script CLI	Strong CLI compatible with EC2 API	—
Security	Baseline + Keystone	Baseline VLAN/firewall VM protection	Baseline + component registration	Host communication using secure shell (SSH) Rivest–Shamir–Adleman (RSA) and secure sockets layer (SSL)
High availability	Swift Ring, Otherwise manual effort	Loan balanced Multinode controller	Primary/secondary Component failover	—
Language	Python, shell scripts	Python, shell scripts	Python, shell scripts	Python, shell scripts
Development model	Public development	Public development	Public development	Public development
Developer engagement	Contributor license agreement	Contributor license agreement	Contributor license agreement	Contributor license agreement
Governance model	Foundation	Technical meritocracy	Benevolent dictator	Benevolent dictator
Production readiness	No, only available through any of the several vendor-specific stacks	Enterprise ready and direct support from developers	Enterprise ready and direct support from developers	Enterprise ready and direct support from developers

Source: From Kranowski, D., CloudStack vs. OpenStack vs. Eucalyptus: IaaS private cloud brief comparison. Business Algorithms, LLC http://www.bizalgo.com October 1, 2012.

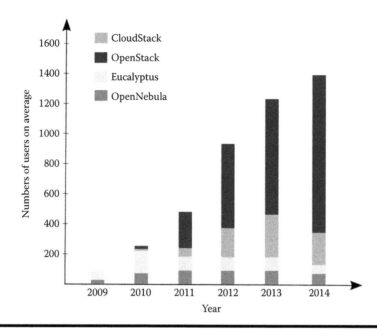

Figure 5.9   Number of monthly users of open-source cloud distribution through the year. (From Jiang, Q., CY15-Q1: Open Source IaaS Community Analysis: OpenStack vs. OpenNebula vs. Eucalyptus vs. CloudStack. University of Sydney, 2015.)

5.4.4.3 VM Migration

Only Eucalyptus does not support VM migration from one resource to another resource.

5.4.4.4 Source Code

Eucalyptus is fully open-source, GPL v3.0, while the other three open-source platforms are fully open-source, Apache v2.0.

5.4.4.5 Governance Model

OpenStack is a foundation with a board of directors, who supervise the strategies of the company. CloudStack follows the Apache meritocracy rules, and both Eucalyptus and OpenNebula follow a centralized, "benevolent dictator" approach. They are managed by a single organization.

5.4.4.6 Production Readiness

From this viewpoint, we can notice that Eucalyptus, OpenNebula, and CloudStack are more "open" than OpenStack. They provide an enterprise-ready open-source cloud solution, while OpenStack gives the production readiness only through some vendor of the specific "stacks." Furthermore, for Eucalyptus, OpenNebula, and CloudStack the commercial support can be purchased directly from the developers and they are not limited editions of enterprise versions. The companies that have purchased OpenStack, after deploying it, are using proprietary software but they are locked to that specific distribution, and there is no possibility to migrate to another vendor's distribution [41].

5.5 OpenStack: A Walk Through

We start this section with a comprehensive quote by Jonathan Bryce (executive director of the OpenStack Foundation) [42]

> At its most basic level, OpenStack is a set of open-source software tools for building clouds. The code that comes out of the OpenStack community is used to deploy compute, storage and networking resources in a data center. OpenStack automates the provisioning and management of those resources. It provides an interface and an API. Users can take control of their application infrastructure environment and manage those resources faster and with greater agility.

OpenStack is a cloud operating system, which goes beyond the simple server virtualization. OpenStack deals with pools of manageable resources and provides the consumer with self-service portals. It provides a user-friendly management layer for controlling, automating, and efficiently allocating the virtualized resources. We now briefly discuss the OpenStack functional procedures in the following section.

5.5.1 OpenStack Architecture

OpenStack basically aims at producing the ubiquitous open-source cloud computing platform that will meet the needs of public and private clouds regardless of size, by being simple to implement and massively scalable [43].

5.5.2 Conceptual Architecture

OpenStack has a modular architecture and it is decomposed into various components: compute (Nova), networking (Neutron/Quantum), identity management (Keystone), object storage (Swift), block storage (Cinder), image service (Glance), and user interface dashboard (Horizon). These components are designed to work together in order to provide a complete IaaS. APIs integrate these OpenStack components, which enable the component-specific services to be used by other components. The modular structure makes OpenStack extendable/customizable to the application areas of the consumer. Figure 5.10 illustrates a simplified view of the conceptual architecture. It is assumed that all of the services are used in the most standard configuration. To illustrate different components of the OpenStack, Figure 5.11 is a regenerated form of Figure 5.10, which more concretely highlights the component names and their integration.

We now discuss the various components of OpenStack depicted in Figure 5.11.

1. *Nova compute node*: Nova is the core component of an infrastructure service. It controls the cloud computing fabric. It is written in Python, it creates and terminates virtual machine (VM) instances via hypervisor's APIs (XenAPI for XenServer/XCP, libvirt for KVM or QEMU, VMwareAPI for VMware, etc.). It has the function to improve utilization and automation. Nova also has a mechanism to cache VM images on compute nodes for faster provisioning. Nova accepts actions from the queue and subsequently performs a series of system commands (as launching a KVM instance) to carry them out while updating the state in the database. It is also possible to store and manage files programmatically through an API.

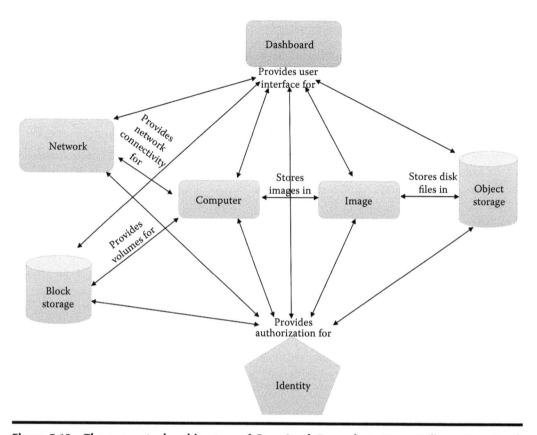

Figure 5.10   The conceptual architecture of OpenStack Example 1. (From Solinea, OpenStack grizzly architecture (revisited), http://solinea.com. June 2015. Accessed: 2016-07-01.)

2. *Neutron networking node*: Neutron provides "network connectivity as a service" between devices managed by other OpenStack services, in the sense that it accepts API requests and then routes them to the appropriate quantum plugin for action. Plugins and agents perform actual actions, for example, they plug/unplug ports, create networks, subnets, and IP addresses. Neutron also has a communication line to route information between the neutron server and various agents. It has a database to store the networking state for particular plugins. Neutron allows users to create their own networks and then link interfaces to them. It has a pluggable architecture to support many popular networking vendors and technologies.

3. *Keystone—Identity management*: Keystone (also called *Authentication*) is a component responsible for the identity and authorization of an operation. It provides user authentication and authorization to all OpenStack components, using user name, password credentials, token-based systems, and AWS-style logins. Keystone works with API requests and provides a single point of integration for policies, configurable catalogues, tokens, and authentication. Every Keystone function has a pluggable backend that permits diverse ways of using the specific service. It maintains standard back ends like SQL, LDAP, and KVS (key-value stores) and creates policies across users and services. We have to note that for the cloud federation, this component might have one of the most important roles for offering a reference, a guardian across clouds.

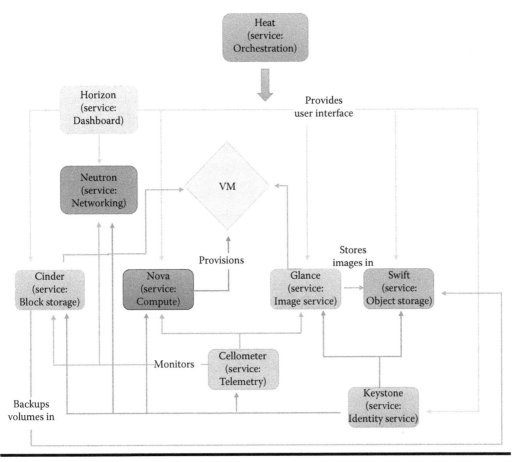

Figure 5.11 The conceptual architecture of OpenStack Example 2: with all the compo-nents. (From Icehouse, Chapter 1, Architecture, in *OpenStack Installation Guide for Ubuntu 12.04/14.04.* June 2015.

OpenStack diversifies two components: OpenStack and Keystone, which "Provides Identity services, together with the administrative and public APIs. Both Identity API v2 and API v3 are supported." Keystone: "Command-line client to access the Identity API."

4. *Swift—Storage*: Swift is grounded on the Rackspace Cloud Files product and is a storage system perfect for scale-out storage. Swift is for redundant storage that can be scaled hori-zontally over the cluster. It is primarily for static data, such as VM images, backups, and archives. It adds new machines, offers redundancy for the files, as well as writing files and other objects to a set of disk drives that can be dispersed on multiple servers around one or more data centers, ensuring data replication and integrity across the cluster.

5. *Cinder—Block storage*: Cinder provides persistent block storage to guest VMs. It is impor-tant to note that this is block storage not file systems like the network file system (NFS) or the common Internet file system (CIFS).

6. *Glance—Image service*: Glance manages a catalog and repository for virtual disk images.

7. *Horizon—User interface dashboard*: It is the control interface and visualizes the basic control and visualization components in a web browser and allows elementary settings.

5.6 Conclusion

In this chapter, we discussed different aspects of the revolutionary technology that is cloud computing. For ease in following the discussed concepts, the chapter starts with briefly describing the fundamentals of cloud computing, followed by service and deployment models. Cloud federation, its drivers, and the concepts therein are discussed. Subsequently, mobile cloud computing technologies are discussed, which incorporate techniques to overcome the lack of flexibility and limitation of the current cloud network as well as mobile networks. Needless to say that future network technologies will mainly be built around cloud computing concepts. We further discussed enablers and paradigms, which impact the designs of future mobile networks in support of emerging mobile cloud computing applications. An architecture for a 5G network was introduced with envisioned features that address various flexibilities, efficiencies, and performance requirements by combining cloud computing, network virtualization, and intelligent control and management. The advancement of mobile networking is backed by revolutionary paradigms, that is, network programmability, autonomous control and management, virtualized functions and components. This makes the mobile network a part of MCC solutions together with cloud computing instead of being a technical constraint for cloud delivery. As a result, cloud computing must be extended outside of the boundaries of the data center.

Moreover, it is important to notice that there are still major concerns for the development of this field. It is limited by certain worries around security, the lack of in-house specialized skills, and the lack of support in the case of Open clouds [44]. This is still relatively true in the other ones. We left, for now, the details about security outside of the scope of our study but it will need to be considered for practical implementation. Cloud Federation Interclouds are going to be part of our new reality since the society needs more and more communication capacities. The old model of the classical capacity is unable to answer the demand of the digital society. Having an overcapacity does not make sense in terms of cost or environmental impact (e.g., the green tech movement). Being under capacity is harmful for companies. Cloud computing was the first step of this evolution. Federated clouds offer the space for bringing the full capacity of this approach, as the Internet did with the possibility of connecting networks on a global scale.

References

1. Introduction to how cloud computing works | HowStuffWorks. http://computer.howstuffworks.com/cloud-computing/cloud-computing.htm, Accessed: 2016-02-23.
2. Moving your infrastructure to the cloud: How to maximize benefits and avoid pitfalls. https://support.rackspace.com/white-paper/moving-your-infrastructure-to-the-cloud-how-to-maximize-benefits-and-avoid-pitfalls/, Accessed: 2016-02-24.
3. I. Foster, Y. Zhao, I. Raicu, and S. Lu, Cloud computing and grid computing 360-degree compared, *Grid Computing Environments Workshop*, 2008, GCE'08, pp. 1–10, IEEE, 2008.
4. L. M. Vaquero, L. Rodero-Merino, J. Caceres, and M. Lindner, A break in the clouds: Towards a cloud definition, SIGCOMM *Computer Communication Review*, Vol. 39, No. 1, pp. 50–55, December 2008.
5. The economics of the cloud, http://news.microsoft.com/download/archived/presskits/cloud/docs/The-Economics-of-the-Cloud.pdf, Accessed: 2016-06-01.
6. P. M. Mell and T. Grance, Sp 800-145, the NIST definition of cloud computing, Technical Report, Gaithersburg, MD, 2011.
7. T. Navarro, The three minute guide to cloud marketplaces. https://www.computenext.com/blog/the-three-minute-guide-to-cloud-marketplaces, Accessed: 2016-02-23.
8. J. Goiri, J. Guitart, and J. Torres, Characterizing cloud federation for enhancing providers' profit, *2013 IEEE Sixth International Conference on Cloud Computing*, pp. 123–130, 2010.
9. R. Buyya, C. Vecchiola, S. Thamarai Selvi, *Mastering Cloud Computing: Foundations and Applications Programming*, Morgan Kaufmann, Waltham, MA, 2013.
10. A. N. Toosi, R. N. Calheiros, and R. Buyya, Interconnected cloud computing environments: Challenges, taxonomy, and survey, *ACM Computing, Surveys*, Vol. 47, No. 1, pp. 7:1–7:47, 2014.

11. N. Pustchi, R. Krishnan, and R. S. Sandhu, Authorization federation in IaaS multi cloud, *3rd International Workshop on Security in Cloud Computing, SCC@ASIACCS '15, Proceedings*, Singapore, April 14, 2015, pp. 63–71, 2015.
12. H. Qi and A. Gani, Research on mobile cloud computing: Review, trend and perspectives, Digital Information and Communication Technology and Its Applications (DICTAP), 2012 Second International Conference on, pp. 195–202. IEEE, 2012.
13. T. Kurze, M. Klems, D. Bermbach, A. Lenk, S. Tai, and M. Kunze, Cloud federation, Cloud Computing 2011, The Second International Conference on Cloud Computing, GRIDs, and Virtualization, pp. 32–38, 2011.
14. K. Subramanian, Defining federated cloud ecosystems, https://www.cloudave.com/15323/defining-federated-cloud-ecosystems, Accessed: 2016-07-01.
15. D. C. Chou. Cloud computing: A value creation model, *Computer Standards & Interfaces*, Vol. 38, pp. 72–77, 2015.
16. H. T. Dinh, C. Lee, D. Niyato, and P. Wang, A survey of mobile cloud computing: architecture, applications, and approaches, *Wireless Communications and Mobile Computing*, Vol. 13, No. 18, pp. 1587–1611, 2013.
17. A. N. Khan, M. L. Mat Kiah, S. U. Khan, and S. A. Madani, Towards secure mobile cloud computing: A survey, *Future Generation Computer Systems*, Vol. 29 No. 5, pp. 1278–1299, 2013.
18. A. R. Khan, M. Othman, S. A. Madani, and S. U. Khan, A survey of mobile cloud computing application models, *Communications Surveys & Tutorials, IEEE*, Vol. 16, No. 1, pp. 393–413, 2014.
19. L. Guan, X. Ke, M. Song, and J. Song, A survey of research on mobile cloud computing, *The 2011 10th IEEE/ACIS International Conference on Computer and Information Science, Proceedings*, pp. 387–392, IEEE Computer Society, 2011.
20. Cisco visual networking index: Global mobile data traffic forecast update, 2014-2019 White Paper, technical report, Cisco VNI, May 2015, http://www.cisco.com/c/en/us/solutions/collateral/service-provider/ip-ngn-ip-next-generation-network/white_paper_c11-481360.pdf
21. X. Jin and Y.-K. Kwok, Cloud assisted P2P media streaming for bandwidth constrained mobile subscribers, The *2010 IEEE 16th International Conference on Parallel and Distributed Systems, ICPADS '10, Proceedings*, pp. 800–805, Washington, DC, IEEE Computer Society, 2010.
22. K. L. Scott and S. Burleigh, Bundle protocol specification, 2007.
23. M. A. Khan and X. T. Dang, A service framework for emerging markets, 2014 21st International Conference on Telecommunications (ICT), pp. 272–276, May 2014.
24. M. Satyanarayanan, P. Bahl, R. Caceres, and N. Davies, The case for VM-based cloudlets in mobile computing, *IEEE Pervasive Computing*, Vol. 8, No.4, pp. 14–23, October 2009,
25. S. Abolfazli, Z. Sanaei, M. Shiraz, and A. Gani, Momcc: Market-oriented architecture for mobile cloud computing based on service oriented architecture, 2012 1st IEEE International Conference on Communications in China Workshops (ICCC), pp. 8–13, IEEE, 2012.
26. B.-G. Chun, S. Ihm, P. Maniatis, M. Naik, and A. Patti, Clonecloud: elastic execution between mobile device and cloud, the *Sixth Conference on Computer Systems, Proceedings*, pp. 301–314, ACM, 2011.
27. E. Cuervo, A. Balasubramanian, Dae-ki Cho, A. Wolman, S. Saroiu, R. Chandra, and P. Bahl, Maui: Making smartphones last longer with code offload, the *8th International Conference on Mobile Systems, Applications, and Services, Proceedings*, pp. 49–62, ACM, 2010.
28. M. Asplund, A. Thomasson, E. J. Vergara, and S. N. Tehrani. Software-related energy footprint of a wireless broadband module, the *9th ACM International Symposium on Mobility Management and Wireless Access, MobiWac '11, Proceedings*, pp. 75–82, New York, NY, ACM, 2011.
29. A. Madhavapeddy, R. Mortier, J. Crowcroft, and S. Hand, Multiscale not multicore: Efficient heterogeneous cloud computing, the *2010 ACM-BCS Visions of Computer Science Conference, Proceedings*, p. 6. British Computer Society, 2010.
30. N. Loutas, E. Kamateri, F. Bosi, and K. Tarabanis. Cloud computing interoperability: The state of play, Cloud Computing Technology and Science (CloudCom), 2011 IEEE Third International Conference on, pp. 752–757, November 2011.
31. ONF Market Education Committee et al., SDN architecture overview, ONF White Paper, 2013.
32. P. K. Agyapong, M. Iwamura, D. Staehle, W. Kiess, and A. Benjebbour, Design considerations for a 5G network architecture, *IEEE Communications Magazine*, Vol. 52 No. 11, pp. 65–75, 2014.

33. ISGNFV ETSI, Network function virtualisation (NFV), Virtual Network Functions Architecture, v1, 1, 2014.

34. A. B. M. Moniruzzaman, K. W. Nafi, and S. A. Hossain, An experimental study of load balancing of OpenNebula open-source cloud computing platform, CoRR, abs/1406.5759, 2014.

35. P. Sempolinski and D. Thain. A comparison and critique of Eucalyptus, OpenNebula and Nimbus, 2013 IEEE 5th International Conference on Cloud Computing Technology and Science, pp. 417–426, 2010.

36. B. Kleyman. Understanding CloudStack, OpenStack, and the cloud API. Accessed: 2016-02-01.

37. OpenStack operations guide. Accessed: 2016-03-11.

38. Q. Jiang, CY15-Q1 Open source IaaS community analysis—OpenStack vs. OpenNebula vs. Eucalyptus vs. CloudStack. http://www.qyjohn.net/?p=3801, Accessed : 2016-02-25.

39. CloudStack vs. OpenStack vs. Eucalyptus: IaaS private cloud brief comparison. http://www.slide-share.net/bizalgo/cloudstack-vs-openstack-vs-eucalyptus-iaas-private-cloud-brief-comparison, Accessed: 2016-03-11.

40. OpenStack community welcome guide. https://www.openstack.org/assets/welcome-guide/OpenStackWelcomeGuide.pdf, Accessed: 2016-03-11.

41. I. M. Llorente. OpenStack, CloudStack, Eucalyptus and OpenNebula: Which cloud platform is the most open? http://opennebula.org/openstack-cloudstack-eucalyptus-and-opennebula-which-cloud-platform-is-the-most-open, Accessed: 2016-03-11.

42. J. Bryce. OpenStack: Driving the software-defined economy. http://www.networkcomputing.com/cloud-infrastructure/openstack-driving-software-defined-economy/1573138704, Accessed: 2016-07-01.

43. R. Schulze. OpenStack architecture and pattern deployment using heat. http://www.iaas.uni-stuttgart.de/lehre/vorlesung/2015_ws/vorlesungen/smcc/materialien/Ruediger%20Schulze%20-%20OpenStack%20Architecture%20and%20Heat%20v2%2008112015.pdf, Accessed: 2016-07-01.

44. The state of the open source cloud 2014. https://www.zenoss.com/documents/2014-State-OS-Cloud-Report.pdf, Accessed: 2016-02-29.

45. OpenStack grizzly architecture (revisited). http://solinea.com/blog/openstack-grizzly-architecture-revisited, Accessed: 2016-07-01.

46. Chapter 1. Architecture—OpenStack Installation Guide for Ubuntu 14.04 -juno. http://docs.openstack.org/juno/install-guide/install/apt/content/ch_overview.html, Accessed: 2016-02-253.

5G RAN VIRTUALIZATION SOLUTIONS

Chapter 6

Software-Defined Networking and Network Function Virtualization for C-RAN Systems

Massimo Condoluci, Toktam Mahmoodi, and Giuseppe Araniti

Contents

6.1 Introduction

The availability of wireless connections is changing the way people interact and communicate and this has brought about a drastic increase in the number of wireless devices as well as the introduction of a vast amount of applications covering heterogeneous areas, from smart cities to smart offices, from advertisement to industrial automation, and so on. Such applications have led to an increasing demand for more bandwidth and have dictated the need for more powerful and faster networks. As a consequence, network operators need novel solutions to enhance the traditional architecture and coverage paradigms that are becoming increasingly overwhelmed. To this aim, *cell densification*, where small (e.g., pico and femto) cells are deployed to increase the coverage of existing macro cells, is a viable solution to effectively handle the extremely huge traffic load of future mobile networks (Andrews et al., 2012). Nevertheless, denser deployments open new challenges (for instance, in terms of interference management, intercell coordination, spectrum allocation, control, and data planes management), which thus call for the adoption of more efficient approaches to network design to guarantee high reliability, flexibility, and low latency.

In this scenario, the *cloud/centralized radio access network* (C-RAN) is considered as a promising solution to boost and optimize network performance (Dawson et al., 2014). C-RAN is based on the idea of decoupling baseband processing from radio units, thus allowing the processing power to be pooled at a central location; this allows for the replacement of the traditional cells with more generic and simpler nodes carrying out minimal tasks (such as radio frequency [RF] operations) and to move other computationally intensive tasks (such as resource allocation, baseband processing, etc.) to a centralized location. C-RAN allows for the reduction of the total cost of ownership (especially capital and operating expenditures) thanks to the shared use of storage/computing/network/radio resources. Therefore, common repositories for network functionality may be used to avoid multiple deployments of the same component (e.g., macro and small cells which use shared resources). C-RAN may be helpful in several scenarios: (1) the *cell configuration, resource assignment*, and *traffic distribution* to the cells; (2) the *activation of the appropriate volume/type of functional/software components* needed to handle a given network situation; (3) the *allocation of functional components to the physical elements*. Nevertheless, effective solutions to guarantee deployment and to efficiently run the C-RAN architecture are needed. In this regard, further steps are needed in decoupling *data delivery from management and control* and decoupling *functionalities from the underlying hardware*.

This chapter discusses two enabling technologies for C-RAN that allow decoupling beyond baseband and radio, that is, software-defined networking (SDN) and network function virtualization (NFV). SDN is an emerging network architecture based on the idea of decoupling the control and data planes; SDN exploits a logically centralized network controller, which works in the control plane, handling the allocation of traffic to network elements in an isolated data plane. Moreover, NFV foresees the implementation of the network function of a network device in a software package running in a virtual container(s), for example, a virtual machine(s), to allow for the decoupling of network functions from the hardware. The NFV introduces flexibility and allows for the quick installation/reconfiguration of network functions by simply installing/upgrading software package(s). Alongside visual depictions of C-RAN systems through SDN and NFV, the pros and cons of these enabling technologies will also be thoroughly discussed in this chapter.

6.2 Software-Defined Networking

In traditional IP networks, the control and data planes are tightly coupled, that is, control and data planes' functionalities run on the same networking devices; this aspect is highlighted in

Figure 6.1. This was considered important for the design of the Internet in its early days: It seemed to be the best way to guarantee network resilience, which was a crucial design goal.

The main drawback of this coupled paradigm is a very complex and relatively static architecture, as addressed by Kim and Feamster (2013). A further issue is related to network management, which is typically handled through a large number of proprietary solutions with their own specialized hardware, operating systems, and control programs. This involves high operating expenditure/capital expenditure (OPEX/CAPEX) as operators have to acquire and maintain different management solutions and the corresponding specialized teams, and this further involves long returns on investment cycles and limits the introduction of innovation.

The *softwarization* paradigm is useful to overcome these limitations as it introduces the following features:

- *The decoupling of control and data planes.* This means that control functionalities will no longer be handled by network devices that act only as packet-forwarding units.
- *Per flow–based forwarding.* This means that all packets belonging to the same flow (identified through the sender/receiver addresses) receive identical service policies at the forwarding devices, instead of having per-packet routing decisions based only on the packet destination's address.
- *Network controller.* Control logic is moved to an external controller, which is a software platform that runs on commodity server technology and provides the essential resources and abstractions to facilitate the programming of forwarding devices based on a logically centralized, abstract network view. This allows for the control of the network by taking into consideration the whole state of the network.
- *Software-based network management.* The network is programmable through software applications running on top of the network controller that interacts with the underlying data plane devices. This allows for a quick network reconfiguration and innovation.

The new network vision based on SDN, whose high-level architecture is depicted in Figure 6.4, will allow for the easier programming of novel network functionalities as well as the optimization of network balancing, as all applications can take advantage of the same network information (i.e., global network view). The switches in Figure 6.4 are SDN network elements running OpenFlow and this allows them to receive information by the SDN controller to configure link parameters (bandwidth, queues, meters, etc.) as well as intranetwork paths. As a consequence, Figure 6.2 highlights that data and control planes are now decoupled as the control plane is removed from the physical links between the switches and it is instead managed by the SDN controller.

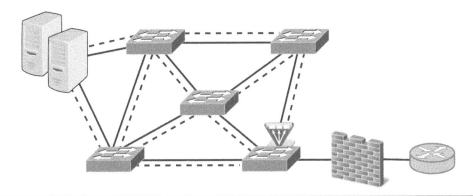

Figure 6.1   Conventional networking with coupled control/data planes.

6.2.1 SDN Architecture

The SDN architecture is depicted in Figure 6.3. Different components may be envisioned, which are presented in more detail in Kreutz et al. (2015). In the remainder of this section, we will provide a global overview of SDN architecture.

6.2.1.1 Entities

SDN architecture is composed of two main elements, that is, *forwarding devices* and *controllers*. The former are hardware- or software-based elements handling packet forwarding, while a controller is a software stack running on a commodity hardware platform.

6.2.1.2 Planes

An SDN network is composed of three different planes. The *data plane* (DP) refers to the plane where devices are interconnected through wireless radio channels or wired cables. The *control plane* (CP) can be considered as the "network brain," as all control logic rests in the applications and controllers, which form the control plane. Finally, the *management plane* (MP) deals with the set of applications that leverage functions such as routing, firewalls, load balancers, monitoring, and so on. Essentially, a management application defines the policies, which are ultimately translated to southbound-specific instructions that program the behavior of the forwarding devices.

6.2.1.3 Interfaces

SDN introduces the concept of a *southbound interface* (SI), which defines: (1) the communication protocol and application programming interfaces (APIs) between forwarding devices and control plane elements and (2) the interaction between control and data planes. Actually, OpenFlow is the most widely accepted and deployed open southbound standard for SDN; other solutions are gaining ground as alternative SIs, such as forwarding and control element separation (ForCES), Open vSwitch database (OVSDB), protocol-oblivious forwarding (POF), OpFlex, OpenState, Revised OpenFlow Library (ROFL), hardware abstraction layer (HAL), and programmable abstraction of datapath (PAD). The *northbound interface* (NI) is a common interface exploited to develop

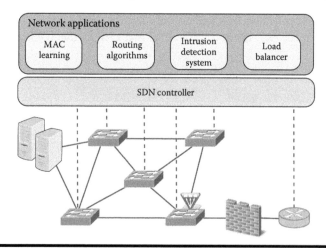

Figure 6.2   Software-defined networking with decoupled control/data planes.

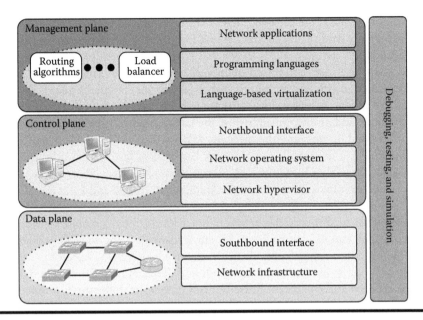

Figure 6.3   SDN architecture with the related planes, layers, and main entities.

applications, that is, the NI abstracts the low-level instruction sets used by SIs to program forwarding devices. A common NI is still an open issue; it may still be a bit too early to define a standard NI, as use cases are still being worked out.

6.2.2 Standardization Activities

The standardization landscape in SDN is already wide. The *Open Networking Foundation* (ONF) is considered as the member-driven organization aimed at promoting the adoption of SDN, with the main contribution being the development of the OpenFlow protocol. The *Internet Research Task Force* (IRTF), has created the Software-Defined Networking Research Group (SDNRG) that is currently investigating SDN in both short- and long-term activities, that is, aiming at identifying the approaches that can be defined, deployed, and used in the near term, as well as identifying future research challenges. Similarly, the *International Telecommunications Union's Telecommunication Sector* (ITU-T) has already started to develop recommendations for SDN. The *Institute of Electrical and Electronics Engineers* (IEEE) has started some activities to standardize SDN capabilities on access networks based on IEEE 802 infrastructure, for both wired and wireless technologies to embrace new control interfaces.

The *European Telecommunication Standards Institute* (ETSI) is working on the *virtualization* of SDN. ETSI considers softwarization and virtualization as complementary features, as both share the goal of accelerating innovation inside the network through the introduction of programmability. Similarly, the 3rd generation partnership project (3GPP) is studying the management of virtualized networks. The main aspects of network virtualization will be treated in the next section.

6.2.3 Data and Control Decoupling in the Mobile Network

It is also interesting to see the transition from a fully coupled data and management/control plane in the mobile network to a relatively decoupled architecture. For the first time the long-term evolution (LTE) core network, that is, the evolved packet core (EPC), has a clear split into: (1) a packet-only data plane, comprised of a E-UTRAN Node B (eNodeB), serving gateway (S-GW), and PDN gateway (PDN-GW), and (2) a management plane to manage mobility, policies, and charging rules, comprised of mobility management entity (MME), policy and charging rules function (PCRF), and home subscriber server (HSS). Although the LTE architecture yields to easier management, it is still not as evolvable, flexible, and programmable as it can be. Furthermore and as mentioned before, the LTE design enforces a significant increase in the backhaul load and in the signaling message, as discussed by Nokia Siemens (2012).

Introducing SDN in the mobile core network has been so far discussed through integration of software agents (possibly Open vSwitch*), installed in all devices, that can be controlled by an SDN controller; examples can be found in Amani et al. (2014) and Errani et al. (2012). The introduction of these agents is mainly intended to maintain the logically centralized nature of the SDN controller, with the distributed solution, in line with the today's mobile architecture design. Considering 2G, 3G, and 4G networks are all simultaneously active in today's mobile network, a clean slate approach is not justifiable. To this end, introducing SDN within the existing operational mobile network is discussed by Mahmoodi and Seetharaman (2014), where the management plane is retained and significant flexibility and programmability are introduced through a new control plane. Since the management plane could also potentially be software-defined, the control plane may, in the long term, subsume the functions offered by the management plane.

6.3 Network Function Virtualization

The proprietary nature of existing hardware appliances as well as the cost of offering the space and energy for a variety of middle boxes limits the time to market of new services in today's networks. Network function virtualization (NFV) is a radical shift in the way network operators design and deploy their infrastructure that deals with the separation of software instances from hardware platform. The main idea behind the virtualization is that virtualized network functions (VNFs) are implemented through software virtualization techniques and run on commodity hardware (i.e., industry-standard servers, storage, and switches), as shown in Figure 6.4.

The virtualization concept is expected to introduce a large set of benefits for telecommunication operators: (1) a capital investment reduction, (2) energy savings by consolidating networking appliances, (3) a reduction in the time to market of new services thanks to the use of software-based service deployment, and (4) the introduction of services tailored to the customer's needs. Furthermore, the concept of virtualization and softwarization are mutually beneficial and highly complementary to each other. For example, SDN can support network virtualization to enhance its performance and simplify the compatibility with legacy deployments.

6.3.1 Architecture

The NFV architecture shown in Figure 6.5 highlights the two major enablers of NFV, that is, *industry-standard servers* and *technologies developed for cloud computing*. Being general purpose servers, industry-standard servers have the key feature of a competitive price, compared with network appliances based on bespoke application-specific integrated circuits (ASICs). Using these servers may come in handy to extend the life cycle of hardware when technologies evolve (this is

---

* Open vSwitch: An Open Virtual Switch, http://openvswitch.org.

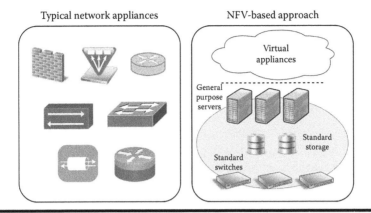

Figure 6.4   The network-virtualization paradigm.

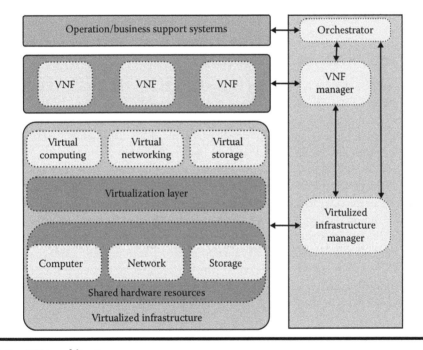

Figure 6.5   NFV architecture.

achieved by running different software versions on the same platform). Cloud computing solutions, such as various hypervisors, OpenStack, and Open vSwitch, enable the automatic instantiation and migration of virtual machines (VMs) running specific network services.

NFV architecture is mainly composed of four different units. The first one is the *orchestrator*, which is responsible for the management and orchestration of software resources and the virtualized hardware infrastructure to realize networking services. The *VNF manager* has the following tasks: instantiation, scaling, termination, updating events during the life cycle of a VNF, and supporting zero-touch automation. The *virtualization layer* is in charge of abstracting the physical resources and anchoring the VNFs to the virtualized infrastructure. The virtualization layer has the key role to ensure that the life cycles of VNFs are independent of the underlying hardware platforms, this is achieved through the use of virtual machines (VMs) and their hypervisors. Finally, the *virtualized infrastructure manager* has the role of virtualizing and managing the configurable computing, networking, and storage resources, and of controlling their interaction with VNFs.

More details on the architecture of NFV can be found in Han et al. (2015).

6.3.2 Reception by Industries

Service providers have shown a keen interest in NFV and this pushed IT companies to investigate different aspects of NFV realization. Leading vendors like Ericsson, Nokia, Alcatel–Lucent, and Huawei have already started to adopt and upgrade their equipment to support NFV (an example can be found in Ericsson, 2014). In addition, companies such as HP have been working closely with Intel to optimize their software on Intel processors in order to achieve higher packet processing computations that enable softwarization and virtualization on commercial off-the-shelf platforms. To this aim, Intel has released the data plane development kit and has scheduled the release of a signal processing development kit in its software development roadmap.

6.4 Role of C-RAN in 5G Systems

The traffic in mobile networks continues to grow and 5G systems need to face unprecedented challenges in terms of *capacity,* that is, simultaneous support of high data-rate traffic and a huge amount of devices. Indeed, according to Cisco (2014), data traffic of about 24.3 EB per month is expected from high-end devices (e.g., smartphones, tablets) by 2019, while Ericsson (2011) predicts 50 billion connected (machine and human) devices by 2020.

To cope with these challenges, cell densification is attracting the interest of mobile network providers to offload data from the creaking traditional network and to extend the coverage (Andrews et al., 2012). Nevertheless, the densification of coverage cells eases the congestion in the radio access network (RAN) due to the larger number of base stations (BSs) to be managed in a restricted area (Bhushan et al., 2014). Consequently, denser deployments bring new challenges in interference management and intercell coordination that dictate new approaches to properly manage such aspects.

The C-RAN has come to the fore as one of the key architectural concepts for future 5G networks and beyond (Boccardi et al., 2014). C-RAN represents a cost-effective approach to addressing the increased density in the RAN.

6.4.1 C-RAN Architecture

The main idea behind C-RAN is the *replacement of self-contained base stations* at each radio mast with shared/cloud-based processing and distributed radio elements. C-RAN architecture is depicted in Figure 6.6 and the related main components are the following:

- *Baseband processing units* (BBUs), that is, the pool of computing resources to provide the signal processing and coordination functionality required by all cells within the area.
- *Fronthaul,* that is, optical fiber/wireless links carrying digitized representations of the baseband data ready for transmission in the RAN.
- *Remote Radio Heads* (RRHs), that is, lightweight radio units and antennas that user equipment connects to via the RAN. RRHs can be used in place of any size of cell from macro down to femto and pico.

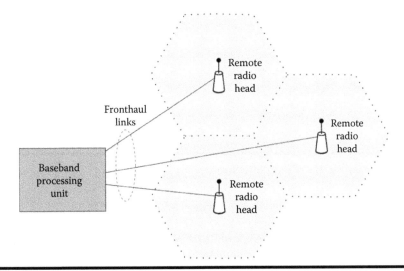

Figure 6.6   C-RAN architecture with centralized baseband processing and remote radio heads.

In this architecture, RRHs, potentially smaller in size compared with traditional base stations, can be located almost anywhere and not necessarily on a dedicated tower. The RRHs, therefore, need only the space for the antenna and access to any fronthaul link.

One of the key goals of C-RAN architecture is achieving significantly easier intercell coordination given that management of RRHs in a given area is handled by a single BS pool, and communication occurs directly within the pool.

6.4.2 Challenges, Limitations, and Enabling Technologies

The C-RAN paradigm offers lower costs and easier deployment of macro/small cells while it also enables the simultaneous management of huge heterogeneity in the RAN. Nevertheless, the network's overall operational efficiency will continue to be limited by the signaling load between the radio access and the evolved packet core (EPC) segments of the network.

The EPC, depicted in Figure 6.7 and defined by 3GPP (2015), is entirely packet-switched with all data sent using an IP and is composed of the following entities:

■ *Mobility management entity* (MME), which handles mobility-related signaling.
■ *Home subscriber server* (HSS), which contains all of the information related to users and subscribers and provides supporting functionalities to the MME.
■ *Policy and charging rules function* (PCRF), which decides the policies and charges each service/user flow.
■ *Serving gateway* (SGW), which forwards/receives data to/from BSs and, in the case of an inter-BS handover, it acts as a mobility anchor.
■ *Packet data network gateway* (PDN-GW), which connects the EPC to external networks.

The EPC is currently facing a significant challenge in terms of signaling load when considering the deployment of small cells. Compared with 2G and 3G or high-speed packet access (HSPA), the 4G long-term evolution (LTE) results in a significantly higher signaling requirement per subscriber, up to 42% compared with HSPA according to Nokia Siemens (2012). Although a portion

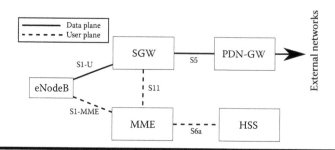

Figure 6.7   The existing 4G EPC architecture.

of this new signaling is required for new services and new types of devices, over 50% of the signaling is related to mobility and paging, due to the greater node density.

To address these issues, *softwarization* and *virtualization* are gaining ground in the mobile networking ecosystem, particularly in conjunction with C-RAN (Chiosi et al., 2012). These two paradigms aim at introducing programmability in the mobile core with the main benefit being the decoupling of the network control and management function from data forwarding, which takes place in the hardware (Granelli et al., 2015). In this direction, significant work has gone toward softwarizing radio access functionalities and toward allowing for their implementation in software packages running on generic processing hardware; this introduces the opportunity of saving cost and time during the reconfiguration tasks of the network (Ganqiang et al., 2015a). An example can be found in Riggio et al. (2014), where the authors presented a software-defined RAN (SD-RAN) controller, where a Python SDK provides a framework for accessing network resource information and scheduling transmissions independent of access technology.

In the remainder of this chapter, we will focus on the main features of a software-based virtualized core network, by highlighting their role in introducing flexibility in the design of 5G systems.

6.5 Role of SDN and NFV for C-RAN Deployments

The virtualization and softwarization paradigms are gaining ground in the mobile networking ecosystem, particularly in conjunction with C-RAN (for instance, refer to Chiosi et al., 2012). In this field, great effort has gone into virtualizing radio access technology as this enables the virtualization of edge functions of the core network without incurring additional hardware costs. In the remainder of this section, we will focus on the recent advances in the virtualization of mobile networks, with particular attention to C-RAN deployments.

6.5.1 Softwarization in the Radio Access

Sofwarization represents an important enhancement in the process toward effective C-RAN deployments by exploiting the novel features of the SDN paradigm.

As discussed by Arslan et al. (2015), the programmability of the SDN architecture allows the data plane to only deal with fast-rule lookups and executes forwarding at fine timescales, whereas new rules can be pushed into longer timescales due to the latency involved in communicating with the controller. In this sense, C-RAN architecture can be seen as a direct extension of SDN's control/data plane separation principle to the RAN, where the C-RAN and SDN complement each other. As an example, Zaidi et al. (2015) proposed to handle control plane tasks such as radio resource management (RRM) or interference coordination logic in an SDN controller implemented in C-RAN architecture in order to orchestrate the parameters of RRHs (data plane): In this case, SDN brings some benefits in terms of distributing the control information triggered by the C-RAN to the involved network entities. Another example is the activation/deactivation of RRHs, which is decided by the C-RAN according to network load and interference level; in this case, SDN updates the path configuration in order to guarantee reliable communication for the newly activated RRHs or to optimize data paths when some RRHs are switched off.

Among the aspects that need to be properly highlighted is the role of SDN in managing the fronthaul link of C-RANs. Zaidi et al. (2015) investigated the benefits of SDN in providing APIs to the RRHs as well as to the core network. When considering in detail how to manage the fronthaul links, it is worth highlighting that the C-RAN decouples the BBUs from the RRHs in terms of physical placement, but there is a one-to-one logical mapping between BBUs and RRHs. As analyzed by Sundaresan et al. (2013), this notion of fixed one-to-one mapping can potentially limit the performance of C-RANs. For instance, mobile users require handovers when moving from one RRH to another one and in this scenario a one-to-many mapping on the fronthaul link could reduce the overhead and optimize network performance. Another aspect to be taken into consideration is that, with the one-to-one mapping, several BBUs are active and generate frames (and thus consume energy in the BBU pool) even if an enhanced capacity may not be needed in all parts of the network or at all times. As an example, when the traffic load is low in a region (e.g., a coverage area of multiple small cell RRHs), a single BBU may be enough to serve the offered load. The SDN paradigm may come in handy to introduce this flexibility in the fronthaul management by treating fronthaul links as network links. Sundaresan et al. (2013) proposed a flexible C-RAN system for RRHs that is based on the introduction of an intelligent controller in the BBU pool that, similar to an SDN controller, dynamically reconfigures the fronthaul (at coarse time scales) based on network feedback to cater effectively to both heterogeneous user and traffic profiles. As a consequence, the amount of traffic demand that is satisfied on the RAN is maximized for both static and mobile users, while at the same time the compute resource usage in the BBU pool is optimized.

6.5.2 Virtualization in the Radio Access

The interest of service providers in virtualizing mobile base stations is growing as this allows for the consolidation of as many network functions as possible in a standard piece of hardware: This introduces the opportunity of handling different mobile network technologies with a single virtualized base station.

The main challenge in the virtualization of mobile networks is related to the physical layer functionalities of base stations. Consequently, virtualization is first considered for implementation in the higher network stack layers. As an example, ETSI (2013) is considering the introduction of virtualization to layer 3 and then to layer 2 of the base stations; layer 3 hosts the functionalities of the control and data plane that connect to the mobile core network while layer 2 hosts the packet data convergence protocol (PDCP), radio link control (RLC), and media access control (MAC) network functions.

The virtualization of layers 2 and 3 (which implements the functionalities of control and data planes) provides the opportunity to offer a centralized computing infrastructure for multiple base stations. Finally, some effort to centralize the functionalities of layer 1 of several base stations is currently in progress, aiming at supporting multiple telecommunications technologies and adapting them for new releases. This may allow for the effective deployment of C-RANs as service providers and will benefit from sharing their remote base stations' infrastructures to achieve better area coverage with minimum CAPEX and OPEX investment. A more detailed overview on the state of the art in the virtualization of mobile networks can be found in Hawilo et al. (2014).

The increases in signaling and more stringent latency requirements for intercell cooperation are placing pressure on network providers that need to properly manage such issues, especially in the context of C-RAN in order to achieve the expected benefits of this technology. To this aim, Dawson et al. (2014) proposed to isolate the EPC from the RAN in order to reduce both radio/core loads. Indeed, considering the legacy 4G deployments, all signaling information of a given flow is passed to the EPC and this presents a significant load if, for instance, a given user regularly moves between small cells or requires enhanced transmission schemes, such as coordinated multipoint (CoMP) transmission, to improve its coverage at the cell edge. A possible solution to reduce this signaling is to allow integration at BSs, in order to group several small cells. The idea proposed by Dawson et al. (2014) is to exploit the C-RAN approach, where macro BSs are visible to the EPC while small cells are visible only to the BS. This approach is named C-RAN BS. In this way, mobility signaling due to the transitions between the macro and small cells is handled at the BS; simultaneously, the EPC still maintains overall vision of user mobility.

The architecture enabling virtualization in the C-RAN is depicted in Figure 6.8. The idea at the basis of the architecture proposed by Dawson et al. (2014) is to extend the concepts of virtual local area networks (V-LANs) and network address translation (NAT), which have long been accepted features of the modern Internet, to mobile networks. On the EPC side of the C-RAN BS, authors introduced two entities: (1) a VLAN controller that is responsible for grouping cells together as virtual cells and (2) a NAT that will represent the virtual cells to the EPC as a single macro cell. The C-RAN BS will be in charge of performing different functions. It will act as a *mobility anchor*, in a similar way as the SGW acts in the EPC, to provide a static endpoint for communications as well as handovers between cells belonging to the same virtual cell. To further reduce signaling with the use of C-RAN BS, it is also expected to have completely new user-centered protocols aimed at redefining mobility management. In this scenario, the VLAN allows the EPC to continue to function without requiring knowledge of RAN changes due to user mobility.

Another element introduced in this architecture is an SD-RAN controller, which describes and provides the methods for polling all available resources available at connected cells. So doing, the C-RAN BS can ensure that only the minimum required resources are active at any time in the whole VLAN, instead of activating the minimum required resources in each cell. The SD-RAN controller would also provide a means of slicing the network resources to allow for RAN sharing between operators in order to deploy and support multitenancy deployments, which are attracting the interest of the 5G research community as outlined, for instance, by Condoluci et al. (2015).

6.5.3 Softwarization and Virtualization in the Mobile Core

The mobile core network is the most important part of the network, and for this reason the virtualization of the mobile core represents the most investigated field in introducing virtualization and softwarization in 5G.

The most recent core network is the evolved packet core (EPC), defined by 3GPP (2015) and discussed in Section 6.4.2. The EPC is a flat all-IP architecture designed to permit mobile broadband services and to support a variety of access technologies. To introduce virtualization in the mobile core, Hawilo et al. (2014) proposed to group the EPC's entities into different segments to achieve less control, signaling traffic and less congestion in the data plane. In the first segment, the MME is migrated with the HSS front-end (HSS FE), which is an application that implements all

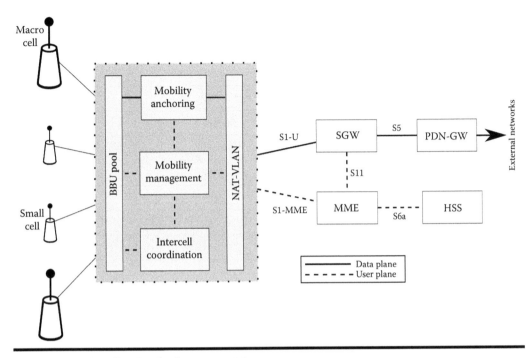

Figure 6.8 Virtualization in the C-RAN BS.

the logical functionality of the HSS but does not contain the user information database. In particular, the HSS FE requests the user information from the user data repository (UDR, the central user information database) and stores these data temporarily in cache memory. This allows for the running of authentication and authorization processes internally, without any data transactions through the network but in a similar way, as if the MME was accessing the complete HSS database. In the second segment, PDN-GW is migrated with the SGW with the aim to minimize the number of nodes involved in the data plane chain. Implementing both PDN-GW and SGW in one VM or VNF will benefit from centralized processing in the data plane. Finally, another segment is composed of the UDR, online charging system (OCS), and offline charging system (OFCS), which are migrated in the PCRF. The idea behind this migration is that the PCRF requests user information to generate the required policies for each established bearer; in this way, information exchange is no longer necessary and this minimizes the latency of policy function generation.

The benefits of grouping network entities are in terms of a reduced amount of transactions among network entities. A numerical example is listed in Table 6.1, which highlights the meaningful reductions in terms of transactions per second offered by the solution proposed by Hawilo et al. (2014) compared with legacy 4G deployments (as discussed by Nokia Siemens, 2012), while introduced benefits are listed in Table 6.2.

When considering the integration of C-RANs in the mobile core, Yang et al. (2015) have analyzed the benefits offered by the joint use of virtualization and SDN by focusing on different aspects. As a first benefit, the authors have considered the traffic offload, which can be beneficial to relieve the load of the core network. In this scenario, virtualization is exploited to instantiate network functionalities such as PDN-GW in the C-RAN while SDN triggers path reconfiguration of data traffic. Another example always focusing on how to relieve the core network load is related to the caching (both data and control functionalities caching) in the C-RAN. In this case, SDN can

Table 6.1 Benefits of Virtualization in Terms of the Number of Transactions

	Signaling (transactions per second)	
Transactions between core elements	*Before grouping*	*After grouping*
MME, eNBs, and S-GW	175,322	175,332
S-GW and P-GW	56,559	0
MME and HSS	1,039,430	173,239
PCRF and P-GW	37,706	37,706
PCRF and UDR	18,853	0
PCRF and OCS	30,164	0
Total Traffic	1,358,044	386,277

Table 6.2 Benefits Introduced by Virtualizing Network Entities

Entities	*Benefits*
• HSS front-end (HSS FE) • Mobility management entity (MME)	• Local interactions between HSS and MME • Fewer networking transactions through vSwitches
• Packet data network gateway (PGW) • Policy and charging enforcement function (PCEF) • Serving gateway (SGW)	• Reduction in the number of nodes processing data plane • Reduction of data forwarding • Improvements in data monitoring and charging
• User data repository (UDR) • Online charging system (OCS) • Offline charging system (OFCS) • Policy and charging rules function (PCRF)	• Reduced fragmentation • Local interaction between the PCRF and the UDR • Local interaction between OCS and PCRF • Central interaction point for OSS/BSS

be useful to analyze the utilization of data links as well as to analyze the end-to-end paths while virtualization is useful to move the content from the PDN-GW to the C-RAN.

6.5.4 Major Research Challenges

The design and the deployment of a software-based virtualized C-RAN architecture are still under investigation. The related challenges have been investigated in Arslan et al. (2015), and are now summarized as follows:

■ *Latency.* The main task of the fronthaul network is to deliver highly delay-sensitive signals to the RRHs. If we consider the LTE frame, novel signals need to be delivered to the RRHs every 1 ms (i.e., the LTE's subframe duration); this becomes more challenging in 5G deployments expected to also operate with shorter subframes. This introduces latency challenges in the fronthaul network, especially in terms of switching procedures.

■ *Communication protocol*. C-RANs are still evolving and there is no consensus on open APIs to send\receive data to\from the RRHs. An admissible trend should be the exploitation of protocols such as the common public radio interface (CPRI), commonly used to carry signals between the indoor and outdoor units of traditional base stations and tailored to be extended for the fronthaul network. However, integrating such protocols with switch operations and catering to low latencies is still a big challenge to be adequately investigated.

■ *Electrical versus optical switching*. The design and the deployment of proper switching solutions represent a key aspect to be taken into consideration as proper switching procedures involve several benefits in the whole C-RAN network. Optical switches may incur a longer reconfiguration time than electrical switches but are advantageous in terms of cost, power consumption, and being data-rate agnostic (Farrington et al., 2010). These and other trade-offs such as operational cost and reliability need to be carefully evaluated before deciding on a particular technology.

■ *Heterogeneity*. This challenge is due to the fact that the fronthaul interfaces may be composed of a mix of fiber, wireless, and copper links. This thus introduces the need of efficient integration strategies using the bandwidth from the available forms of physical fronthaul to support the logical configurations made by the controller.

■ *Security*. SDN/NFV-based systems should obtain a security level close to that of a proprietary hosting environment for network functions. Nevertheless, security attacks are expected to increase when implementing network functions in a virtualized environment. In addition to the hypervisor, which should be protected to prevent any unauthorized access or data leakage, other processes such as data communication and VM migration should run in a secure environment. Finally, the exploitation of APIs, exploited to provide programmable orchestration and interaction with its infrastructure, introduce a higher security threat to VNFs, as considered in Cloud Security Alliance (2013).

■ *Reliability and stability*. Reliability is an important requirement for network operators, as they need to guarantee the service reliability and service-level agreements; this should not be affected when considering SDN/NFV deployments. The challenges deal with the fact that the flexibility of service provisioning may require the consolidation and migration of VNFs according to the traffic load as well as the user demand and this may involve reliability degradations. Furthermore, network operators should be able to move VNF components from one hardware platform onto a different platform, which consequently may introduce delays, while still satisfying the service continuity requirement.

■ *SDN controller*. The exploitation of SDN in wireless networks introduces new challenges for the SDN controller that needs to orchestrate and manage the control plane of the network by taking into account a radio access system composed of several base stations; this exacerbates the issues in terms of load balancing and traffic/mobility management.

6.6 Conclusions

In this chapter, we highlighted how current trends in the development of the RAN cannot be supported by the existing 4G core infrastructure. We further illustrated that the deployment of C-RAN still needs to handle several challenges, such as high signaling overhead and increasing demands for low latency, which still affect the network in the case of centralized intelligence.

We have discussed the benefits introduced by virtualization and softwarization paradigms in the network design of the next-to-come 5G systems, and we discussed about the role of these two novel paradigms as enablers for the deployment of C-RAN. We summarized the state-of-the-art on the exploitation of virtualization and softwarization for C-RAN and, finally, we provided the related research challenges and outlined the future research trends.

Acknowledgment

This work has been supported in part by the 5GPP VirtuWind (Virtual and programmable industrial network prototype deployed in operational Wind park) Project.

References

1. 3GPP, Network architecture. Technical Specification 23.002, 2015.
2. Amani, M., Mahmoodi, T., Tatipamula, M., and Aghvami, H., Programmable policies for data offloading in LTE network, paper presented at the IEEE International Conference on Communications, Sydney, Australia, June 2014.
3. Andrews, J.G., Claussen, H., Dohler, M., Rangan, S., and Reed, M.C., Femtocells: Past, present, and future, *IEEE Journal on Selected Areas in Communications*, Vol. 30, No. 3, pp. 497–508, 2012.
4. Arslan, M., Sundaresan, K., and Rangarajan, S., Software-defined networking in cellular radio access networks: Potential and challenges, *IEEE Communications Magazine*, Vol. 53 No. 1, pp. 150–156, 2015.
5. Bhushan, N., Li, J., Malladi, D., Gilmore, R., Brenner, D., Damnjanovic, A., Sukhavasi, R., Patel, C., and Geirhofer, S., Network densification: The dominant theme for wireless evolution into 5G, *IEEE Communications Magazine*, Vol. 52, No. 2, pp. 82–89, 2014.
6. Boccardi, F., Heath, R., Lozano, A., Marzetta, T., and Popovski, P., Five disruptive technology directions for 5G, *IEEE Communications Magazine*, Vol. 52, No. 2, pp. 74–80, 2014.
7. Chiosi, M., Clarke, D., Willis, P., Reid, A., Feger, J., Bugenhagen, M., and Sen, P., Network functions virtualisation: An introduction, benefits, enablers, challenges and call for action, paper presented at the SDN and OpenFlow World Congress, Darmstadt, Germany, October 2012.
8. Cisco, Cisco visual networking index: Global mobile data traffic forecast update, White Paper, pp. 2013–2018, 2014.
9. Cloud Security Alliance, The notorious nine cloud computing top threats in 2013, White Paper, 2013.
10. Condoluci, M., Sardis, F., and Mahmoodi, T., Softwarization and virtualization in 5G networks for smart cities, paper presented at the EAI International Conference on Cyber Physical Systems, IoT and Sensors Networks, Rome, Italy, October 2015.
11. Dawson, A.W., Marina, M.K., and Garcia, F.J., On the benefits of RAN virtualisation in C-RAN based mobile networks, paper presented at the Third European Workshop on Software Defined Networks, Budapest, Hungary, September 2014.
12. Ericsson, More than 50 billion connected devices, White Paper, 2011.
13. Ericsson, Telefonica and Ericsson partner to virtualize networks, White Paper, 2014.
14. Errani, L.L., Mao, Z.M., and Rexford, J., Towards software-defined cellular networks, paper presented at the European Workshop on Software Defined Networking, Washington, DC, October 2012.
15. ETSI, Network function virtualization: Use cases, White Paper, 2013.
16. Farrington, N., Porter, G., Radhakrishnan, S., Bazzaz, H.H., Subramanya, V., Fainman, Y., Papen, G., and Vahdat, A., Helios: A hybrid electrical/optical switch architecture for modular data centers, paper presented at the ACM SIGCOMM, New York, NY, October 2010.
17. Ganqiang, L., Caixia, L., Lingshu, L., and Quan, Y., A dynamic allocation algorithm for physical carrier resource in BBU pool of virtualized wireless network, paper presented at the International Conference on Cyber-Enabled Distributed Computing and Knowledge Discovery, Xi'an, China, September 2015.

18. Granelli, F., Gebremariam, A.A., Usman, M., Cugini, F., Stamati, V., Alitska, M., and Chatzimisios, P., Software defined and virtualized wireless access in future wireless networks: Scenarios and standards. *IEEE Communications Magazine*, Vol. 53, No. 6, pp. 26–34, 2015.

19. Han, B., Gopalakrishnan, V., Lusheng Ji, L., and Lee, S., Network function virtualization: Challenges and opportunities for innovations. *IEEE Communications Magazine*, Vol. 53 No. 2, pp. 90–97, 2015.

20. Hawilo, H., Shami, A., Mirahmadi, M., and Asal, R., NFV: State of the art, challenges, and implementation in next generation mobile networks (vEPC). *IEEE Network*, Vol. 28 No. 6, pp. 18–26, 2014.

21. Kim, H., and Feamster, N., Improving network management with software defined networking, *IEEE Communications Magazine*, Vol. 51, No. 2, pp. 114–119, 2013.

22. Kreutz, D., Ramos, F.M.V., Esteves Verissimo, P., Esteve Rothenberg, C., Azodolmolky, S., and Uhlig, S., Software-defined networking: A comprehensive survey, *Proceedings of the IEEE*, Vol. 103, No. 1, pp. 14–76, 2015.

23. Mahmoodi, T., and Seetharaman, S., Traffic jam: Handling the increasing volume of mobile data traffic, *IEEE Vehicular Technology Magazine*, Vol. 9, No. 3, pp. 56–62, 2014.

24. Nokia Siemens, Signalling is growing 50% faster than data traffic, White Paper, 2012.

25. Riggio, R., Marina, M., and Rasheed, T., Programming software-defined wireless networks, paper presented at the ACM Annual International Conference on Mobile Computing and Networking, Maui Hawaii, September 2014.

26. Sundaresan, K., Arslan, M.Y., Singh, S., Rangarajan, S., and Krishnamurthy, S.V., FluidNet: A flexible cloud-based radio access network for small cells, paper presented at the 19th Annual International Conference on Mobile Computing & Networking, New York, NY, September 2013.

27. Yang, C., Chen, Z., Xia, B., and Wang, J., When ICN meets C-RAN for HetNets: An SDN approach, *IEEE Communications Magazine*, Vol. 53, No. 11, pp. 118–125, November 2015.

28. Zaidi, Z., Friderikos, V., and Imran, M.A., Future RAN architecture: SD-RAN through a general-purpose processing platform, *IEEE Vehicular Technology Magazine*, Vol. 10, No. 1, pp. 52–60, March 2015.

Chapter 7

Software-Defined Networking in the World of C-RAN

Bolagala Sravya and Hrishikesh Venkataraman

Contents

Over the last 3–5 years, with more than 70% of the traffic in wireless networks coming from indoors, the network operators have been increasingly looking at small cells to complement macro cells. However, in the last 18–24 months, operators, particularly China Mobile and KT Telecom, have been working on having a centralized radio access network (C-RAN) network; wherein the cell head is limited to being a remote radio head (RRH) while the baseband unit (BBU) of all cells are hosted together in a centralized location. C-RAN primarily separates the radio frequency (RF) and baseband functionalities. While the RF would be handled by a compact RRH, the centralized BBU would be responsible for all operations, configurations, and resource allocation across the coverage area. This could either be a data center or located in a cloud (the reason why C-RAN is alternatively called *cloud-RAN*). Recently, China Mobile, in collaboration with Intel, carried out a detailed investigation. C-RAN not only enables dynamic resource management across different cells, depending on real-time factors like the number of users in a cell, the traffic load, channel conditions, and so on, but also provides a host of other advantages like capital expenditure (CAPEX) and operating expenditure (OPEX) savings, increased asset utilization, energy savings, and so on.

Having said that, one of the primary requirements for C-RAN is the centralized controller. Given that today's wireless network is quite heterogeneous and the components are typically from different independent vendors, a fast emerging aspect for C-RAN is the control of networking through software. In this regard, *software-defined networking* (SDN) is an emerging network architecture wherein the networks are controlled by software applications.

7.1 Background on Need of SDN

Typically, in current wireless networks, the implementation of required features is done through proprietary commands that are typically vendor specific. However, the addition of new features to networks and an increase in network protocols have greatly increased *network complexity*. With a cloud-based network architecture, the need to configure security and quality of service (QOS) policies will become still more complicated resulting in heavy investment in scripting language skills or in the automation of configuration changes. Furthermore, significant investment would be needed in terms of time and energy to figure out the incorrectly entered line of a security policy or access control list (ACL). In addition, with a heterogeneous network environment—with LTE, Wi-Fi, small cells, and coexistence with legacy networks—removal of an application from the network will require significant changes in the configuration and hardware-based setup. It should be noted that eventually, it would become almost impossible to remove all of the policies associated with it from millions of network devices [1]. Furthermore, in order to scale the network to meet the heterogeneous network requirements, a periodic redesign of the network would be needed.

On the other hand, SDN serves as a framework that would overcome the limitations in the network's architecture. It aims to separate traditional network traffic into three components: data, how the data is sent, and the purpose that it serves, as shown in Figure 7.1. The primary idea of this architecture is to decouple the network control logic and the underlying hardware (switches and routers) by enabling the control plane to be directly programmable. SDN will allow the users to dynamically manage millions of network devices, services, traffic paths, and QOS policies using APIs (application programming interfaces) [2]. SDN will enable better traffic management to handle scalability, the delivery of critical data, increased bandwidth requirements, and the faster provision of network services. The SDN would provide a network where

■ Millions of forwarding devices are controlled and managed through a single command.
■ The behavior of routers and switches are changed on a fly.
■ Network resources are used independent of their physical location.
■ The size of the network is changed dynamically.
■ The performance of the network is increased by optimizing network device utilization.
■ Fast network failure handling is achieved.
■ Users can configure firewalls, load balancers, Intrusion Detection Systems (IDS), and middleware dynamically on demand.

Notably, the use of SDN architecture in a 5G network overcomes the limitations of multihop wireless networks, provides advanced caching techniques to store data at edge networks, and gives operators greater freedom to balance operational parameters.

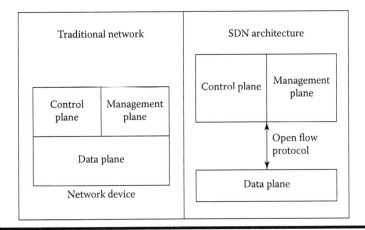

Figure 7.1 **Comparison between traditional network and SDN architecture.**

7.2 SDN Architecture

The hierarchical architecture of SDN is a composition of three different layers, namely application, control and infrastructural layers as shown in Figure 7.2 [3,4]. All of the applications and services that define network behavior are a part of the application layer. All of the components of the network (hardware devices) reside in an infrastructural layer. The core of SDN is the control layer, software that interacts with both infrastructure and the application layer. It appears as a logical switch used to control and manages the entire network.

7.2.1 Infrastructure Layer

Similar to traditional networks, SDN architecture also contains network devices (routers, switches, and middleware appliances), but now they are just forwarding devices, that is, a dumb hardware device without a brain. The embedded software of all of these data plane devices is replaced with a centralized control logic. All of the data-forwarding devices and data-processing devices that are hardware-based or software-based reside in this layer. The data plane handles packets (forwarding,

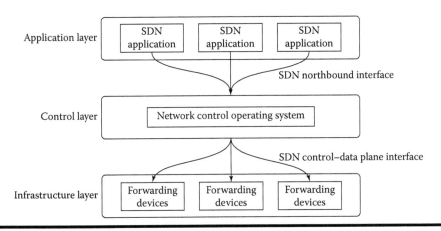

Figure 7.2 **Details of SDN architecture.**

dropping, changing packets, etc.) in the data path, based on the instructions received from the controller. In other words, the data plane is usually the termination point for controller services and applications. A data plane device, known as a *forwarding device*, is specialized in packet forwarding. The work of these forwarding devices is based on a pipeline of flow tables. The path of a packet is defined and handled based on its travel through a sequence of flow tables. When a packet arrives at the forwarding device it firstly checks the flow table for the matching rule, if it matches, then it will execute the corresponding actions on the matched packet and then it increments the counter that keeps the statistics of matching packets in the flow table. On the other hand, when there is no rule found for a packet, it will be discarded. However, to avoid this, a default rule is configured in the flow table that informs the switch to send the packet back to the controller.

The possible actions on a packet, based on flow table rules, include

1. Forwarding the packet to an outgoing port
2. Encapsulating and forwarding to the controller
3. Dropping the packet
4. Sending it to the next flow table

This layer also includes an operational plan that manages the operational state of the network device, for example, whether the device is active or inactive, the number of ports available, the status of each port, and so on. It relates to network device resources such as ports, memory, and so on. The communication between SDN data plane devices and the controller is through an interface called *SDN control–data plane interface* (SDN CDPI). OpenFlow is the widely accepted and standard southbound interface for SDN. Moreover, there are other API proposals such as forwarding and control element separation (ForCES), Open vSwitch database (OVSDB), protocol-oblivious forwarding (POF), OpFlex, OpenState, the Revised OpenFlow Library (ROFL), the Hardware Abstraction Layer (HAL), and the programmable abstraction of datapath (PAD).

7.2.2 Control Layer

The field of operating systems has advanced to a stage where developing applications became easier, making the life span of systems better with an increase in productivity. Rather than providing device-specific instructions, they make machines more flexible by providing abstractions (high-level programming APIs) for accessing and managing the underlying resources (hard drive, network adapter, CPU, memory, etc.). In addition, they also provide security protection mechanisms (firewalls). Unlike operating systems, traditional networks still provide the user's lower level, device-specific instruction sets to manage and configure the network devices. Moreover, the idea of abstracting device characteristics and providing an abstract interface is still absent today. Present-day networks eventually result in increasing network problems and complexity.

SDN promises to ease the burden of solving networking problems by providing a logically centralized network control operating system (NOS). The core idea of NOS is to provide abstractions (APIs) to developers making their way easier to control network devices. Moreover, a developer no longer needs to bother with the low-level details (data distribution among routing elements) because the systems create a new environment resulting in innovation at a faster pace by reducing the complexity of creating new network protocols and network applications. NOS plays a crucial role in SDN architecture as it is the main source for providing control logic APIs to generate the network configuration based on the policies defined by the network operator. It abstracts the lower level details of forwarding devices (regarding connection, interaction, etc.) and provides a high-level programming platform. The SDN controller is a logically centralized entity that provides the following features:

1. The translation of the requirements from the SDN application layer into commands to be installed in the data plane, dictating the behavior of the forwarding devices
2. The making of decisions about where to send traffic
3. The provision of the SDN applications with an abstract view of the network

For instance, consider a routing application whose aim is to define the routing path of the packets from one point to another. Based on the user input, the SDN centralized NOS has to, decide on the path to use and install the respective forwarding rules in all forwarding devices on the chosen path. Notably, the failure in the NOS (single point of failure) disturbs the whole network while a distributed controller can improve the control plane's resilience and scalability. A logically centralized, physically distributed controller is the best solution for overcoming these drawbacks.

Significantly, the applications on the application layer interact with the upper part of the control layer through northbound interfaces such as programming languages like NetCore. The lower part of it interacts with the forwarding devices on the data plane. The network control should provide all the functionalities that the network applications use in building its logic, like statistics, notifications, device management, the shortest path for forwarding, and security mechanisms. In addition, it should be able to receive and forward events. One of the touch jobs of the controller is to maintain security mechanisms between services and applications. For example, the rules generated by high priority services should not be overwritten with rules created by applications with a lower priority. Furthermore, network applications can be seen as the "network brains." They implement the control logic that will be translated into commands to be installed in the data plane, dictating the behavior of the forwarding devices.

7.2.3 Application Layer

Finally, the SDN applications are programs that directly communicate to the SDN controller to specify their network requirements and desired network behavior through northbound interfaces. In addition, they are provided with an abstracted view of the network for their internal decision-making purposes. The application layer of SDN consists of the SDN application's logic and northbound interface (NBI) drivers.

7.3 Technical Challenges in SDN

The centralized controller of SDN offers a whole gamut of applications [2] both in wireless networks and in databases. These include

1. Dynamic bandwidth allocations for traffic without human intervention on a need-by-need basis
2. Traffic congestion control and the rerouting of traffic on failure without causing a network outage
3. Node recovery and restarting from remote and complex topology maintenance for the provider

4. Dynamic traffic analysis and action processing.
5. Single point configuration is a huge benefit that service providers would like to leverage.

However, there are still several challenges including open problems that need to be addressed before SDN can be adopted at an enterprise level. For instance, SDN goes down if the processing time of the incoming packets is greater than a traditional switch or if it not able to provide the shortest routing paths and good security. Because of these reasons, it is necessary to invest in the performance of SDN data and control planes, which has been a major research challenge. This section discusses the technical aspects to be considered while building an efficient SDN architecture [5].

7.3.1 Scalability

Besides the complexity of designing standard APIs for connecting the control and data planes, scalability limitations may arise. When the bandwidth, the number of switches, the number of end hosts, and the flows increase the controller may not handle it and the requests can be queued. The existing controllers can handle requests that are sufficient for campus and enterprise networks. But what about the data centers with millions of virtual machines? And an increase in virtual machines may cause controller overhead and flow limitations causing limitations on network scalability. The performance of the network depends on switch resources and controller performance. Flow setup delays and overhead may pose a challenge to network scalability. The SDN platform may cause the limited visibility of network traffic, making troubleshooting nearly impossible. With this loss of visibility, troubleshooting is hindered and scalability limitations emerge. In order to minimize the proliferation of flow entries, the controller should use header rewrites in the network core. The flow entries will be at the ingress and egress switches.

In this regard, improved network scalability can be ensured by enabling a virtual machine and virtual storage migration between sites. Another solution for scalability is building a distributed flow management architecture that can be scaled up to meet the requirements (large numbers of hosts, flows, and rules) of large networks. A viable solution to the challenge of scale is proposed in the controller-based robust network (CORONET) SDN architecture, which is scalable to large networks because of the virtual LAN (VLAN) mechanism installed in local switches. It has fast recovery from switch or link failures, supports scalable networks, uses alternative multipath routing techniques, works with any network topology, and uses a centralized controller to forward packets. Another solution, DevoFlow, minimized the cost of controller visibility associated with every flow setup and reduced the effect of flow-scheduling overhead, thus enhancing network performance and scalability.

7.3.2 Reliability

In traditional networks, if one or more network devices fail, network traffic is routed through alternative nearby nodes to maintain flow continuity. However, in centralized controller architecture (SDN) where only one central controller is in charge of the whole network, if the controller fails, the whole network may collapse. A new network technique should be developed to maintain the reliability of the network. To overcome this, a distributed architecture is proposed where another standby controller handles the network until the master controller comes back.

7.3.3 Controller Placement

The controller placement problem influences every aspect of a decoupled control plane, from flow setup latencies to network reliability, to error handling and to performance. For example, long propagation delays may limit the availability and convergence time. This has practical implications for software design, affecting whether controllers can respond to events in real time or whether they must push forwarding actions to forwarding elements in advance. This problem includes controller placement with respect to the available network topology and the number of controllers needed.

7.3.4 Controller–Application Interface

Presently, there is no standard for the interactions between controllers and network applications. If we consider the controller as a "network operating system," then there has to be a defined interface by which applications can access the underlying hardware, interact with other applications, and utilize system resources, where in the application developer does not have any knowledge on implementation details of the controller. While several controllers exist, their application interfaces are still in the early stages of development and independent from each other.

7.3.5 Efficient Resource Management

Emerging self-organizing networks extend the range of infrastructure-based networks or handle connectivity disruptions. Self-organizing networks may thus enable a variety of new applications such as cloud-based services, vehicular communication, community services, healthcare delivery, emergency response, and environmental monitoring. Efficient data delivery over wireless access networks will become essential, and self-organizing networks may become a prevalent part of the future Internet.

A major challenge of future networks is the efficient utilization of resources as the available wireless capacity is inherently limited. This is due to a number of factors including the use of a shared physical medium compounded, wireless channel impairments, and the absence of managed infrastructure.

7.3.6 Security

Since SDN is an open-source technology, many users will not want to expose their network to a potential hacker. Programmable SDN architecture needs intelligent security models because SDN systems are handled by the network administrator, who configures the network as required through software. Security needs to be developed in architecture to protect the controller securely where the tenants sharing the infrastructure are completely isolated. The controller should be able to alert the administrators in case of any sudden attack and to limit control communication during an attack.

7.4 Future of SDN

The *Internet of things* (IoT) refers to a state in which all the real-world objects will be connected via the Internet where many intelligent devices and management platforms are interconnected to enable a "smart world" around us. From home automation and smart manufacturing to smart utility meters, healthcare, and smart farming, this world is becoming hyperconnected. This concept demands a new technology to manage the devices, secure the data they generate continuously, and to store, sort, and analyze it in real time to deliver instant results. SDN is a promising and easily deployable solution to address these needs. For instance, e-commerce is a business model which runs over the Internet with billions of customers. The information/data from a customer's smartphone such as the monitoring of the response to the products (taking pictures, browsing behavior, etc.) can be used to deliver customized offers to encourage an immediate sale. SDN can not only be used for centralized networking, but also can be of tremendous benefit in managing large and diverse volumes of data, a faster analysis, and providing rigorous security to ease privacy concerns. The C-RAN networking architecture on the wireless side can be used for easier infrastructure deployment and network management. Further, the concept of SDN can be applied to this architecture by creating virtual RAN. This would help in traffic management and in the creation of a dynamic environment [6].

Through the use of predefined policies for plug-and-play setup, SDN would allow for the rapid and easy addition of new types of IoT sensors. By abstracting network services from the hardware on which they run, SDN would allow for the automated, policy-based creation of virtual load balancers, and quality of service for various classes of traffic. Importantly, the ease of adding and removing resources would reduce the cost and risk of IoT experiments by allowing the reuse of the network infrastructure when no longer needed. Significantly, SDN will make it easier to find and fight security threats through the improved visibility they provide to network traffic, right to the edge of the network. It would also make it easy to apply automated policies to redirect suspicious traffic. Further, by centralizing configuration and management, SDN would allow IT to effectively program the network to make automatic, real-time decisions about traffic flow. Finally, it would not only allow for the analysis of sensor data, but also about the health of the network located close to the network; which could also be used to prevent traffic jams and security risks. The centralized configuration and management of the network and the abstraction of network devices would make it far easier to manage applications that run on the edge of the IoT [7].

SDN still has many challenges to overcome before becoming a preferred and deployable mechanism. To begin with, since it is an open-source technology, security would be a major concern that needs to be addressed first, before being accepted by both the users and operators. Second, the current network management policies only include a single device or single-path focus. The operator's focus on the network manager has been only on how SDN helps or destroys the network. However, in reality, SDN is much bigger and a lot of work still remains to be done to make it acceptable by the users [8].

7.5 Conclusions

The chapter begins by providing an introduction to the need of SDN. The new SDN paradigm is then briefly explained and compared with traditional networks. Further, following a bottom-up approach, an in-depth overview of SDN architecture is provided that includes the (1) infrastructure layer, (2) control layer, (3) and application layer. Subsequently, the challenges faced by SDN are then explained. Finally, SDN would need more time to mature and also, the telecommunication industry would need further time to synchronize the devices with the network's requirements.

References

1. F. Alam, I. Katib and A.S. Alzahrani, New networking era: Software defined networking, *International Journal of Advanced Research in Computer Science and Software Engineering*, Vol. 3, No. 11, pp. 349–353, November 2013.
2. Open Networking Foundation. Software-defined networking definition, https://www.opennetworking.org/sdn-resources/sdn-definition. (Accessed: 14 July, 2016.)
3. D. Kreutz, M.V.R. Fernando, P. Verissimo, C.E. Rothenberg, S. Azodolmolky and S. Uhlig, Software-defined networking: A comprehensive survey, *Proceedings of IEEE*, Vol. 3, No. 1, pp. 14–76, January 2015.
4. SDxCentral, SDN & NFV use cases defined, https://www.sdxcentral.com/sdn-nfv-use-cases/. (Accessed: 21 July, 2016.)
5. M. Jammal, T. Singh, A. Shami, R. Asal and Y. Li, Software defined networking: State of the art and research challenges, *Computer Networks*, Vol. 72, pp. 74–98, 2014.
6. Y. Chenchen, Z. Chen, B. Xia and J. Wang, When ICN meets C-RAN for HetNets: An SDN approach, *Proceedings of IEEE*, Vol. 53, No. 11, pp. 118–125, November 2015.
7. Network World, Software-defined networking will be a critical enabler of the Internet of things, http://www.networkworld.com/article/2932276/sdn/software-defined-networking-will-be-a-critical-enabler-of-the-internet-of-things.html. (Accessed: 20 July, 2016.)
8. Network World, SDN vital to IoT, http://www.networkworld.com/article/2601926/sdn/sdn-vital-to-iot.html. (Accessed: 20 July, 2016.)

Chapter 8

Managing Mobility with SDN: A Practical Walkthrough

Xuan Thuy Dang and Manzoor Ahmed Khan

Contents

8.1 Software-Defined Networking: An Overview

Recent years have witnessed a tremendous growth in the demand for mobile data communication. According to the latest Cisco Visual Networking Index update [1], global mobile data traffic grew 69% in 2014 and reached 2.5 EB per month at the end of 2014, which was up from 1.5 EB per month at the end of 2013. In the next 5 years, this number is predicted to increase nearly tenfold, with a compound annual growth rate CAGR of 57% until 2019, reaching 24.3 EB per month by 2019.

This mobile data demand resulted from various emerging market trends: an increased use of smart mobile devices, advances in cellular networks, an increase in mobile video usage, and the adoption of the mobile Internet of things (IoT). Smart device markets constantly introduce new types of devices. Tablet computers have dominated laptop usage but its growth went down quickly with the introduction of smartphones with larger screens and lightweight laptops, which has a similar form to a tablet but is more suitable for mobile work and life. All these devices are equipped with powerful computing capabilities for demanding multimedia processing, as well as high-speed network connectivity with the latest cellular technologies. In wireless communication, there has been a fast evolution toward higher-generation cellular networks from 2G to 3G, 4G, or long-term evolution (LTE). In the past, the transition to 3G was a push to mobile data usage. With faster and higher bandwidth provided, mobile multimedia services gained popularity over simple voice calls, for example, over-the-top (OTT) content, voice-over Internet protocol (VOIP), or video calls. The recent adoption of cloud-based data and computing services has made mobile access the main method of service delivery. Currently, this mobile lifestyle has outgrown the capacity of 3G and 3.5G networks and is catalyzing the transition to the even faster and more ubiquitous mobile network of 4G or LTE. More powerful smart devices in combination with high-speed connectivity have changed the IT landscape from being networkcentric to service- and user-centric. Video content created and consumed by mobile users will account for a great share of mobile data usage. Finally, the adoption and fast growth of the IoT combined with big data analytics will result in billions of smart devices, for example, sensors, vehicles, surveillance cameras, and so on, which are wirelessly connected with cloud-base processing services and add a significant amount of data to the mobile networks.

The mobile data demand has put pressure on mobile network operators to search for innovations, in order to meet the new performance dimensions of the next-generation (5G) mobile network, for example, the number of connected devices, bandwidth, lower delay, among other things, which continue to increase by several orders of magnitude. Mobile networks increasingly move their significance toward services and users. As a result, network operators and owners need to provide ubiquitous connectivity and can no longer create revenues and differentiate themselves based on network infrastructure. Reducing operation and expansion costs is crucial for growth. To meet the aforementioned future mobile data demand, there are three main solution dimensions: more cell sites, an improved spectral efficiency, and more spectrum. While adding spectrum creates more immediate bandwidth, the license cost is high, given its scarceness. Moreover, the use of millimeter or event light for wireless communication requires new transceivers, which leads to wide-spreading changes in end-user devices and network infrastructure. In contrast, the other two solutions directly address the limitations of current mobile networks, which result from the lack of flexibility of a monolithic infrastructure. The deployment of new cells, including small cells, and the taking advantage of an improved spectral efficiency, both urge for a rethinking of mobile network infrastructure. User mobility and direct device-to-device communication are important requirements for the network design. Increased network capacity may be achieved by offloading mobile data to Wi-Fi or other technologies based on an unlicensed spectrum. Additionally, interoperation between small cells enables improvements in both frequency reuse and network density. These approaches require flexible mobile network architecture and the global management and orchestration of different network segments, especially in radio access networking (RAN).

Reengineering mobile networks may benefit from recent advances in cloud computing and network-virtualization technologies. Designing services for the cloud has become the essential approach for providers to realize significant cost reductions, which are enabled by the advantages of a cloud operating model: on-demand, multitenancy, elasticity, and real-time measurement. While application services are increasingly deployed in largely centralized data centers, mobile network infrastructure spreads over different network segments, each of which consists of specialized hardware devices and specific network protocols. This results in high operation and expansion costs, and a lack of agility against fluctuating user demands. As said, despite the flattening effect of current network-virtualization technologies, for example, virtual LAN (VLAN), tunneling, and packet labeling, mobile networks still rely largely on hardware devices requiring the manual configuration of thousands of parameters, and on complex network management. More flexible virtualized network architectures are needed in order to realize cloud-based operation models for mobile networks.

At this point, software-defined networking (SDN) [2] is an emerging network-virtualization paradigm with a high potential for enabling new designs toward the cloud network vision. This paradigm is different from current network technologies, in which the forwarding behavior of network devices must be configured directly with control and management software embedded in the network appliances. The concept of SDN is the separation of network control and packet forwarding, or in other words, the separation of the control plane (CP) and the data plane (DP). Network control and management are implemented by a logically centralized controller, which configures packet forwarding in routers to create flows of packets in the data plane. A flow is a series of packets passing through routers according to some flow rules. The controller installs these forwarding rules in the routers' flow tables, which are applied for packets with certain matching patterns. The separation enables a flexible, application-specific control of network devices while maintaining the line-rate packet-forwarding capability of network devices. Figure 8.1 shows the logical architecture of an SDN controller that interacts with both the upper application layer (northbound) and lower layer of network devices (southbound). The northbound interface allows controller logic to be integrated into an application context using service-oriented integration protocols. Southbound interfaces and open standard, vendor-neutral protocols enable SDN controllers to work with a wide range of network devices. Because of this architecture, SDN controllers are also referred to as *network operating systems*

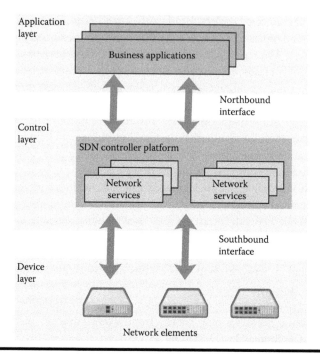

Figure 8.1 SDN architecture overview. (From ONF Market Education Committee et al., SDN architecture overview, ONF White Paper, 2013.)

with control logic abstracted from low-level hardware devices. OpenFlow [2] is such a southbound protocol, which allows the controller to write flow rules into the devices' flow tables, and to collect statistics from those devices. Real-time monitoring data of a global network state is shared with network applications to facilitate the configuration and optimization of the network as a whole.

The OpenFlow protocol allows control intelligence to be logically centralized in the control plane by facilitating the enforcement of control on data plane devices. The logical centralization implies freedom for the deployment of physical network control infrastructure from data plane devices. Multiple instances of the SDN controller can be distributed in order to realize reliability through redundancy, and scalability through the scaling out of hardware or virtualized computing resources. The OpenFlow protocol specifies the expression of the control logic in the form of forwarding actions, which are applied by the switches for the packets of the defined flows. The packets are matched with certain flows based on their layer 2 to layer 4 header fields. Actions and matches are the important parts of a flow's entry, which are written to the network device's flow table and managed by the controller using methods defined by the protocol. Examples of flow matching are to inspect the source/destination IP address of transmission control protocol (TCP) packets, the media access control (MAC) address of in/outbound packets, or packets with specific multiprotocol label switching (MPLS)/VLAN tags. Examples of actions are forwarding packets to specific ports or to the controller, modification of the packet header, or the application of certain flow entries on different tables.

Flow entries can be sent by the controller to network devices in a proactive or reactive manner. The former applies when flow entries are defined before forwarding devices receive packets of a certain flow. In the latter case, a switch may receive packets of a new flow without a matching flow table entry. The unknown packet is sent to the controller for further inspection and the creation of a new match and action for the flow. Once the new flow entry is reactively added to the switch's flow table, subsequent packets of the flow are handled without the intervention of the controller.

There are several benefits of SDN for the realization of flexible, virtualized network infrastructures, of which a few prominent ones are discussed as follows:

- Global network view: SDN provides a centralized view of the entire network, which appears as a single logical switch to high-level policies, thus enabling an easier and more efficient form of network management [4].
- Flexibility and programmability: SDN helps resolve the concerns raised between definitions of network policies and their implementation, which is the basic ingredient of the envisioned network flexibility. A decoupled and logically centralized control plane provides a simpler environment for modifying network policies that is, instead of relying on hard-coded protocols and control logic implemented by the switches, the network control logic may easily be implemented/adapted through high-level languages and software components. Load balancing, mobility management, path computation, and traffic prioritization are some of the examples of native SDN applications.
- Reduced capital expenditure (CAPEX): When it comes to cloud providers such as Amazon, Google, and so on, they are supposed to deploy switches/routers from the same vendor to ease the network reconfiguration and routing. SDN with its unified control allows for the redrafting of faster policies, network reconfiguration, and resource distribution. In addition, SDN also eases the lives of cloud service consumers by enabling them to create virtual flow slices; for example, the OpenFlow protocol enables consumers to create slices without being aware of the physical network infrastructure [5].
- Cross-tenants resource optimization: The SDN concept is a good fit to ensure the improved cross-site performance isolation for tenant-specific traffic optimization in applications similar to cloud-based data centers [5].
- Simplified implementation: Having abstracted the control logic to centralized control, SDN provides the network managers with sophisticated application interfaces to implement network control logic using high-level programming languages such as C++, Java, or Python, and so on. The control logic implementation can be tested and debugged more easily using network emulation. Moreover, centralized control simplifies the verification of control logic, compared with distributed protocols, and enables stricter notions of consistency during network updates (strict vs. eventual consistency).
- Improved performance: SDN implements the control functionalities in software, which may follow a reactive or proactive vision of network management. Needless to mention that proactive approaches introduce performance improvements in the network control and management. SDN's provision of the global network view creates a suitable environment for modeling and developing proactive network management approaches.

SDN technology is a promising means toward future, cloud-based mobile network infrastructures, in which not only control functions, but also forwarding functionalities can be implemented in software and hosted in data centers. This opens up a new approach to softwarizing networks, that is, network function virtualization (NFV) [6]. However, many aspects of mobile networking need to be considered for their architecture. One of them is, for example, the service provisioning for future connected vehicles with high-level mobility in heterogeneous small cell deployment. In the next sections, we take a bold step trying to tackle such requirements with the tools provided by current SDN controllers.

8.2 An Introduction to SDN Controllers

SDN-based network research has quickly grown as proof of the concept of programmable flows [7], which are gaining popularity among network device vendors and cloud network operators seeking alternatives for current complex network deployments, and among researchers seeking radical designs for future networks. The huge interest in SDN is, however, hindered by the lack of controller implementation, which provides the needed features to thoroughly investigate SDN-based solutions. Because of the difference to other network technologies, which can be studied by simulations and emulations, the separation of the control and forwarding planes in SDN introduces additional delays between them, especially in reactive scenarios. The study of SDN performance requires realistic experiments with SDN controllers and the control plane network channels. However, researchers are short of resources for implementing the many features needed to study future networks from the ground up. Besides, there are great efforts from the industry, which result in numerous proprietary and open-source SDN controllers. But these implementations firstly aim at features that provide replacements for the functionalities of existing network devices. For the purpose of researching SDN in future networks, we set out to find suitable controller platforms for the implementation of, and experimentation with, novel future network scenarios.

In the literature there exists several comparisons of various SDN controllers [8–10]. These works discuss many aspects of evaluating the controllers such as architectural features, efficiency, and applicable use cases. Given the wide range of application domains for SDN controllers, it is challenging to discuss all of their possible features and purposes. However, the papers provide common views of selected controllers regarding their architectural features, for example, northbound and southbound interfaces and the controller OS, as well as their functional evaluation, performance, security, and reliability. The authors in [9] study recently matured controllers (POX, Ryu, Trema, Floodlight, OpenDaylight) based on these criteria: transport layer security (TLS) support, network emulation, open-source, supported interfaces, graphical user interface (GUI), documentation, programming language, and support for the OpenStack network, among other things. While the first three criteria are mandatory, the remaining diverse criteria are dynamically weighted by their adapted analytic hierarchy process (AHP). In contrast to the highlighted analysis method, the authors in [8] evaluate popular controllers (NOX, POX, Beacon, Floodlight, OpenMUL, Maestro, Ryu) with benchmark tools, "hcprobe," using a real test bed for a control plane channel. The measurements include performance parameters (throughput, latency), security (a malformed message), and reliability. Despite providing detailed views of popular SDN controllers, most comparative works lack the discussion of their applicability in broader SDN-based network solutions. Instead, the evaluation of performance and security aspects is only helpful for selecting network controllers for the deployment of current network operations.

8.2.1 SDN Controller in Future Networks

Our main focus is the applicability of SDN controllers in future network solutions and their capability to support experimental development. Figure 8.2 depicts a vision of the future network infrastructure, in which various SDN-based use cases are seen to replace inflexible network segments to realize efficient, flow-based mobile networks. The following discussions of future network components aim to identify the required features of SDN controllers, which serve as important selection criteria for their application in future network solutions.

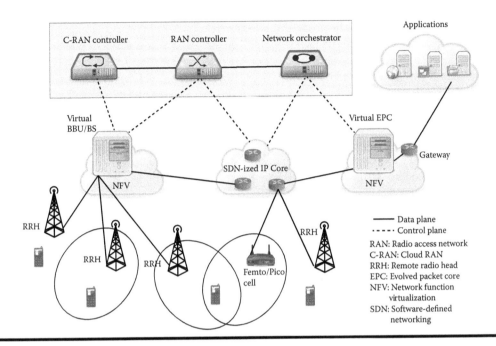

Figure 8.2   Future mobile network architecture.

8.2.1.1 Software-Defined Network Architectures

Future requirements for high performance and efficiency lead networks toward massively flexible architectures. The component networks (RAN, front/backhaul, core, edge networks) are designed to be implemented, deployed, and maintained by software processes. Programmable characteristics allow for the rapid composition of component networks, the capability of network function orchestration, portability and scalability to demand. Abstracted network services and control interfaces allow application services and network life cycles to be jointly managed resulting in better resource utility, reduced costs, and new service models. Key-enabling technologies for flexible networks are network virtualization, SDN, and cloud computing. Network virtualization allows network resources to be sliced and granted to multiple tenants. Software-based network functions are removed from dedicated hardware devices and implemented as software components hosted on cloud platforms. SDN's separation of control logic from data planes allows data plane components to be put in a pool of composable elements. The dynamic deployment of network infrastructures and services can be carried out by a global management service by combining and enforcing policies on various cloud-based network resources.

8.2.1.2 Cloud-RAN

The deployment of small cell RAN is a cost-effective expansion of mobile wireless networks. Base stations with small coverage and support for heterogeneous wireless technologies (HETNET), for example, the global system for mobile communications (GSM), code division multiple access (CDMA), universal mobile telecommunications system (UMTS)/high-speed packet access (HSPA), LTE, LTE-advanced (LTE-A), and Wi-Fi, enable denser networks with higher throughput and extended coverage to an indoor environment. However, the efficacy of RAN is affected by interference, mobility management, and the maintenance of a large number of cells. Cloud-RAN (C-RAN) architecture is an innovative approach to overcome those challenges of small cell RAN. This architecture splits baseband units (BBUs) from remote radio heads (RRH), which were collocated in the current network architectures. Advances in long-distance and low-delay fronthaul networks enable such a separation. Common public radio interface (CPRI) or open base station architecture initiative (OBSAI) protocols provide a connection between RRHs and BBUs over wired (Fiber, Ethernet, WDM) or wireless (Microwave) networks. This allows the centralized deployment of BBUs for signal processing functionality.

The benefit of this centralized architecture is twofold. More processing capacity can be deployed for the central BBUs for advanced interference control techniques such as enhanced intercell interference coordination (ICIC), and resource sharing such as carrier aggregation and coordinated multipoint (CoMP). Further, with the application of SDN and NFV, BBU functionality can be virtualized in a pool of virtual BBUs (vBBUs), which provides a software-definable way of resource allocation, mobility, and interference management, and the scalability of the cloud service model.

The separation of the elements of previously monolithic network architectures requires a logically centralized RAN control entity as depicted in the RAN part of Figure 8.2. The controllers manage the service and operational aspects of the elements such as policies, access control, monitoring, and data flows, connecting those elements and services in fronthaul, backhaul, and core networks.

8.2.1.3 Software-Defined Cloud Network

The term *software-defined cloud networking* (SDCN) extends the notion of virtualization to networking resources. Such network abstraction permits separate control over the logical provisioning and physical management of network resources, which paves a path for the automated orchestration of the network. SDCN corresponds to the capability that allows each aspect of the cloud environment to be managed by the software. A specific use of this concept is the software-defined data center, where all the infrastructural elements (storage, processing, networking, etc.) are virtualized and delivered as a service. Given that the network is virtualized and efficiently orchestrated, the service providers are able to meet the needs of different tenants, users, applications, and devices. The anticipated complex management of a huge number of virtualized services in future data centers will be carried out by softwarized control components, which basically is the software implementation of deployment, provisioning, configuration procedures, and so forth. Cloud-based data centers comprise a huge number of physical servers and switches connecting these servers. Each server further hosts a number of virtual machines, which may belong to different users. These virtual machines are virtually networked, which may be (re)configured when necessary. Obviously with an increasing number of users, the network management complexity inflates and may no longer be managed manually or with traditional configuration approaches. This is where the SDN concept becomes useful, it should accomplish the following requirements:

■ Dynamically configure the network to meet new/adapted users' demands
■ Ensure the service quality agreed upon by users and service providers
■ Efficiently support mobile users
■ Enable the dynamic interstakeholder relationships
■ Implement the efficient traffic engineering solutions
■ Provide resilience and reliability

8.2.2 SDN Controller Comparison

In the future network visions that were just discussed, the SDN controller takes a central role in the design and implementation of the network's architecture. Future network solutions are being built on emerging technologies and concepts. Many of them are being researched or experimented with. Prototyping of the solution's components also relies on the tools and software developed while researching specific problems. As a result, these solution prototypes cannot be tested in realistic operation conditions. SDN enables the flexible creation of virtual networks for testing and experimenting on production network infrastructures. It is important that the solution prototypes are built with as many features as required by the running systems. This allows a fast and smooth integration of the solutions in a productive infrastructure. We evaluate some popular SDN controllers for their applicability in the development of network solutions for the selected future network use cases. Some criteria are listed as follows:

- Southbound plugins: Support for legacy and future network protocols
- Application orchestration: Support for interoperability with other networks applications. This can be, for example, flexible, standardized application integration, protocols and methods
- Scalability: The capability and support for horizontal scaling (protocol, design).
- Programming language: Support for components and tools developed with multiple programming languages
- Software framework: Developed based on software frameworks for modularity and manageability
- Cloud support: Features for integration with a cloud computing platform
- Policy enforcement: Support for policy-based network control
- Virtual network overlay: Support for network overlay and multitenant provisioning

Some controllers are evaluated based on the given requirements and the results are summarized in Table 8.1. The support for selected criteria is indicated with a maximum of three stars.

8.3 OpenDaylight Controller: An Inside Out

OpenDaylight (ODL) controllers consists of a set of protocol implementations and applications, which can be packaged together to provide the intended control functions. From a programmer's

Table 8.1 SDN Controllers in Comparison

–	ODL	Floodlight	Beacon	Trema	Ryu	POX
Southbound plugins	***	*	*	*	**	*
Application orchestration	***	**	—	—	—	—
Scalability	***		—	—	—	—
Programming language	***	**	**	**	**	**
Software framework	***		**	—	—	—
Cloud support	***	***	—	—	***	—
Policy enforcement	***	**	*	—	—	—
Virtual network overlay	***	*	—	***	***	***

perspective, OpenDaylight's components are managed by a lightweight open service gateway initiative (OSGI) container called *Karaf*, which basically is a service platform for the Java programming language that implements a complete and dynamic component model. As a result, applications or components, coming in the form of bundles for deployment, can be remotely installed, started, stopped, updated, and uninstalled without requiring a reboot. The management of Java packages/classes is specified in great detail. The application's life-cycle management is implemented via application programming interfaces (APIs) that allow for the remote downloading of management policies. The service registry allows bundles to detect the addition of new services, or the removal of services, and to adapt accordingly. Being built on Karaf allows ODL to be modular, flexible, and highly extendable as a framework.

8.3.1 OpenDaylight Terminology

Building on top of OSGI architecture, each ODL component is packaged as an independent bundle. Together they implement different building blocks of the SDN's architecture, for example, southbound, northbound, and control logics. While being managed by Karaf, these components need to be glued together creating a complete SDN control system. For this purpose, the ODL controller implements a middleware called a *service abstraction layer* (SAL), which enables communication and coordination between the components. As a result, the ODL controller becomes a framework, allowing different versions of a certain component, or a new functionality to be plugged into the control application. In the following paragraphs, we provide short details of the ODL framework's concepts, which may cause confusion when starting with ODL application development.

8.3.1.1 Karaf Distribution

Apache Karaf is a lightweight OSGI container. It is used as the main packaging and distribution method of OpenDaylight as a controller product. Karaf is the application platform for the OpenDaylight controller's components, analogous to some popular modular web application containers, which host Java implementations of a web application's frontend, backend, and database interaction. We use Karaf to refer to the OpenDaylight controller when discussing the software bundles and components.

8.3.1.2 Bundle and Features

The implementation of the controller's functionality is compiled and packaged as a modular Java package called *bundle* in order to be managed by Karaf. Inside the Karaf container, all of the code packages are treated as bundles, regardless of if they implement user interfaces, OpenFlow protocols, an application logic, and so on. *Feature* is another definition relating to Karaf. It is a collection of bundles, whose combined code implements a certain functionality. Features are used in the sense that when they are loaded, the functionality they implement is added to the controller. As an example, the OpenFlow plugin feature includes, among other things, an OpenFlow protocol implementation bundle, a flow rules manager bundle, and bundles implementing remote procedure calls (RPCs).

SAL is the "service abstraction layer," which is the middleware of the OpenDaylight framework. It enables loose coupling between the components of an SDN controller while preserving the cohesion of their functionalities.

8.3.1.3 Plugin and Service

OpenDaylight components communicate over the SAL middleware. The bundles implementing ODL components are plugins to the SAL. Each plugin implements a certain functionality of the controller and is also referred to as a service. The services exchange data over SAL. If a service needs data from another service, it is called *consumer service* and its counter part is *provider service*. A service can also be both types.

8.3.2 OpenDaylight Controller

OpenDaylight is the open-source platform for building a modular, extensible, scalable, and multiprotocol SDN controller. It supports the independent development of various protocols, applications, and network services by providing an abstraction layer with flexible provisioning and data-exchange mechanisms between software modules. Generic and specialized network solutions built with the OpenDaylight platform will have reusable and compatible solution components. Being an open-source platform with support for both separation and interoperability between component projects, OpenDaylight gained great momentum and contribution from the community. As a result, OpenDaylight has become an ecosystem with a fast-growing number of features. Figure 8.3 shows the diversity of network applications and services available on the platform. OpenDaylight's software modules can be divided into three groups with reference to the SDN controller's architecture:

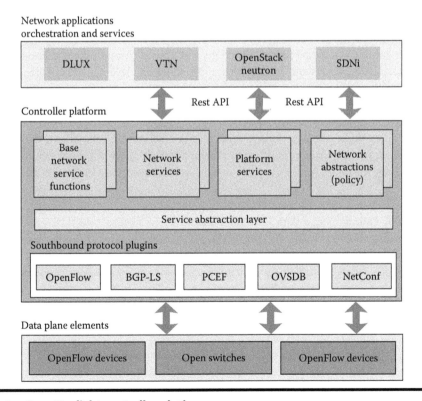

Figure 8.3   OpenDaylight controller platform.

- Northbound application and services
- Controller platform services
- Southbound plugins and protocols

8.3.2.1 OpenDaylight Protocol Plugins

OpenDaylight protocol plugins are crucial for the controller to configure data plane elements and to get information about the network state. Protocol plugins are independent, pluggable modules that provide network intelligence to other component and network applications. Standard and specific protocols for vendor-specific network elements can be implemented as plugins allowing OpenDaylight network applications to extend their services to heterogeneous network infrastructures. In addition to standard protocol plugins—for example, the simple network managing protocol (SNMP), locator/identifier separation protocol (LISP), or border gateway protocol (BGP)—support for emerging protocols is quickly developed. The OpenFlow plugin provides support for the evolving OpenFlow protocol, an open-standard protocol for flow-based switches. It is important that multiple versions of the protocol are supported. This makes OpenDaylight the controller and integration platform for both production and experimental infrastructures. The OVSDB plugin enables the communication with OpenFlow switches by using a database management protocol to operate on the data store for flow tables on those switches. It is developed and used to provide switch status for the OpenStack cloud service components, which enable OpenDaylight the control of the OpenStack virtual network.

8.3.2.2 OpenDaylight Controller Platform Services

The OpenDaylight controller platform consists of network control functionalities, which are implemented by service plugins. These control functions are exposed through the northbound interface, which is a set of (REST) APIs and services that applications can leverage to manage their network infrastructures. The protocol plugins form southbound interfaces, through which the control functions can interact with the underlying infrastructure. Controller platform services implement two main functions: base network service functions and other solution-specific service functions.

The base network service functions provide platform service and network-specific functions, which are designed to be common building blocks for a complex network service. Some of the most common functions, which are also used for our implementation, are described as the following:

- *The topology manager* stores and handles information about the managed networking devices. It maintains in a data store the network devices' states and their interconnections. It is notified about network changes by the southbound plugins and other services in order to keep the data store updated.
- *The statistics manager* implements statistics collection, sends statistics requests to all managed switches, and stores statistics reports in the data store. The statistics manager also exposes northbound APIs to provide information on the switch ports, flow, meter, table, group statistics, and so on.
- *The switch manager* provides network nodes (switches) and node connectors (switch ports) details. Information about the discovered network components are managed by switch manager in the data. It also provides northbound APIs to get information on the discovered nodes and port devices.

■ The forwarding rules manager (FRM) manages basic OpenFlow forwarding rules, resolves their conflicts, and validates them. The forwarding rules manager communicates with southbound (OpenFlow) plugins and loads OpenFlow rules into the managed switches.

■ The inventory manager queries and updates information about switches and ports managed by OpenDaylight, guaranteeing that the inventory database is accurate and up-to-date. It also manages notifications to inform other services of changes in the data store.

■ The host tracker is provided by a l2s witch project, which implements l2 switching logics. The host tracker stores information about the end hosts (data layer address, switch type, port type, and network address), and provides APIs that retrieve end-node information. The host tracker relies on address resolution protocol (ARP) to track the location of the hosts.

Other solution-specific functions are also placed in the controller platform. They provide application-specific APIs to the northbound interface and make use of network information from the southbound interface. However, these services interact and rely on the base network functions for common network operations and implement a more intelligent control logic to be applied to the infrastructure. For example, VTN Manager, OVSDB Neutron provides the specific APIs required by a virtual network and OpenStack applications.

8.3.2.3 OpenDaylight Network Applications and Orchestration

OpenDaylight supports the autogeneration of representational state transfer (REST) APIs using a REST configuration. REST is a HTTP-based resource query protocol, which is widely used for the integration of web services. It helps eliminate the east–west interface required by the integration of OpenDaylight applications with external applications, resulting in a more simple and modular controller platform. Application integration and orchestration are handles at the network application layer.

8.3.3 OpenDaylight as a Software Framework

Figure 8.4 gives a different view of the OpenDaylight platform from a software development perspective. A service abstraction layer plays the central role of the software framework.

8.3.3.1 Northbound Services: Consumer Plugin

Software designers use the terms *northbound* and *southbound* to refer to a functionality implementation or a component of the controller. Implementations of network applications, orchestration, services, and user interfaces are business use–case specific. They are placed above the software abstraction layer (SAL). Bundles belonging to core controller services, functions, and extensions are also placed here. Within the OpenDaylight framework, plugins are differentiated between consumer and provider plugins. Consumer plugins register with the SAL to receive notification events when there are changes to the system status. For example, an event is created when a packet is sent from a switch to the controller. Consumer plugins may desire changes to the status of network elements. They ask SAL to return appropriate RPC implementations for their purposes. As such, consumer plugins often implement northbound bundles.

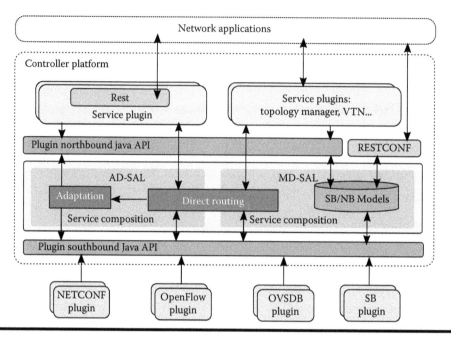

Figure 8.4   OpenDaylight controller platform. (From OpenDaylight Wiki: MD-SAL Architecture. https://wiki.opendaylight.org.)

8.3.3.2 Southbound Protocols: Provider Plugin

The plugins implementing protocols and vendor-specific interfaces allow the controller to interface with hardware elements in the data plane. They are the providers of network information and the carriers of instructions to the control network devices. The implementations of operations on the data plane are exposed in the form of RPCs. The plugins register their RPCs with SAL so that requests for RPCs from consumer plugins are routed to the appropriate RPC for implementation. In model-driven-SAL (MD-SAL), provider plugins also register with SAL to operate on an MD-SAL internal data store, which SAL uses to maintain the states of the controller and network elements. Modifications to this data store result in notification events sent out by SAL to the other plugins.

8.3.3.3 Service Abstraction Layer

The service abstraction layer (SAL) is the main difference between OpenDaylight and other OpenFlow-centered controller platforms. It is considered as an attempt to simplify the interface development in OpenDaylight. The abstraction of SAL serves the purpose of the unification of the northbound and southbound APIs of the controller. With the help of this abstraction, different data structures can be used and northbound services can be written in various programming languages. The SAL also supports multiple protocols on the southbound API and it provides consistent services for modules and applications.

SAL makes OpenDaylight a programming framework for network applications, which extends the OSGI framework by its own implementation of a middleware that provides mechanisms for communication and coordination between OpenDaylight bundles. SAL connects data-providing bundles with those consuming data. It therefore is basically a data-exchange and adaptation mechanism between plugins.

8.3.3.4 Model-Driven Network Programmability

Network infrastructure in production consists of large numbers of forwarding elements. The devices can be managed and configured manually or by using vendor-specific protocols. This greatly limits the automatic and dynamic reconfiguration of the devices. SDN and OpenFlow enable a programmatic approach and standard to address such limitations. However, the capability of the network controller to transactionally manage a device's configuration state is needed.

A model-driven approach is being increasingly used in the networking domain to describe the functionality of network devices, services, policies, and network APIs. OpenDaylight enforces this approach by way of the adoption of the Internet engineering task force (IETF)'s NETCONF and RESTCONF [12] protocols and YANG modeling language for the abstraction of network devices and services. A model may be used by devices to manage its own attributes and can be included in the model for the development of their plugins and application.

NETCONF is an IETF network management protocol that defines configuration and operational conceptual data stores and a set of create, retrieve, update, and delete (CRUD) operations that can be used to access these data stores. In addition to the data stores' CRUD operations, NETCONF also supports simple remote procedure call (RPC) and notification operations. NETCONF operations are realized on top of a simple call (RPC) layer. NETCONF uses XML-based data encoding for the configuration and operational data, as well as for its protocol messages.

YANG was originally developed to model configuration and state data in network devices, but it can also be used to describe other network constructs, such as services, policies, protocols, or subscribers. YANG is tree- structured rather than object-oriented; data are structured into a tree and it can contain complex types, such as lists and unions. In addition to data definitions, YANG supports constructs to model remote procedure calls (RPCs) and notifications, which make it suitable for use as an interface description language (IDL) in a model-driven system.

RESTCONF is a REST-like protocol that provides a programmatic interface over HTTP for accessing data defined in YANG using the data stores defined in NETCONF. Configuration data and state data are exposed as resources that can be retrieved with the HTTP GET method. Resources representing configuration data can be modified with the HTTP DELETE, PATCH, POST, and PUT methods. Data are encoded in either XML or JSON.

8.3.4 OpenDaylight SAL: A Closer Look

The service abstraction layer (SAL) is designed to separate southbound plugins, which interface with a data plane, and network services, which provide northbound APIs for network applications. The layered architecture allows the controller to support multiple southbound protocols and to provide a uniform set of services and APIs to applications through a common set of APIs. As a result, SAL implements a middleware with mechanisms for the composition of the loosely coupled consumer and provider services and facilitates request routing and data adaptation between them.

The original SAL was API-driven (AD-SAL) 4, request routing between consumers and providers and data adaptations are all statically defined at compile/build time. When a northbound service requests an operation on a given node, AD-SAL routes the request to a southbound plugin based on its type, which serves a given node instance. AD-SAL also supports service abstraction. Service requests can be made to an abstract southbound plugin API. The adaptation is applied to the abstract API in order to be routed to the appropriate plugin. The drawback with AD-SAL is the static coding of request routing and data adaptation for each plugin, limiting interoperability and fast development.

A new model-driven architecture, MD-SAL, was implemented to replace AD-SAL. In MD-SAL, all data models and services are modeled using the YANG language. All plugins provide data to the SAL and consume data from the SAL through the API generated from the data model. MD-SAL provides request routing between the plugins but no service adaptation. Service adaptation is implemented in MD-SAL as a plugin that performs model-to-model translation between two APIs. Requesting routing in the MD-SAL is done on both protocol type and node instances, since node instance data are exported from the plugin into the SAL (the model data contains routing information).

The OpenDaylight development environment includes tools that generate this code (codecs and Java APIs). The tools preserve YANG data-type hierarchies and retain the data tree hierarchy (providing normal Java compile time–type safety) and data-addressing hierarchies. A plugin's APIs are resolved when the plugin is loaded into the controller. The SAL does not contain any plugin-specific code or APIs and is therefore a generic plumbing that can adapt itself to any plugins loaded into the controller.

From the infrastructure's point of view, there is no difference between a protocol plugin and an application/service plugin. All plugin life cycles are the same, each plugin is an OSGi bundle that contains models that define the plugin's APIs.

8.3.5 MD-SAL Architecture

The model-driven service abstraction layer (MD-SAL) is an infrastructure that provides service messaging and data storage functionality for the abstraction of a user-defined plugin module by its data and interface models. It enables the unification of northbound and southbound APIs and the data structures used in various services and components of the OpenDaylight SDN Controller. The data model and APIs of a service module are prototyped by developers while SAL's plumbing layer just works when the service is deployed on the controller platform. This eliminates the interdependency in the development of SAL and network services, guaranteeing compatibility between services components.

The infrastructure for the service prototyping requires some important architectural components: data definition language (DDL), data-access patterns, a core runtime environment (RTE) supporting DDL and data access, technology-independent services on top of the RTE, and a core set of technology-specific data models.

MD-SAL infrastructure is developed with a model-driven approach. A domain-specific language, YANG, is selected as the modeling language for services and data abstractions. Some key features that the language provides are

- Modeling the structure of XML data and functionality provided by controller components
- Defining the semantic elements and their relationships
- Modeling all of the components as a single system
- A decentralized extension mechanism, extensible language, and data-type hierarchy
- Existing tools: NETCONF and YANG tools

The advantages of a schema language like YANG allows for self-describing data, which can be provided to requesting controller components and applications without further processing. Utilizing a schema language simplifies the development of controller components and applications.

A developer of a module that provides some functionality (a service, data, functions/procedures) can define a schema and thus create simpler, statically typed APIs for the provided functionality, and thereby lower the risk of an incorrect interpretation of data structures exposed through the service abstraction layer.

Details of MD-SAL designs and their implementation are kept on OpenDaylight Wiki [11]. We consolidate them in the following sections to capture a complete and simple view of the architecture.

8.3.5.1 Basic Concepts

Basic concepts are building blocks that are used by applications, and from which MD-SAL derives its services and behavior based on the mapping of basic concepts to developer-supplied YANG models [11].

- *Data Tree* All state-related data are modeled and represented as a data tree, with the possibility to address any element/subtree. The data tree is described by YANG schemas.
- *Operational Data Tree* Reported state of the system, published by the providers using MD-SAL. This represents a feedback loop for applications to observe the state of the network/system.
- *Configuration Data Tree* The intended state of the system or network, populated by consumers, which expresses their intention.
- *Instance Identifier (Path)* Unique identifier of a node/subtree in a data tree, which provides unambiguous information on how to retrieve a node/subtree from conceptual data trees.
- *Notification* An asynchronous transient event (from the perspective of a provider) which may be consumed by consumers and they may act upon it.
- *RPC* An asynchronous request–reply message pair; when a request is triggered by a consumer and sent to the provider, and which in the future replies with a message.
- *Mount* is a logically nested MD-SAL instance, which may use a separate set of YANG models; it supports its own RPCs and notifications and it allows for the reuse of device models and a particular context in networkwide contexts without having to redefine the device models in the controller. Mount is basically a logical mount of a remote conceptual data store.

8.3.5.2 MD-SAL Infrastructure Services

The MD-SAL provides a variety of functions required for adaptation between providers and consumers. This common model-driven infrastructure allows developers of applications and plugins to develop against one set of APIs that are derived from a single model: Java-generated APIs, data object model (DOM) APIs, and REST APIs.

- *RPC* call router routes RPC calls between consumers and providers.
- *Notification* provides a subscription-based mechanism for the delivery of notifications from publishers to subscribers.
- *Data broker* routes data, reads from consumers to a particular data store, and coordinates data changes between providers.
- *Mount manager* creates and manages mounts.

The implementation of these SAL functions requires the use of two data representations and two sets of SAL plugin APIs.

- The binding-independent data format/APIs is a data object model (DOM) representation of YANG trees. This format is suitable for generic components, such as the data store, the NETCONF connector, RESTCONF, which can derive behavior from the YANG model itself.
- The binding-aware data format/APIs is a specific YANG to Java language binding, which specifies how Java data transfer objects (DTOs) and APIs are generated from a YANG model. The API definition for these DTOs, interfaces for invoking/implementing RPCs, and interfaces containing notification callbacks are generated at compile time. Codecs to translate between the Java DTOs and DOM representation are generated on demand at runtime. Note that the functionality and performance requirements for both data representations are the same.

The two types allow the data/APIs of the providers to be exposed without any coding required. MD-SAL currently exposes the following transport/payload formats [11]:

- Intra-JVM communication using generated DTOs (Java YANG binding)
- Intra-JVM communication using the YANG DOM model
- HTTP consumer-only APIs using Restconf, XML, and JSON as payload
- Cross-process APIs using ZeroMQ and XML as payload
- Cross-JVM communication using Akka

8.3.5.3 MD-SAL Design

The data-handling functionality is separated into two distinct brokers: a binding-independent DOM broker that interprets YANG models at runtime and is the core component of the MD-SAL runtime, and a binding-aware broker that exposes Java APIs for plugins using a binding-aware representation of data (Java DTOs). These brokers, along with their supporting components are shown in Figure 8.5.

The DOM broker uses YANG data APIs to describe data and instance identifiers specific to YANG to describe paths to data in the system. Data structures in the binding-aware broker that are visible to applications are generated from YANG models in YANG tools. The DOM broker relies on the presence of YANG schemas, which are interpreted at runtime for functionality-specific purposes, such as RPC routing, data store organization, and the validation of paths.

The binding-aware broker relies on Java APIs, which are generated from YANG models, and on common properties of Java DTOs, which are enforced by code generation. Therefore, data transfer optimizations (zero-copy) are possible when a data consumer and a data provider are both binding-aware.

The binding-aware broker connects to the DOM broker through the BA-BI connector, so that binding-aware consumer/provider applications/plugins can communicate with their respective binding-independent counterparts. The BA-BI connector, together with the mapping service, the schema service, the codec registry and the codec generator implement dynamic late binding: the codecs that translate YANG data representations between a binding-independent (DOM) format and DTOs, which are specific to Java bindings, are autogenerated on demand.

The physical data store is pluggable, MD-SAL provides an SPI through which different data store implementations can be plugged in.

The mount concept and the support for APIs generated from models allow for applications talking to NETCONF devices to be compiled directly against device models. There is no need for

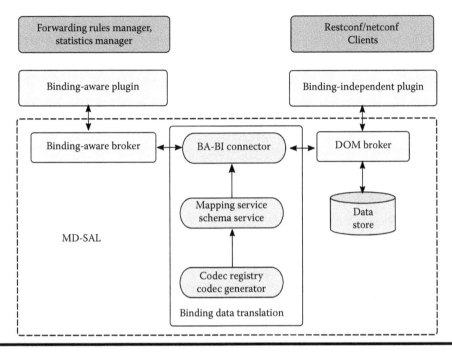

Figure 8.5   MD-SAL design. (From OpenDaylight Wiki: MD-SAL Architecture. https://wiki. opendaylight.org.)

controller-level models that represent devices. Device models are loaded into the controller from a NETCONF device when the controller connects to the device, and apps can work directly with them.

8.4 Mobility Management Application in SDN Environment

Being designed for mobility is among the most important features of the future communication network. Mobile data traffic grew rapidly in recent years with the increased number of mobile devices and the amount of broadband connectivity provided by 4G networks. The demand for services and data access on mobile networks is increasing at the same rate in the next few years. Innovations in mobile systems, especially mobile access networks, are needed to meet future network performance requirements. User and device mobility adds an additional dimension to the challenges for mobile systems to provide a huge bandwidth and very low latency to a vast number of mobile and M2M devices. Mobility management has a great impact on the design of protocols and the architecture for next-generation mobile networks.

Mobility management guarantees continuous sessions and uninterrupted data access for mobile devices. IP protocol has been the main protocol for the global Internet. However, it was not designed for mobile computing systems. The evolution toward mobile Internet has created architecture and protocols to connect mobile systems with the Internet. Currently, there are two main forms of mobile architecture in the mobile domain. One form of architecture is driven by the 3rd generation partnership project (3GPP), which sets standards for 2G, 3G, and the current 4G's LTE system. The other form of architecture is designed for device mobility in IP-based networks with IEEE's mobile IP protocols: mobile IP (MIP), MIPv6, proxy mobile IPv6 (PMIPv6), and their derivatives.

Although mobile connectivity is supported, both systems feature a centralized architecture with a central mobility anchor and dedicated mobility management entity for each mobile domain. In LTE systems the local mobility anchor is P-GW and device mobility is handled by a mobility management entity (MME). The respective elements in PMIP systems are a local mobility anchor (LMA) and mobile access gateway (MAG). These centralized, specialized designs have some scalability and flexibility problems that result in some cost and performance issues in order to meet future demands. For example, given the huge and unpredictable use of mobile data, overprovisioning becomes a costly and less timely expansion approach. The complexity of those systems also infers high operation costs and additional end-to-end delays. Current mobile systems have operational and performance limits while mobile data demand keeps growing in terms of bandwidth, latency, and service availability.

The advancement of cloud computing and especially the emergence of SDN technologies have opened up new design approaches for future mobile networks. Networks become more agile and manageable. SDN enables flow-based connectivities in the data plane, which can be programmed from a remote-controlled plane. Forwarding networks are flatter and more dynamic with software-definable flows and data paths. This flexibility enables cloud computing models, for example, multitenancy, on-demand, or granular resource slicing, to be applied in future designs of core, transport, and access networks. The logically centralized control plane enables the concentration of control logic. More complex and global network control can be implemented on an unlimited virtualized platform. Such a design with a constrained capacity for specialized forwarding devices makes them more complex and expensive. On the other hand, cloud computing when applied to the data plane greatly reduces operational costs and enables fast deployment and autonomous management. Network function virtualization (NFV) enables physical forwarding devices to be reimplemented in software functions, which can be hosted servers specialized for line-rate packet processing. With many parts of the network being virtualized and programmable, intelligent software designs, for example agent technologies or big data, are employed to create systems with autonomous management and performance efficiency.

We experiment with simple software-defined mobility management in an IP-based access network for mobile vehicles. A clean design is proposed, which is based on SDN and cloud computing technologies.

8.4.1 Use Case Scenario, Challenges and Technologies

Data communication in mobile vehicles finds more and more realistic applications, for example, entertainment, connected driving assistance, autonomous driving, and safety. This will add significant challenges with the mobile access networks. We aim at a realization of a roadside access network that supports a traffic information service for mobile vehicles. The cloud-based information service is hosted in a data center and accessible over the Internet. It collects data from different sources, for example, traffic reports, weather forecasts, sensor data from vehicles, and calculates relevant traffic information for vehicles in each local area. Mobile vehicles need mobile network infrastructure to provide connectivity with the application servers for uploading sensor data and receiving traffic information.

Relying on current mobile broadband infrastructure (LTE) incurs unfavorable conditions for operators. Firstly, the sparse deployment of macrocells may not provide constant bandwidth for the transfer of sensor data and service data traffic. Second, system performance may decrease due to the maintenance of connectivity for a large number of mobile vehicles and the management of their mobility. Third, operational and expansion costs are not paid off by the changing demand of a road traffic environment. During traffic congestion there are a large number of mobile nodes with peak demand, while at another time there is no service request. The drawbacks of the current network infrastructure must be avoided in the envisioned system with the following objectives:

■ Reliable data delivery with constant connectivity and access to multiple networks
■ Guaranteed service availability for mobile devices
■ Energy and performance management for flexible, demand-driven network operation

Several network technologies were developed to address the special requirements of data communication. SDN-based network control allows these technologies to be efficiently integrated and managed with the current network infrastructure. Disruption-tolerant networking (DTN) addresses the lack of reliability in a network with disrupted connectivity. Disconnections can result from the operation environment, such as geographical obstructions or high mobility. Constant end-to-end links in a normal communication network cannot be assumed. DTN enables mobile nodes and the capability of storing data packets (bundles) for a long period of time. The mobile nodes exchange data bundles using a bundle protocol (RFC5050) [13] when they are in contact by way of any of the direct communication technologies, for example, Wi-Fi, Bluetooth, or even offline data transfer. Forwarding algorithms have been developed, which increase the success of delivery and minimize the resource usage. Implementations of DTN routers are available [14]. Applying DTN to our scenario helps to increase the reliability of traffic information services for mobile vehicles.

Another technology, information-centric network (ICN) [15], is promising for mobility support, resource efficiency, and service availability. In ICN, data packets are routed based on their "names." Data names follow a schema that allow for the identification of a data source and the specific data object provided. Requests for data are forwarded by routers upstream. This creates paths between requesting nodes and data sources. Data objects are sent back through the established paths. ICN protocol has a natural cache mechanism, in which data objects are cached on intermediary routers for each received request. Subsequent requests for the same objects are served by the nearest routers containing replications of the objects. Using ICN results in the efficient distribution of data where needed and a decreased service response time. One of the ICN implementations is the CCNx project [16]. The characteristics of ICN help to achieve the service quality required by a traffic information service in our scenario, where only geographically relevant information is delivered to the areas where vehicles are located.

8.4.2 Network Architecture

The network design for our scenario is depicted in Figure 8.6, which consists of three segments: a Wi-Fi access network, aggregation network, and core network. The network devices are OpenFlow-based and managed by a centralized SDN controller.

The access network consists of Wi-Fi roadside access points (RSU), which are installed along the roads and provide wireless access for mobile vehicles. These network spreads large geographical areas that provide wide coverage. In order to increase reliability in a highly mobile environment, mobile ad hoc communication and disruption-tolerant network (DTN) technologies may be employed. DTN enables data to be stored, carried by a mobile host, and forwarded to the next host if direct connectivity is available. This results in a DTN-enabled wireless mesh network, which provides both direct device-to-device communication and infrastructural network access.

The aggregation network consists of interconnected OpenFlow switches and provides backhaul for the transport of large amounts of data to and from access networks. Broadband wired and wireless technologies enable low latency connectivity between the switches and RSUs. The

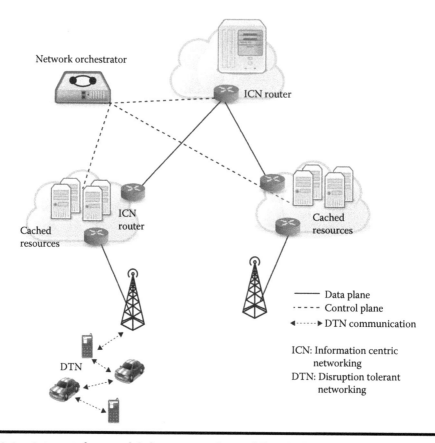

Figure 8.6   Integrated network infrastructure for mobile vehicles.

switches directly connected with an access network aggregate and forward traffic between multiple RSUs and the core network. The aggregation network provides data-centric routing by the installation of ICN routing function on the switches. Additionally, resource elasticity is provided by virtual ICN cache elements. Given the fact that object caching on the switches is limited due to the design for packet processing of switch devices, virtual cache units are dynamically assigned to optimally selected aggregation switches. These cache units act as virtual storage provided by the local cloud infrastructure and connected with the network on demand by the SDN controller. Cloud infrastructure management combined with network control functions results in a dynamically orchestrated aggregation network.

A core network provides Internet access for the access network and connectivity to application servers hosted in data centers. Given the large geographical deployment, Internet gateways can be provided by different local Internet infrastructure providers. However, the gateways are managed by the centralized SDN controllers to work in accordance with aggregation switches.

8.4.3 Mobility Management Application on SDN Controller

An SDN mobility management application (MMA) is designed to provide the required flexibility for the envisioned mobile network. We focus on the function that manages the aforementioned virtual ICN cache. Figure 8.7 shows the components of the MMA relatively in the OpenDaylight (ODL) software framework and their interactions with other OpenDaylight plugins.

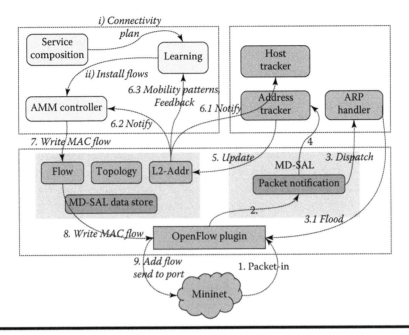

Figure 8.7   Mobility management application architecture.

The relevant ODL components are depicted. In the southbound layer, the OpenFlow plugin implemented with an ODL controller handles OpenFlow communication with forwarding elements. While the OpenFlow plugin is described here as the main provider of network information, additional southbound plugins and protocol may be used to provide useful network information. For example, the Push Access Protocol (PAP) WAP plugin implements a protocol for the management and monitoring of Wi-Fi access points. In the SAL layer, packet notification is an adaptation between an OpenFlow southbound service and the packet-handling northbound services. MD-SAL data store contains network status data that is needed by the MMA. In the ODL control layer, ARP Handler, Address Tracker, and Host-Tracker plugins handle ARP packets and provide topology information, which is used by MMA plugins. The proposed MMA plugins are depicted in an ODL control layer. They carry out functions to react with network topology changes, to coordinate with external cloud management (OpenStack), and to enforce the projected network control. The *Learning* plugin is the central part of an MMA application. Updated information from the network and available cache resources from OpenStack's cloud management is processed by the plugin in order to produce an optimal allocation of the ICN cache in an aggregation network. If an additional cache should be attached to a switch or RSU due to an increased demand, the Learning plugin indicates a request for a virtual cache unit to be created. At the same time, new links are created to connect related switches with the newly created cache. Optionally, a machine-learning method may be applied for the calculation of future demands and the proactive modification of the network state. Information regarding available virtual resources is provided by the *Service Composition* plugin. It provides northbound API for interaction with OpenStack management, which allows for the querying state of virtual cache resources. If additional cache units are required by the Learning plugin, through the same API, the Service Composition plugin sends a request to cloud management for their provision. The *MMA-Controller* plugin translates the calculated topology adaptation by the Learning plugin to a set of flow rules to be updated on relevant switches and caches. Figure 8.7 describes a complete process and interaction between the plugins, in which the MMA-Controller registers changes in the network state and carries out the respective adaptations. The host's mobility in the data plane results in changes in the network state that are reported to the SDN controller. When a new host attaches to an RSU, its sends ARP packets to the network. RSUs are configured to forward all ARP packets as "Packet-In" to the controller. Packet-Ins are first handled by the OpenFlow plugin. It sends notifications to the consumer plugins that registered with MD-SAL to receive packet events. The ARP headers are dispatched to the ARP-Handler plugin and Address-Tracker plugin. The ARP Handler just makes sure that the ARP packet is forwarded from the RSU to other switches in the network. The Address-Tracker plugin updates the MD-SAL data store with the new L2 link and host MAC-Address in the network. The Host-Tracker plugin registered with MD-SAL for notifications about changes to certain nodes in the data store. When a new link is added to the data store, Host-Tracker updates the additional information of the connected host. With the same mechanism, MMA's Learning and MMA-Controller plugins are notified of the latest changes in network. The Learning component calculates adaptations to the network with full topology information as described earlier in this section. Finally, the MMA-Controller writes the flow rules to the node in MD-SAL data store, which represents the RSU. MD-SAL's Flow Rule Manager service will make sure the rules are written to RSU's flow table using the OpenFlow protocol. To summarize, we have described the architecture and elements of a mobile access network, which is designed for a more efficient delivery of a transport information service to mobile vehicles. The architecture of an OpenDaylight SDN controller is provided with detailed interaction of its components.

8.5 Implementation of Proposed Mobility Management Solution with ODL and Mininet

This section provides a detailed walkthrough of the steps to implement the MMA-Controller plugin described in Section 8.4.3. We focus on the important programming patterns in order to implement control logic and to make use of the available ODL plugins and services.

8.5.1 Development Environment

At the time of this writing, the stable OpenDaylight release is Lithium. The following system requirements are provided to build the OpenDaylight controller.

- Operating system: 64 bit Linux (Fedora 22), kernel version 4.2.8-200.fc22.x86_64.
- Oracle Java 1.8 version: 1.8.0_66
- Maven version 3.3.9
- Git version control is useful for the development

The emulation of a data plane and device mobility is hosted on a separated KVM-based virtual machine with the same operating system. It should also works with other Linux-based systems installed on a virtual machine with Virtualbox 5.0 virtualization tools. Installed on the virtual machine are the following:

- OpenvSwitch version 2.32 provides OpenFlow switch implementation
- Mininet version 2.1 provides emulation of the OpenFlow data plane network

8.5.2 Generate MD-SAL Project Skeleton with Maven

Maven is selected as the build system for OpenDaylight projects. An "archetypes" project is available, which can be used to generate common project structures and a code template. In a working directory, the following command will create an MMA project skeleton:

```
mvn archetype:generate -DarchetypeGroupId=org.opendaylight.controller \
 -DarchetypeRepository=http://nexus.opendaylight.org/content/
repositories/opendaylight.snapshot/ \
  -DarchetypeCatalog=http://nexus.opendaylight.org/content/repositories/
opendaylight.snapshot/archetype-catalog.xml
    -DappName=MMA
```

Maven will ask for the type of project to be generated.

```
Choose archetype:
1: http://nexus.opendaylight.org/content/repositories/opendaylight.
napshot/archetype-catalog.xml -> org.opendaylight.controller: config-
module-archetype (Archetype for new module managed by configuration
subsystem)
2: http://nexus.opendaylight.org/content/repositories/opendaylight.
snapshot/archetype-catalog.xml -> org.opendaylight.controller:
opendaylight-karaf-distro-archetype (-)
3: http://nexus.opendaylight.org/content/repositories/opendaylight.
snapshot/archetype-catalog.xml -> org.opendaylight.controller:
opendaylight-configfile-archetype (Configuration files for md-sal)
4: http://nexus.opendaylight.org/content/repositories/opendaylight.
snapshot/archetype-catalog.xml -> org.opendaylight.controller:
opendaylight-karaf-features-archetype (-)
5: http://nexus.opendaylight.org/content/repositories/opendaylight.
snapshot/archetype-catalog.xml -> org.opendaylight.controller.
archetypes:odl-model-project (-)
6: http://nexus.opendaylight.org/content/repositories/opendaylight.
snapshot/archetype-catalog.xml -> org.opendaylight.controller:
opendaylight-startup-archetype (-)
7: http://nexus.opendaylight.org/content/repositories/opendaylight.
snapshot/archetype-catalog.xml -> org.opendaylight.dlux:dlux-app (-)
8: http://nexus.opendaylight.org/content/repositories/opendaylight.
snapshot/archetype-catalog.xml -> org.opendaylight.toolkit:md- sal-app-
simple (-)
Choose a number or apply filter (format: [groupId:]artifactId, case
sensitive contains): : 8
```

There are templates available for each module type. We select the template for *md-sal-app-simple* by inputting its index, 8. Continuing the interactive generation process, Maven asks for standard project properties, which can be given as follows:

```
Define value for property 'groupId': : de.tutorial.odl.mma
Define value for property 'artifactId': : mma-controller
Define value for property 'version': 1.0-SNAPSHOT: :
Define value for property 'package': de.tutorial.odl.mma: :
[INFO] Using property: appName = MMA
```

```
[INFO] Using property: modelFields = \{"title":"string",
"desc":"string"\}
Confirm properties configuration:
groupId: de.tutorial.odl.mma
artifactId: mma-controller
version: 1.0-SNAPSHOT
package: de.tutorial.odl.mma
appName: MMA
modelFields: \{"title":"string", "desc":"string"\}
 Y: : Y
```

There are some details that are specific to the OpenDaylight project. First, the property *appName* is set to *MMA*. This is defined in the archetype generation command with the parameter *-DappName=MMA*. Second, the property *modelFields = {"title":"string", "desc":"string"}* is the default JSON object representation of a node, which is used for saving the state of a forwarding element in an MD-SAL data store. The JSON string could be modified to better suit the network element managed by the module under development. Alternatively, a file containing a more complex description can be given. Our module does not need a specific model and the default can be accepted. After the generation process, the OpenDaylight modules are listed as follows:.

```
.
    Archetype_Next_Steps.README
    consumer
        META-INF
        pom.xml
        src
            main
    features
        pom.xml
        src
            main
    generate
        pom.xml
        src
            main
    model
        META-INF
        pom.xml
    pom.xml
    provider
        META-INF
        pom.xml
        src
            main
    web
        pom.xml
                    src
                        main
```

The *generate module* is a helper module that is used immediately after a generation process. Maven archetypes cannot provide the additional configuration required by the project, which is accomplished by this module. We execute the "generate module" with the following command and remove it afterward:

```
cd generate
mvn clean install -Dgen
cd ..
rm -rf generate
mvn clean install
```

The *model module* contains the sample YANG file that defines our "model." The generated file contains sample contents of a YANG file. Java code is autogenerated from the YANG file. There are a few exceptions when writing complex YANG files. For now, we are not modifying this module.

The *provider module* is set up with a service that implements any remote procedure calls (RPC) that were defined in the model's YANG files. Additionally, it automatically sets the application up with access to the following MD-SAL services:

■ DataBroker for reading, writing, and listening to changes on models in the data store
■ RpcRegistryService for registering our RPC implementation, or, invoking other RpcImplementations defined by other modules
■ NotificationProviderService for sending any notifications defined in the YANG file

The *consumer module* is where we write an application that consumes the RPC services provided by the provider module. In the consumer module, only initial access to the RpcRegistryService was set up, however, with a few modifications access to the DataBroker and NotificationProviderService is possible.

The *web module* provides an application that allows for the definition of customer REST APIs.

The *features module* Karaf features a directory that provides a list of sample features to enable the provider, consumer, and the web.

8.5.3 Generate Karaf Distribution Project

The Karaf distribution project is where the OSGI-based Karaf container is configured. It should include basic ODL controller bundles and third-party bundles, which provide additional control functions. We also generate Karaf the distribution project using a Manven archetype:

```
mvn archetype:generate -DarchetypeGroupId=org.opendaylight.
    controller \
  -DarchetypeRepository=http://nexus.opendaylight.org/content/
     repositories/opendaylight.snapshot/ \
      -DarchetypeCatalog=http://nexus.opendaylight.org/content/
          repositories/opendaylight.snapshot/archetype-catalog.xml
```

Maven again asks to choose the archetype. At index 2 the *opendaylight-karaf-distro-archetype* can be selected. In the next step, the latest archetype version should be selected, *1.3.0-SNAPSHOT*. The module properties are the same as in the previous generation's processes, except for the *repoName* property. In this case, the value is *mma*, which is the name of the git repository for this project.

To complete the distribution project, the pom.xml file needs to be edited to contain some dependencies. The MMA-Controller plugin is dependent on services provided by the OpenFlow plugin and Host-Tracker service from the l2-switch project. Their implementation is added to the dependency list as follows:

```
<dependency>
  <groupId>org.opendaylight.controller</groupId>
  <artifactId>features-mdsal</artifactId>
  <classifier>features</classifier>
  <version>1.2.0-SNAPSHOT</version>
  <type>xml</type>
  <scope>runtime</scope>
</dependency>
<dependency>
  <groupId>org.opendaylight.openflowplugin</groupId>
  <artifactId>features-openflowplugin</artifactId>
  <classifier>features</classifier>
  <version>0.1.2-SNAPSHOT</version>
  <type>xml</type>
  <scope>runtime</scope>
</dependency>
<dependency>
  <groupId>org.opendaylight.l2switch</groupId>
  <artifactId>features-l2switch</artifactId>
  <classifier>features</classifier>
  <version>0.2.2-SNAPSHOT</version>
  <type>xml</type>
  <scope>runtime</scope>
</dependency>
```

8.5.4 Karaf Features Module

Apache Karaf supports the provisioning of applications and modules using the concept of Karaf features. A *feature* is a simple way of provisioning an application in Karaf. It contains information about the application, such as a name, version, description, set of bundles, configurations (files), and the set of dependency features. When a feature is installed, Karaf will automatically resolve and install all of its bundles, configurations, and dependency features described in the feature from maven repositories.

This feature module contains a features.xml file, which contains the description of a set of features. A features XML descriptor is named a "features repository." Before being able to install a feature, you have to register the features repository that provides the feature (using feature:repo-add command as described in Section 8.5.6).

MMA-Controller will be implemented based on the provider module. So its dependency on l2switch bundles, OpenFlow plugin bundles, and MD-SAL bundles needs to be reflected in the XML descriptor. We modify features.xml as follows:

```
<repository>mvn:org.opendaylight.openflowplugin/features-
openflowplugin/${openflow.plugin.version}/xml/features</ repository>
<repository> mvn:org.opendaylight.controller/features-restconf/${ mdsal.
version}/xml/features</repository>
<repository>mvn:org.opendaylight.l2switch/features-l2switch/${ l2switch.
version}/xml/features</repository>
```

```
<feature name='odl-MMA-provider' version='${project.version}'>
<feature version='${yangtools.version}'>odl-yangtools-common</ feature>
<feature version='${yangtools.version}'>odl-yangtools-binding</ feature>
<feature version='${mdsal.version}'>odl-mdsal-broker</feature>
<feature version="${l2switch.version}">odl-l2switch-hosttracker</
feature>
<bundle>mvn:de.tutorial.odl.mma/${artifactName}-model/${project.
version}</bundle>
<bundle>mvn:de.tutorial.odl.mma/${artifactName}-provider/${project.
version}</bundle>
<configfile finalname="${config.configfile.directory}/05-MMA-provider-
config.xml">
mvn:de.tutorial.odl.mma/${artifactName}-provider/${project.version }/xml/
config</configfile>
</feature>
...
```

Additional feature external repositories are added, where the bundles are specified. The *odl-l2switch-hosttracker* is available from the l2switch repository and we can add it as a dependency to an *odl-MMA-provider* feature. On loading odl-MMA-provider, Karaf will load hosttracker and all of the features that it depends on.

8.5.5 Implementation of MMA-Controller Plugin

The generated provider module project is selected for the implementation of MMA control logics. The MMA-Controller can be implemented only with services from other plugins, for example, Packet Processing, Flow Writer, or Topology Manager. Although it is possible to implement MMA-Controller as consumer service, the decision to use generated code for a provider service allows for further development of the plugin to provide useful services. This makes the MMA-Controller both a consumer and a provider service. One of the advantages of a provider project is that it is generated with MD-SAL services and is API-available.

8.5.5.1 Generating Java Data Objects from YANG Model

In project source code, the YANG file *MMA-provider-impl.yang* contains a YANG model of the provider's service. The model is used by a *yang-maven-plugin* to generate Java code for its implementation. It contains configurations that direct the generation of Java code that wires the provider's service into MD-SAL's configuration subsystem: RPC, notification, and MD-SAL data-broker dependencies. The module's pom.xml is configured to apply the maven-plugin when the project is built. We run the first command:

```
mvn clean install
```

The newly generated Java code is placed in *yang-gen-config* and *yang-gen-sal* folders as configured. The folders contain Java classes that provide MD-SAL API for the provider service's implementation. Other autogenerated classes where we can start with the MMA-Controller's implementation are described in the following section.

MMAProviderModule.java when the provider bundle is loaded, MD-SAL gets an instance of the implemented service by calling the *MMAProviderModule.createInstance()* method. This class gets references to MD-SAL API (Data broker, RPC Registry, Notification) and passes them to the provider service instance. As a result, the reference to the configuration subsystem services is made available to the provider service, allowing it to interact with the other SAL service's implementation. The module registers itself with MD-SAL through an RPC Registration API. When a request for the MMAProvider service is received, MD-SAL retrieves an instance of the MMAService and returns its reference to the requesting service.

```
@Override
public AutoCloseable createInstance() {
  final MMAProvider appProvider = new MMAProvider();

  DataBroker dataBrokerService = getDataBrokerDependency();
  appProvider.setDataService(dataBrokerService);

  RpcProviderRegistry rpcRegistryDependency =
    getRpcRegistryDependency();
  final BindingAwareBroker.RpcRegistration<MMAService>
    rpcRegistration =
          rpcRegistryDependency
            .addRpcImplementation(MMAService.class,
              appProvider);

  //retrieves the notification service for publishing notifications
  NotificationProviderService notificationService =
    getNotificationServiceDependency();
```

8.5.5.2 MMA-Controller Implementation Classes

8.5.5.2.1 Registering Services with MD-SAL RPC in MMAProvider.java

This class contains MMA-Controller mobility management implementation. It instantiates a switch manager implementation and delegates to it the handling of switch events. The code listing shows how the ODL Controller's basic network services are made available. The packet processing service provides utilities for the handling of data packets. The SAL flow service provides methods to set up a flow, update a flow, or delete a flow on a node, which will trigger a flow rule manager service to update flow rules in the forwarding device's flow table. References to these services can be requested from the RPC registration service with their class name, because they are registered with the RPC registration system.

```
switchManager = new SwitchManagerImpl();
switchManager.setNotificationService(this.notificationService);
switchManager.setDataBroker(this.dataService);

switchManager.setPacketProcessingService(this.rpcService.
   getRpcService(PacketProcessingService.class));
// Flow services
SalFlowService salFlowService = this.rpcService.getRpcService(
   SalFlowService.class);
FlowWriterService flowWriterService = new FlowWriterServiceImpl(
   salFlowService);
switchManager.setSalFlowService(salFlowService);
switchManager.setFlowWriterService(flowWriterService);
```

8.5.5.2.2 Event Notification from Services with SwitchManagerImpl.java

On initialization SwitchManager implementation instantiates specific switch handler implementations with references to network services that it obtained from RPC registration. The switch handlers are event handlers, which are managed by the event dispatcher classes *PacketInDispatcherImp* and *NodeEventDispatcherImpl*. The dispatchers are registered with the MD-SAL notification service to receive event notifications from other services.

```
switchHandler = new SwitchHandlerFacadeImpl();
// Services dependancy
switchHandler.setPacketProcessingService(packetProcessingService);
FlowManager flowManager = new FlowManagerImpl();
flowManager.setSalFlowService(salFlowService);
flowManager.setFlowWriterService(flowWriterService);
switchHandler.setFlowManager(flowManager);

switchHandler.setFlowWriterService(flowWriterService);
switchHandler.setSalFlowService(salFlowService);

// Event listeners holder
PacketInDispatcherImpl packetInDispatcher = new
    PacketInDispatcherImpl();
NodeEventDispatcherImpl nodeEventDispatcher = new
    NodeEventDispatcherImpl();
HostMobilityEventListenerImpl hostMobilityEventListener =
 new HostMobilityEventListenerImpl(dataBroker);
switchHandler.setPacketInDispatcher(packetInDispatcher);
packetInRegistration = notificationService.
    registerNotificationListener(packetInDispatcher);

switchHandler.setNodeEventDispatcher(nodeEventDispatcher);
switchHandler.setHostMobilityEventListener(
    hostMobilityEventListener);
hostMobilityEventListener.registerAsDataChangeListener();

// Listen to Node Appeared Event
NodeListener nodeListener = new NodeListener();
nodeListener.setSwitchHandler(switchHandler);
inventoryListenerReg = notificationService.
    registerNotificationListener(nodeListener);
```

8.5.5.2.3 Notification on Packet-In in PacketInDispatcherImpl.java

The packet-in event is generated by the OpenFlow plugin service when the southbound plugin receives a packet-in from a forwarding device. The *PacketInDispatcherImpl* is registered to receive the event and must implement the *PacketProcessingListener* interface. It implements the *onPacketReceived()* callback method, which handles the event. In the method body, PacketInDispatcherImpl() identifies the switch that sends packet-in and calls its respective switch handlers.

```
InstanceIdentifier<?> ingressPort = notification.getIngress().
getValue();
```

```
InstanceIdentifier<Node> nodeOfPacket = ingressPort.
firstIdentifierOf(Node.class);

PacketProcessingListener nodeHandler = handlerMapping.get( nodeOfPacket);
if (nodeHandler != null) {

    nodeHandler.onPacketReceived(notification);
}
```

8.5.5.2.4 Notification of Node Status in Data Store with NodeListener.java

The *OpendaylightInventory* service allows other registered services to receive events when a switch is managed by the controller. The events indicate the state of the switch in the data store, for example, "node connector removed," "node connector updated (appeared)," and "node removed and node updated." The listeners must implement the *OpendaylightInventoryListener* interface. *NodeListener* is registered with the inventory service to call the switch handler when a switch appears.

```
public class NodeListener implements OpendaylightInventoryListener  {
 private final Logger _logger = LoggerFactory.getLogger( NodeListener.
class);
   private SwitchHandler switchHandler;
 public void setSwitchHandler(SwitchHandler switchHandler) {
  this.switchHandler = switchHandler;
 }

 @Override
 public void onNodeConnectorRemoved(NodeConnectorRemoved
nodeConnectorRemoved) {
  //do nothing
 }
 @Override
 public void onNodeConnectorUpdated(NodeConnectorUpdated
  nodeConnectorUpdated) {
  //do nothing
 }
 public void onNodeRemoved(NodeRemoved nodeRemoved) {
  //do nothing
 }

 @Override
 public void onNodeUpdated(NodeUpdated nodeUpdated) {
  switchHandler.onNodeAppeared(nodeUpdated);
 }
```

8.5.5.2.5 Notification of the State of Any Element in a Data Store with HostMobilityEventListenerImpl.java

This is a sample of a listener implementation that directly registered for an event from the MD-SAL data store. When there is a state update of a node in a data tree, the store notifies plugins that listen to the event of that node. *HostMobilityEventListenerImpl* detects host mobility by watching for events, when hosttracker service updates the *Addresses* and *HostNode* operational data store. It must implement the *DataChangeListener* interface and register for node events as follows:

```
@Override
public void registerAsDataChangeListener() {
 log.info("Register As DataChangeListener");

 InstanceIdentifier<Addresses> addrCapableNodeConnectors =
      InstanceIdentifier.builder(Nodes.class)
      .child(org.opendaylight.yang.gen.v1.urn.
opendaylight.               inventory.rev130819.nodes.Node.class)
      .child(NodeConnector.class)
      .augmentation(AddressCapableNodeConnector.class)
      .child(Addresses.class).build();

 this.addrsNodeListerRegistration = dataService. registerDataChangeListen
er(LogicalDatastoreType.OPERATIONAL, addrCapableNodeConnectors, this,
DataChangeScope.SUBTREE);

 InstanceIdentifier<HostNode> hostNodes =
InstanceIdentifier. builder(NetworkTopology.class)
      .child(Topology.class, new TopologyKey(new
TopologyId(                topologyId)))
      .child(Node.class)
      .augmentation(HostNode.class).build();
 this.hostNodeListerRegistration = dataService. registerDataChangeListener
(LogicalDatastoreType.OPERATIONAL, hostNodes, this, DataChangeScope.
SUBTREE);

 InstanceIdentifier<Link> lIID = InstanceIdentifier.
builder( NetworkTopology.class)
      .child(Topology.class, new TopologyKey(new
TopoloqyId(                topoloqyId)))
      .child(Link.class).build();

 this.addrsNodeListerRegistration = dataService. registerDataChangeListener
(LogicalDatastoreType.OPERATIONAL,  lIID, this, DataChangeScope.BASE);
}
```

An instance identifier for the data node of interest must be given in order to register its listener with the data store. The network state is stored in an operational data store and this must be indicated. Date change of scope is set to track all changes to the child node of the subtree. There is a difference between the configuration and operational data stores. The configuration store is where "requests" are stored and the operational store is where the "network state as discovered from the network" is stored. So flows are requested by being placed in the configuration store, but after they are configured on the forwarding device and ODL "discovers" them that data is put in the operational store.

After successfully registering with the data store for data changes, a data change listener provides its callback method to handle data change events.

```
@Override
public void onDataChanged(final AsyncDataChangeEvent<
InstanceIdentifier<?>, DataObject> change) {
```

```
  // handle event here
  exec.submit(new Runnable() {
@Override
public void run() {
 if (change == null) {
  log.info("In onDataChanged: No processing done as change even
   is null.");
  return;
 }
 Map<InstanceIdentifier<?>, DataObject> updatedData =
change.getUpdatedData();
 Map<InstanceIdentifier<?>, DataObject> createdData =
change. getCreatedData();
 Map<InstanceIdentifier<?>, DataObject> originalData =
change. getOriginalData();
 Set<InstanceIdentifier<?>> deletedData = change.getRemovedPaths
 ();

 for (InstanceIdentifier<?> iid : deletedData) {
  if (iid.getTargetType().equals(Node.class)) {
   Node node = ((Node) originalData.get(iid));
   InstanceIdentifier<Node> iiN =
(InstanceIdentifier<Node>)            iid;
   HostNode hostNode = node.getAugmentation(HostNode.class);
   if (hostNode != null) {
    log.debug("Deleted - HostNode: {}", hostNode);
    /*---- Handle HostNode Deleted ----*/
   }
  } else if (iid.getTargetType().equals(Link.class)) {
   log.debug("Deleted - Link: {}, Original data: {}",
iid,   originalData.get(iid));
    /*---- Handle Link Deleted ----*/
  }
 }
 for (Map.Entry<InstanceIdentifier<?>, DataObject> entrySet
:     updatedData.entrySet()) {
  InstanceIdentifier<?> iiD = entrySet.getKey();
  final DataObject dataObject = entrySet.getValue();
  if (dataObject instanceof Addresses) {
   log.debug("Updated - Addresses: {}", dataObject);
   /*---- Handle Addresses Updated ----*/
   packetReceived((Addresses) dataObject, iiD);
  } else if (dataObject instanceof Node) {
   log.debug("Updated - Node: {}", dataObject);
  }
 }

 for (Map.Entry<InstanceIdentifier<?>, DataObject> entrySet
:     createdData.entrySet()) {
  InstanceIdentifier<?> iiD = entrySet.getKey();
  final DataObject dataObject = entrySet.getValue();
  if (dataObject instanceof Addresses) {
   log.debug("Created - Addresses: {}", dataObject);
   packetReceived((Addresses) dataObject, iiD);
```

```
  } else if (dataObject instanceof Node) {
    log.debug("Created - Node: {}", dataObject);
  } else if (dataObject instanceof Link) {
    log.debug("Created - Link: {}", dataObject);
  }


 }
}
  });
}
```

8.5.5.2.6 Write Flow Rules to Network Elements in FlowManager.java

We have walked through various methods to capture the network state in real time. This final code listing demonstrates the methods to adapt forwarding elements in the data plane. First a *Flow* object is instantiated for a flow rule. This code listing shows the steps for building a flow rule, which tells a switch to forward all ARP packets to the controller as Packet-Ins.

```
private Flow createArpToControllerFlow(Short tableId, int priority) {
 // start building flow
 FlowBuilder arpFlow = new FlowBuilder()
   .setTableId(tableId) //
   .setFlowName("arp2cntrl");

 // use its own hash code for id.
 arpFlow.setId(new FlowId(Long.toString(arpFlow.hashCode())));
 EthernetMatchBuilder ethernetMatchBuilder = new EthernetMatchBuilder()
   .setEthernetType(new EthernetTypeBuilder()
     .setType(new EtherType(Long.valueOf(KnownEtherType.
Arp. getIntValue())))).build());

 Match match = new MatchBuilder()
   .setEthernetMatch(ethernetMatchBuilder.build())
   .build();

 List<Action> actions = new ArrayList<Action>();
 actions.add(getSendToControllerAction());
 if(isHybridMode) {
  actions.add(getNormalAction());
 }

 // Create an Apply Action
 ApplyActions applyActions = new ApplyActionsBuilder().setAction(actions)
   .build();

 // Wrap the Apply Action in an Instruction
 Instruction applyActionsInstruction = new InstructionBuilder()
   .setOrder(0)
   .setInstruction(new ApplyActionsCaseBuilder()
     .setApplyActions(applyActions)
     .build())
   .build();
```

```
// Put the Instruction in a list of Instructions
arpFlow
  .setMatch(match)
  .setInstructions(new InstructionsBuilder()
    .setInstruction(ImmutableList.of(applyActionsInstruction))
    .build())
  .setPriority(priority)
  .setBufferId(OFConstants.OFP_NO_BUFFER)
  .setHardTimeout(flowHardTimeout)
  .setIdleTimeout(flowIdleTimeout
  .setCookie(new FlowCookie(BigInteger.valueOf(flowCookieInc.
getAndIncrement())))
  .setFlags(new FlowModFlags(false, false, false, false, false));

 return arpFlow.build();
}
```

The flow rule is written to configuration data store by SAL flow service. The flow path in the data store is identified by an instance identifier object.

```
private InstanceIdentifier<Flow> buildFlowPath(NodeConnectorRef
   nodeConnectorRef, TableKey flowTableKey) {

 // generate unique flow key
 FlowId flowId = new FlowId(String.valueOf(flowIdInc.
getAndIncrement()));
 FlowKey flowKey = new FlowKey(flowId);

 return InstanceIdentifierUtils.generateFlowInstanceIdentifier(
nodeConnectorRef, flowTableKey, flowKey);
}
```

The provided flow path in configuration store is update with the flow created previously.

```
private Future<RpcResult<AddFlowOutput>> writeFlowToConfigData(
InstanceIdentifier<Flow> flowPath, Flow flow) {
 final InstanceIdentifier<Table> tableInstanceId = flowPath.<Table>
firstIdentifierOf(Table.class);
 final InstanceIdentifier<Node> nodeInstanceId = flowPath.<Node>
firstIdentifierOf(Node.class);
 final AddFlowInputBuilder builder = new AddFlowInputBuilder(flow);
 builder.setNode(new NodeRef(nodeInstanceId));
 builder.setFlowRef(new FlowRef(flowPath));
 builder.setFlowTable(new FlowTableRef(tableInstanceId));
 builder.setTransactionUri(new Uri(flow.getId().getValue()));
 return salFlowService.addFlow(builder.build());
}
```

8.5.6 Testing the Controller with Mininet

At this point we can compile all modules in the project directory:
```
mvn clean install
```

After the build is finished, Karaf distribution can be started as follows:

```
./distribution-karaf/target/assembly/bin/karaf
```

After karaf is fully started we need to activate some ODL basic features.
feature:install odl-restconf odl-mdsal-apidocs odl-dlux-all
This will activate restconf, apidocs, and the dlux UI of the ODL controller. As the result, the web UIs are now available at the following links. The default username and password are admin/admin.

```
localhost:8080/index.html
localhsot:8181/apidoc/explorer/index.html
```

Prior to loading the *odl-MMA-provider* feature, we must first add the feature repository. This is not needed if we add the repository as a dependency for a distribution-karaf module. However, during development, we will add the repository manually. After the installation of feature modules, the features.xml are available in the Maven repository:

```
~/.m2/repository/de/tutorial/odl/mma/features-MMA/1.0-SNAPSHOT/ features-
MMA-1.0-SNAPSHOT-features.xml
```

We add that maven location in Karaf so the bundle can be found:

```
repo-add mvn:de.tutorial.odl.mma/features-MMA/1.0-SNAPSHOT/xml/ features
```

To check if the feature is now available to karaf, we can find the bundle in the features list:
feature:list — grep -i mma
Now we can let Karaf download and activate the *odl-MMA-provider* feature.

```
feature:install odl-MMA-provider
```

8.5.6.1 Testing with Mininet

Upon starting, mininet will find a controller, so it is important to start Karaf with all the needed features first. We start mininet with a simple topology:

```
mn --topo single,3 --mac --switch ovsk,protocols=OpenFlow13 --controller
    remote,ip=10.10.11.44,port=6633
```

When a virtual switch in mininet is detected, *odl-MMA-provider* will install some default flows, which can be seen using the OVS command:

```
ovs-ofctl -O OpenFlow13 dump-flows s1
```

8.6 Conclusion

Future networks will have to cope with unprecedented demands for higher capacity, lower delay, higher QoE, more devices, reduced costs, among other things. In addition, cloud-based service provisioning becomes the first choice for application service providers to take advantage of resource elasticity, cost saving, and reliability. Mobile cloud computing, which enables access to cloud-based applications over a mobile network, requires the interplay between cloud and mobile network infrastructures. Given the limitation of current mobile networks, the full potential of cloud computing cannot be brought to mobile users. Future mobile networks designed for mobile cloud computing need to be more agile, elastic, and efficient.

New network paradigm and technologies, that is, SDN, NFV, and Cloud-RAN, are some of the important enablers toward realizing a future mobile network infrastructure. The technologies allow virtualization of all network segments. Network resources of each segment from core to RAN are dynamically sliced and orchestrated in order to efficiently deliver application data to mobile users. As a result, overall resources are optimized according to users' demands and to operators' operational constraints. Initial work has been carried out by the research community, which provides the concepts and new industrial products that support the vision, and is being deployed. However, the wide adoption of the new technologies is still absent while a next-generation mobile network is becoming closer on the timeline. Although the products come with support for SDN and NFV, their deployment is experimental alongside legacy system.

More studies are needed to thoroughly investigate the many aspects of revolutionizing the network paradigm in order to accelerate its adoption. The research community is in need of the tools to experiment with SDN and NFV in a near-production environment. This enables a fast and smooth transition of research results into reality and encourages joint efforts from both the research and industry communities. This chapter focuses on OpenDaylight, an SDN network controller, which is the most suitable for such a requirement from a research and experimentation perspective, and it is widely supported by market-leading network vendors. Some use cases of future networks are analyzed in terms of the vision of their architecture in its support of future mobile cloud applications. The chapter also walks through the implementation of an OpenDaylight application in order to investigate the handling of the user's mobility in a future SDN network.

One important aspect of the SDN paradigm is the control plane and its impact on the overall network performance. A large body of work focuses on the data plane and on network virtualization. It is assumed that network policies are translated to network settings and configurations, which are immediately enforced by SDN controllers on data plane elements. However, in most cases there is no ideal control network without reliability and delay constraints. It is more likely that the control plane and data plane share the same network substrate, which might be virtualized and isolated for their purposes. Such a separation mechanism, interdependence, encapsulation, and resource allocation between control and data planes are themselves complex topics for research on future networks.

References

1. Cisco, Cisco visual networking index: Global mobile data traffic forecast update, 2014–2019 White Paper, technical report, Cisco VNI, pp. 1–3, May 2015.
2. ONF Market Education Committee et al. Software-defined networking: The new norm for networks, ONF White Paper, p. 7, 2012.
3. ONF Market Education Committee et al. SDN architecture overview, ONF White Paper, p. 3, 2013.
4. I. F. Akyildiz, A. Lee, P. Wang, M. Luo, and W. Chou, A roadmap for traffic engineering in SDN-OpenFlow networks, *Computer Networks*, Vol. 71, pp. 1–30, October 2014.
5. F. Hu, Q. Hao, and K. Bao. A survey on software-defined network and OpenFlow: From concept to implementation. *Communications Surveys Tutorials, IEEE*, Vol. 16, No. 4, pp. 2181–2206, 2014.

6. ISGNFV ETSI, Network functions virtualisation (NFV), Virtual Network Functions Architecture, v1, 1, 2014.
7. K. K. Yap, R. Sherwood, M. Kobayashi, Te-Yuan Huang, M. Chan, N. Handigol, N. McKeown, and G. Parulkar. Blueprint for introducing innovation into wireless mobile networks, in the *Second ACM SIGCOMM Workshop on Virtualized Infrastructure Systems and Architectures, VISA '10, Proceedings*, pp. 25–32, New York, ACM, 2010.
8. A. Shalimov, D. Zuikov, D. Zimarina, V. Pashkov, and R. Smeliansky. Advanced study of SDN/OpenFlow controllers, in the *9th Central & Eastern European Software Engineering Conference in Russia, Proceedings*, p. 1, ACM, 2013.
9. R. Khondoker, A. Zaalouk, R. Marx, and K. Bayarou, Feature-based comparison and selection of software defined networking (SDN) controllers, *Computer Applications and Information Systems (WCCAIS), 2014 World Congress on*, pp. 1–7, IEEE, 2014.
10. S.-Y. Wang, H.-W. Chiu, and C.-L. Chou, Comparisons of SDN OpenFlow controllers over estinet: Ryu vs. nox, *ICN 2015*, p. 256, 2015.
11. OpenDaylight wiki, OpenDaylight Controller: MD-SAL architecture. https://wiki.opendaylight.org/view/OpenDaylight_Controller:MD-SAL:Architecture. (Accessed: 1 February 2016.)
12. R. Enns, M. Bjorklund, J. Schoenwaelder, and A. Bierman, Rfc 6241, network configuration protocol (netconf), 2011.
13. K. L. Scott and S. Burleigh, Bundle protocol specification, 2007.
14. W. B. Pöttner, J. Morgenroth, S. Schildt, and L. Wolf, Performance comparison of DTN bundle protocol implementations, *the 6th ACM Workshop on Challenged Networks, Proceedings*, pp. 61–64, ACM, 2011.
15. Van Jacobson, D. K. Smetters, J. D. Thornton, M. F. Plass, N. H. Briggs, and R. L. Braynard, Networking-named content, *the 5th International Conference on Emerging Networking Experiments and Technologies, Proceedings*, pp. 1–12. ACM, 2009.
16. CCNx protocol. http://www.ccnx.org/releases/ccnx-0.8.2/doc/technical/CCNxProtocol.html. (Accessed: 1 February, 2016.)

Chapter 9

Autonomic Network Management

Manzoor Ahmed Khan

Contents

9.1 Introduction

The evolution of mobile technology has been driven by the ever-increasing demands for high data rates and diverse applications. This has significant implications for the network infrastructure providers or mobile operators. The huge imbalance in the growth rates of data throughputs and operators' revenue implies that both capital expenditure (CAPEX) and operation expenditure (OPEX) need to be reduced. Furthermore, the challenges on the technical front grow rigid due to the complexity and scale of the modern mobile communication system. Operators pursuing approaches of combining heterogeneous access technologies to boost their network services adds another layer of complexity in network management. Therefore, it is believed that the traditional (mainly human-controlled) network management paradigm necessitates a shift toward a self-organization and self-optimization system, which assists in enacting the goal of reduced OPEX. The implication of self-x network management is to enable the networks to organize and optimize their parameters by themselves and to minimize human intervention [1]. Most of the proposals to realize self-x network management are at large inspired by the biological systems that exhibit autonomic behavior, such as self-healing, self-management, and so on. This entails that for networks to fully implement the self-x vision, the following autonomic principles need to be implemented: (1) the ability to translate business goals into low-level network configurations; (2) the in-time sensing of contextual changes in the networks and the timely reporting of them to proper network segment(s); (3) the implementation of an optimal control behavior upon sensing contextual changes, which ensures that the system's functionality adapts to meet the requirements of the changing environment; (4) the capability to observe the impact of its extended control strategy and to learn to converge with an optimal strategy.

It is believed that, based on the operator's defined policies, there are a few high-level performance indicators and network configuration parameters that are necessary to monitor and control for realizing the self-organizing network's (SON) vision. In this chapter, a thorough discussion of the requirements and realization of self-x network management is provided. The chapter starts by providing the vision of self-x network management, which is followed by a brief discussion of the essential terminologies and background information. The fundamental requirements that support realizing the envisioned self-x network management are discussed as basic constituents, the relevant activities, mainly EU projects, are gauged on these constituent blocks to analyze their focus. The chapter also presents the details of a contributed solution.

9.2 Essential Terminologies: An Overview

This section provides a brief discussion of the essential concepts and describes the fundamental terminologies that assist in understanding the contents of this chapter.

9.2.1 Autonomic Networking

The term *autonomous* is derived from the Greek work *autonomous*, which means "auto law." "Autonomous" further forms the basis for the term *autonomic*, which describes a tendency to be autonomous under any circumstances, functionally independent, and under no voluntary control [2]. Inspired by the concept of "autonomic computing," presented by IBM in 2001 [3], the autonomic networking targets achieve the self-management of complex networking procedures by employing the fancy concept of a control loop. Thus, a generalized definition of autonomic networking is given as follows:

Definition 9.1 *The mechanism in the telecommunication networks that attains the defined objectives in the dynamically changing environment by managing its own self without external intervention.*

9.2.2 Cognitive Networking

Contrary to the *cognitive radios*, cognitive networking (CN) has a bigger scope, that is, covering all seven open systems interconnection (OSI) layers. Different researchers come up with different CN definitions; however, most of them [4,5] are in agreement on the following components of the definition: (1) the knowledge plane, (2) decision mechanism, (3) environment perception, (4) scope definition, and so on. This leads to the following high-level definition of cognitive networking:

Definition 9.2 *A network with cognitive processes that aims at attaining end-to-end goals by perceiving the environment, learning from the experiences, and adapting its actions (subactions) accordingly.*

9.2.3 Self-Organizing Networks

The vision of SONs is fully based on the concept of self-configuration, self-optimization, and self-healing. Intuitively, one may claim that the SON vision is a specialized case of autonomic networking, where its scope is confined to the network management and control of cellular networks. This discerns the following definition of the SON vision:

Definition 9.3 *The networks with SON functionalities that target the reduction of the O&M costs by automating them. SON functionalities for O&M procedures are categorized into three basic categories, namely: (1) self-configuration, (2) self-optimization, and (3) self-healing.*

9.2.4 Basic Agent Terminologies and Concepts

Agent technologies are expected to play a vital role in bringing the vision of self-x network management into being a reality. Agents enable software designers and developers to structure applications around autonomous, communicative components, leading to the construction of software tools and infrastructure to support the design metaphor [6]. Agent technology is thought to be a suitable candidate for addressing the challenges of future network management, which deals with dynamic and open environments encamping heterogeneous technologies and spanning organizational boundaries. The distributed agent computing may help network management with catering to effective computation for expeditiously changing circumstances and perilously increasing information. The following briefly describes a few agent-relevant terminologies adhering to this chapter:

- *Intelligent agent*: An agent is anything that can be viewed as perceiving its environment through sensors and acting upon that environment through effectors. It is capable of carrying out autonomous actions to meet the objective(s).
- *Agent environment:* Agents interact with their environment. The environment drives the scope of the agent's interaction and its methodology. The agent's environment may be categorized as (1) accessible/inaccessible, (2) deterministic/nondeterministic, (3) static/dynamic, and (4) continuous/discrete [7]. In the context of this work, the agents' environment is defined as partially accessible, discrete, and dynamic. The inaccessibility and dynamicity of the environment is agent position–specific, that is, agents residing in the core deal with a different environment than the one positioned in the access network part of the network stretch.
- *Agent functions*: Agents continuously implement the three stages, namely (1) environment perception, (2) decision, and (3) decision execution. A generic representation of such a control cycle is given in Figure 9.1.

    Stage 1—Monitoring and measurement collection: This stage concerns how the environment can be perceived by agents. The agents capture the state and events of a given environment. Needless to mention that this stage is impacted by the way that environmental functionalities are implemented. In the context of autonomic network management, the agent at this stage may capture network status at the radio access network (RAN) or core level, the antenna's Tx power, congestion level, and so on.

    Stage 2—Analysis and decision making: This stage maps perception to actions based on the implemented logic for decision making. The agent may simply react to triggers, where triggers are the consequence of the perception and measurements collected at *stage 1*.

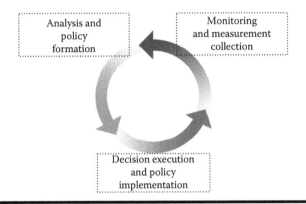

Figure 9.1   The cognitive control loop with three abstract stages.

Stage 3—Decision execution: This stage implements the controlled outcome of the decision stage. This stage affects the external environment of the control loop. The actions may be implemented by actuators, they may as well trigger other actions.

9.3 Self-X Network Management: Setting the Stage

To implement autonomic principles for network management, among the enormous aspects of self-managed networks, a careful selection is imperative to realizing the objectives of this work. The intention here is to gather the requirements and core properties, which assist to comprehend the optimum realization of a self-x network management framework. It should be noted that the requirements highlighted in this section feed the holistic solution and in no way negate the findings of the research literature. The requirements, rather, set the stage by identifying the core capabilities and components, which the author strongly believes are prerequisites for any model of self-x network management. This dictates that for developing self-x network management, the following building blocks and solution concepts should be developed and implemented. In Sections 9.3.1 through 9.3.6, we provide a brief discussion of these building blocks.

9.3.1 Dynamic Policy Formulation

The self-x network management framework should play a central role, that is, enable a wider network view and allow for a centralized policy description. By "policy" here, business-level policies are meant, which should then be transformed into low-level network configuration policies. The dynamic adaptation of high-level policies provides dynamic (re)configuration of different network segments.

9.3.2 End-to-End Reconfiguration

This corresponds to the ability to enforce self-x decisions in all parts of the network stretch. Given that quality of experience (QoE) maximization is the global objective of operators, users are bound in service-level agreements (SLAs) with networks. User satisfaction does not degrade as long as the SLA is fulfilled, which provides continuous control and monitoring from the management framework [8]. This requires the self-management of all the network segments. However, the network monitoring and control parameters vary with respect to the network segment. Intuitively, the different segments may be provided with separate network management systems to comprehend efficient distributed control. This demands the close interaction of these distributed management systems to guarantee end-to-end SLAs.

9.3.3 Cognition

The self-x management framework will meet its objective only if it is provided in a timely manner with all of the measurements/information required for monitoring and controlling. Alternatively, self-x management is effective if the environment is known to the management framework. However, with unfamiliar environmental and technical challenges, the self-x management system may lead to suboptimal decisions. For a solution to exhibit autonomic behavior in all of the environment, it should provide a mechanism that integrates the redesign/reconfiguration as part of the system. One notable solution is to implement the system processes through cognitive control loops. This corresponds to the cycle comprising of multiple stages (analogous to those discussed in Section 9.2). The functions carried out within these stages are driven by the environment, where the control cycle is applied.

9.3.4 Recursion and Conflict Management

Recursion is also worth considering along with the influential characteristic of self-managed networks [8]. If the envisioned framework is to realize the self-management of all of the network segments, the self-management capabilities should be recursively applied. However, in the envisioned heterogeneous wireless network paradigm, the self-management decision for some functionalities may result in a range of conflicts when executed simultaneously. These conflicts result in decreased system stability and a suboptimal solution. Therefore, the relationships in decision/control cycles should be carefully crafted so that the self-managed networks procure the global objective.

9.3.5 Knowledge Management

Knowledge management as defined in [9]: *Knowledge management is an integrated intervention concept which is concerned with possibilities of shaping the organization knowledge base.* This is another imperative aspect to deal with when realizing self-x network management. This building block should save all of the data received from the environment, which should also implement the mechanisms to infer further knowledge based on the received/stored data, which may be accomplished by approaches like: data mining, data aggregation, filtering, data abstraction, and so on.

9.3.6 Measurements and Data Collection

These correspond to the approaches implemented to collect the required data/information from the environment and present these to a decision mechanism. The efficient monitoring and measurement collection techniques play a vital role in realizing self-x network management. What to monitor? where? and at what time? are the most critical questions for solution approaches. The crux of this enabling building block is to make the right information available at the right time without increasing the system overhead.

Having defined the building blocks, the following provides the author's understanding of cognitive network management:

Definition 9.4 *The mechanism that uses control loops for distributed decision making for attaining the high-level goals based on properly structured knowledge gained from concretely determined measurements. The mechanism should incorporate an effective conflict management approach.*

9.4 Relevant Approaches: An Evaluation

This section surveys the most relevant EU projects. It starts by providing brief discussion on the contributions and focus of each project, which is followed by Table 9.1. The table summarizes the projects in terms of the building blocks of the proposed *self-x control and management framework* definition. Each cell in the table highlights the focus of the related project in the column component. Based on an analysis of the projects, I grade the contribution of each project for different constituent components using three levels: appreciable focus (represented by medium gray in Table 9.2), moderately focused (represented by light gray in Table 9.2), and briefly discussed (represented by dark gray in Table 9.2). Table 9.2 presents a symbolic summary of the projects' focuses on different building blocks.

9.4.1 FOCALE

In 2006, Strassner et al. introduced their model of an autonomic networking system called FOCALE (foundation observe compare act, learn, reason) in the book chapters of [10,11] and a series of papers [7,12,13]. A prototype of FOCALE had been under development at the Motorola Research Lab for Autonomic Computing, however, apparently the lab had to close down in 2008.

The FOCALE autonomic architecture has been designed to simplify the complex task of network management by introducing autonomic managers to legacy network devices. To achieve this, FOCALE creates a "lingua franca" which maps the vendor- and technology-specific functionality of legacy devices to a common platform. Based on this common platform FOCALE then introduces multiple autonomic control loops to achieve adaptive control according to changed context information and policies. The FOCALE architecture consists of several components that together form an autonomic management element (AME). The AME has several repositories for different kinds of knowledge, including repositories for policies, object models and semantically enriched finite state machines that are stored in the directory enabled networks–next generation (DEN-ng) information model.

9.4.2 Self-NET

Self-NET (self-management of cognitive future Internet elements) [14] is a specific targeted research project (STREP) of the 7th Framework Programme (FP7) and has finished in October 2010. Self-NET is aimed at introducing, designing, and validating a new paradigm for cognitive self-managed elements of the future Internet. As such, the design principle of Self-NET is to achieve a high autonomy of network elements that implement the paradigms of self-awareness, self-management, and self-optimization in order to allow for a distributed network management. To achieve this Self-NET proposes a distributed cognitive cycle for system & network management (DC-SNM) [15] to facilitate the distribution of network management in a hierarchical fashion. The DC-SNM consists of three management- and (re)configuration-making levels. With

Table 9.1 Focus Description of EU Projects on Relevant Components from This Work's Perspective

Reference	Control Loop	Measurement	Knowledge Managements	Conflict Management
Focale	Adjustment—When one or more reconfiguration actions must be performed. Maintenance—It is triggered when some anomalies are detected. Each time the adjustment loop is run, it is followed by the maintenance loop. Domains not identified.	Relies on SNMP-like measurements, however, the focus on measurements and data collection is limited, that is, it is generally assumed that vendor-specific data are available.	It is argued that the DEN-ng information model that specifies data models is not enough to capture the semantic behavior of managed entities. Thus, Focale uses the combination of UML-augmented with ontological information to address the UML deficiencies. The main focus remains on the model-based translation layer, which introduces complexities specifically when granularities of implementation are discussed.	Focale does not explicitly elaborate on the conflict management. However, their vision of moving the autonomic manager outside of the loop and multiple loops implies their solution.
E³	Hierarchical multiple loops namely inner, middle, and outer loops. The scope of the inner loop is confined to RATs, the middle loop to the intra operator, and the outer loop covers the interoperator interaction scope.	It identifies measurement requirements for various scenarios and their generation entities, for example, in CDMA load balancing, interference measurements collected from the UE are translated into link quality. Although the basics for the measurements are discussed, E³ does not detail concrete measurement metrics.	The project contributes very little in the direction of KM. It suggests, on an abstract level, a block that is responsible for transforming obtained information into knowledge and experience. No techniques/ approaches/interaction with other entities are detailed for knowledge management.	Owing to the fact that the project uses multiple control loops, one may infer that conflict management has been taken care of. However, the focus of the project in this direction lags behind when it comes to concretely discussing its proposed solution for heterogeneous wireless networks.

Self-NET	Three-tier architecture with multiple and hierarchical control loops. Two types of cognitive agents, namely NECM and NDCM. NECM implements two control loops: (1) flexible and (2) enhanced. The former reacts to well-known network problems. Whereas the latter requires event correlation and reasoning.	Self-Net comments that it uses existing standard means of monitoring, however, the focus of the project remains less on the side of elaborating somewhat concrete measurement collection approaches/metric for different use cases.	The project proposes a full knowledge life cycle. The raw data is filtered and transformed into usable information by a "filtering and correlation entity," the situation deduction is carried out through "Reasoner." For handling different situations, ontology-based knowledge management is proposed.	Self-Net highlights on the abstract level the conflict management, for example, it is argued that to resolve the conflict graph that describes the associations between CAs and states is necessary.
Socrates	Three types of decision domains: (1) distributed, (2) centralized, and (3) hybrid. Control loops are not explicitly mentioned.	Particularly focusing on LTE, the project highlights most of the parameters, measurements, and their dependencies on one another for different decisions and so on.	The project simply highlights the data format of the different measurements and does not elaborate on the normaliziation/transformation of the data for SON procedures.	The project highlights two types of conflicts, namely the (1) parameter value and (2) metric value. To perform such conflict management, the project proposes three phases of algorithm development: (1) self-optimization of individual mechanisms, (2) self-optimization of multiple mechanisms, and (3) overall self-optimization.
EFIPSANS	The project proposes four hierarchical level control loops, namely (1) protocol intrinsic, (2) functional block, (3) node, and (4) network-level loops. All the loops are assigned with the specified tasks.	A monitoring loop is proposed for measurement collection. This loop is a function-specific control loop, where the monitoring functions are mainly driven by both protocol- and network-level functions. However, a concrete approach or specific measurement parameters are not discussed.	The project assumes that knowledge is available to different control processes following the hierarchical structure of control loops. It is also assumed that the knowledge is in an understandable format. However, the emphasis on the detailing/contributing the knowledge management has remained noticeably low.	The project addresses conflict management by defining the control loops' design requirements, that is, care must be taken to avoid conflicts between interacting control loops. However, the specific scenarios and conflict situations are not listed.

Table 9.2 Focus of EU Projects on Relevant Components from This Work's Perspective

Ref.	Scope	Control Loop	Measurement	Knowledge Management	Conflict Management
A	Autonomic Network Control and Management				
B	Generic Future Internet Self-x Network Elements				
C	Self-organizing Networks (4th Generation)				
D	Cognitive Networks (Heterogeneous WN)				
E	Autonomic Network Control (Heteroge- neous)				

Sources: [A] Focale, [B] Self-NET, [C] Socrates, [D] E³, [E] Efipsans.

Note: Medium gray, Appreciably focused; light gray, moderately focused; dark gray, briefly discussed.

the levels, the authors define abstractions from the functional layers of the network management domain, namely the network management layer, cognitive agent layer, and, finally, the technology layer on the lowest level. Let us now briefly discuss the processes carried out on these levels:

■ *Lowest level*: In the scope of single network elements (such as routers) local agents (LA) implement a simple, reactive cognitive cycle that consists of the following: (1) monitoring—to perceive internal and environmental conditions by gathering data from the network element via vendor-specific sensors and by exchanging messages with other LAs on the current network status; (2) decision making—LAs are reactive agents without learning capabilities that decide on well-known situations, other decisions are propagated to the middle level; and (3) execution—involves (self-)reconfiguration, software-component replacement, or reorganization and optimization actions.

■ *Middle level*: In the scope of a network domain, domain agents (DA) orchestrate LAs that belong to the same network compartment. Opposed to LAs, the DAs are utilizing learning techniques that extend the MDE cycle to address network anomalies that require a broader perspective on the network than an LA has. As such DAs are responsible for handling the situations that LAs were not able to solve by applying their learning mechanisms to classify probable solutions to a specific problem. The output of this learning process is used to update the LA's knowledge base and to consolidate and improve its decision making process. DAs can also exchange their learned knowledge with their peers in order to enrich their knowledge bases.

■ *Highest level*: In the scope of the network management level, the operator defines a set of high-level goals that are incorporated into the framework in the form of policies and rules stored in a policy repository. Both local and global agents receive their objectives from the network management level. The agents on the other hand report unknown situations to the network.

Therefore, the DC-SNM cycle is realized as a multiagent system with two distinct types of agents, namely the network element cognitive manager (NECM, implements LA functionality) running on network elements and the network domain cognitive manager (NDCM, implements DA functionality) that is associated with NECMs that are associated with the same compartment. Self-NET's scope on evolutionary cognitive future Internet elements motivates research on knowledge acquisition and inference for situation awareness, dynamic protocol composition, self-management, dynamic compartment formation, and decision making.

9.4.3 SOCRATES

The EU FP7 project SOCRATES (self-optimization and self-configuration in wireless networks) [16] was completed in December 2010. The goal of the SOCRATES project is to develop solutions for self-organization within the scope of LTE that consider all elements of the system. Human operators should only be involved to feed the system with policies for the desired system behavior and to manage failures that cannot be solved automatically. The gains expected from the SON's functionality range from OPEX and CAPEX reductions to optimized network efficiency and improved service quality.

In order to achieve this goal, SOCRATES identifies the requirements for self-organization functionality in LTE and defines a set of 25 use cases [17] that are divided into the subcategories of self-configuration, self-optimization, and self-healing. With self-configuration newly added base stations (eNodeBs) configure themselves in a "plug-and-play" fashion. Self-optimization is performed continuously by existing base stations to optimize their operational algorithms and parameters in response to changing traffic and environmental conditions. Finally, self-healing is applied in the event of a cell or site failure to alleviate the resulting coverage/capacity gap. To realize these functionalities SOCRATES follows a bottom-up approach. Algorithms for each use case are developed and simulated in a reference simulation scenario before looking into issues that result from conflicts between integrated SON use cases. Guidelines for the clustering of radio parameters (to be tuned by the self-organization algorithms) into so-called functional groups as well as the interrelationships and dependencies between the use cases are described in [18].

A similar approach is chosen for the overall framework that implements the use cases. First, each use case is analyzed regarding its preferred architecture before deciding on the final system design. Three potential architectural forms have been considered for the use cases, namely centralized, distributed, and hybrid forms [19,20]. Finally, a subset of the use cases has been implemented within the scope of the work packages 3 and 4; however, the corresponding project deliverables are not available to the public domain.

9.4.4 End-to-End Efficiency Project (E³)

The EU FP7 project end-to-end efficiency (E³) [21] lasted two years before finishing in December 2009. The main objective of the E³ project is the introduction of cognitive wireless systems into a B3G communication network scenario in order to evolve current heterogeneous wireless infrastructures into an integrated, scalable, and efficiently managed B3G cognitive system framework.

To overcome the complexity of such a future communication environment, the E^3 consortium has set out four top-level objectives [22]:

■ The design of a cognitive radio system exploiting the capabilities of reconfigurable networks and self-adaptation to a dynamically changing environment.
■ To enable a gradual, nondisruptive evolution of existing wireless networks in accordance with user requirements.
■ To define a means of increasing the efficiency of wireless network operations, in particular by optimally exploiting the full diversity of the heterogeneous radio ecospace, both from the operators' and users' perspectives.
■ To increase system management efficiency for network operation and (re)configuration, building on cognitive system and distributed self-organization principles.

E^3 aims to achieve its objectives by conducting business and systems research, developing management functionality for cognitive systems, and conducting extensive prototyping and validation work. The specification of the E^3 functional architecture/system architecture is listed as one of the main achievements of the project. The components of E^3 architecture can be organized into a set of six pillars; namely (1) autonomic radio entity management, (2) cognition enablers, (3) reconfiguration management, (4) flexible spectrum management, (5) the SON, and (6) radio resource management.

An overview on the E^3 system architecture is provided in [23] together with the proposed scenarios and the information model that provides the main informational concepts and their interrelations. The system scenarios are grouped into three categories according to their key technical aspects, namely their spectrum management-, cognitive radio-, and self-x-related aspects. Based on these system scenarios use cases have been derived, whose requirements then serve as a basis for the specification of the E^3 system architecture, including the definition of the main building blocks and the interfaces between them.

9.4.5 EFIPSANS

The exposing the features in IP version six protocols that can be exploited or extended for the purposes of designing or building autonomic networks and services (EFIPSANS) project [24] introduced a standardizable reference model for autonomic networking and self-management called the *Generic Autonomic Network Architecture* (GANA) *Reference Model*. The GANA reference model defines decision elements (DEs) at different abstraction levels of functionality ranging from within devices to the overall network architecture. The DEs perform autonomic management and the control of their associated managed entities (MEs) as well as cooperating with each other in order to drive the self- management functionality of the network. MEs are started, configured, monitored, and dynamically controlled by DEs—in EFIPSANS terminology the DE drives a control loop over the associated MEs. The GANA model defines a framework of hierarchical control loops with associated DEs on four levels:

■ Protocol level
■ Abstracted functions level
■ Node level
■ Network level

With the help of these control loops EFIPSANS develops so-called autonomic behaviors that implement self-management features (from this perspective GANA provides a model for designing and engineering autonomic behaviors). An *autonomic behavior* is defined as the collection of behaviors or subbehaviors that drives the entities of a network to reach a final desired goal. These behaviors are managed by the entities of the network and, in doing so, create the self-managing network.

The autonomic behaviors considered in EFIPSANS come from seven categories of autonomic functionality [25]: (1) autonomic routing and forwarding, (2) autodiscovery and autoconfiguration, (3) mobility and autonomicity, (4) QoS and autonomicity, (5) resilience and survivability, (6) self-monitoring, and (7) autonomic fault management.

A set of seven overall objectives has been defined for the EFIPSANS project [25]: (1) the specification of some of the autonomic behaviors to be implemented in different networking environments, such as self-adaptive routing in the core network; (2) the examination and identification of those existing characteristics related to the IPv6 protocols that can be exploitable to be used in the development of the autonomic behaviors; (3) the investigation and creation of the IPv6 protocol extensions that are necessary for implementing the different autonomic behaviors defined; (4) workout the framework for complementary network component and algorithms, which assist in realizing the autonomic behaviors; (5) the investigation and creation of the network components, algorithms, and paradigms necessary for implementing the different autonomic behaviors defined (6) the selection of those autonomic behaviors among the defined ones to be implemented and demonstrated in a testbed scenario; and (7) the industrialization and standardization of the autonomic behavior specifications (ABs) and the protocol extensions with the help of the standardization bodies.

9.4.6 Agent-Based Approaches

In the recent past, research activities concerned with agents' application in computing, energy conservation, and networking environments has gained great attention from the research community, for example, [26–31]. However, this section concentrates on the approaches that involve multiagents being deployed in the networking environment for carrying out network maintenance and healing activities. Gerard et al. in [32] propose an interpretation of the autonomic networking paradigm and description of a situated based knowledge plane. Authors apply the proposed concept for resource regulation in IP military networks. It is claimed that the knowledge plane is the only information center that is responsible for providing the necessary information to all other components of the system. Based on the preceding claim, authors highlight the basic requirements for a knowledge plane:

■ Knowledge plane information should be useful, rich, pertinent to different mechanisms.
■ The knowledge plane should be able to precompute the data, correlate them, and maintain them within a specific rich format.
■ The knowledge plane should disseminate information to where it is required.

The proposed knowledge plane is based on multiagent systems. Basically, the authors propose a calculus-based approximation method for determining the necessary knowledge pieces, the proposed approach of approximation is driven by two factors, namely (1) the number of interfaces per node within the topology and (2) the maximum distance where the information is shared. It was analyzed that the cost of sharing knowledge in a network grows exponentially with the increasing number of hops, for example, the cost for broadcasting information over the whole network would be about 1000 times the cost for broadcasting information to a 4 hops radius area. In their distributed knowledge plane, the authors propose that agents take two basic roles: (1) the resource diagnostic agent—in this role, the agents' goals are specified, or (2) resource manager—in this role, the agents build and consolidate their knowledge from peers' information and act when necessary. However, this paper can be graded as a contribution in the direction of knowledge plane/information management only. It does not detail the interactions among different agents and the possible conflicting situations.

Jiang Xie et al. discuss the distributed constraint optimization problem in cognitive radio networks (specifically focusing on resource allocation in WLANs) [33]. Authors solve the problem of resource allocation using multiagents. Authors propose a third-party-based hierarchical resource management architecture, where an intermediate layer entity (i.e., a local network controller) controls a number of WLAN APs in a similar fashion as a base station controller controls the NodeBs or base transceiver stations (BTSs) in the universal mobile telecommunication system (UMTS) or the global system for mobile communications (GSM) access networks. Although the paper suggests an agent-based solution, the agents' interaction, knowledge management, conflict management, and so on are not detailed. Furthermore, the scope of the solution, scenario, and solution approaches are limited.

The application of multiagent solutions for network management is discussed in [34,35], where the authors propose a task decomposition approach driven by task priorities and their interdependencies. To realize their task scheduling and decomposition approach in the network management configuration, the authors propose a multiagent-based network management framework. A directed graph approach is used to capture the interdependencies of both control and data tasks. Authors claim that the proposed scheduling algorithms take care of conflict issues in general. Two agent types, namely scheduling and common agents, are proposed, where the former is the type that executes the proposed scheduling algorithms for distributing various subtasks among the group of agents. The papers in general present a multiagent network management framework, however, various aspects remain unaddressed. For example, in autonomic networking, how are the priorities assigned (static/dynamic), or in case of dynamic priority assignment, what factors drive these and how are the interactions, knowledge management, and conflicts taken care of in the multientities" environment(s)? One approach that addresses such issues is contributed by Ana et al. in [36], which focuses on the learning aspects in the multiagent-based solution for interference reduction in a multiple cognitive radios (CR) environment.

9.5 Proposed Self-X Network Management Framework

This section details the contributed concepts and components for realizing the envisioned self-x management framework. A fitting communication architecture is proposed, which assists in deploying management control cycles for distributed decision making while still enabling the autoreconfiguration of an end-to-end network stretch. For improved self-x functionalities, approaches for intercontrol-cycle communication, knowledge management, and learning are proposed. In what follows next, more details of the contributed concepts are provided.

9.5.1 Autonomic Control Agent

An intelligent software agent is expected to play a crucial role in realizing self-x network management solutions. We propose to deploy intelligent agents in different network segments for distributed network management. The proposed agent endows the following fundamental characteristics: (1) communication, (2) autonomy, (3) cooperation, (4) responsiveness, and (5) learning. To implement these characteristics, we design and develop the cognitive control agent. Figure 9.2 shows an abstract

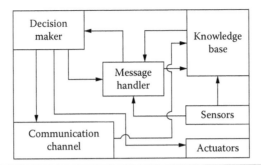

Figure 9.2   The internal architecture of the proposed cognitive agent.

internal architecture of the proposed cognitive agent. The functional component of the node's agent architecture, which comprehends the aforementioned characteristics, are illustrated as follows:

9.5.1.1 Decision Maker Component

This component enables the agent's autonomy. It provides the agent with control over its actions by reacting to the network status defining its environment. The decision may be based on different parameters' values observed from the environment through its own sensors, data patterns/aggregated data from the knowledge base, or the data from other agents. The decision is propagated to actuators for execution.

9.5.1.2 Message Handler Component

This component encompasses multiple functionalities, namely a (1) buffer, (2) iter, and (3) interrupt handler. The need for buffer functionality in the proposed agent is evident from the fact that sensory data may be periodic with very short intervals. Thus, buffering this data is necessary for further action. When it comes to the interrupt handler functionality of the component, the idea is that the message handler contains operational values/threshold values of different parameters, these values may be tuned by the operator policies or optimization algorithms (that are executed in the decision-making component and which result in tuning the parameter threshold values). Thus, as soon as the sensory data exceed the threshold value of the parameter, an interrupt is generated toward the decision-making component that kicks off the decision mechanism. It should be noted that no matter what approach is followed (i.e., event-based or periodic) for sensory data collection, the communication between the message handler and the decision maker remain interrupt based. The filter functionality of the component carries out the interagent communication task, that is, when the other agents need information from this agent, the information request is filtered and sent to the knowledge-base component of the agent. However, in case the interagent communication requires the agent to kick the decision mechanism off, then the message handler forwards the message to the decision maker (higher level policy implementation can be an example of such a scenario).

9.5.1.3 Sensor and Actuator Components

As evident from their names, these components are responsible for collecting measurements and executing decisions, respectively. An agent can have any number of such components depending on its position in the network; for example, an agent residing in the core network may need to gather information from the core entities and the underlying radio access technologies.

9.5.1.4 Communication Channel Component

This component enables the agent to communicate with other agents and with its user. In this work, we propose to position agents in different segments of the network. These agents will need to communicate for implementing the network policies. Hence, enabling efficient communication among the distributed agents is imperative. The communication channel component equips the proposed cognitive agents with the required communication capabilities.

9.5.1.5 Knowledge-Base Component

It is an accepted fact that a mobile network exhibits a very dynamic behavior, where the level of dynamicity varies in different segments in the network stretch. For instance, wireless characteristics vary more frequently than those parameters buried in higher layers of the network. Thus, to reach the optimal decisions for network management, the decisions are based on various parameters, of which vital inputs come from the knowledge-base component. This component does not only hold the environment data collected through sensors but also implements various approaches to form the data patterns/aggregate the available data. It should be noted that the learning aspects are introduced in this component. Table 9.3 presents the summary of these components and their functionalities. It should be noted that the proposed agent's design is strongly driven by the operations they will be performing in the proposed self-x management framework. Proposed

Table 9.3 Summary of the Functionalities of Proposed Agent's Functionalities

Component	Description
Message handler	Every received message is stored in the memory. The message handler is executed on a regular basis and represents the execution cycle. The execution frequency can be adjusted. It checks the messages that are in the memory and, passing a threshold, it can start the decision maker.
Decision maker	The decision maker accesses the stored data in the memory in order to make proper decisions.
Knowledge base	The knowledge base holds the memory, where all the knowledge is stored. It gives access to messages and other kinds of stored knowledge.
Sensors	A sensor is a passive adaptor. It senses data from the outside world and stores it in the memory for further use.
Actuators	An actuator is an active adaptor. It changes settings, can write a log or execute anything that was decided earlier.
Communication channel	The communication channel organizes the communication with other agents. It invokes send actions, packet messages, and can be notified of certain (self-defined) messages that are written into the memory in order to react immediately.

agents implement the cognition by executing the cognitive control loop similar to the one shown in Figure 9.3.

During the first stage, the agent perceives its environment via its sensors. The environment parameter values are then analyzed and processed in the second stage. The decision mechanism is provided with different parameter types including processed and raw data. The data processing may include data abstraction and the introduction of learning vision to the perceived data for computing proactively estimating the parameter values. The decisions are executed by the agents via their actuators.

9.5.2 Agent Architecture Realization

To realize the proposed agent architecture, we adapt the JIAC (Java-based intelligent Agent Componentware) [37], which is developed by the research institute of the author. It is based on component-oriented architecture that allows for the creation of a software agent from different software components [38]. Each needed ability, like understanding different communication protocols, knowledge processing, and action managing, as well as scheduling can be found in a special component. JIAC agents are programmed using Jadl++ (JIAC agent description language). It allows for the semantic description of services in terms of their preconditions and effects. JIAC's main focus remains on (1) introducing robustness, scalability, modularity, and extensibility; and (2) the dynamic addition and removal of services, agents, and nodes at runtime. The integration of agents with service-oriented architecture is the core aspect of JIAC. Owing to its use of powerful discovery and messaging infrastructure, JIAC agents can be distributed transparently over the network, or even beyond network boundaries. JIAC agents in the distributed agent platform can interact with each other by means of service invocation, by sending messages to individual agents or multicast channels, and by complex interaction protocols. Each individual agent's knowledge is stored in a tuple space-based memory. Finally, JIAC agents can be remotely monitored and controlled at runtime via the Java Management Extension Standard (JMX). Each agent contains a number of default components, such as an execution cycle, a local memory and

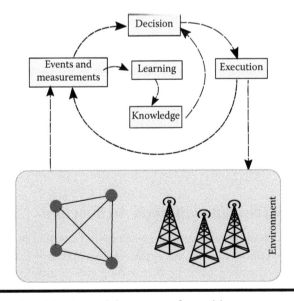

Figure 9.3   The internal architecture of the proposed cognitive agent.

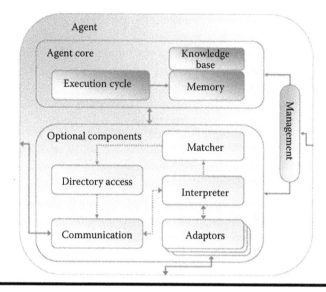

Figure 9.4   The mapping of the functional components of the proposed agent to the JIAC functional components.

the communication adaptors. The agents' behaviors and capabilities are implemented in a number of so-called AgentBeans. AgentBeans support very flexible activation schemes: A bean may be executed at regular intervals or according to a life-cycle change, such as initialization, or starting. Furthermore, the structure of each agent contains a number of standard components, such as an execution cycle, a local memory, and the communication adaptors. For ready reference, the functional components of JIAC agents are highlighted in Figure 9.4.

In the following, we briefly describe the involved functional components of JIAC agents.

- *Memory*: It provides the contents to an agent's interpreter for managing the calls to services. It also enables the monitoring of the current state of execution.
- *Knowledge base*: This block facilitates the reasoning and inference of the agent. It is basically a semantic memory rather than a simple object store.
- *Adapters*: These correspond to the agent's connection to the outside world. This is a sensor/effector concept, where all of the agent's actions are represented by action declarations.

To realize the proposed agent's functionalities, we make use of the JIAC's capabilities. JIAC's functional components are used to achieve the required functionalities of the proposed agents. Figure 9.5 depicts the mapping of the proposed agent over JIAC's functional components, which correspond to the components we used for realizing the proposed agent.

9.5.3 Hierarchical Telecommunication Architecture

It is believed that a hierarchical cellular structure leads toward enacting the requirements of future networks. It helps to decompose the network functionalities and defines the control steps, which in turn simplifies network management by distributing the control logic along the stretch of the network. A four hierarchical layers reference architecture is proposed, which corresponds to a telecommunication chain interconnecting various network segments. Figure 9.6 pictorially

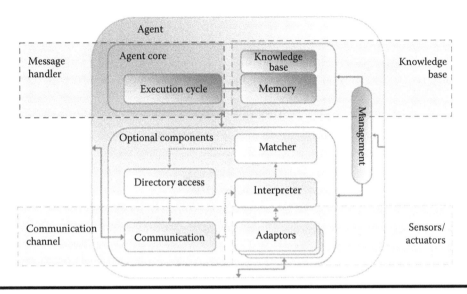

Figure 9.5 The mapping of the functional components of the proposed agent to the JIAC functional components.

presents the proposed hierarchical layers of a telecommunication chain, which is decomposed into policy, cluster, cell, and user levels. The naming of proposed levels is inspired by major network entities or stakeholders residing at those levels. The levels encamp various network operations, which knit together to complete the E2E service requirements. This dictates that optimization and automation of the operations at these levels add to the overall autonomic network management, obtaining the global objective function. Telecom market evolution and user-centricity strengthen the assumption that operators are forced to deviate from traditional objective functions, that is, throughput maximization, resource utilization, and call blocking minimization and focus on an increasingly satisfied user pool. Thus, setting the global objective function, with the proposed hierarchical architecture, a global objective may be defined as an aggregation of various local objective functions, where the local objectives may be specific to network operations carried out at different hierarchical layers. In Figure 9.6, we pictorially present the proposed hierarchical architecture. It can be seen that on each hierarchical layer, we propose to deploy the proposed cognitive agent, which implements the cognitive control loop.

In the following, we discuss details of these agents and their functionalities in the proposed architecture.

9.5.3.1 Coordinator Agent

It is responsible for capturing an operator's policies and translating them into local objective functions. It has the global network view and also takes care of an interoperator's SLA negotiation and resource sharing. It also interacts with cluster agents for policies propagation, network management, and assisting in decision instances promoted from lower levels. For instance, the potential point to implement network-based congestion avoidance/load offloading approaches is given by the coordinator agent; that is, by the (1) simultaneous use of RANs for extending services to the end users, (2) prioritizing of different service and user types on different RANs, and (3) by the sharing of the resources of the under-loaded RAN with the overloaded RAN. The coordinator

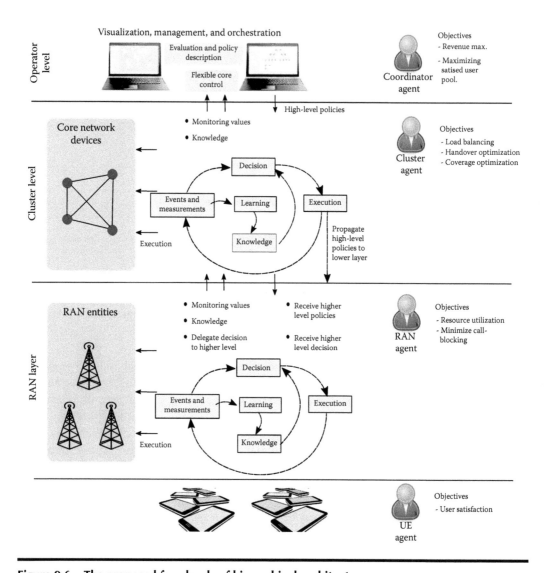

Figure 9.6   The proposed four levels of hierarchical architecture.

agent may also be used to implement the interoperator resource sharing approaches, for example, wireless LAN (WLAN) is owned by operator 1 and long-term evolution (LTE) by operator 2, then interoperator interactions for resource sharing approaches, infrastructure utilization level agreements, and SLAs are carried out by the coordinator agent. However, it should be noted that the information relevant to estimated resource demands for interoperator resource sharing is aggregated from the cluster agents [39].

9.5.3.2 Cluster Agent

This agent resides in the core network. In the downstream (i.e., from server to end user), the cluster agents associate and control the communication activities for a number of access points (Aps). Intuitively, the geographical area covered by all its cells is the footprint of the cluster agent, and the aggregated radio resources of all the cells may be termed as the *cluster radio resources*. A cluster may consist of homogeneous or heterogeneous RAN technologies; the number of access technologies within a cluster is driven by the operators' policies. An operator may have various cluster entities in a geographical area, which implement the cluster-level cognitive control cycle. In addition, the intercluster entities' interactions may be carried out for efficient resource utilization, congestion avoidance, and many other objective functions (these objective functions are detailed in Section 9.6.1. It should further be noted that the involvement of this entity in different objective functions is fully dependent on the system configuration and the integration approaches used for integrating different network technologies and the ownership of technologies.

9.5.3.3 Cell Agent

The entities at this level may be an access point, eNodeB, or NodeB depending on the underlying technology specifications. In addition, introducing cognition at the cell level by implementing a cell-specific control loop, it is also involved in vertical (with agents on higher/lower levels) and horizontal (with peer agents) interactions. For instance, a cell is associated with its core network via the cluster agent in the upstream and is responsible for extending services to the users over radio resources in the downstream. The position of the agent clearly indicates the following three interaction instances:

- Its interaction with the cluster agent—such an interaction is mainly event-based for different objective functions, for example, if the load balancing at the intercells' interaction cannot be carried out at the cell level, the cell cluster agent's interaction is carried out for cluster-level load balancing. Similarly, for inter-eNB handovers, the cluster cell agents' interactions are involved. Depending on the single and multioperator settings, this interaction mainly focuses on resource allocation, load balancing, and the handovers.
- Its interaction with UE—the interaction mainly focuses on the physical layer measurements' extension to the entities sitting at the higher layers for different decision making. The interaction at this layer plays a vital role for the decision made in network selection.
- Its interaction with peer entities at the horizontal level—based on the single and multiple operator settings, the interaction at this level is basically for radio resource sharing and handover optimization.

9.5.3.4 UE Agent

This is the end-user device that is equipped with functionalities similar to that of current smart phones. The required intelligence is introduced by deploying a UE agent on the entity, where the UE agent is responsible for implementing user-level objective functions and carrying out UE cell agents' interactions for different objective functions. It should be noted that most of the mentioned interactions involve a UE agent for measurement value extension. However, the UE agent may be actively involved in the decision making of intelligent network/transmission frequency/data-rate selection which is expected to help the optimization problem converge to an equilibrium state much faster. The claim in the preceding sentence is driven by the fact that introducing the intelligence distributed among different entities and delegating some of the decisions to UE will reduce the control signaling and require less information for decision making.

9.6 Translation Function

In this work, we propose the concept of *objective function translation*. As indicated in Section 9.5.3, various network operations are specific to different hierarchical levels in the proposed architecture. Hence, the optimization of those operations in a defined network's scope may be carried out by what are termed *local objective functions*. An operator policy may involve single or multiple such local objective functions. Thus, when it comes to realizing the vision of policy formulation and execution the proposed concept of objective functions translation is of paramount importance. For instance, the operator crafts a policy by configuring various high-level parameters. The translation of this policy will vary for different time and geographical regions based on the network status and network deployment. The contributed policy translation function ensures the optimal translation of a global objective function (high-level goal/operator policy) into a local objective function. We propose that translation function consists of spatial (l) and temporal (t) factors, as well as a dynamic network status (ρ), operator preferences (ψ), and network technology preferences (ω). These arguments are configured by a policy maker. The translation function then selects a set of local objective functions that best meet the desired goals of the global objective function. Figure 9.8 shows an example of the translation of a global objective function into various local objective functions. As can be seen, the user satisfaction function (global objective function) is translated into load balancing, handover optimization, and so on. We propose the local objective functions relationship as a weighted sum, where the coefficient of each local objective function is the associated weight for that local objective function. This is represented as

$$ G := w_1\left(t, \psi, \rho, l, \omega\right), \ldots, w_n\left(t, \psi, \rho, l, \omega\right) \tag{9.1} $$

such that

$$ \sum_{i=0}^{n} wi = 1 $$

To assign the values to the associated weights, we propose the use of ontology. Hence, the weight computation is greatly impacted by the arguments by function. To better explain the weight computation, we briefly discuss its computation in our developed demonstrator with the help of Figure 9.7.

As can be seen in the figure, the operator's high-level policies are configured in our developed network management and visualization framework. The objective function translation tool then collects the relevant parameter values (e.g., those captured from the operator and emulation environment). These parameter values are passed to the function, where with the help of implemented ontologies, the function's functions are computed. More on the objective function and their relationships are provided in Section 9.6.1.

9.6.1 Relationships among Different Objective Functions: A Generic Overview

This work translates the global objective into various local objectives. A global objective may be defined in terms of different parameters, depending on its translation into local objective

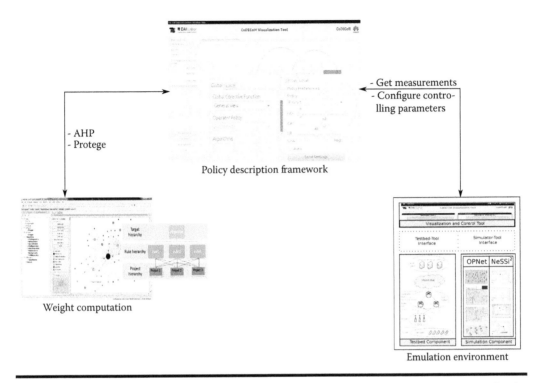

Figure 9.7 **The stages of the local objectives' associated weight computation stages in the developed demonstrator.**

functions and thus into controlling parameters. We further note that the relationships are defined based on the following question: How does an objective function impact the other objective function(s), that is, considering this particular objective function may have a positive or negative impact on the other objective functions? *Negative impact* here indicates the conflicting optimization parameters of the objective (impacting and impacted) objective functions. These impacts may be translated into dependencies, where the scales of dependencies are captured by associating weights to each relationship. Thus, assigning the mentioned weights to the relationships, the objective functions form a hierarchy and define different paths toward achieving the global objective function; for example, refer to Figure 9.8, in which throughput/user QoE may be achieved via (1) Load balancing → Congestion avoidance → Throughput maximization or (2) Call admission control → Congestion avoidance → Throughput maximization. It should be noted that the number of hops in attaining the global objective does not indicate the cost/complexity of the optimization problem. Instead, the level of contribution of the local objective function(s) in attaining the systemwide goals (global objective) is driven by the accessible information and controlling parameters specific to the local objective functions. We also believe that the decision for selecting different local objective functions is sensitive to operator-deployed infrastructure, and temporal and spatial indices. Thus, we claim that the translation of the objective function into local objective functions is dependent on operator policies. Intuitively, there exists a relationship between the local objective of the global objective function. Such a relationship's formulation may be automated using the operator's preferences and ontologies, which are functions of different geographical regions and user populations. The claim in the preceding paragraph dictates that

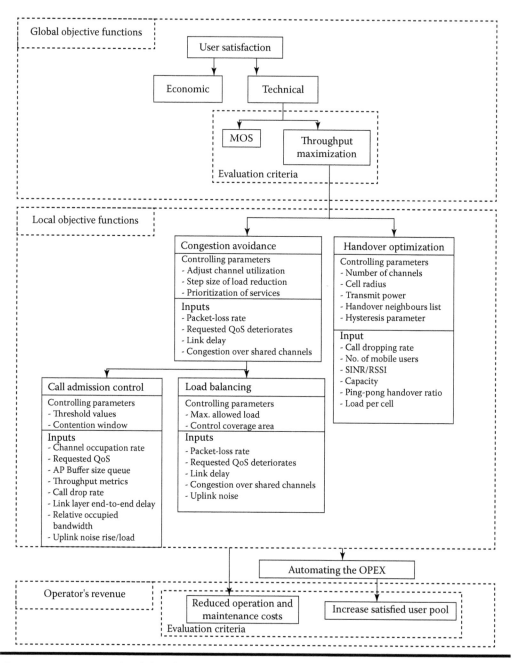

Figure 9.8 An example of the objective function translation into local objective functions.

operator policies set the weight value, or that the setting of these weight values may be automated using ontologies that are functions of different geographical regions and user populations, as explained in Section 9.6

In what follows next, a discussion on the commonly known objective functions and their potential relationships is provided.

9.6.2 Global Objective Function

In the perspective of this work, we consider two main global objective functions, namely *user satisfaction* and operators' revenue, although any number of global objective functions may be considered. By the *global objective function*, we mean the system-wide function that evaluates the fitness of alternative actions in different system settings. In the context of this work, the global objective functions are translated into various local objective functions. Each local objective may involve interactions among different stakeholders, as evident from the description of a proposed architecture where on each hierarchical level, the decision(s) of stakeholders depend on various parameters (criteria). It is necessary to define a fitness value (value ranges) per criterion that allows for a satisfaction and aspiration analysis following the multicriteria decision-making theory. This dictates that an alternative action to the criteria is satisfactory if it fulfills certain satisfaction requirements and it is ideal if the value of the considered criteria reaches certain aspiration levels. The fitness value must include the information provided for each criterion (satisfaction limits or worst permissible values, and the aspiration level or ideal value). This further dictates that global objective functions will be defined as an aggregation of several individual criteria for different simultaneous or sequential decision instances.

9.6.2.1 User Satisfaction Function

Next-generation wireless networks together with smart phone evolution have opened new opportunities to deliver mobile services to users. The concepts of resource virtualization and cloud computing are driving the redesign of ICT infrastructures. When combined with terminal mobility, "always on" devices, and "always on" services, these concepts will impose strong requirements on the capacity, availability, and reliability of wireless access networks. Users will require seamless access to their virtual resources and services in the cloud irrespective of their physical location and activity (e.g., walking, driving) while using their smartphones, tablet, netbooks, and notebooks. The different sections of mobile communication networks (from wireless access, to backhaul and transport) will be deeply affected by these scenarios of ubiquitous wireless access to cloud services that amount to an already significant increase in traditional services (e-mail, browsing, video download, and audio and video streaming) [40].

The current business models of mobile telecommunication operators are based on the concept of the so-called walled gardens: operators run their strictly closed infrastructures, and base their revenue-generating models on their capacity to retain current customers, acquire new ones, and effectively enact both technological and economic barriers to prevent users from being able to utilize services and resources offered by other operators. The radio spectrum resources are statically owned by operators and the exchange of such resources among operators is only possible with long-term agreements (like the agreements between a mobile virtual network operator—MVNO and a traditional operator that owns the "radio" resources). We believe that this approach is not suitable to support the envisaged evolution of telecommunication.

Having accepted that future telecommunication services will be user-centric, operators will be interested in increasing their satisfied user pool for different extended services. Broadly categorizing the services into real-time and non-real-time services, we propose the generic metric for measuring the user satisfaction for both real-time and non-real-time traffic. Intuitively, these services are characterized by different application QoS requirements. In the following, we discuss briefly the application requirements for real-time and non-real-time applications. More details on this can be found in the author's earlier work [40]. Table 9.4 summarizes the quality metrics for different applications.

Table 9.4   Summary of the Proposed User Perception for RT and NRT Applications

MOS	RT Perceived Quality	NRT Perceived Quality
5	Excellent	Imperceptible
4	Good	Perceptible but not annoying
3	Fair	Slightly annoying
2	Poor	Annoying
1	Bad	Very annoying

9.6.2.2 Operator Profit Function

When it comes to defining the *pro t* function of the operator, it may be captured by a quasi-concave-like function, that is, it may consist of gain and cost components. These components may further be the functions of different parameters, where the parameters may be both technical and nontechnical. For instance, when the operators' profit function is modeled so that operators increase their profit in increasing the satisfied user pool while optimally utilizing their resources and reducing the incurred costs. This dictates that users' satisfaction is tied to both technical (service quality) and economic (service cost) parameters. However, it should be noted that other influencing parameters include market dynamics and operator policies, and so on.

In this work, we will confine our discussion to modeling user satisfaction in the technical indices. Looking at the system from the operators' perspective, operators aim at increasing the satisfied user pool by optimizing various local objective functions, for example, handover optimization, load balancing, resource scheduling, implementing cross-layer optimization approaches, and so on. In Figure 9.8, we present the translation of a global objective function into local objective functions.

It should be noticed that the translation of a QoE global objective function into local objective functions is strongly based on the operator's policies, which are further driven by the spatial and temporal dynamics. For instance, an operator may implement different policies in different geographical regions; similarly, an operator adapts the policies for different time periods based on resource demands, and so on. One may interpret the global objective function's translation into local objective functions as an end-to-end optimization solution. Going one step ahead, given that the network is up and running, the operators on one hand are interested in optimally utilizing the available resources and on the other hand they also strive to reduce the operation and maintenance costs. One possible way to reduce the operation and maintenance costs is to autonomically implement control and management in the network.

9.6.3 Local Objective Functions

This section presents an overview of local objective functions, which assist in optimizing the global objective functions.

9.6.3.1 Load Balancing

Although no formal definition of the term *load balancing* exists in the literature, the research community defines it in different ways. Evidentially, the main component of the term *load balancing* is "load"; hence, giving any definition to the term *load* leads to a concrete definition of load balancing.

In the perspective of this work, we define "load" as the ratio of required to total resources. If the amount of required resources of all users connected to an AP is greater or equal to its total resources, this AP is then considered to be overloaded. This further provides a concrete definition of the required resources. In connection with this, we propose the user types; namely, excellent, good, and fair users for different application types (e.g., elastic and rigid applications with different bandwidth requirements). Each user is characterized by his/her preferred QoS requirements, which we translate into a user satisfaction function. Let the AP (*A*) load be denoted by *L*, which is given by

$$L = \frac{1}{B} \sum u_{c,k} \forall c \in \left\{ \text{app.classes} \right\} \& k \in \left\{ \text{user types} \right\} \tag{9.2}$$

where:

Index *k* represents the user type
  c represents an element from the set of the application classes
  B represents the total available capacity of the AP

When it comes to defining load balancing in this work, we define *load balancing* as the process of load distribution over the available (homogeneous/heterogeneous) system infrastructure and radio resources. The motivation for such an objective comes from the fact that the approaches used for load balancing achieve an overall better performance relative to some selected metric. In general, it can be thought of as a task migration mechanism in order to place the tasks at the right resources. Load-balancing algorithms (centralized or distributed) with system-specific complexities achieve this objective.

9.6.3.2 Link Adaption

The term *link adaptation*, in its broader sense, denotes the matching modulation, coding, and other signal/protocol parameters to condition the radio link. This task may be carried out by the adaptive modulation schemes, where the channel quality indicator (CQI) is derived from signal-to-interference-plus-noise ratio (SINR) measurements made by the receiver. There are various adaptation approaches such as (1) fixed link adaptation, (2) differentiated link adaptation, (3) fast link adaptation, and (4) window-based link adaptation. In this work, we consider an extended version of the link adaptation definition, that is, where the link adaptation local objective function is not confined to physical-level characteristics, instead it should encamp both the channel condition and backhaul network conditions. Furthermore, for solutions implementing simultaneous connectivity over multiple interfaces, in which case the proposed link adaptation incorporates the load balancing (over homogeneous/heterogeneous wireless access networks and in the core network) concepts at the network side and maintains the user satisfaction at the user side.

9.6.3.3 Handover Optimization

This work basically provides the ability to implement different optimization problems with subdomains of the system domain. Thus, by *handover optimization*, we mean dynamic policy-based integrated vertical and horizontal handover optimization, as shown in Figure 9.9. We aim at attaining

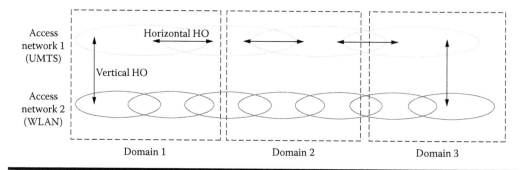

Figure 9.9 Handover optimization of the local objective function.

the following main goals of handover optimization: to (1) minimize the number of handover failures, (2) minimize the number of unnecessary handovers, (3) minimize the absolute number of initiated handovers, (4) minimize handover delay, (5) maximize the total time of the user being connected to the best cell, and (6) minimize the impact of handover on system and service performance.

These objectives are attained by implementing interagent interactions. We envision such a local objective function as an element in the package of a global objective function; for example, proposed agents interact with each other to minimize the end-to-end delay of a mobile user, which in turn will impact the user-received throughput and add to user satisfaction.

9.6.3.4 Congestion Avoidance

By definition, congestion avoidance corresponds to the techniques used, which monitor network traffic load to anticipate and avoid congestion at common network bottlenecks. There are various mechanisms for congestion avoidance in the literature, for example, random early detection (RED), weighted random early detection (WRED), distributed WRED (DWRED), and so on. We translate the congestion avoidance into load balancing, call admission control, handover optimization, and so on.

9.7 Inter-Agents Interaction for Self-X Network Management

This section focuses on illustrating the interaction among different cognitive agents for carrying out self-x network management and dynamically executing operator policies across the network stretch. In this connection, we provide the detailed interagents' interactions for different global and local objective functions.

9.7.1 Inter-Agents Interaction for QoE/Throughput Maximization

Considering user-perceived QoE to be a global objective function, which may be translated into a number of local objective functions (for details refer to Section 9.6.1), when it comes to implementing an interaction for attaining this objective function in the proposed architecture, most of the proposed agents are involved in the interaction depending on the configuration. The interaction among the involved entities is presented in the sequence diagram given in Figure 9.10. As

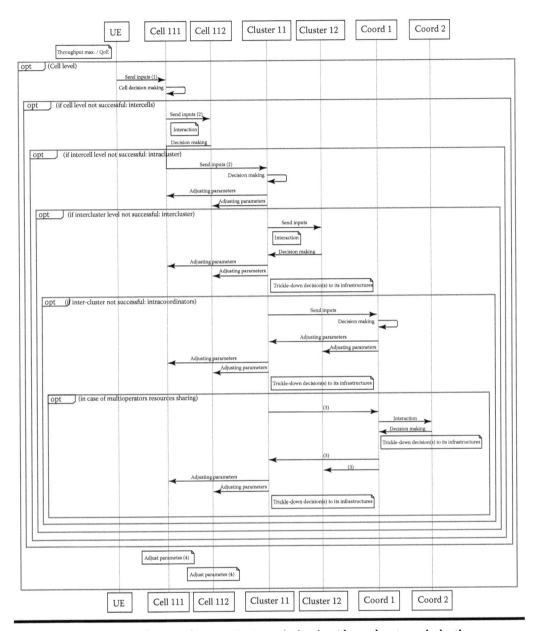

Figure 9.10   Sequence diagram for user QoE maximization/throughput maximization.

can be seen the trigger for throughput optimization/user QoE maximization is generated by the UE agent, that is, in terms of MOS values in the inter-UE cell agents' interaction. Upon receiving the trigger(s), the cell agent carries out the intercell agents' interaction, depending on the operator policy (by *operator policy* here we mean, the translation of global objective into local objectives), for attaining different local objectives. Assume that the intercell agents' interaction may not resolve the problem of optimally setting the transmitting power or transmission rate, in such a case, the interaction is extended and the cluster agent is involved (as shown in the sequence diagram given

Table 9.5 Control Parameters and Inputs for Throughput Optimization

Inputs	Agent	Controlling Parameters	Agent
MOS	UE	Transmit power	Cell, (Cluster, Coordinator)
BER	UE and Cell	Transmit rate	Cell, (Cluster, Coordinator)
SNR	UE	—	—

Table 9.6 Control Parameters and Inputs for Handover Optimization

Inputs	Agents	Controlling Parameters	Agent
Call dropping rate	Cell	No. of channels	Cell
No. of mobile users	Cell	Transmit power	Cell
SNR/RSSI	UE	Handover neighboring lists	Cell
Capacity	Cell	Cell radius	Cell
Ping-pong handover ratio	Cluster	Hysteresis	Cell
Load per cell	UE	—	—

in Figure 9.10 and explained in Table 9.5). The cluster agent has a wider vision about its cells, and thus, is in a better position to tune the controlling parameters for different cells within the cluster. Along similar lines, if the objective function still needs to be optimized, intracluster followed by intercluster interaction will take place. This completes the proposed hierarchical interactions, which (as also claimed in Section 9.5.3) results in both fully distributed and seldomly centralized decision making. In addition to intercluster interaction, the coordinator agent comes into play when multioperator resource sharing approaches need to be realized. The interentities' interaction for user QoE maximization is further detailed with the help of the sequence diagram and the flowchart given in Figure 9.10 .

9.7.2 Inter-Agents Interaction for Handover Optimization

In this section, we detail the interaction of proposed agents for attaining a handover optimization objective function with the aid of Table 9.6 and Figure 9.11.

9.7.3 Inter-Agents Interaction for Link Adaptation

In this section, we detail the interaction of proposed agents for attaining a link adaptation objective function with the aid of Figure 9.12 and Table 9.7.

9.7.4 Inter-Agents Interaction for Call Admission Control

In this section, we detail the interaction of proposed agents for attaining a call admission control objective function with the aid of Figure 9.13 and Table 9.8.

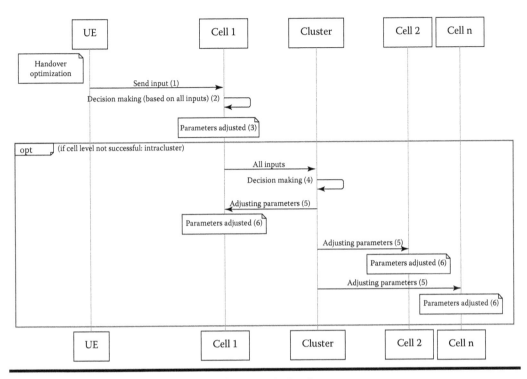

Figure 9.11   Sequence diagram for handover optimization.

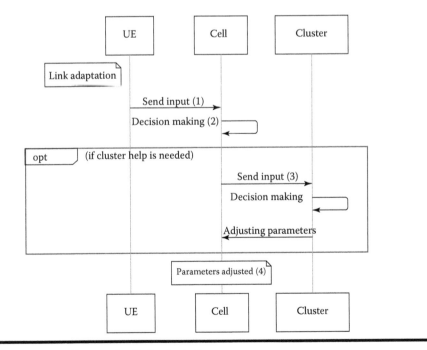

Figure 9.12   Sequence diagram for link adaptation.

Table 9.7 Control Parameters and Inputs for Link Adaptation

Inputs	Agents	Controlling Parameters	Agent
RSSI of received frames	UE	Threshold values	Cell
Application QoS deteriorates	UE	Transmission frequency	Cell
Deterioration of res. Utilization	Cell	Modulation and code rate	Cell
—	Cell	Scheduling weight	Cell
—	—	Resource reservation	Cell

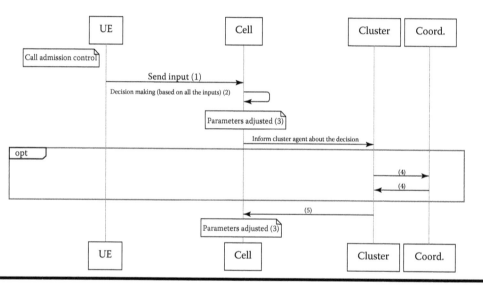

Figure 9.13 Sequence diagram for call admission control.

Table 9.8 Control Parameters and Inputs for Call Admission Control

Inputs	Agents	Controlling Parameters	Agent
Channel occupation rate	Cell	Threshold values	Cell
Requested QoS	UE	Contention window	Cell
Throughput metric	Cell	—	—
Call drop rate	Cell	—	—
L2 E2E delay	Cell	—	—
Relative occupied b/w	Cell	—	—
Uplink noise/load	Cell	—	—
Shared channel utilization	Cell	—	—

9.7.5 Inter-Agents Interaction for Load Balancing

In this section, we detail the interaction of proposed agents for attaining a load-balancing objective function with the aid of Figure 9.14 and Table 9.9.

9.7.6 Inter-Agents Interaction for Congestion Avoidance

In this section, we detail the interaction of proposed agents for attaining a congestion avoidance objective function with the aid of Figure 9.15 and Table 9.10.

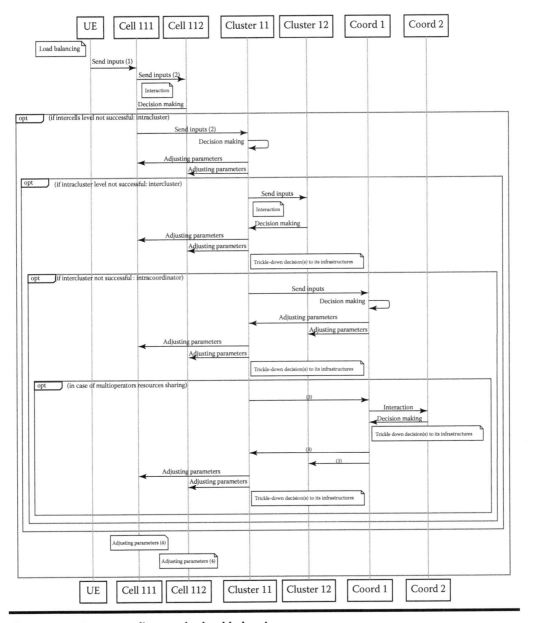

Figure 9.14 Sequence diagram for load balancing.

Table 9.9   Control Parameters and Inputs for Load Balancing

Inputs	Agents	Controlling Parameters	Agent
Packet loss rate	Cell/UE	Max. allowed load	Cell
Requested QoS	UE	Control coverage area	Cell
Link delay values	Cell	—	—
Congestion over shared channel	Cell	—	—
Uplink noise	Cell	—	—

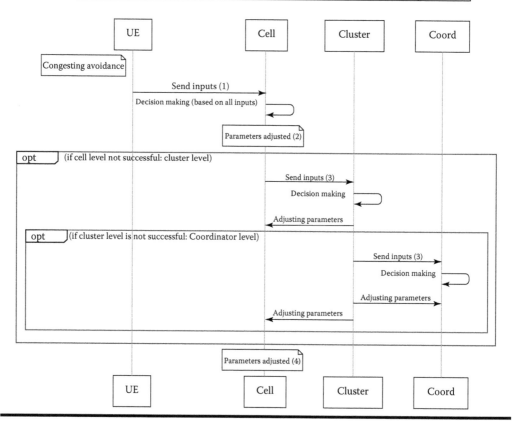

Figure 9.15   Sequence diagram for congestion avoidance.

9.8 Use Case: Operator's Policy for Mobile Users in Congested Area

As can be seen in Figure 9.8, in this use case, the global objective function is user satisfaction. Let us denote this by G. As it may be noticed, G in turn is translated into operators' revenue. Let us assume that the operator is to attain G in a geographical region, where the operator owns multiple heterogeneous wireless access technologies. Users within the area are mobile and their UE devices are equipped with multiple interfaces. Consider that the operator is faced with defining a policy for attaining G (which may be interpreted as a subdomain) in the mentioned geographical region for

Table 9.10   Control Parameters and Inputs for Congestion Avoidance

Inputs	Agents	Controlling Parameters	Agent
Packet loss rate	Cell	Adjust channel utilization	Cell
Requested QoS	UE	Step-size of load reduction	Cell
Link delay values	Cell	Prioritization of services	Cell
Congestion over shared channel	Cell	—	—

busy hours. One intuitive policy is what we show in Figure 9.8, in which G is translated into two levels of a local objective function. Let these levels be represented by $L_{x,y}$, where the index x represents the level and index y represents the number of local objective functions at any level. In this scenario:

$$G = L_{1,1}, L_{1,2} \qquad (9.3)$$

where:

$L_{1,1}$ represents the congestion avoidance
$L_{1,2}$ represents the handover optimization

The choice of such objective functions' translation is justified by the scenario description, that is, operators will aim at avoiding congestion and optimizing handovers with a view to maintaining the user-preferred service QoS perception. In Figure 9.9, one may observe a further decomposition of a first-level local objective function, that is, $L_{1,1} = L_{2,1}, L_{2,2}$, where $L_{2,1}$ represents the load balancing and $L_{2,2}$ represents the call admission control, or, to put it differently, congestion avoidance = (load balancing, call admission control). Such a decomposition of the first-level local objective function is justified by the fact that the local objective function (i.e., congestion avoidance) may be attained by implementing various approaches. The intuitive ones include load balancing/sharing over the available infrastructural resources and by implementing call admission control. This dictates that now the operation for attaining G is as follows:

$$G = \left(L_{2,1}, L_{2,2} \right), L_{1,2} \qquad (9.4)$$

One may further notice that it contains two components, where the first component represents the multiple local objectives of the second level and the later component represents the first-level local objective function. The elements of these components may have different priority levels, which are set by the operator preferences. For instance, an operator prioritizes the load balancing more than handover optimization whereas call admission control has the least priority in the considered scenario. Operator priorities over various local objective functions are defined by the weights associated with each local objective function. This further provides a clear relationship between local objective functions. In the perspective of this work, we propose the objective functions' relationship as a weighted sum approach, where the coefficient of each local objective function is the associated weight to the local objective function.

$$G = w_1 \left(t, \psi, \rho, l, \omega \right) L_{2,1} + w_2 \left(t, \psi, \rho, l, \omega \right) L_{2,2} + w_3 \left(t, \psi, \rho, l, \omega \right) L_{1,2} \qquad (9.5)$$

such that

$$w_1\left(t,\psi,\rho,l,\omega\right)+w_2\left(t,\psi,\rho,l,\omega\right)+w_3\left(t,\psi,\rho,l,\omega\right)=1 \qquad (9.6)$$

As can be seen, $w_1(t,\psi,\rho,l,\omega)$ is the function of time t, geographical location l, operator preference profile ψ, access network technology ω, and dynamic network status ρ. This would mean that the priority of the objective function varies in the mentioned parameters, that is, for the considered geographical region, the operator's policies may vary in time. The values of the associated weights may be computed by using various approaches including analytical hierarchy process (AHP), gray relational analysis (GRA), and so on.

9.8.1 Trigger Generation for Considered Use Case

As explained, the decision instances are initialized by the trigger mechanism and follow the operator preferences, that is, each input for the triggering mechanism is weighted according to operator policies. The triggering mechanism of any decision instance may receive multiple inputs belonging to single or multiple objective functions. In the case given in Section 9.8, the decision of generating a trigger is straightforward, that is, when the value of any input crosses the predefined threshold value, the decision mechanism is triggered. When it comes to a triggering mechanism, these are fed with inputs for multiple objective functions, in this case, each input of the particular local objective function. To illustrate this, let us consider Figure 9.16 for this scenario. As can be seen, there are two decision instances residing at cellular and cluster levels, thus two triggering mechanisms. These triggering mechanisms are fed with inputs from four hierarchical levels, namely UE, cell, cluster, and coordinator agent levels. The measurement inputs for different local objectives may be the same or different. We summarize such inputs for the considered scenario in Table 9.11 for the heterogeneous wireless network domain. We also know that each decision instance controls

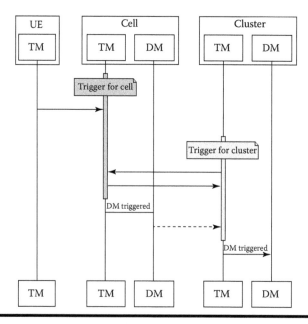

Figure 9.16 Sequence diagram showing the triggering and decision mechanism concept.

Table 9.11 Explanation of Measurements and Controlling Parameters for the Considered Scenario

Local OF	Wt	Measurement	Point of Presence	Controlling Parameters
Load balancing	0.5	Number of users per cell	Cell	1. Maximum allowed load 2. Cell coverage area 3. Interface selection
		Packet loss rate	E2E	
		Requested QoE deteriorates	UE	
		Delay	Cell, Cluster	
		Congestion over shared channel	UE	
		Technology preferences	Coordinator	
Handover optimization	0.3	Call dropping rate	Cell	1. Maximum allowed load 2. Cell coverage area, 3. HO neighboring list 4. Hysteresis parameters 5. Interface selection
		Number of users per cell	Cell	
		SINR/RSSI	UE	
		Available capacity	Cell	
		Technology preference	Coordinator	
CAC	0.2	User preference change	UE	1. Threshold value 2. Congestion threshold 3. Interface selection
		Channel occupation rate	Cell	
		Throughput metric	UE, Cell	
		Delay	E2E	
		Technology preferences	Coordinator	

various controlling parameter(s). Such decision instances within the decision maker may be triggered by the measurement of a single local objective function/multiple objective functions. In this case, it is triggered by a multiple objective function and it may result in a cooperative or conflicting situation. By *cooperative*, we mean the situations where adapting the controlling parameter has the same effect on all of the involved objective functions, whereas the conflicting situation is the converse to being cooperative, that is, an objective function may require adapting the controlling parameter differently than that of the other local objective functions. In both of the mentioned situations, the weight associated with measurements turns out to be the deciding factor for resolving the conflicts. The conflict resolution is basically carried out by prioritizing the objective functions (Figure 9.17).

9.8.2 Inter-Entities Interaction for Considered Use-Case

It should be noted that the trigger for any local objective function may arrive at anytime. In the following, we discuss the interaction among proposed cognitive agents for the considered use case

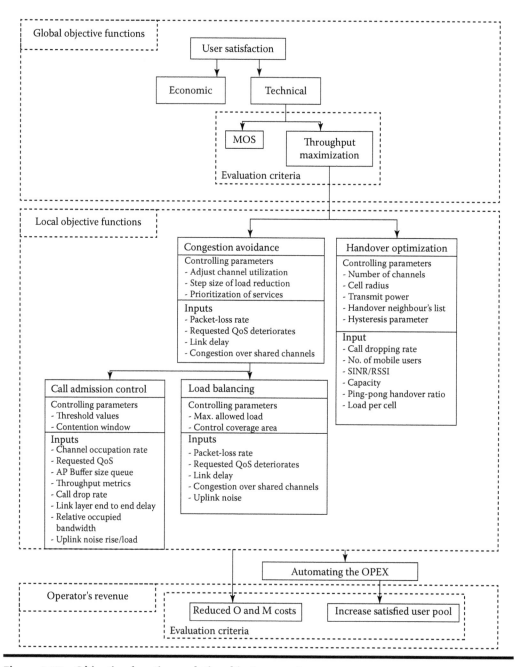

Figure 9.17   Objective functions relationship (use case).

scenario. Assume that the operator defines the policy. Assume that the parameter values of the weight computation function results in the following weight values for the local objective functions: load-balancing = 0.5, handover optimization = 0.3, and call admission control = 0.2.

Based on Table 9.11, we have the controlling parameters given in the last column of the table, which may add to attaining the overall global objective function. In Table 9.12, we arrange the controlling parameters in descending order.

Values of different controlling functions impact different local objective functions differently. One may interpret the global objective function as the following controlling functions:

$$G = w_1\left(t,\psi,\rho,l,\omega\right)\left(C_1 + C_2 + C_3\right) + w_2\left(t,\psi,\rho,l,\omega\right)C_4 + w_3\left(t,\psi,\rho,l,\omega\right)\left(C_5 + C_6\right) \qquad (9.7)$$

9.9 Concluding Remarks

In this chapter, a self-x network management framework is discussed. An IP-based, simplified (flat) core, network-based hierarchical architecture is proposed that includes different components, intelligent agents, their functionalities, and their interactions in different configurations (e.g., mobility management, call admission, link adaption, etc.). A detailed discussion on the translation of objective functions that assist in realizing self-x network management and dynamic policy formulation, is provided. In Table 9.13, we summarize the main outcomes of the proposed framework.

Table 9.12   Prioritized List of Controlling Parameters

Controlling Parameters	Priority	Associated Weights
Max. allowed load	1	0.8
Interface selection	1	0.8
Coverage area definition	1	0.8
Congestion threshold value	2	0.7
Neighboring list	3	0.2
Hysteresis	3	0.2

Table 9.13   Summary of the Proposed Components of the Self-X Network Management

Dimension	Proposed Component	Proposed Approach
End-to-end approach	Distributed control mechanism	Self-adapting control and management processes by enabling the use of various learning and bargaining approaches.
	Environment perception and measurements	Applied concrete measurement methodologies to heterogeneous wireless networks including emerging technologies.
	Knowledge modeling and exploitation	Adapt Self-NET-based approach for a knowledge life cycle. This work aims at making use of knowledge management for conflict management by introducing the learning-based ontology approaches.
Hands on approach	Implementation of all ideas on demonstrator	
	Agile combination of theoretical and physical research	

References

1. Barth, U., and Kuehn, E., Self-organization in 4G mobile networks: Motivation and vision, *Wireless Communication Systems (ISWCS), 2010 7th International Symposium*, pp. 731–735, 2010.
2. Gaiti, D., Pujolle, G., Al-Shaer, E., Calvert, K., Doboson, S., Leduc, G., and Martikainen, O., editors, *Autonomic Networking, First International IFIP TC6 Conference (AN 2006)*, Paris, pp. 27–29 September, Springer.
3. IBM. (2001). Autonomic manifesto. www.research.ibm.com/autonomic/manifesto.
4. Balamuralidhar, P., and Prasad, R., A context driven architecture for cognitive radio nodes. *Wireless Personal Communications*, Vol. 45, No. 3, pp. 423–434, 2008.
5. Thomas, R. W., DaSilva, L. A., and MacKenzie, A. B., Cognitive networks, *First IEEE International Symposium on New Frontiers in Dynamic Spectrum Access Networks, 2005*, pp. 352–360, 2005.
6. Luck, M., McBurney, P., and O.S.S.W., *Agent Technology, Computing as Interaction: A Roadmap for Agent-Based Computing*. University of Southampton Department of Electronics & Computer Science; illustrated edition, September 2005.
7. Strassner, J., OFoghlu, M., Donnelly, W., and Agoulmine, N., Beyond the knowledge plane: An inference plane to support the next generation Internet, *Global Information Infrastructure Symposium, 2007. GIIS 2007*. First International, pp. 112–119, 2007.
8. Johnsson, M., Jennings, B., and Botvich, D., Inherently self-managed networks: Requirements, properties and an initial model, *Integrated Network Management (IM), 2011 IFIP/IEEE International Symposium*, pp. 1200–1207, 2011.
9. Schmitz, C., *Self-Organized Collaborative Knowledge Management*, Kassel, University Press GmbH, 2007.
10. John Strassner, N., and Agoulmine, E. L., Focale: A novel autonomic networking architecture, Latin American Autonomic Computing Symposium (LAACS), Campo Grande, Mato Grosso, Brazil, 2006.
11. Agoulmine, N., editor, *Autonomic Network Management Principles from Concepts to Applications*, Burlington, MA: Academic Press, 2011.
12. Jennings, B., van der Meer, S., Balasubramaniam, S., Botvich, D., O Foghlu, M., Donnelly, W., and Strassner, J., Towards autonomic management of communications networks, *Communications Magazine, IEEE*, Vol. 45 No. 10, pp. 112–121, 2007.
13. Raymer, D., Meer, S. v. d., and Strassner, J., From autonomic computing to autonomic networking: An architectural perspective, *Engineering of Autonomic and Autonomous Systems, 2008. EASE 2008. Fifth IEEE Workshop*, IEEE Computer Society, pp. 174–183, 2008.
14. Self-net EU Project.
15. Self-net deliverable 2.3, Final report on self-aware network management artefacts.
16. Socrates EU FP7 project homepage: http://www.fp7-socrates.org/.
17. Socrates Project, D2.1: Use cases for self-organizing networks. http://www.fp7-socrates.eu/files/Deliverables/SOCRATES_D2.1%20Use%20cases%20for%20self-organising%20networks.pdf
18. Socrates Project, D2.4: Framework for the development of self-organization methods. http://www.fp7-socrates.eu/files/Deliverables/SOCRATES_D2.4%20Framework%20for%20self-organising%20networks.pdf.
19. Socrates Project, D2.5: Review of use cases and framework. http://www.fp7-socrates.eu/files/Deliverables/SOCRATES_D2.5%20Review%20of%20use%20cases%20and%20framework%20(Public%20version).pdf.
20. Socrates Project, D2.6: review of use cases and framework ii. http://www.fp7-socrates.eu/files/Deliverables/SOCRATES_D2.6%20Review%20of%20use%20cases%20and%20framework%20II.pdf.
21. End-to-end efficiency (e3), eu fp7 project, https://ict-e3.eu/. http://www.fp7-socrates.eu/files/Workshop1/SOCRATES%20workshop%20Santander_Wolfgang%20Konig.pdf.
22. E3. Project approach. In www.ict-e3.eu/project/approach/approach.html. http://cordis.europa.eu/pub/fp7/ict/docs/future-networks/projects-e3-factsheet_en.pdf.
23. E3, P., D2.3: Architecture, information model and reference points, assessment framework, platform independent programmable interfaces, deliverable.

24. EFIPSANS, EU FP7 project, http://www.efipsans.org/.
25. Chaparadza, R. EFIPSANS: Spirit and vision. http://secan-lab.uni.lu/efipsans-web/images/stories/EFIPSANS%20Spirit%20and%20Vision.pdf.
26. Gavalas, D., Greenwood, D., Ghanbari, M., and O'Mahony, M., An infrastructure for distributed and dynamic network management based on mobile agent technology, *Communications, 1999, ICC '99, 1999 IEEE International Conference*, Elsevier, Vol. 2, pp. 1362–1366, 1999.
27. Nicklisch, J., Quittek, J., Kind, A., and Arao, S., Inca: An agent-based network control architecture, the *2nd International Workshop on Intelligent Agents for Telecommunication Applications (IATA'98)*, LNCS, Proceedings, pp. 143–155. Springer, 1998.
28. Nagata, T., and Sasaki, H., A multi-agent approach to power system restoration, *Power Systems, IEEE Transactions on*, Vol. 17 No. 2, pp. 457–462, 2002.
29. Chavez, A., Moukas, R., and Maes, P., A multi-agent system for distributed resource allocation, *Proceedings of the First International Conference on Autonomous Agents, Challenger: A Multi-agent System for Distributed Resource Allocation*, ACM Press, pp. 323–331, 1997.
30. Cao, J., Jarvis, S. A., Saini, S., Kerbyson, D. J., and Nudd, G. R., ARMS: An agent-based resource management system for grid computing, *Scientific Programming*, Vol. 10, No. 2, pp. 135–148, 2002.
31. Lee, G., Faratin, P., Bauer, S., and Wroclawski, J., A user-guided cognitive agent for network service selection in pervasive computing environments, Pervasive Computing and Communications, 2004, PerCom 2004, *Proceedings of the Second IEEE Annual Conference*, pp. 219–228, 2004.
32. Nguengang, G., Bullot, T., Gaiti, D., Hugues, L., and Pujolle, G., Advanced autonomic networking and communication, chapter autonomic resource regulation, *IP Military Networks: A Situatedness Based Knowledge Plane*, pp. 81–100, Birkhäuser Basel, Basel, 2008.
33. Xie, J., Howitt, I., and Raja, A., Cognitive radio resource management using multi-agent systems, *Consumer Communications and Networking Conference, 2007, CCNC 2007, 4th IEEE*, pp. 1123–1127, 2007.
34. Bo, L., Junzhou, L., and Wei, L. Multi-agent based network management task decomposition and scheduling, *2013, IEEE 27th International Conference on Advanced Information Networking and Applications (AINA)*, pp. 41–46, 2005.
35. Liu, B., Li, W., and Luo, J., Agent cooperation in multi-agent based network management, *Computer Supported Cooperative Work in Design, 2004, The 8th International Conference on, Proceedings*, Vol. 2, pp. 283–287, 2004.
36. Galindo-Serrano, A. and Giupponi, L., Aggregated interference control for cognitive radio networks based on multi-agent learning, *Cognitive Radio Oriented Wireless Networks and Communications, 2009, CROWNCOM '09, 4th International Conference on*, pp. 1–6, 2009.
37. JIAC, Java-based intelligent agent componentware, DAI Labor, Technical University Berlin, Germany, http://www.jiac.de/, 2014.
38. Sesseler, R., Keiblinger, A., and Varone, N., Software agent technology in mobile service environments, Workshop on M-Services at the 13th International Symposium on Methodologies for Intelligent Systems (ISMIS), 2002.
39. Khan, M. A., Toker, A. C., Troung, C., Sivrikaya, F., and Albayrak, S., Cooperative game theoretic approach to integrated bandwidth sharing and allocation, IEEE, 2010.
40. Manzoor Ahmed Khan, U. T., User utility function as QOE, 10th International Conference on Networks, ICN 2011, St. Maarten, the Netherlands Antilles, 2011.

Chapter 10

Distributed Data Aggregation and Compression and Compression for 5G Virtual RAN IoT Sensor Applications

Nikos Deligiannis and Spyridon Louvros

Contents

10.1 Introduction*

The Internet of things (IoT) and the technology around machine-to-machine (M2M) communications [1] are seeing fast adoption, with growth taking place at a breathtaking pace, from two billion objects connected to the Internet in 2006 to a projected 50 billion by 2020. The main goal is the seamless wireless (or wired) connection of a massive amount of smart devices through unique schemes such that they cover a wide range of applications, like smart cities, smart health, smart monitoring, and smart mobility. Smart cities, for example, is an urban development vision to integrate and leverage multiple information and communication technology solutions in a secure fashion to manage city assets, such as local departments' information systems, transportation systems, hospitals, water supply networks, waste management, and law enforcement. The main goal is to drive competitiveness, sustainability, economic growth, energy efficiency, and to improve citizens' healthcare and, in general, their quality of life. The successful deployment of smart cities calls for a unified ICT infrastructure to support the heterogeneous set of applications for urban development. The great majority of these devices used the standard wireless sensor and actuator networking (WSAN) technology based on IEEE 802.15.4. However, IoT-based applications require the adoption of more advanced communication technologies, such as 4G/long-term evolution (LTE), which are capable of providing services of higher quality.

10.1.1 Background and Motivation

This recent thrust toward machine-to-machine (M2M) communications [2,3] and the integration of wireless sensor networks with the generic Internet infrastructure via IPv6 over low-power wireless personal area networks' (6LoWPAN) support at the network layer [4,5] call for the development of new data sensing and aggregation mechanisms that increase the efficiency of such networks. Especially in the latest cloud and virtual RAN architectural forms of 5G technology, such mechanisms will be the motivation for enhanced capacity improvements with green energy policies.

Cloud radio access networking (cloud-RAN) can provide significant assets to the IoT since it can optimize the spectrum access for multiple heterogeneous devices, prioritizing access to network resources according to the service request in both a centralized and a distributed manner. Signaling between devices that use different communication technologies is decreased and their information exchange is accelerated through the local remote unit. Furthermore, cloud-RAN

---

* Parts of this work have been published in [42,56,65,68]. N. Deligiannis' research is supported by the VUB Strategic Research Programme M3D2.

architecture can significantly reduce excessive hardware costs, since they only require centralized management and operation, while the installation of new remote units can be done with a simple SDR device and the required software. Finally, with the advent of 5G connectivity as a basic technological pillar for the IoT [6], cloud-RAN could efficiently integrate the heterogeneity of the involved devices and their efficient coexistence, since it can easily be integrated with existing IoT middleware platforms, playing the role of communication manager.

Wireless sensor networks (WSNs) operate under austere constraints in terms of energy resources, computational capabilities, and available bandwidth [7]. Many WSN applications (e.g., temperature or humidity monitoring, wireless visual sensors) involve a high density of sensors within specific radio environments, thereby sensors' readings are highly correlated. In order to minimize the amount of information transmitted by the sensors (saving 5G network capacity), this redundancy needs to be removed by efficient data compression mechanisms that have low computational demands. In addition, as information is sent over error-prone wireless channels (i.e., LTE, LTE-advanced [LTE-A], and 5G), effective data protection mechanisms are required to provide reliable communication.

In this setting, distributed source coding (DSC) is considered a key technology for WSNs [8]. DSC is rooted in the information-theoretic results by Slepian and Wolf [9]—on lossless compression of correlated sources—and by Wyner and Ziv [10]—on lossy compression with side information at the decoder. The multiterminal source coding theory [11] extended these results to an arbitrary number of correlated sources [12]. DSC designs [8,13,14] exploit the correlation among the sensors' readings at the decoder, that is, the base station or sink node. In this way, efficient compression is obtained by shifting the complexity to energy-robust nodes and keeping the sensors' computational and energy demands to a minimum. In addition, energy expensive data exchange between sensors is avoided. Moreover, as Slepian–Wolf coding is realized by channel codes (e.g., Turbo [15], low-density parity-check [16], or Raptor [17] codes), distributed joint source-channel coding (DJSCC) [18] designs offer resilience against communication channel errors [18]. Hence, it is recognized [8,19,20] that, in correlated data gathering by energy-constrained WSNs, DSC schemes have distinct advantages over predictive coding systems that apply complex adaptive prediction and entropy coding at the encoder.

10.1.2 Contributions

This chapter focuses on the problem of efficiently aggregating data collected by heterogeneous sensor devices on the cloud-RAN (C-RAN). We review the background in C-RAN architecture and propose a new scheme that combines wireless sensor networks with the C-RAN cloud. The novel contribution of the work stems from the proposal of several coding schemes that are suitable for (1) allowing for low-complexity operations at the sensors, while still (2) achieving high-compression performance and (3) offering robustness against errors in the transmission channel. We evaluate the proposed approaches in two different application domains: (1) the collection of temperature measurements from distributed sensors and (2) privacy-preserving monitoring via low-resolution visual sensors. The proposed coding approaches are based on the theory of DSC; in this context, this chapter offers an additional fundamental contribution. In particular, we study the problem of Wyner–Ziv coding and manage to extend the no-rate-loss property to the case where the source and the side information are binary and the dependency is given by a Z-channel.

10.1.3 Chapter Outline

Regarding the remainder of the chapter: Section 10.2 overviews the cloud-RAN architectural details and provides a short historical flashback. Section 10.3 entails the proposed solution for the coupling of a centralized C-RAN architecture with a wireless sensor network, whereas Section 10.4 describes the fundamentals behind distributed compression and presents a novel information-theoretic result in the domain. Sections 10.5 and 10.6 present our distributed data compression and transmission solutions for the temperature-measuring sensors and visual sensors, respectively. Finally, Section 10.6 draws the conclusions of the chapter.

10.2 Background on Cloud-RAN

10.2.1 Historical Note on Industrial Developments

C-RAN (i.e., cloud-RAN) or V-RAN (i.e., virtual RAN) is lately considered to be a rational combination of enhanced radio technologies with IoT over cloud computing–based cellular network architecture [1,21]. The technology is a good candidate for future 5G mobile network infrastructures and it is fully backward compatible with all existing cellular evolutions in the global system for mobile communications/general packet radio service (GSM/GPRS), wideband code division multiple access/high-speed packet analysis (WCDMA/HSPA), and LTE [22]. While preparing their network infrastructure for future 5G deployment, operators have currently proposed C-RAN implementations over existing 3G and 4G topologies to mitigate the expected cost investment. This is because 4G networks become mature in terms of their services and capacity, pushing for more investments and network expansions. Indeed there are many challenges nowadays for operator networks according to [23].

C-RAN history goes back to 2010, when it was introduced in public for the first time by the China Mobile Research Institute at the 1st C-RAN International Workshop, Beijing, China on 21 April 2010. Since then, ZTE, IBM, Huawei, and Intel have initially signed a memorandum of understanding (MoU) for multilateral collaboration and research to develop and implement this new technology. Later on (in December 2010), during the 4th International Mobile Internet Conference, more telecom players joined that common effort, like Orange, Ericsson, Nokia Siemens Networks, and Alcatel–Lucent. What was missing yet was a proof of the concept since all of the ideas were only on paper and not in the firmware. In the 40th ITU Telecom Exhibition, China Mobile, together with its partners (ZTE, Huawei, IBM, Orange Labs Beijing, and Beijing University of Posts and Telecommunications), presented four different C-RAN systems based on open and proprietary platforms. In April 2011, the Next Generation Mobile Network Alliance (NGMN) established a working group called the *Project Centralised RAN* (P-CRAN) to further study and propose requirements and standards for C-RAN solution. Since then, several conferences, meetings, and standardization congresses have accommodated C-RAN modules and sessions resulting in open-platform solutions, which are based on ARM and ASOCS technology.

10.2.2 Overview of the C-RAN Architecture

Dominant market mobile technology vendors (Ericsson, Nokia, Huawei) in late 2010s made an effort and pushed the International Telecommunication Union (ITU) and 3rd Generation Partnership Project (3GPP) to include new forms of distributed firmware base station (DBS) architecture in the standards. In this new architecture, the radio base station unit (RRU) was separated from the main cabinet digital processing baseband unit (BBU). The RRU was mounted on top of the antenna tower back-to-back with the antenna, reducing the radiofrequency (RF) feeder losses for outdoor applications, see Figure 10.1.

Fiber-optic links provide much more flexibility to the network/transmission as well as superior cost-effective deployments exploiting existing urban area infrastructures for distances of up to a

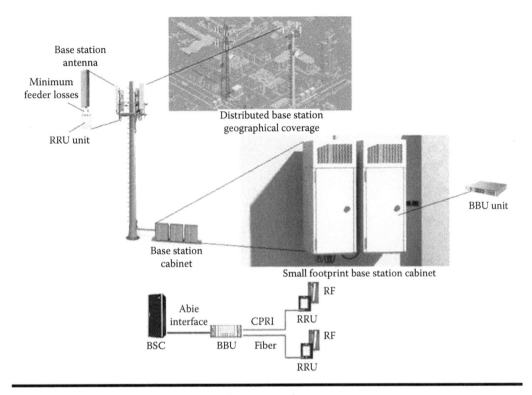

Figure 10.1 Distributed base station solution: Outdoor coverage.

few kilometers using single mode long-range fiber-optic cables with dense wavelength division multiplexing (DWDM) technologies. Another deployment solution is the indoor scenario where RRU was enclosed into the same box with a low-transmission power antenna and mounted into corridors, floors, or ceilings and harmonized with indoor building architectures. BBU units can be installed in the basements of buildings and connected with short-range fiber links (plastic optical fibers, or POF) with the RRUs, we refer toFigure 10.2.

Cloud-RAN is the next-evolution step, ahead of DBS, based on existing ideas of RRU and BBU. It is, however, introducing advanced technologies over radio, moving processing load functions to cell-edge devices (mobile edge computing solutions), and exploiting optical network technology for RAN transmission and backhaul network topology [24], a solution known as a *C-RAN partial centralized solution*, see Figure 10.3.

Regarding the radio enhancements, RRUs are no longer just simple radio amplifiers with a combiner/filter but become more sophisticated and intelligent, introducing a data compression function to lessen the transport network capacity, fast Fourier transform/inverse fast Fourier transform (FFT/IFFT) functions for orthogonal frequency division multiplexing-based (OFDM-based) radio interface networks (LTE-A) to lessen the load on BBUs, as well as interference coordination functions [23]. However, the most important aspect is the remote radio head (RRH) unit that together with the RRU provides more intelligent and flexible antenna solutions for beamforming and multiple-input multiple-output (MIMO) capabilities. On the other hand, the RRH/RRU and the BBU are interconnected over fiber technologies, based on the latest common public radio interference (CPRI) standards, with low-cost coarse wavelength division multiplexing/dense wavelength division multiplexing (CWDM/DWDM) optical networking achieving large-scale

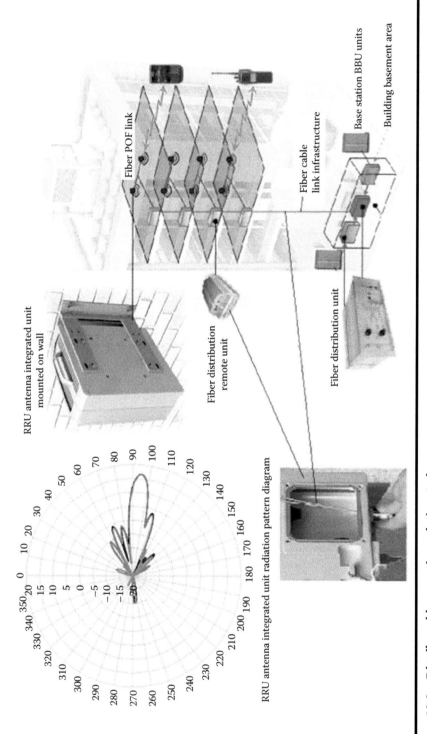

Figure 10.2   Distributed base station solution: Indoor coverage.

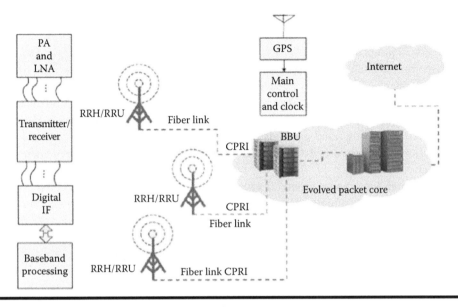

Figure 10.3 Partially centralized C-RAN implementation.

centralized base station deployment with an emphasis on capital expenditure/operational expenditure (CAPEX/OPEX) optimization, see Figure 10.3. The BBU technology is based on the latest IT and blade-server technologies that use real-time virtualization cloud computing with shared and redundant computing resources over the cloud.

There are many different proposals in the international literature for network architectural deployments. The architectural deployment depends on the application, network topology, and existing mobile network infrastructure. If someone would like to categorize the different architectural deployments, three of them (according to the authors' opinion) are going to be the most dominant in the market. The first is known as a *typical centralized deployment over a large scale*, where a large number of remote RRHs/RRUs are deployed over a large geographical area and are all connected through fiber links to a centralized pool BBU on cloud server. Typical ranges are 15–20 km over fiber links for LTE-A solutions, 30–40 km for 3G, and 60–80 km for 2G. This is a very good solution for dense and heterogeneous multilayer networks, reducing cost deployments for both indoor and outdoor layers. A different architecture is known as *collaborative radio technologies support*, where different pooled BBUs over the cloud are allowed to interconnect with each other using Gbps links in order to improve mobility and scalability scenarios. Finally, the latest proposal is known as *real-time virtualization*, where RRUs and BBUs are not provided from the same vendor; furthermore, the BBU is based on an open platform over the cloud.

10.3 Proposed Solution: Combining Centralized C-RAN with WSNs

Choosing a network architecture that allows for the efficient and secure interworking of a large number of heterogeneous devices is a challenging research topic. This is because all of the differences between the various communication technologies and protocols, in terms of their carrier frequency, bandwidth, modulation and coding schemes, packet structures, and packet sizes. A simple example is the following: A smartphone with 3G access can only exchange information with sensor devices (that communicate based on the ZigBee protocol) via a third device that translates all the necessary protocols and sends back the sensed data. In urban environments, the excessive radio intercommunication generated by a huge amount of sensing devices can severely impact the network performance. This is even more serious if we consider that (a) the industrial, scientific, and medical (ISM) radio bands are already affected by interference from sources other than wireless networks; and (b) WSANs are very susceptible to other wireless transmissions. Hence, a key challenge refers to finding novel methods for the compression, aggregation, and prioritization of the information sent by the IoT devices, which are also robust to transmission errors due to collisions or interference.

In this chapter, we propose an architecture that marries the benefits of wireless sensor networks and mobile cloud computing. In contrast to existing work on the topic—see for example [25]—our system is based on (1) a centralized C-RAN approach for the cloud and (2) a novel distributed data compression and aggregation framework that builds on the theory of DSC.

A reliable architecture for connecting heterogeneous IoT networks can be realized by integrating the benefits of cognitive radio [26] and cloud-RAN [1,21] frameworks. The cloud-RAN architecture comprises the following:

- A cloud with centralized server units that manage base station resources
- The distributed radio units that are located at remote sites
- Radio links between the centralized unit and the remote sites with high bandwidth and low latency

Compared with standard forms of C-RAN architecture proposed for LTE, this architecture makes use of radio units at remote sites that are capable of handling the simultaneous connections of various communication technologies. Hence, the costs of installing multiple units for each communication technology are avoided, since only one radio unit has to be installed at each site. Also, the network management decisions (i.e., spectrum assignment, routing, scheduling, etc.) can be made either locally at each radio unit (when they are related to users on each cell) or centrally by the centralized server units (when interaction with the neighbor cells is required, or for optimizing local decisions). Radio units are reprogrammable and, hence, any updates regarding the communication protocols, installation of additional technologies, or implementation of new networking standards, can be done easily, thereby saving significant hardware costs. More importantly, since SDR can simultaneously handle different communication technologies, such as IEEE 802.11, 3G, 4G/LTE, or IEEE 802.15.4, the remote units act as different virtual base stations (VBS) [22].

The cloud has a number of centralized server units that are able to perform an optimized management of the available network resources since it has a global view of the available resources at each radio unit. It can easily apply runtime resource reconfiguration to balance potential unit overloads or to change frequency bands in case of increased interference. Also, the architecture can easily adapt to nonuniform traffic via the load-balancing capability of the distributed pool of base stations. This pool can share the signaling, traffic, and channel occupancy information of the active users in order to optimize the radio resource management decisions. Spectral efficiency is improved via the cognitive radio mechanisms for the intelligent management of spectrum resources that can be applied to the SRUs together with joint processing and scheduling.

We therefore adhere to a real-time virtualization solution and we consider a C-RAN *fully centralized approach* where baseband signal processing units are implemented on a pooled BBU according to Figure 10.4. This approach provides superior flexibility to operators selecting different

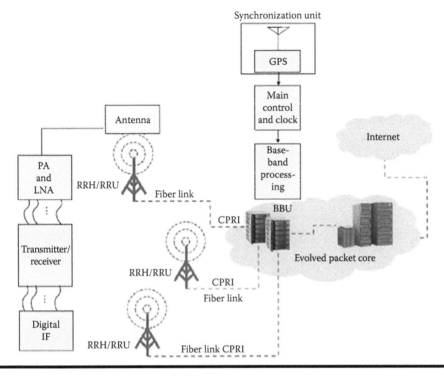

Figure 10.4 Fully centralized C-RAN implementation for real-time virtualization.

vendors for baseband and radio deployments and load balancing on the BBU cloud server is possible with different configurations among 2G, 3G, LTE, LTE-A, and different vendor providers per day. However, the major drawback is the expected high data volume between RRH/RRU and BBU over the fiber links.

Following the C-RAN fully centralized approach, sensor networks in a fully deployed 5G indoor application level could be organized into groups of neighboring sensor nodes called *clusters*. Each cluster comprises an elected coordinator called a *cluster head* (CH) and the peripheral nodes (see Figure 10.5).

Peripheral nodes measure diverse data such as temperature or visual data, apply compression and error protection mechanisms, and transmit the resulting data packets to the base station via their corresponding CH. The latter are group coordinators that organize data transfer, sleeping periods, and data aggregation within each group, as well as convey the encoded data to the base station. In addition, each CH measures and transmits its own data. Each peripheral node has the processing capacity needed to become a CH. To prevent CH battery depletion, the CH changes periodically based on energy criteria [27]. When the residual energy of the CH turns low, another CH is elected among the peripheral nodes. In this way, energy consumption is balanced within the cluster and the network lifetime increases [27]. The cluster formation abides by well-known cluster tree solutions for IEEE 802.15.4-based media access control (MAC) protocols in WSNs, for example, the IEEE 802.15.4 GTS [28]. Alternatively, we can consider more recent solutions for the MAC, which apply decentralized multichannel coordination—they apply cross-channel synchronization and intrachannel desynchronization by means of pulse-coupled oscillators [29,30].

The IEEE 802.15.4 router (sink) will collect all sensor data and will forward them to the outdoor LTE unit, which will forward them to the LTE RRU and then to the cloud-RAN (blade-server approach) for further data analysis, see Figure 10.5.

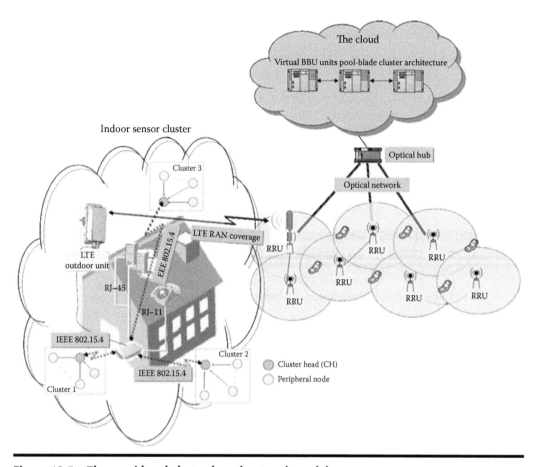

Figure 10.5   The considered cluster-based network model.

The wireless sensor devices have limited computational resources and operate under limitations in terms of energy budget; they are typically battery powered and/or they can be equipped with an energy-harvesting module [7]. Furthermore, the wireless links for the sensors to the network backbone as well as the backbone itself adhere to constraints in terms of bandwidth. The problem becomes more evident when considering that the number of nodes is high (according to the IoT vision) and that the data rates of the applications become higher (e.g., we refer to visual sensor network applications). Many WSN applications (e.g., temperature or humidity monitoring, or wireless visual sensors) involve a high density of sensors within specific radio environments; therefore, the sensors' readings are highly correlated. In order to minimize the amount of information transmitted by the sensors (saving 5G network capacity), this redundancy needs to be removed by efficient data compression mechanisms that have low computational demands. In addition, as information is sent over error-prone wireless channels (i.e., LTE, LTE-A, and 5G), effective data protection mechanisms are required to provide reliable communication.

In what follows, we first present the fundamentals of distributed compression and we propose a new theoretical result with a profound impact in this framework. Then, we present two application scenarios for our framework: (1) a distributed joint source–channel coding system for collecting temperature data and (2) a low-cost distributed video coding system for visual sensor networks.

10.4 Distributed Source Coding Fundamentals and New Results

The theory of DSC originates from two landmark information theory papers: the first [9] by Slepian and Wolf in 1973, and the second [10] by Wyner and Ziv in 1976.

10.4.1 Slepian–Wolf Coding

Consider the compression of two correlated, discrete, i.i.d. random sources X and Y. In traditional (predictive) coding, both the encoder and the decoder have access to the statistical dependencies between the sources. According to Shannon's source coding theory [31], the achievable lower rate bound for lossless compression is given by the joint entropy, $H(X,Y)$. Adhering to an unorthodox coding perspective, a distributed coding scenario considers the sources to be independently encoded and jointly decoded, exploiting the intersource correlation at the decoder side.

Figure 10.6 illustrates the concept, in which sources X and Y are encoded by separate encoders at rate R_X and R_Y, respectively, but jointly decoded by a set of linked decoders, producing the reconstructed signals $\hat{X}$ and $\hat{Y}$. The DSC scenario was first studied by Slepian and Wolf [9].

When the compression is lossless, the achievable rate region for decoding X and Y with an arbitrarily small error probability is given by the Slepian–Wolf theorem [9]:

$$R_X \geq H(X \mid Y)$$
$$R_Y \geq H(Y \mid X)$$
$$R_X + R_Y \geq H(X,Y)$$

(10.1)

where $H(X|Y)$ is the conditional entropy of X given Y and $H(Y|X)$ is the conditional entropy of Y given X. The inequalities in Equation 10.1 reveal that even when correlated sources are coded independently, a total rate equal to the joint entropy suffices to achieve lossless compression. Hence, according to information theory, the lossless distributed encoding of i.i.d-correlated sources does not have any compression efficiency loss compared with joint encoding. It is important to point out that Slepian and Wolf [9] proved the achievability of their distributed compression scheme for independently and identically distributed (i.i.d) correlated sources. However, their result has been extended to any arbitrary correlated sources that satisfy the asymptotic equipartition property, for example, the case of any jointly ergodic source [12].

Functional Slepian–Wolf coding is based on algebraic binning [32] constructed using channel coding. Two principal directions for realizing an algebraic binning approach have been reported

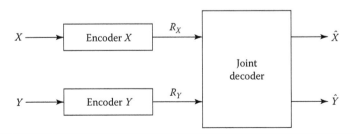

Figure 10.6   Distributed compression of two correlated, i.i.d., discrete random sequences, X and Y.

in the literature. The first method consists of a syndrome-based scheme, rooted in the landmark paper of Wyner [33]. The second method is known as the *parity-based scheme*.

10.4.1.1 Syndrome Approach

In [33], Wyner partitioned the source alphabet into disjoint sets, similar to the cosets of a linear channel code tailored to a particular correlation model, compressing the source into syndromes. Specifically, assume that we have binary sources X and Y and a correlation noise N given by N $\sim B(p_c)$. Namely, the correlation channel is the binary symmetric channel (BSC) with crossover probability p_c. The probability mass function (pmf) of the BSC is given by

$$p(x\,|\,y) = \begin{cases} (1 - p_c)\delta(x) + p_c\delta(x-1), & y = 0 \\ p_c\delta(x) + (1 - p_c)\delta(x-1), & y = 1 \end{cases} \tag{10.2}$$

where $\delta(x)$ is the Dirac delta function.

To compress the binary *n-tuple* $\mathbf{x}$, the Wyner's syndrome–based encoder employs an (n,k) linear channel code C constructed by the generator matrix $\mathbf{G}_{k \times n} = [\mathbf{I}_k | \mathbf{P}_{k \times (n-k)}],^*$ where $\mathbf{I}$ and $\mathbf{P}$ represent the unit and the parity matrix, respectively. The corresponding $(n-k) \times n$ parity-check matrix of C is $\mathbf{H}_{(n-k) \times n} = \left[\mathbf{P}^T_{k \times (n-k)} \,|\, \mathbf{I}_{n-k} \right]$. The encoder forms the syndrome $(n-k)$-*tuple* as $s = \mathbf{x}\mathbf{H}^T$, and transmits it to the decoder. Then, the decoder applies a decoding function on the received syndrome and the side information to derive the error vector $\mathbf{e}$. Finally, the encoded source sequence is reconstructed as $\hat{\mathbf{x}} = \mathbf{e} \oplus \mathbf{y}$, where $\oplus$ is the exclusive-OR (XOR) operator [33].

Wyner's methodology was used by [13] for practical Slepian–Wolf code design based on conventional channel codes, such as block and trellis codes. Alternatively, Liveris et al. [16] engineered a syndrome-based code design rooted in the state-of-the-art low-density parity-check (LDPC) codes, that achieves a compression performance very close to the Slepian–Wolf limit. Furthermore, Varodayan et al. [34] developed a rate-adaptive LDPC syndrome–based code that achieves various puncturing rates, while maintaining very good performance.

10.4.1.2 Parity Approach

In the parity-driven coding approach, parity-check bits, rather than syndrome bits, of a systematic channel code are employed to index the Slepian–Wolf bins. Specifically, in order to encode the binary *n-tuple* $\mathbf{x}$, a parity-based Slepian–Wolf encoder deploys an $(n + r,n)$ systematic channel code C' defined by the generator matrix $\mathbf{G}'_{n \times (n+r)} = \left[\mathbf{I}_n \,|\, \mathbf{P}'_{n \times r} \right]$. The encoder develops a parity bits *r-tuple* $\mathbf{p} = \mathbf{x}\mathbf{P}'$, which constitutes the compressed information, and sends it to the decoder. Thereafter, the decoder produces an $(n + r)$-*tuple* $\mathbf{g} = [\mathbf{y}_{1 \times n}|\mathbf{p}]$ by attaching the side information *n-tuple* $\mathbf{y}_{1 \times n}$ to the received parity bits *r-tuple* $\mathbf{p}$. By decoding $\mathbf{g}$ on the channel code C', the designed parity-based Slepian–Wolf decoder yields the decoded code word $\hat{\mathbf{c}} = \hat{\mathbf{x}}\mathbf{G}'_{n \times (n+r)}$. The systematic part of the latter is extracted, and constitutes the reconstruction $\hat{\mathbf{x}}$ of the encoded source array [18].

Practical Slepian–Wolf codes following the parity-based approach have been engineered, anchored in a state-of-the-art capacity approaching binary linear codes, such as Turbo [15] and low-density parity-check (LDPC) [18] codes. These code designs have shown great performance,

---

* To simplify the presentation, the linear code is assumed to be systematic.

namely, very close to the Slepian–Wolf bound. Moreover, as it will be explained below, these designs offer inherited robustness against transmission errors, and allow for a range of rates based on modified puncturing patterns.

For distributed compression under a noiseless transmission scenario the syndrome-based Slepian–Wolf scheme is optimal, as it can achieve the theoretic bound with the shortest channel code word length. Nonetheless, in order to address distributed compression in a noisy transmission scenario the parity-based Slepian–Wolf scheme is preferable, as it can derive a distributed joint-source channel coding (DJSCC) scheme* [17,18]. Specifically, let the capacity of the communication channel be given by $C \le 1$, and assume that the transmitted parity bits of the parity-based Slepian–Wolf code are increased to $R_X > H(X|Y)/C$. According to the DJSCC theory, the added parity bits' redundancy can be employed to protect against the errors occurred in the communication medium.

10.4.2 Wyner–Ziv Coding

Figure 10.7 shows the general arrangement of Wyner–Ziv coding or lossy compression with decoder side information. Let X and Y be two statistically dependent i.i.d. random sequences, where X is independently encoded and jointly decoded, using Y as side information, to form a reconstructed sequence $\hat{X}$, yielding an expected distortion $D = E\left[d\left(X, \hat{X} \right) \right]$.

The formal definition of the Wyner–Ziv coding problem is as follows [10]: For a specific distortion metric $d\left(x^n, \hat{x}^n \right)$, that is, $d{:}A_{X^n} \times A_{\hat{X}^n} \to \mathbb{R}^+$, a Wyner–Ziv code $\left(R_{X|Y}^{WZ}, D \right)$ is defined by [10] an encoding function:

$$f_n^{WZ} : A_{X^n} \to \left\{ 1, 2, \ldots, 2^{nR_{X|Y}^{WZ}} \right\} \tag{10.3}$$

and a decoding with side information function:

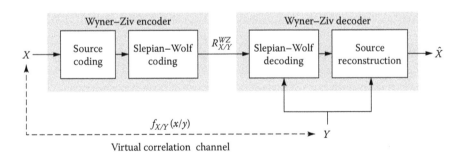

Figure 10.7 **Lossy compression with side information at the decoder (the Wyner–Ziv problem). The correlation between the source and the side information is expressed through a virtual communication channel.**

---

* The syndrome-based Slepian–Wolf bits can only compress but not protect against communication channel errors. Therefore, the syndrome-based approach requires separate source and channel coding designs. According to the Shannon separation theorem [26] separate designs are asymptotically optimal. In practice, however, good designs are employing DJSCC [49].

$$g_n^{WZ} : A_{Y^n} \times \left\{ 1, 2, \ldots, 2^{nR_{X|Y}^{WZ}} \right\} \to A_{\hat{X}^n} \tag{10.4}$$

where A_{Y^n} is the alphabet of the random variable corresponding to the side information. The distortion corresponding to the Wyner–Ziv $\left(R_{X|Y}^{WZ}, D \right)$ code is given by

$$D = E\left[d\left(X^n, g_n^{WZ}\left(Y^n, f_n^{WZ}\left(X^n \right) \right) \right) \right] \tag{10.5}$$

where $\hat{X}^n = g_n^{WZ}\left(Y^n, f_n^{WZ}\left(X^n \right) \right)$ is the reconstructed sequence.

Derived by the Wyner–Ziv theorem [10], the rate-distortion function with decoder side information is given by

$$R_{X|Y}^{WZ}(D) = \inf_{f(u|x)} \left\{ I(X;U) - I(Y;U) \right\} \tag{10.6}$$

where the infimum is taken over all reconstruction functions $\varphi: A_{Y^n} \times A_{U^n} \to A_{\hat{X}^n}$ and conditional probability density functions (pdfs) $f(u|x)$, such that

$$\iiint\limits_{y,x,u} f(x,y) f(u|x) d(x, \varphi(y,u)) \, dx\,dy\,du \le D \tag{10.7}$$

Note that U is an auxiliary random variable satisfying the following Markov chains [10]:

$$U \leftrightarrow X \leftrightarrow Y \tag{10.8}$$

$$X \leftrightarrow (U, Y) \leftrightarrow \hat{X} \tag{10.9}$$

The first Markov chain, that is, Equation 10.8, indicates that, in Wyner–Ziv coding, the selection of the auxiliary U codebook is independent of the side information Y. Furthermore, the second Markov chain, given by Equation 10.9, designates that the reconstruction function $\varphi(y,u)$ in Equation 10.6 is independent of the source signal X.

In case the side information is also available to the encoder, the predictive coding rate-distortion function is given by

$$R_{X|Y}(D) = \inf_{f(\hat{x}|x,y)} \left\{ I\left(X;\hat{X} \right) - I\left(Y;\hat{X} \right) \right\} \tag{10.10}$$

where the minimization is over all conditional pdfs $f\left(\hat{x}|x,y \right)$ for which the joint pdf satisfies the distortion constraint, that is,

$$\iiint\limits_{x,y,\hat{x}} f(x,y) f(\hat{x}|x,y) d(x,\hat{x}) \, dx\,dy\,d\hat{x} \le D \tag{10.11}$$

According to the theoretic proof derived by Wyner and Ziv [10], a rate loss compared with traditional predictive coding is sustained when the encoder does not have access to the side information, namely,

$$R_{X|Y}^{WZ}(D) - R_{X|Y}(D) \geq 0 \tag{10.12}$$

However, Wyner and Ziv [10] further demonstrated that equality in Equation 10.12 holds for the quadratic Gaussian case, that is, the case where X and Y are jointly Gaussian and a mean-square distortion metric $d(x,\hat{x})$ is used. Later, Pradhan et al. [20] generalized the Wyner–Ziv equality to include sources defined by the sum of arbitrarily distributed side information Y and independent Gaussian noise N, that is, $X = Y + N$. What is more, assuming generic source statistics, Zamir [35] proved that the rate loss, due to the exploitation of the side information at the decoder side only, is upper bounded by 0.5 bits per sample, namely,

$$0 \leq R_{X|Y}^{WZ}(D) - R_{X|Y}(D) \leq \frac{1}{2} \tag{10.13}$$

10.4.2.1 Practical Wyner–Ziv Coding

In essence, practical Wyner–Ziv coding combines quantization followed by Slepian–Wolf coding of the quantization indices. In effect, Wyner–Ziv coding is a joint source-channel coding problem. To operate closely to the Wyner–Ziv bound, one needs to employ both source codes, for example, trellis coded quantization (TCQ), that minimize source coding loss and sophisticated channel codes, for example, Turbo and LDPC codes, that can approach the Slepian–Wolf limit. Except for channel decoding, the side information is also used at the decoder to perform source reconstruction. In this way, the side information diminishes the imposed distortion of the reconstructed source $\hat{X}$.

In more detail, initial practical Wyner–Ziv code designs, focused on finding good nested codes among lattice- and trellis-based codes for the quadratic Gaussian case. In [32], Zamir et al. introduced nested lattice codes, demonstrating their optimality for (prohibitively) large dimensions. Motivated by the latter theoretical scheme, Servetto [36] proposed specific nested lattice constructions, based on similar sublattices for the high correlation case. Recent results have shown that trellis-based nested codes can realize high-dimensional nested lattice codes. In DSC using syndromes (DISCUS) [13], scalar quantization or TCQ, for source coding combined with scalar coset codes or trellis-based coset codes, for channel coding, were employed for Wyner–Ziv coding.

However, as dimensionality increases, lattice source codes approach the source coding limit much faster than lattice channel codes approach the capacity. Hence, the need for outstanding channel codes, that is, codes with higher dimensionality compared with source codes, is highlighted in order to approach the Wyner–Ziv bound. This observation has induced the second wave of Wyner–Ziv code design, which is based on nested lattice codes followed by binning, entitled *Slepian–Wolf coded nested quantization* (SWC-NQ) [37]. Under high-rate assumptions, asymptotic performance bounds of SWC-NQ were derived in [37], where it was shown that ideal Slepian–Wolf coded one-/two-dimensional (1-D/2-D) nested lattice quantization performs 1.53/1.36 dB worse than the Wyner–Ziv bound function (with a probability at almost one).

The third practical approach to Wyner–Ziv coding considers nonnested quantization followed by efficient binning, realized by a high-dimensional channel code. In this approach, the performance loss with respect to the Wyner–Ziv bound is only due to quantization without knowledge of side information at the encoder. Considering ideal Slepian–Wolf coding and applying high-rate assumptions [38], have shown that scalar quantization coupled with ideal Slepian–Wolf coding leads to a 1.53 dB gap from the Wyner–Ziv bound. This gap is the same as the one incurred by entropy-constrained scalar quantization in the nondistributed case [39]. In [40], Yang et al. have shown that at high rates, TCQ with ideal Slepian–Wolf coding performs 0.2 dB away from the Wyner–Ziv limit (with a probability of almost one).

10.4.3 New Result: Extending the No-Rate-Loss Property of Wyner–Ziv Coding

Although Wyner and Ziv investigated the doubly symmetric binary source coding case, limited light has been shed until now on the case where the correlation is expressed by an asymmetric channel. Recent advances in Wyner–Ziv video coding, however, have demonstrated the benefit of adopting an asymmetric correlation channel model that can lead to performance improvements compared with using a symmetric channel model [41]. In [34], Varodayan et al. studied the performance of low-density parity-check accumulate codes for the practical Slepian–Wolf coding [9] of a binary source with decoder side information under the most widely studied asymmetric correlation channel model, that is, the Z-channel.

Motivated by these advancements, Deligiannis et al. [42] studied the rate-distortion performance of binary source coding with side information when the correlation is expressed by a Z-channel and the Hamming distance is used as a distortion metric. For coding with side information available to both the encoder and the decoder the rate-distortion function is derived in [43]. However, for Wyner–Ziv coding, the setting of this function is unknown. We have derived the rate-distortion function for Wyner–Ziv coding under the aforementioned setup and surprisingly, we have proved that there is no rate loss compared with source coding with side information available to both the encoder and the decoder.

Our result can be summarized in the following theorem:

Theorem [42]: Consider binary source coding in the presence of side information with the Hamming distance as a distortion metric. When the correlation between the source and the side information is expressed by a Z-channel, Wyner–Ziv coding does not suffer a rate loss compared with source coding with side information available at both the encoder and the decoder. Specifically,

$$R_{WZ}^{Z}(D) = R_{(X|Y)}^{Z}(D) = (1 - q + qp_0)\left[h\left(\frac{qp_0}{1 - q + qp_0}\right) - h\left(\frac{D}{1 - q + qp_0}\right)\right]$$

where $q = \Pr[X = 1]$ parameterizes the probability distribution of the binary source to be encoded and $h(\cdot)$ is the binary entropy function, $h(p) = -p\log_2 p - (1 - p)\log_2 (1 - p)$ with $p \in [0, 1]$. The dependence between the source and the side information Y is expressed by a Z-channel, with crossover probabilities:

$$p(y \mid x) = \begin{cases} 0, & x = 0 \text{ and } y = 1 \\ p_0, & x = 1 \text{ and } y = 0 \end{cases}$$

In order to verify our theory, we used an implementation of the Blahut–Arimoto algorithm for the R-D problem with two-sided state information [44], adapted such that it generates the R-D points for binary source coding with decoder side information, under Z-channel correlation. We vary the distribution of the source X, by modifying $q = \Pr[X = 1]$, as well as the crossover probability of the Z-channel, by modifying p_0. Figure 10.8a presents the Wyner–Ziv R-D performance for a uniform source with varying crossover probability for the Z-channel, while Figure 10.8b depicts the R-D when the correlation channel is kept constant and the source distribution is varying. The figures corroborate the perfect match of our theoretical R-D function with the experimental R-D points obtained with the Blahut–Arimoto algorithm, full lines for the former and, respectively, discrete values for the latter. Moreover, the variation of $p(U|X)$ with the distortion, as obtained by the Blahut–Arimoto algorithm for two different pairs of p_0 and q, is depicted in Figure 10.9a and b. It can be observed that $p(U|X)$ exhibits an asymmetric behavior. In particular, it is noteworthy that, for $p(U|X) = (0.3, 0.3)$, $p(U|X)$—that is, the channel between X and the inverse of U—approximates a Z-channel ($a \approx 1$) for any $D \in [0, 0.09]$.

10.5 Distributed Joint Source-Channel Coding System for Temperature Monitoring

Several works have proposed DSC constructions for wireless sensors monitoring temperature. A scheme realizing Slepian–Wolf (SW) coding for two sensors measuring the temperature in a room

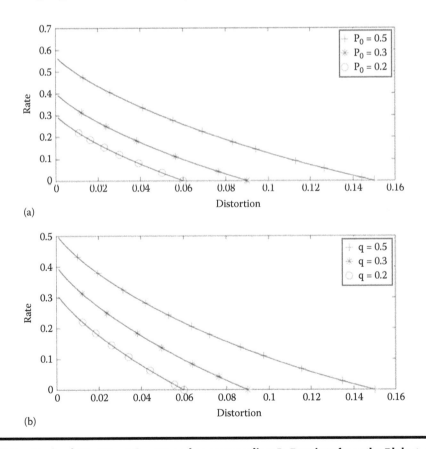

(a)

(b)

Figure 10.8 Derived $R^Z_{WZ}(D) = R^Z_{(X|Y)}(D)$ and corresponding R-D points from the Blahut–Arimoto algorithm: (a) $p_0 = 0.5$, $p_0 = 0.3$, $p_0 = 0.2$, and $q = 0.3$; (b) $p_0 = 0.3$, and $q = 0.5$, $q = 0.3$, $q = 0.2$.

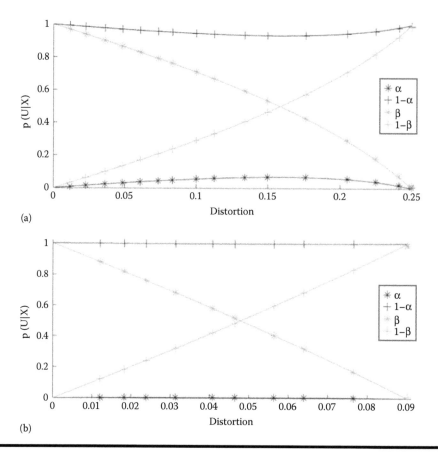

Figure 10.9 *p*(*U*|*X*) obtained from the Blahut–Arimoto algorithm: (a) $p_0 = 0.5$ and $q = 0.3$; (b) $p_0 = 0.3$, and $q = 0.3$.

was devised in [45]. The construction of [45] was extended to a cross-layer design by modeling the interaction between DSC and the medium access control (MAC) layer [46]. A Wyner–Ziv code design comprising quantization followed by binarization and LDPC encoding was proposed in [47]. Considering a multisensory scenario, the author of [48] introduced a multiterminal code design in which SW coding was simply replaced by entropy coding, whereas the joint-source reconstruction at the decoder was realized by Gaussian process regression. The authors of [49] studied multiterminal source coding under physical models of heat diffusion, focusing heat conduction in solid bodies (rail temperature–monitoring applications).

Existing coding schemes for temperature data collected by sensors, see [47,48,50–53], focus only on data compression. We describe our design that addresses joint compression and error-resilient data transmission. Since a medium access control (MAC) protocol is used, transmission is performed over a set of parallel channels. In this setup, our distributed joint-source channel coding (DJSCC) design mitigates channel impairments without requiring packet retransmissions at the MAC layer, thereby leading to significant energy savings for each end device.

Our scheme uses asymmetric SW coding realized by Raptor codes [54], the newest class of rateless channel codes. Our design is specifically tailored to the requirements of temperature monitoring by WSNs, as it is based on nonsystematic Raptor codes that achieve good performance for short code lengths. Experimental results using a proprietary WSN deployment show that our system introduces notable compression gains (up to 30.08% in rate reduction) with respect to the baseline scheme that performs arithmetic entropy coding of the data.

10.5.1 DJSCC System Architecture

In the proposed architecture, which is shown in Figure 10.10, the correlation between the data collected from the sensors within each cluster is exploited by means of Slepian–Wolf coding. Particularly, let N be the total number of sensor nodes within a cluster, with the Nth node denoting the CH. According to the proposed coding scheme, the CH encodes its collected discrete information, denoted by $\tilde{X}_N$, at a rate $R_{\tilde{X}_N} \geq H\left(\tilde{X}_N\right)$. Each of the $N-1$ peripheral nodes within the cluster encodes the gathered discrete data using asymmetric SW coding. That is, the corresponding encoding rates are $R_{\tilde{X}_n} \geq H\left(\tilde{X}_n \mid \tilde{X}_N\right), n = 1, 2, \dots, N-1$. Since the information is transmitted over wireless links, channel encoding is required. Transmission is performed over the 16 channels of the IEEE 802.15.4 physical layer (PHY) and intersensor interference is mitigated via the utilized MAC layer cluster tree coordination [28]. On account of the MAC protocol, the multiple access channel becomes a system of parallel channels. Conventional error protection, by means of channel encoding, is performed for the encoded data of the CH (see Figure 10.10), while the proposed DJSCC is performed at the peripheral nodes. Assuming a statistical model for the cluster-level temperature data correlation, the base station decodes the information from the peripheral nodes using the decoded temperature data collected from the CH as side information.

10.5.2 Correlation Modeling

Temperature readings from sensors are typically modeled as jointly Gaussian, namely, the spatial correlation is characterized by a multivariate Gaussian distribution [45,47,48]. This assumption is also typically encountered in information-theoretic studies [19], code designs [40], and correlation estimation works [55].

We have proposed a novel modeling approach for the spatial correlation of the sensors' measurements [56]. Contrary to the multivariate Gaussian model, typically considered in state-of-the-art works [45,47,48,55], our approach models the marginal distributions of the data using kernel

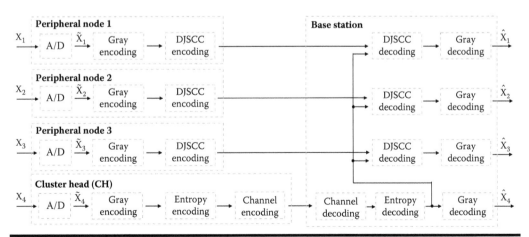

Figure 10.10   Our distributed joint source-channel coding architecture based on asymmetric Slepian–Wolf coding.

density estimation and expresses the correlation using a copula function [57]. In this way, our approach offers higher modeling accuracy than the conventional multivariate Gaussian model, leading to significant coding improvements.

In effect, via our WSN deployment, we show that, when using the conventional multivariate Gaussian model, the proposed DJSCC system brings systematic energy savings at the sensor nodes by up to 17.49% with respect to the baseline system. When the proposed copula-function-based model is used in the DJSCC system, the energy savings increase up to 24.36% compared with the baseline system.

10.5.3 Experimental Results on Compression Performance

Within an indoor office environment, we deployed a wireless sensor network (WSN) comprising 16 nodes gathering temperature data. The utilized hardware for the sensors and the base station (sink node) is described in Table 10.1.

Within each cluster of the network architecture, the number of sensor nodes was $N = 4$ and they were chosen to be colocated; three of them being peripheral nodes and the fourth being the CH. The sink node was connected to a desktop computer where data collection and decoding took place. The IEEE 802.15.4 guaranteed time slot (GTS) [28] was used for the intracluster super-frame beaconing and the scheduling of packet transmissions. All residual transmission impairments incurred from external sources (e.g., interference from colocated IEEE 802.15.4 or Wi-Fi networks) were mitigated via the default PHY layer protection or the proposed DJSCC scheme.

Table 10.1 Hardware Specification of the Different Nodes in the Wireless Sensor Network

Peripheral or CH Node
Microcontroller Atmel ATmega 1281
Transmitter AT86RF230
Dual-chip antenna
Microchip MCP9700AT temperature transducer (−40°C to +150°C)
TAOS luminosity intensity transducer TSL250R
Li-polymer battery—3.7 V
Battery charger with USB port
Dimensions: 60 × 33 mm
Base station (sink node)
Microcontroller Atmel ATmega 1281
Transmitter AT86RF230
Dual-chip antenna
USB-UART bridge for connection to PC USB port
Dimensions: 48 × 21 mm

Table 10.2 Comparison of Average Encoding Rates (in bits/data block)

	$\tilde{X}_1$	$\tilde{X}_2$	$\tilde{X}_3$	$\tilde{X}_4$
Entropy coding	452	496	512	471
Proposed with MG	319	356	358	—
Gain w.r.t. entropy coding (%)	29.43	28.23	30.08	—
Proposed with CF	263	312	303	—
Gain w.r.t. entropy coding (%)	41.81	37.10	40.82	—
Gain w.r.t. MG model (%)	17.56	12.36	15.36	—

Note: The data from the 4th node in the cluster is always entropy coded.

We aggregated $m = 40$ consecutive measurements to construct a data block of size $k = m \times b = 640$ bits, where $b = 16$ bits is the bit depth of the A/D converter within each sensor.

During the training stage, data collected over a three-day operation of the WSN were used to derive the parameters of a copula function–based model. To evaluate the compression performance and the error-resilience capability of the proposed system we collected additional data (different from the training data) over the 30-day operation period of the system.

We have compared the compression performance of the proposed system against the performance of the baseline system, which performs arithmetic entropy coding of each sensor's readings. In both cases, lossless encoding is achieved, that is, the decoded temperature values of each node match the corresponding measured values. The average encoding rates (in bits per encoded datablock) achieved with the baseline system and the proposed system are reported in Table 10.2. The results show that, when using the conventional multivariate Gaussian model, the proposed system reduces the required rate for compression by up to 30.08% compared with the baseline system. When the proposed copula function–based model is used, the obtained improvements in rate reduction over the baseline system can reach up to 41.81%.

10.6 Distributed Video Coding for Low-Resolution Visual Sensors

Low-power visual sensors with modest frame resolutions can be fabricated at low costs; nevertheless, low-resolution video may still prove adequate for regular video processing tasks. In this context, the visual sensors presented in [58] captured video of 30 × 30 pixels, which was effectively used to perform edge detection, background removal, and face detection. Low-cost and low-power characteristics together with video processing capabilities create the opportunity to engineer video-based applications with advanced functionality in a reasonable price range. For instance, in [59], occupancy maps for a single room covered by four low-resolution visual sensors were built. Up to four individuals could be tracked based on video captured at 64 × 48 pixels [59]. The potential of low-resolution visual sensors organized in a network for posture recognition was suggested in [58,60].

Moreover, autonomous battery-powered wireless sensors ease installation by evading a cabled setup and are less invasive in nature. In addition, the low resolution of the recorded data may evade privacy-related constraints.

A high-performance compression system is an essential component in wireless video applications. Significant rate reductions induce an important decrease in power consumption by the wireless transmission of the recording devices, thereby prolonging battery life. Alternatively, efficient coding of the captured video could increase the frame rate of the transmitted sequence at the same cost in transmission power. In addition, a compression system that offers efficient compression at a minimal computational complexity would have a distinct edge. Reducing the number of operations during encoding reduces the associated power consumption, thereby extending battery life. Unfortunately, contemporary video coding standards, H.264/AVC [61] or H.265/HEVC [62], primarily focus on achieving high-compression performance. Although remarkable compression performance is achieved, the computational load during encoding constitutes a substantial burden under power-constrained conditions. The available coding options for wireless visual sensors with limited resources boil down to the low-complexity profiles of current standards; for example, H.264/AVC Intra [61] or high-performance image codecs such as JPEG compression.

In contrast to the common video coding standards [61,62] that follow a predictive coding paradigm, distributed video coding (DVC) offers an alternative to video coding architecture. DVC systems are specifically designed to provide competitive video compression performance at low encoding complexity. Applying Wyner–Ziv coding principles to video allows for the transfer of the computationally expensive task of generating accurate temporal predictions from the encoder to the decoder.

This chapter describes a novel transform-domain Wyner–Ziv video coding architecture, specifically designed to handle extremely low-resolution video captured by visual sensors such as the 1K-pixel sensor of [58]. The proposed system quantizes the original frames in the DCT domain after which the quantization indices are encoded using a powerful channel code. In this context, this work proposes a new code word formation technique suitable for extremely low-resolution frames. Existing methods would yield very short code words that severely weaken the performance of the channel code. A second crucial component for achieving high-compression performance in DVC, is the generation of high-quality temporal predictions at the decoder. In this regard, the proposed system features an efficient switched-current (SI) generation technique, suitable for low-resolution data. The proposed system is evaluated on data obtained from the mouse camera motes of [58]. Experimental results show that the proposed DVC architecture outperforms H.264/AVC Intra, a low-complexity profile of the H.264/AVC standard.

10.6.1 Transform-Domain DVC Architecture

The schematic overview of the proposed Wyner–Ziv video coding system for 1K pixel visual sensors is given in Figure 10.11.

10.6.1.1 Encoder

The proposed system operates in the transform domain, employing a 4×4 discrete cosine transform (DCT). Therefore, to accommodate an integer number of blocks per dimension, the data gathered with the sensor from [58] is padded from 30×30 to 32×32 pixels. Then, the (padded) sequence is organized into groups of pictures (GOPs) and is decomposed into key frames, that is, the first frame in a GOP, and Wyner–Ziv (WZ) frames. The key frames, denoted by K, are coded using H.264/AVC Intra [61] in main profile, configured with context-adaptive variable length coding (CAVLC). The WZ frames, denoted by W, are transformed using the 4×4 integer

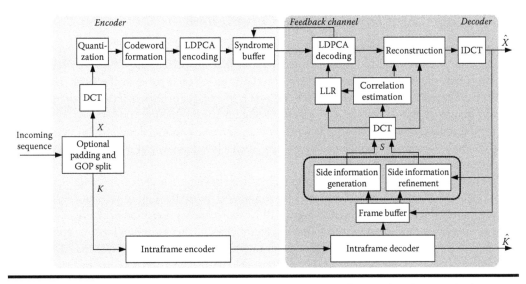

Figure 10.11 Block diagram of the proposed Wyner–Ziv video codec for 1K-pixel camera sensors.

approximation of the DCT and the derived DCT coefficients are grouped into 16 coefficient bands that are subsequently quantized. The DC and AC coefficients are quantized using uniform and dead-zone scalar quantizers, respectively, and the resulting indices are split into bit planes. Then, multiple bit planes belonging to different frequency bands are grouped to form code words, which are fed to a low-density parity-check accumulate (LDPCA) encoder [34]. Bit-plane grouping is carried out to create sufficiently large code words that benefit the performance of practical Slepian–Wolf coding. Then, the derived syndrome bits per code word are transmitted in portions upon the decoder's request using a feedback channel, following the design from [38].

10.6.1.2 Decoder

At the decoder, the key frames are intradecoded and stored in a reference frame buffer. The decoder first generates a motion-compensated prediction of a WZ frame to serve as initial side information in the DCT domain. Correlation channel estimation (CCE), as in [63], is subsequently carried out in order to express the statistical correlation between an original WZ frame and its side information. The obtained correlation model derives the required *a priori* information to LDPCA decode an initial set of code words from the WZ frame. The bit planes belonging to the decoded code words are grouped into quantization indices and minimum mean squared error (MMSE) reconstruction [64] is performed, yielding a decoded version of the WZ frame coefficients. side information refinement is performed using motion-compensated prediction between every partially decoded WZ frame and the reference frames from the buffer. The resulting refined version of the side information is then used to reinitiate CCE and log-likelihood ratio (LLR) formation—see also [63]. These updated LLRs are used to LDPCA decode an additional set of code words to further improve the reconstruction of the partially decoded WZ frame. This side information refinement and decoding operation is recursively executed until all information has been decoded.

Details on side information refinement are provided in [65]. After the final refinement round, all the encoded DCT coefficients have been decoded and the inverse DCT yields the decoded WZ frame, which is displayed and stored in the reference frame buffer for future referencing.

10.6.2 Code Word Formation and Quantization

Designed for QCIF resolutions or above, current DVC systems [38,66,67] consider predefined quantization matrices (QMs). Each frequency band β is quantized with $2^{L\beta}$ levels (i.e., L_β bit planes), where the number of levels is given by the value of each band in the QM. Then, code words are formed independently for each bit plane of the quantization indices belonging to a specific frequency band. For the considered resolution of the padded frames, that is, 32×32, every band contains 64 coefficients. Hence, following the conventional design from [38,66,67] the LDPCA code word length would also be 64 bits. Such a low code length would vastly undermine the performance of LDPCA codes.

We create LDPCA code words by grouping bitplanes belonging to different bands. Specifically, each code word always contains 2 bit–planes belonging to 4 specific frequency bands that together compose a so-called band group (BG). Figure 10.12 shows the composition of the BGs. This code word formation is motivated by the following reasons. First, this grouping leads to a code word length of 512 bits, which can support good performance of LDPCA codes [34]. Second, this band grouping still provides adequate flexibility to boost the compression performance by means of side information refinement, as proposed in [65]. Third, by assembling just 2 consecutive bit planes per band in one code word, the benefit of layered WZ coding [64], concerning LLR calculation and CCE refinement, is maintained. The proposed code word composition puts constraints on the design of the quantization matrices (QMs). In effect, every band belonging to the same BG_i, $i = \{0, 1, 2, 3\}$ needs to be quantized with the same number of levels. In other words, for each BG_i, $i = \{0, 1, 2, 3\}$, the number of quantization levels $2^{L\beta}$, with $(\beta \bmod 4) = i$, must be equal. Also, the number of bit planes per band must be a multiple of 2, that is, $L_\beta \bmod 2 = 0$ must hold for every frequency band $\beta = \{0, 1, ..., 15\}$. Under these constraints, a compatible set of QMs, targeting a wide rate range, is designed.

10.6.3 Side Information Generation and Refinement

The objective of employing motion-compensated interpolation, or briefly MCI, in the decoder of a Wyner–Ziv video coding system is to create a motion-compensated prediction of an encoded WZ frame based on two already decoded reference frames, that is, one previous and one following a frame. Seeing the fact that this prediction acts as side information to the original WZ frame, the higher its resemblance to the latter, the higher the compression performance of the developed Wyner–Ziv video coding system. This subsection summarizes the state-of-the-art MCI method employed in the DISCOVER [67] reference DVC system, incorporating modifications and extensions proposed by Deligiannis et al. [66].

The schematic representation of the developed MCI technique is depicted in Figure 10.13. The frame interpolation module first performs block-based motion estimation between two already

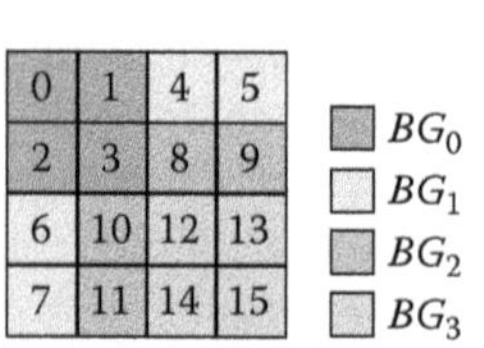

Figure 10.12 Grouping of individual DCT bands $\beta = \{0, 1, ..., 15\}$ to form band groups BG_i, $i = \{0, 1, 2, 3\}$ and in turn code words, where $i = \beta \bmod 4$ with mod being the modulo operation.

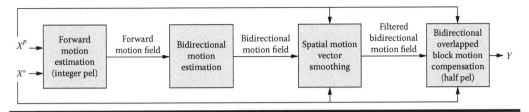

Figure 10.13   Schematic diagram of motion-compensated interpolation. (From Deligiannis, N. et al., *Proc. International Conference on Digital Signal Processing (DSP)***, 2011; Artigas, X., et al.,** *Proc. Picture Coding Symposium (PCS)***, 2007.)**

decoded reference frames (i.e., one previous and one following frame), and the resulting motion vectors are intercepted in the current frame. Next, for each block in the current frame, the closest intersecting vector is split into two parts and treated as a bidirectional motion vector. The vectors are then further refined with half-pel accuracy. The ensuing motion field is smoothed using a median filter. In DISCOVER's MCI method, the side information frame is generated block-by-block using simple bidirectional motion compensation. However, the MCI technique employed in the work of Deligiannis et al. [66] advances over the latter by deploying bidirectional overlapped block motion compensation.

10.6.3.1 Forward Motion Estimation

In the first stage, for each WZ frame, X forward block-based motion estimation with integer-pixel accuracy is performed between the previous and the next reference frame, denoted by X^p and X^n, respectively. As a hierarchical motion predictive structure is considered (see Figure 10.14) the reference frames are the already decoded previous and next key and/or WZ frames. Note that the reference frames are initially low-pass filtered (with a 3×3 mean filter) in order to improve the reliability of the motions vectors. In this setting, for each block in the next reference frame, forward block motion estimation involves finding the best matching block in the past reference frame, within a certain search range. This operation is sketched in Figure 10.15. Similar to [67], the error metric (EM) employed for block matching is a modified version of the sum of absolute differences (SAD) metric, which favors smaller motion vectors [67], that is,

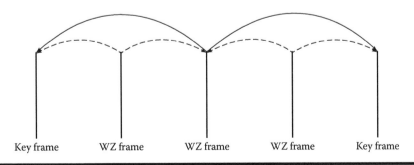

Figure 10.14   Hierarchical bidirectional motion prediction structure as employed by the motion-compensated interpolation method for GOP a size of 4.

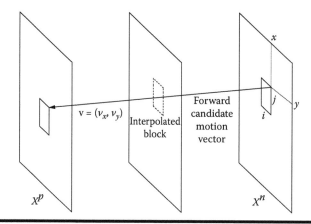

Figure 10.15   Forward motion estimation.

$$EM\left(x, y, \mathbf{v} = \left(v_x, v_y\right)\right) = \left(1 + k \parallel \mathbf{v} \parallel\right) \cdot$$

$$\sum_{j=0}^{N-1} \sum_{i=0}^{N-1} |X^n\left(Nx + i, Ny + j\right) - X^p\left(Nx + i + v_x, Ny + j + v_y\right)$$

where:

x and y	respectively, denote the top-left coordinates of the block for which motion estimation is performed
N	denotes the block size
i and j	are, respectively, the column and row coordinates of the pixels in the block
$\mathbf{v} = \left(v_x, v_y\right)$	represents the candidate motion vector
k	is a constant set to $k = 0.05$ [67]

In compliance with prior art [67], a block size of $N = 16$ and a search range of $\rho = 32$ pixels is employed in the forward motion estimation algorithm.

10.6.3.2 Bidirectional Motion Estimation

The resulting unidirectional motion field, denoted by MF_F, is thereafter used to derive the bidirectional motion field, MF_B, between the interpolated frame and the reference frames, as depicted in Figure 10.16. In particular, similar to [67], the points where the motion vectors of MF_F intercept the interpolated frame are determined first. For each block in the interpolated frame, the motion vector for which the intercept point is closest to the top-left corner of the block is selected. This motion vector v is subsequently scaled with the ratio between the distance of the interpolated frame to the previous reference frame and the distance between both reference frames, yielding the new forward motion vector for the block. Observe that this ratio is always ½ since hierarchical prediction is used. Similarly, the backward motion vector of the interpolated block is determined by scaling the inverted motion vector $-v$ by ½. This operation generates the initial bidirectional motion field between the interpolated frame and both reference frames.

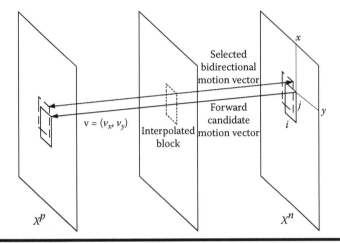

Figure 10.16 Extrapolation of the bidirectional motion field from the unidirectional one. For each block in the current (i.e., interpolated) frame, the closest intercepting vector is found, shifted to the top-left corner of the block, and then divided into a bidirectional motion vector.

Subsequently, the obtained bidirectional motion field is further improved. The algorithm searches for symmetric motion vector pairs, corresponding to linear motion trajectories, around the initially determined motion vector pair. This operation is schematically described in Figure 10.17. The procedure employs the SAD between the referred blocks in the previous and next reference frames as an error metric and supports half-pel motion estimation accuracy. The required interpolation for half-pel motion estimation is performed using the 6-tap interpolation filter of H.264/AVC [61].

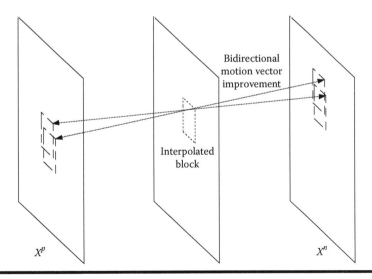

Figure 10.17 Improvement of the initially obtained bidirectional motion field by using symmetric motion vector pairs.

10.6.3.3 Spatial Motion Vector Smoothing

The ensuing bidirectional motion field is spatially smoothed by applying a weighted vector media filter [67]. This is done in order to improve the spatial coherence of the obtained bidirectional motion field, thereby aiming at removing outliers, that is, motion vectors that are far from the true motion field. Specifically, for each block B_l in the interpolated frame, the weighted median vector filter proposed in [67] looks for candidate motion vectors at neighboring blocks, which can better represent the motion in the block. According to this method, the spatially smoothed motion vector for an interpolated block B_l is given by

$$\mathbf{v} = \arg\min_{\mathbf{v}_l}\left\{\sum_{m=1}^{M} w_m \parallel \mathbf{v}_l - \mathbf{v}_m \parallel\right\} \qquad (10.15)$$

where $\mathbf{v}_{\{m=1\}}$, $\mathbf{v}_{\{m=2\}}$, ..., $\mathbf{v}_{\{m-1\}}$, ..., $\mathbf{v}_{\{m=M\}}$, are the motion vectors derived by the refined bidirectional motion estimation of the block under consideration and its M-1 neighbors, and w_m, $m = 1, ..., M$, are weights determining the strength of the median filter. These weighting factors are obtained as

$$w_m = \frac{1}{\mathrm{SAD}\left(B_l, \mathbf{v}_m\right)} \qquad (10.16)$$

where the SAD metric evaluates the matching error between the reference blocks for each block B_l compensated with the bidirectional vector $\mathbf{v}_m$.

It is important to mention that extensive experimentation has shown that spatial motion vector smoothing is mainly beneficial for common intermediate format (CIF) rather than for quarter-CIF (QCIF) sequences. Based on this evaluation, when a QCIF sequence is coded no subsequent motion field smoothing is performed in our MCI method, as explained in [66].

10.6.3.4 Motion Compensation

Once the final bidirectional motion field is derived, the side information frame is obtained by performing motion compensation. In the MCI method developed for the DISCOVER codec, a simple bidirectional motion compensation approach is followed. In particular, for the pixels belonging to block B, bidirectional motion compensation is defined by

$$Y_B\left(i, j\right) = \frac{1}{2}\left\{X_B^P\left(i - v_x, j - v_y\right) + X_B^n\left(i + v_x, j + v_y\right)\right\} \qquad (10.17)$$

where $Y_B(i,j)$ corresponds to a pixel location in the block B in the motion-compensated frame, and $X_B^P\left(i - v_x, j - v_y\right)$, $X_B^n\left(i + v_x, j + v_y\right)$ represents the corresponding pixels in the best matching bocks, identified by the derived symmetric bidirectional motion vector $v = (v_x, v_y)$, in the previous and next reference frame, respectively.

In contrast to the latter method, in the MCI [66] algorithm by Deligiannis et al., *bidirectional overlapped block motion compensation (OBMC)* is performed. Rather than predicting by using a single symmetric motion vector per block, OBMC predicts using motion vectors from the blocks in a neighborhood around the interpolated block. Hence, by introducing OBMC, the presented MCI technique produces an interpolated frame which exhibits *reduced prediction error* energy at the pixel level, and in turn increases the performance of Wyner–Ziv coding. Moreover, *blocking artifacts*, typically appearing at block boundaries, are vastly diminished, thereby increasing the visual quality of the decoded frame.

In the proposed MCI technique, bidirectional OBMC is performed as follows. Initially, based on the previously obtained bidirectional motion field, the proposed approach derives a forward and a backward overlapped block motion-compensated frame, denoted by $\tilde{Y}^p$ and $\tilde{Y}^n$, respectively. Each of these frames is obtained by using the corresponding motion field (i.e., forward or backward) and by applying OBMC. Note that OBMC may employ an adaptive nonlinear predictor. However, in the designed methodology a fixed linear predictor, in particular a *raised cosine window* is used. This means that OBMC is actually implemented as a windowed motion compensation method (Figure 10.18). In this case, translated blocks are first scaled by the window, and the overlapping fractions are summed. In this way, a pixel in position (i, j) in the block B in the forward overlapped block motion-compensated frame $\tilde{Y}^p$ is predicted as

$$\tilde{Y}_B^p(i,j) = \Sigma_{m=1}^{M} w(i_m, j_m) X_{B_m}^p(i - v_{m,x}, j - v_{m,y}) \qquad (10.18)$$

where:

$m = 1, \dots, M$ indexes the block of which the window contains the compensated pixel

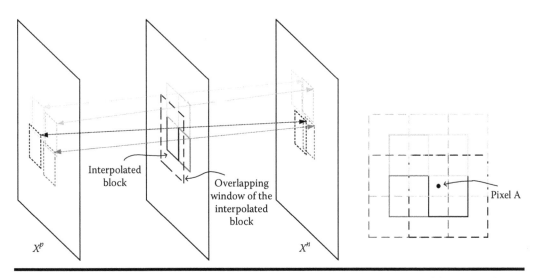

Figure 10.18 **Example of overlapped block motion compensation with a fixed linear predictor. The blocks in the block lattice are represented by continuous lines, the overlapping windows are indicated by dashed lines, and the motion vectors by dotted lines. For convenience, the blocks and their corresponding overlapping windows are sketched on the right. The pixel A belonging to the black block is predicted by four motion vectors, namely, the motion vector of the black block and the motion vectors of its three neighboring blocks.**

$w(i_m, j_m)$ is the corresponding scaling factor of the mth overlapping window

$X_{B_m}^p \left(i - v_{m,x}, j - v_{m,y} \right)$ is the candidate predictor pixel in the previous reference frame belonging to the mth overlapping window

Similarly, the backward overlapped block motion-compensated frame $\tilde{Y}^p$ can be found as

$$\tilde{Y}_B^n (i, j) = \Sigma_{m-1}^M w \left(i_m, j_m \right) X_{B_m}^n \left(i + v_{m,x}, j + v_{m,y} \right) \tag{10.19}$$

Finally, the derived *forward* and *backward* overlapped block motion-compensated frames are averaged yielding the final side information pixel values, that is,

$$Y_B (i, j) = \frac{1}{2} \left\{ \tilde{Y}_B^p (i, j) + \tilde{Y}_B^n (i, j) \right\} \tag{10.20}$$

10.6.3.5 Motion Refinement

Having decoded the coefficients belonging to a band group, BG_i, the decoder obtains access to the partially decoded WZ frame and hence it has more knowledge of the original WZ frame. This knowledge is utilized to improve the quality of the SI used to decode the coefficients of the following band group, BG_{i+1}. To this end, the decoder applies the successively refined OBMEC technique from [65] using the partially decoded WZ frame and the reference frames.

10.6.4 Experimental Results

The designed system is evaluated on four sequences obtained with the mouse camera motes of [58], where the position of the camera during recording remained fixed and the scene was set up to contain different degrees of motion. All sequences contain 450 frames of 30×30 pixels, have a frame rate of 33 Hz, and a bit depth in which every pixel is 6 bits. The considered sequences are organized in a GOP of size 2, 4, and 8 and the proposed system is compared against H.264/AVC Intra [61] in main profile with CAVLC. H.264/AVC Intra is one of the finest intra-frame codecs available and is a well-known reference in Wyner–Ziv video coding. During the experimental evaluation, the proposed codec was configured as follows. Both MCI- and overlapped block motion estimation and compensation–based (OBMEC-based) SI generation modules used a block size of 4 4 pixels. The search range for the forward motion estimation step of the proposed MCI as well as the during the bidirectional motion field refinement operation was set to 4. During side information refinement the search range of OBME was also put to 4.

Figure 10.19 shows snapshots of every sequence after mirror padding to 32×32 pixels, while the compression results are shown in Figure 10.20. The *coffee* sequence displays a single person who is seated and leisurely sips a cup of coffee (see Figure 10.19a). Hence, the degree of motion is very low. This is reflected by the results in Figure 10.20a, where the proposed system vastly outperforms H.264/AVC Intra. The utilized SI generation method is very successful in exploiting the temporal correlation at the decoder, since the linear motion assumption of MCI holds well under low-motion conditions. What is more, the longer the GOP size, the better the performance, since temporal redundancy is efficiently exploited over more frames.

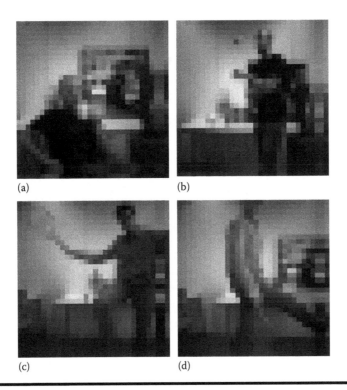

(a) (b)

(c) (d)

Figure 10.19 Snapshots of video sequences captured with the mouse sensor of [58].

In the *juggling* sequence, the motion content increases. Although the portion of the frame containing the juggling pattern contains very fast complex movements, the region is relatively confined (see Figure 10.19b). The results in Figure 10.20b show that the proposed system outperforms H.264/AVC Intra over the entire rate region, where the largest gains are recorded at low to medium rates. Also, the performance of the proposed codec for the different GOP sizes tend to converge, since the temporal correlation is less easy to exploit over longer GOPs.

Tennis depicts a person executing elaborate swings with a racket together with exaggerated leg movement (see Figure 10.19c). Hence, the sequence contains very high motion over the entire frame. It is well-known that such motion conditions are highly favorable to H.264/AVC Intra. Nevertheless, Figure 10.20c shows that the performance of the proposed codec outperforms H.264/AVC Intra at low to medium rates, while at the highest rate the performance of H.264/AVC Intra is slightly superior. When the motion patterns are complex, the linear motion assumption of MCI does not hold. As a result, the initial MCI-based SI reduces in quality, in particular for large GOPs. Nevertheless, the performance of the proposed system is similar for all GOP sizes. This is due to the success of the SI refinement method. At every refinement stage, a part of the original WZ frame is reconstructed which serves as a good basis for accurate OBME-based SI generation which transcends a linear motion model. This means that from the first refinement stage onwards, the efficiency of exploiting the temporal redundancy over large GOPs increases.

The last sequence, *sillywalks*, shows a member of Monty Python's Ministry of Silly Walks traversing the scene (see Figure 10.19d). The proposed codec significantly outperforms H.264/AVC Intra, as shown in Figure 10.20d. The performance for the larger GOPs surpasses the performance

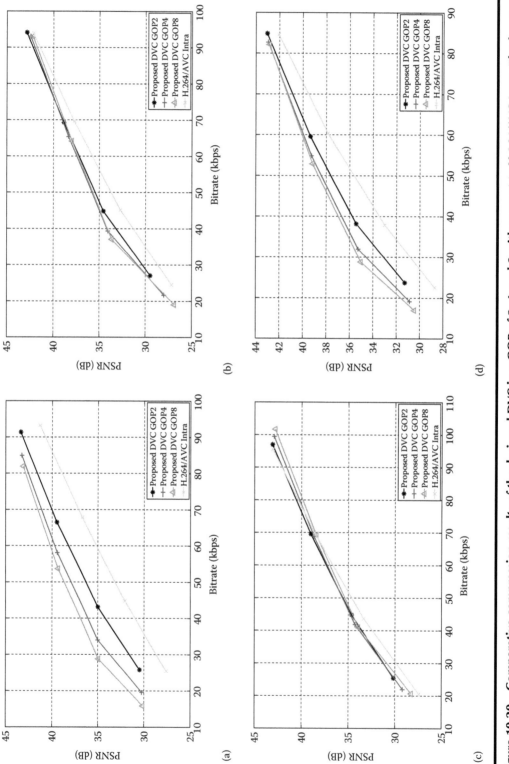

Figure 10.20 Comparative compression results of the designed DVC in a GOP of 2, 4, and 8 with respect to H.264/AVC Intra. The four test sequences were obtained with the mouse camera mote from [58] at a frame rate of 33 Hz and are composed of 450 frames each.

for a GOP of 2, which suggests that both the MCI- and OBME-based temporal predictions deliver high-quality SI. However, compared to the *coffee* sequence, the motion content is significantly higher, which causes the performance on a GOP of 4 and 8 to converge, where the loss in MCI accuracy is compensated by the success of SI refinement in the longer GOP.

10.7 Conclusion

We have presented a new approach to distributed data aggregation from wireless sensor networks to the C-RAN. Our approach combines a centralized C-RAN architecture for the mobile cloud and a cluster head-based architecture for the wireless sensor network. We have also demonstrated our approach in two application domains: (1) the distributed aggregation of temperature measurements and (2) distributed video coding of visual data obtained with wireless visual sensors. The architectural forms we have proposed provide high compression efficiency and therefore they take care of the limitation in bandwidth of the systems. The developed tools allow for low complex encoding at the sensor node, which is energy efficient and it enables the prolonged operation of these devices. Furthermore, we have shown that the developed solutions provide robustness against errors in the transmission medium. As such, our architectural forms are suitable for the aggregation of diverse data from the wireless sensors to the cloud, where they can be further processed and analyzed.

References

1. E. Z. Tragos, and V. Angelakis, Cognitive radio inspired M2M communications, *16th International Symposium on Wireless Personal Multimedia Communications (WPMC)*, pp. 1–5. IEEE, 2013.
2. G. Wu, S. Talwar, K. Johnsson, N. Himayat, and K. D. Johnson, M2m: From mobile to embedded internet, *IEEE Communications Magazine*, Vol. 49, No. 4, pp. 36–43, 2011.
3. Y. Zhang, R. Yu, S. Xie, W. Yao, Y. Xiao, and M. Guizani, Home M2M networks: Architectures, standards, and QOS improvement, *IEEE Communications Magazine*, Vol. 49, No. 4, pp. 44–52, 2011.
4. L. Atzori, A. Iera, and G. Morabito, The internet of things: A survey, *Computer Networks*, Vol. 54, No. 15, pp. 2787–2805, 2010.
5. G. Mulligan, The 6lowpan architecture, *Proceedings of the 4th Workshop on Embedded Networked Sensors. ACM*, pp. 78–82, 2007.
6. M. Peng, Y. Li, Z. Zhao, and C. Wang, System architecture and key technologies for 5G heterogeneous cloud radio access networks, *IEEE Network*, Vol. 29, No. 2, pp. 6–14, 2015.
7. J. Yick, B. Mukherjee, and D. Ghosal, Wireless sensor network survey, *Computer Networks*, Vol. 52, No. 12, pp. 2292–2330, 2008.
8. Z. Xiong, A. D. Liveris, and S. Cheng, Distributed source coding for sensor networks, *IEEE Signal Processing Magazine*, Vol. 21, No. 5, pp. 80–94, 2004.
9. D. Slepian and J. Wolf, Noiseless coding of correlated information sources, *IEEE Transactions on Information Theory*, Vol. 19, No. 4, pp. 471–480, 1973.
10. A. D. Wyner and J. Ziv, The rate-distortion function for source coding with side information at the decoder, *IEEE Transactions on Information Theory*, Vol. 22, No. 1, pp. 1–10, 1976.
11. T. Berger, Multiterminal source coding, *The Information Theory Approach to Communications*, G. Longo, Ed. New York, NY, Springer-Verlag, pp. 171–231, 1977.
12. T. M. Cover, A proof of the data compression theorem of Slepian and Wolf for ergodic sources (Corresp.), *IEEE Transactions on Information Theory*, Vol. 21, No. 2, pp. 226–228, March 1975.
13. S. S. Pradhan and K. Ramchandran, Distributed source coding using syndromes (DISCUS): Design and construction, *IEEE Transactions on Information Theory*, Vol. 49, No. 3, pp. 626–643, March 2003.

14. V. Stankovic, A. D. Liveris, Z. Xiong, and C. N. Georghiades, On code design for the Slepian–Wolf problem and lossless multiterminal networks, *IEEE Transactions on Information Theory*, Vol. 52, No. 4, pp. 1495–1507, April 2006.

15. J. Garcia-Frias, Compression of correlated binary sources using turbo codes, *IEEE Communication Letters*, Vol. 5, No. 10, pp. 417–419, October 2001.

16. A. D. Liveris, Z. Xiong, and C. N. Georghiades, Compression of binary sources with side information at the decoder using LDPC codes, *IEEE Communication Letters*, Vol. 6, No. 10, pp. 440–442, October 2002.

17. M. Fresia, L. Vandendorpe, and H. V. Poor, Distributed source coding using raptor codes for hidden Markov sources, *IEEE Transactions on Signal Processing*, Vol. 57, No. 7, pp. 2868–2875, July 2009.

18. Q. Xu, V. Stankovic, and Z. Xiong, Distributed joint source-channel coding of video using raptor codes, *IEEE Journal on Selected Areas in Communication*, Vol. 25, No. 4, pp. 851–861, May 2007.

19. R. Cristescu, B. Beferull-Lozano, and M. Vetterli, Networked Slepian–Wolf: Theory, algorithms, and scaling laws, *IEEE Transactions on Information Theory*, Vol. 51, No. 12, pp. 4057–4073, December 2005.

20. S. S. Pradhan, J. Kusuma, and K. Ramchandran, Distributed compression in a dense microsensor network, *IEEE Signal Processing Magazine*, Vol. 19, No. 2, pp. 51–60, March 2002.

21. A. Checko, H. L. Christiansen, Y. Yan, L. Scolari, G. Kardaras, M. S. Berger, and L. Dittmann, Cloud RAN for mobile networks: A technology overview, *IEEE Communications Surveys and Tutorials*, Vol. 17, No. 1, pp. 405–426, 2015.

22. Z. Zhu, P. Gupta, Q. Wang, S. Kalyanaraman, Y. Lin, H. Franke, and S. Sarangi, Virtual base station pool: Towards a wireless network cloud for radio access networks, *8th ACM International Conference on Computing Frontiers*, p. 34, May 2011.

23. China Mobile Research Institute, C-RAN: The road towards green RAN, White Paper, version 2.5, October 2011.

24. C. Chen, J. Huang, W. Jueping, Y. Wu, and G. Li, Suggestions on potential solutions to C-RAN, NGMN Alliance project P-CRAN Centralized Processing Collaborative Radio Real Time Cloud Computing Clear RAN System, version 4.0, January 2013.

25. C. Zhu, H. Wang, X. Liu, L. Shu, L. T. Yang, V. Leung, A novel sensory data processing framework to integrate sensor networks with mobile cloud, *IEEE Systems Journal*, Vol. 10, No. 3, pp. 1125–1136, September 2016.

26. Y. Zhang, R. Yu, M. Nekovee, Y. Liu, S. Xie, and S. Gjessing, Cognitive machine-to-machine communications: Visions and potentials for the smart grid, *IEEE Network*, Vol. 26, No. 3, pp. 6–13, 2012.

27. K. Akkaya and M. Younis, A survey on routing protocols for wireless sensor networks, *Ad Hoc Networks*, Vol. 3, No. 3, pp. 325–349, May 2005.

28. A. Koubâa, M. Alves, M. Attia, and A. Van Nieuwenhuyse, Collisionfree beacon scheduling mechanisms for IEEE 802.15.4/Zigbee cluster tree wireless sensor networks, *7th International Workshop on Applications and Services in Wireless Networks (ASWN), Proceedings*, 2007, pp. 1–16.

29. G. Smart, N. Deligiannis, R. Surace, V. Loscri, G. Fortino, and Y. Andreopoulos, Decentralized time-synchronized channel swapping for ad hoc wireless networks, *IEEE Transactions Vehicular Technology*, Vol. 65, No. 10, pp. 8538–8553, October 2016.

30. N. Deligiannis, J. F. C. Mota, G. Smart, and Y. Andreopoulos, Fast desynchronization for decentralized multichannel medium access control, *IEEE Transactions on Communications*, Vol. 63, No. 9, pp. 3336–3349, September 2015.

31. C. E. Shannon, A mathematical theory of communication, *Bell System Technical Journal*, Vol. 27, pp. 379–423, July 1948.

32. R. Zamir, S. Shamai, and U. Erez, Nested linear/lattice codes for structured multiterminal binning, *IEEE Transactions on Information Theory*, Vol. 48, No. 6, pp. 1250–1276, June 2002.

33. A. Wyner, Recent results in the Shannon theory, *IEEE Transactions on Information Theory*, Vol. 20, No. 1, pp. 2–10, January 1974.

34. D. Varodayan, A. Aaron, and B. Girod, Rate-adaptive codes for distributed source coding, *Signal Processing Journal, Special Issue on Distributed Source Coding*, Vol. 86, No. 11, pp. 3123–3130, November 2006.

35. R. Zamir, The rate loss in the Wyner-Ziv problem, *IEEE Transactions on Information Theory*, Vol. 42, No. 11, pp. 2073–2084, November 1996.

36. S. Servetto, Lattice quantization with side information, IEEE Data Compression Conference, DCC 2000, March 2000.

37. Z. Liu, S. Cheng, A. Liveris, and Z. Xiong, Slepian–Wolf coded nested quantization (SWC-NQ) for Wyner-Ziv coding: Performance analysis and code design, IEEE Data Compression Conference, DCC 2004, Snowbird, UT, March 2004.

38. B. Girod, A. Aaron, S. Rane, and D. Rebollo-Monedero, Distributed video coding, *Proceedings of the IEEE*, Vol. 93, No. 1, pp. 71–83, January 2005.

39. D. Taubman and M. W. Marcelin, *JPEG2000: Image Compression Fundamentals, Standards, and Practice*. Norwell, MA: Kluwer Academic Publishers, 2002.

40. Y. Yang, S. Cheng, Z. Xiong, and W. Zhao, Wyner-Ziv coding based on TCQ and LDPC codes, Asilomar Conference on Signals, Systems, and Computers, Pacific Grove, CA, November 2003.

41. N. Deligiannis, J. Barbarien, M. Jacobs, A. Munteanu, A. Skodras, and P. Schelkens, Side-information-dependent correlation channel estimation in hash-based distributed video coding, *IEEE Transactions on Image Processing*, Vol. 21, No. 4, pp. 1934–1949, April 2012.

42. N. Deligiannis, A. Sechelea, A. Munteanu, and S. Cheng, The no-rate-loss property of Wyner-Ziv coding in the Z-channel correlation case, *IEEE Communications Letters*, Vol. 18, No. 10, pp. 1675–1678, October 2014.

43. Y. Steinberg, Coding and common reconstruction, *IEEE Transactions on Information Theory*, Vol. 55, No. 11, pp. 4995–5010, November 2009.

44. S. Cheng, V. Stankovic, and Z. Xiong, Computing the channel capacity and rate-distortion function with two-sided state information, *IEEE Transactions on Information Theory*, Vol. 51, No. 12, pp. 4418–4425, December. 2005.

45. F. Oldewurtel, M. Foks, and P. Mahonen, On a practical distributed source coding scheme for wireless sensor networks, *IEEE Vehicular Technology Conference (VTC Spring), Proceedings*, pp. 228–232, May 2008.

46. F. Oldewurtel, J. Ansari, and P. Mahonen, Cross-layer design for distributed source coding in wireless sensor networks, *2nd International Conference on Sensor Technologies and Applications (SENSORCOMM), Proceedings*, pp. 435–443, August 2008.

47. F. Chen, M. Rutkowski, C. Fenner, R. C. Huck, S. Wang, and S. Cheng, Compression of distributed correlated temperature data in sensor networks, *the Data Compression Conference (DCC), Proceedings*, p. 479, March 2013.

48. S. Cheng, Multiterminal source coding for many sensors with entropy coding and Gaussian process regression, *the Data Compression Conference, Proceedings*, p. 480, March 2013.

49. B. Beferull-Lozano and R. L. Konsbruck, On source coding for distributed temperature sensing with shift-invariant geometries, *IEEE Transactions on Communication*, Vol. 59, No. 4, pp. 1053–1065, April 2011.

50. K. C. Barr and K. Asanovic, Energy-aware lossless data compression, *ACM Transactions on Computational Systems*, Vol. 24, No. 3, pp. 250–291, 2006.

51. D. I. Sacaleanu, R. Stoian, D. M. Ofrim, and N. Deligiannis, Compression scheme for increasing the lifetime of wireless intelligent sensor networks, *20th European Signal Processing Conference (EUSIPCO), Proceedings*, pp. 709–713, August 2012.

52. F. Marcelloni and M. Vecchio, A simple algorithm for data compression in wireless sensor networks, *IEEE Communications Letters*, Vol. 12, No. 6, pp. 411–413, June 2008.

53. M. Vecchio, R. Giaffreda, and F. Marcelloni, Adaptive lossless entropy compressors for tiny IoT devices, *IEEE Transactions on Wireless Communications*, Vol. 13, No. 2, pp. 1088–1100, February 2014.

54. A. Shokrollahi, Raptor codes, *IEEE Transactions on Information Theory*, Vol. 52, No. 6, pp. 2551–2567, June 2006.

55. J. E. Barceló-Lladó, A. M. Pérez, and G. Seco-Granados, Enhanced correlation estimators for distributed source coding in large wireless sensor networks, *IEEE Sensors Journal*, Vol. 12, No. 9, pp. 2799–2806, September 2012.

56. N. Deligiannis, E. Zimos, D. M. Ofrim, Y. Andreopoulos, and A. Munteanu, Distributed joint source-channel coding with copula-function-based correlation modeling for wireless sensors measuring temperature, *IEEE Sensors Journal*, Vol. 15, No. 8, pp. 4496–4507, August 2015.
57. P. K. Trivedi and D. M. Zimmer, *Copula Modeling: An Introduction for Practitioners*, Vol. 1. Delft, The Netherlands: NOW Pub., 2007.
58. M. Camilli and R. Kleihorst, Mouse sensor networks, the smart camera, *ACM/IEEE International Conference on Distributed Smart Cameras (ICDSC), Proceedings*, pp. 1–3, August 2011.
59. S. Grunwedel, V. Jelaca, P. Van Hese, R. Kleihorst, and W. Philips, Multi-view occupancy maps using a network of low resolution visual sensors, *ACM/IEEE International Conference on Distributed Smart Cameras (ICDSC), Proceedings*, August 2011.
60. S. Zambanini, J. Machajdik, and M. Kampel, Detecting falls at homes using a network of low-resolution cameras, *IEEE International Conference on Information Technology and Applications in Biomedicine, (ITAB), Proceedings*, November 2010.
61. T. Wiegand, G. J. Sullivan, G. Bjntegaard, and A. Luthra, Overview of the H.264/AVC video coding standard, *IEEE Transactions on Circuits and Systems for Video Technology*, Vol. 13, No. 7, pp. 560–576, July 2003.
62. G. J. Sullivan, J.-R. Ohm, W.-J. Han, and T. Wiegand, Overview of the high efficiency video coding (HEVC) standard, *IEEE Transactions on Circuits and Systems for Video Technology*, Vol. 22, No. 12, pp. 1649–1668, December 2012.
63. N. Deligiannis, A. Munteanu, S. Wang, S. Cheng, and P. Schelkens, Maximum likelihood Laplacian correlation channel estimation in layered Wyner-Ziv coding, *IEEE Transactions on Signal Processing*, Vol. 62, No. 4, pp. 892–904, February 2014.
64. S. Cheng and Z. Xiong, Successive refinement for the Wyner-Ziv problem and layered code design, *IEEE Transactions on Signal Processing*, Vol. 53, No. 8, pp. 3269–3281, August. 2005.
65. N. Deligiannis, F. Verbist, J. Slowack, R. Van de Walle, P. Schelkens, and A. Munteanu, Progressively refined Wyner-Ziv video coding for visual sensors, *ACM Transactions on Sensor Networks*, Special Issue on New Advancements in Distributed Smart Camera Networks, Vol. 10, No. 2, pp. 1–34, January 2014.
66. N. Deligiannis, M. Jacobs, J. Barbarien, F. Verbist, J. Škorupa, R. Van de Walle, A. Skodras, P. Schelkens, and A. Munteanu, Joint DC coefficient band decoding and motion estimation in Wyner-Ziv video coding, *International Conference on Digital Signal Processing (DSP), Proceedings*, July 2011, pp. 1–6.
67. X. Artigas, J. Ascenso, M. Dalai, S. Klomp, D. Kubasov, and M. Quaret, The DISCOVER codec: Architecture, techniques and evaluation, *Picture Coding Symposium (PCS), Proceedings*, November 2007.
68. F. Verbist, N. Deligiannis, W. Chen, P. Schelkens, and A. Munteanu, Transform-domain Wyner-Ziv video coding for 1-K pixel visual sensors, ACM/IEEE International Conference on Distributed Smart Cameras, ICDSC'13, Palm Springs, CA, October–November 2013.

Chapter 11

5G C-RAN Uplink Cross-Layer Optimization to Support Massive Traffic Sensor Network Services

Spyridon Louvros and Nikos Deligiannis

Contents

11.1 Introduction*,†

It is mainly expected that 5G technology and cloud-radio access networks (C-RAN) will provide, apart from traditional user equipment (UE) handset Internet connectivity, adequate coverage, and a capacity for sensor network services and traffic. What distinguishes 5G networks from other existing and legacy systems is the effort to provide the native and efficient support of single-user multisector communication with two or more different sectors, which may efficiently lead to advanced throughput as well as new requested frequency bands. 5G requirements for throughput, latency, accessibility, and quality of service (QoS) could be feasible and cost-effective through the virtualization of nodes and C-RAN solutions. The Internet of things (IoT) as well as machine-to-machine (M2M) and device-to-device (D2D) communications are the major perspectives on the new era of wireless 5G services, supported over a wide range of physical deployments, from distributed base stations to centralized cloud-RAN deployments or distributed edge clouds.

11.1.1 Background and Motivation

Whatever might be at the end of the final 5G-network architecture for future IoT services, it should definitely be both feasible for implementation from the operator's perspective as well as cost-effective from the operator's deployment and investment points of view, in order to gradually be adopted into the existing 3G and 4G legacy cellular networks. The supporting key technology options, toward flexibility and enhanced performance, are the usage of mobile network functions, software-defined (SDN) mobile network control, as well as the joint optimization of mobile access and core network functions [1]. What would be expected of 5G mobile network architecture, would be the inclusion of both physical and virtual (also related to cloud) network functions, as well as edge cloud computing and centralized cloud deployments. Consequently, the 5G mobile network needs to integrate the most known and globally accepted network scheme of long-term evolution–advanced (LTE-A) [1] on the RAN level (the current and modified definition of RAN as *cloud-RAN*) as well as in terms of security functions [2]. The Next Generation Mobile Networks (NGMN) Alliance [3] requires the integration of RAN technologies far beyond the existing 3GPP interworking proposals toward 5G C-RAN access technologies [4]. 5G C-RAN mobile network architectures should be capable of supporting not only the expected enormous growth of mobile downlink but mostly the expected IoT sensor-based uplink data traffic generated by customer devices in smart cities [5] platforms and user applications. The most common implementation is the transformation of legacy wireless macrocell networks into cloud-based architecture on C-RAN, comprising large numbers of small cells complemented with macrocells for ubiquitous geographical coverage [6].

11.1.2 Book Chapter Contribution

In this chapter, we propose, aligned with 5GPPP [7] as well as 3GPP, LTE, and LTE-A [8], the substitution of legacy baseband units (BBUs) and remote radio units (RRUs) with cloud radio access networks (C-RANs) [9], considering some radio access–related restrictions. The C-RAN

---

* Part of this work is the result of research in mobile cloud & network services (MCNS), Cyprus.
† Part of this work is the result of consultancy in Teledrom AB for Ericsson next-generation mobile network deployments.

architectural splitting, BBU–RRU, approach [10] introduces many restrictions on media access control (MAC) to physical cross-layer design as well as on cell planning capacity, especially for uplink throughput and accessibility performance. Considering specific applications, like future smart cities with IoT sensor-traffic load, where high bandwidth is a definite demand with stringent delay and synchronization requirements between the RRUs and remote computing cloud mainframes, these demands are becoming really restrictive. Finally, a C-RAN virtualization proposal, performance, and cell planning methodology should be aligned with the worldwide operator demands on traffic load and with new network deployments for cost efficiency. Moreover, most of the operators are pushing toward the reframing and utilization of existing LTE-A and heterogeneous networks (HetNets) to minimize cost and optimize the infrastructure investment. Indeed, following world-dominant vendor proposals, the LTE-A architecture enriched with radio splitting and BBU–RRU over broadband optical backhaul is the dominant candidate to smoothly migrate toward the full deployment of 5G [11,12].

11.1.3 5G C-RAN Next Generation Mobile Network (NGMN) Scenario

Among the proposed 5G C-RAN architectures with a nondominant standardized solution so far—though 5GPP with enhanced LTE-advanced network functionality (LTE-A) is already a promising and good candidate for a worldwide standard—the most popular due to its cost-effectiveness and simplicity in terms of network implementation is the C-RAN centralized solution. Most world-dominant vendors are proposing the LTE-A network architecture and functionality to support the C-RAN approach and to migrate toward 5G. The C-RAN concept is proposed to be based on a centralized baseband processing pool of equipment, serving a number of clustered distributed radio access nodes [13]. In legacy operator networks such as LTE-A and heterogeneous networks, where coordinated functionality and real-time processing are essential to performance interference as well as to mobility and synchronization improvements, the cloud-RAN approach is easily accommodated. Furthermore, the cell planning principles are quite similar to LTE-A with extra restrictions and demands adapting to the specific traffic and service. Ericsson has lately (early 2016) proposed a combination of powerful software features to combine cloud-RAN with LTE-A technology and to deliver extreme application coverage with huge peak cell throughputs over existing 4G operator infrastructures, in an effort toward 5G networks aligned with 3GPP and 5GPPP standards and proposals [14].

In such architectures, a large number of remote radio handlers (RRH)/RRUs are deployed over a large geographical area, all connected over fronthaul fiber links (dark fiber links), toward a centralized pool BBU on a cloud server with typical cell coverage ranges of 15–20 km over fiber links for LTE-A solutions [15]. It is widely accepted that using RRH/RRU-distributed units over a radio interface introduces advanced technologies over radio access networks, moving processing load functions to the cell-edge devices (mobile edge computing solutions) and exploiting IP/Ethernet with an emphasis on multiprotocol label switching (MPLS) over optical network technology for the RAN transmission and backhaul network topology [4]. With such a design any kind of traffic could be accommodated over a well-planned LTE-A network, including traditional IP subscriber web traffic, cloud services, and sensor-based traffic as well as generic IoT services of any kind. Following the fully centralized C-RAN approach, indoor sensor network topologies in a well deployed indoor application could be organized into different topology cluster groups with a primary sink and transmit, in a wide sense, dense periodic measurement reports (temperature, image, video, or streaming applications) [16]. The sensor cluster formation abides by well-known cluster tree architectures for IEEE 802.15.4-based MAC protocols in wireless sensor networks

(WSNs), for example, the IEEE 802.15.4 GTS [17]. The IEEE 802.15.4 router (also known as a *sink*) will collect all sensor data and forward them to the LTE-A indoor UE known as *customer premise equipment* (CPE), a customer device to provide uplink/downlink coverage connectivity. That CPE will transmit over the uplink all IEEE sensor MAC transport blocks toward an appropriate RRH/RRU unit in a maximum coverage distance of 15–20 km, depending on the cell planning and accessibility connectivity. Finally, RRH/RRU will forward traffic, using fronthaul fiber optical networks, to the cloud-RAN (blade-server approach) for further data analysis and finally to the ISP network [18] (Figure 11.1).

11.2 C-RAN Design Considerations

Following the cellular vendor proposals [5,14] and 3GPP/5GPPP standards [7,8], the design of the C-RAN proposed architecture of Figure 11.1 is governed by legacy LTE-A and HetNet cell planning principles. Furthermore, the latest proposals from researchers [19, pp. 97–98], have indicated the necessity to integrate 5G RAN technology into the existing 4G infrastructure and have emphasized the similarity between LTE/LTE-A and 5G cell planning methodologies. 4G Americas has also released a white paper indicating the evolution of 5G as an enhancement of LTE-A and 4G technologies with a similar RAN approach [20]. Consequently, RAN design is similar to 4G with special requirements on the service, the UE, and the network deployment like cloud-RAN and sensor-based IoT traffic.

There are, however, three major restrictions to differentiate and complicate the design, restrictions that definitely have to be fulfilled in order to optimize the C-RAN LTE-A performance:

- *C-RAN interference considerations*: First of all, the study and proof of interference mitigation on a distributed random channel band selection.
- *Signal-to-interference-plus-noise ratio* (*SINR*) *considerations*: The major concern is related to uplink cell planning and optimization issues, in such a way as to guarantee adequate SINR for accepted service accessibility as well as integrity (throughput) performance.
- *Cross-layer considerations*: Last but not least, is the cross-layer approach regarding the LTE-A MAC to physical layer planning. The preselected sensor network IEEE MAC transport blocks will have to be fitted into an optimized LTE-A MAC transmission mechanism in order to minimize retransmissions and hence optimize capacity and throughput.

11.3 C-RAN Interference Considerations

C-RAN radio network design over LTE-A cloud-based architecture for IoT services, considering mix sensors and UE-based packet-switched (PS) traffic applications, emphasizes mostly, CPE uplink coverage for sensor-based traffic [18] (Figure 11.1). In such a scenario, uplink is always weaker than downlink and accessibility [21] as well as integrity [22]; consequently ensuring the uplink budget [23] and considering the appropriate signal-to-interference requirements $SINR_{\text{target}} = \gamma_{\text{target}}^{\text{uplink}}$ the IoT sensor-based QoS traffic is guaranteed [18]. Since adequate intercell interference is expected in the area, the radio planner should restrict the intercell distance d and also configure properly the allowed maximum transmitted power of neighbor LTE-A outdoor units in the cell area, $P_{\text{max},ul}^{UE}$ [24]. The allowed maximum transmitted power $P_{\text{max},ul}^{UE}$ is an operator-configured parameter with the extra restriction to be always less than the hardware maximum

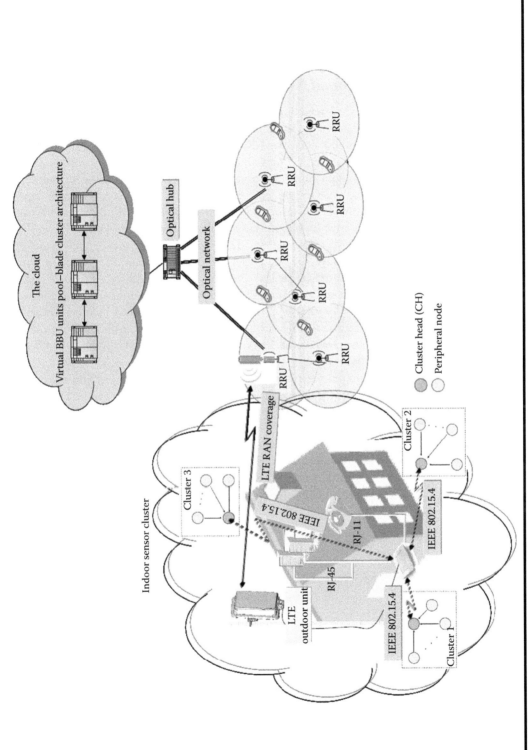

Figure 11.1 **Proposed centralized C-RAN network for indoor sensor network traffic.**

available LTE-A outdoor CPE customer unit power P_0^{UE}, that is, $P_{\max,ul}^{UE} \leq P_0^{UE}$. This optimum setting will ensure expected uplink neighbor cell (intercell) interference to be bounded into levels below an acceptable threshold [24].

11.3.1 Noise Floor (Background Noise) Level Estimation

Background Noise N depends on the background environmental temperature and is expected to differentiate daily as well as based on latitude coordinates. Estimation follows the basic principles of statistical physics (thermodynamics) since the RRH/RRU antenna receiver (Figure 11.1) is subject to temperature differences during day- and nighttime. Environmental temperature T°K defines the amount of molecular random vibrations inside the metal crystal structure contributing to the additive white Gaussian noise (AWGN) N_t. From such random vibrations, molecular energy subject to environmental temperature T°K is expected to be $E \sim kT$, where k is the Boltzmann constant $k = 1.38 \cdot 10^{-23}$ [J/°K]. Such energy follows Gaussian distributions with mean value $\langle E \rangle \sim k\langle T \rangle$ and mean power $\langle P \rangle \sim k\langle T \rangle \Delta t$ over Δt time periods. Taking into account $\Delta t = 1/\Delta f$, where Δf is the channel bandwidth, the mean noise spectral power density is $N_t \sim k\langle T \rangle / \Delta f$ [W/BW]. For $\Delta f = 1$ Hz, we define the mean noise power density per unit of bandwidth $N_t \sim k\langle T \rangle$ [W/Hz]. Substituting the Boltzmann constant value and considering a typical environmental temperature of $\langle T \rangle = 290°$K (almost 18°C), then $N_t = 10\log k\langle T \rangle = -174$ [dBm/Hz]. In LTE-A indoor and pico/micro cells, the bandwidth unit of scheduled resources is one physical resource block (PRB) = 180 kHz and then the expected noise power density is $N_t \cdot RB_{BW} = k\langle T \rangle \cdot 180$ kHz [W] or $N_t \cdot RB_{BW}$ [dB$_m$] = $10\log k\langle T \rangle + 10\log 180$ kHz.

Noise floor level, however, might be increased due to the transceiver's electronic equipment noise figure. This noise figure is the contribution of the operational temperature of electronic equipment due to quantum noise and is estimated from basic physics principles to be $N_f = N_f^{LNA} + ((N_f^R L_{pathloss}^{feeder}) - 1/G_{LNA})$, where N_f^{LNA} is the contribution of the preamplifier (low-noise amplifier, LNA), which exists mostly after the receiving antenna and before the receiving unit equipment. Such an LNA contributes to the improvement of the uplink-received signal before its signal processing functions. N_f^R is the noise contribution of the receiving unit increased by the feeder losses $L_{pathloss}^{feeder}$ and underestimated from the signal-over-noise gain G_{LNA}. Typical values fall into $N_f = 3$ [dB] for $L_{pathloss}^{feeder} = 1$ and $G_{LNA} = 1$. Summarizing background noise per PRB is estimated as the following [25]:

$$N = N_t \cdot RB_{BW} \cdot N_f = N_t \cdot RB_{BW} \cdot \left(N_f^{LNA} + \frac{\left(N_f^R L_{pathloss}^{feeder}\right) - 1}{G_{LNA}} \right) \tag{11.1}$$

with typical values of $N = -119$ [dB$_m$].

11.3.2 Expected Intercell Interference Estimation

Among all major limitations of 5G networks, the most important and difficult one to coordinate is the high expected cochannel intercell interference in both downlink and uplink [26]. This is mainly because with LTE-A as well as HetNets and 5G evolving networks with a high density of sensor-based and handset devices, the densely overlaid and multilayer heterogeneous network's deployment is a common RAN design practice. Moreover, with the trend to increase service capacity by fully reusing all of the available channel bandwidth per sector (which extends up to 100 MHz), the expected intercell interference is inevitable. 3GPP and lately 5GPPP have proposed [27], through several advanced SON optional features, many different and effective techniques to coordinate intercell interference and finally mitigate the expected grade of service (GoS). Techniques such as intercell interference coordination (ICIC) [28], or joint scheduling in conjunction with cell planning [29], are quite familiar among network planners and optimizers. Although intercell interference is affected by cell planning and the geographical distribution of dense 5G RRH/RRU units, estimating intercell interference, I_{RB} per PRB of 180 kHz, is of extreme importance for the expected per-cell SINR target. Following a semianalytical model of analysis, consider $i \in \{1, 2, \ldots, 6\}$ neighboring cells surrounding the serving cell of radius R and intercell distance $d = 3/2\ R$, according to Figure 11.2, with different cell loads (the number of active subscribers and used PRB $k \in \{1, 2, \ldots, q_i\}$ per neighbor cell) that contribute to the overall uplink intercell interference [30]. All cells (serving and neighbors) have the same geographical coverage area; expected uplink interference is $I_{RB,n}[W]$ per physical resource block (PRB), where the available number of n PRBs depends on the channel bandwidth BW_{cell} $\in \{5, 10, 15, 20, 40, 60, 80, 100\}[MHz]$ and of course the number of PRBs is restricted by $n \in \{1, 2, \ldots, (BW_{cell}/[180\,kHz]) - BW_{guardband}\}$.

The expected interference per PRB $I_{RB,n}[W]$ is [31]

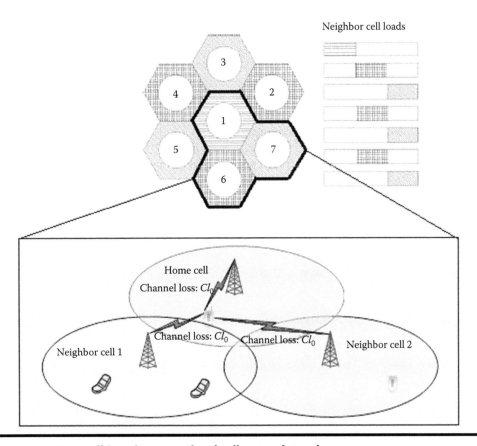

Figure 11.2   Intercell interference–related cell network topology.

$$I_{RB,n}[W] = \sum_{i=1}^{6} \left(f_i \cdot \varphi_i \cdot pr_{n,i}(\lambda) \cdot \sum_{k=1}^{q_i} \frac{P_{q_i,i}^{UE,RB}[W] \cdot G_{q_i,i}^{T}\left(\theta_{q_i,i}\right) \cdot G_{q_i,i}^{R}\left(\theta_{q_i,i}\right)}{L_{q_i}} \right) \qquad (11.2)$$

where:

$P_{q_i,i}^{UE,RB}[W]$ is the expected transmitted power of the q_i activated uplink CPE on the ith cell

$G_{q_i,i}^{T}(\theta_{q_i,i})$ is the antenna gain of the q_i activated user uplink CPE on the ith cell with an angle of transmission $\theta_{qi,i}$

$G_{q_i,i}^{R}(\theta_{q_i,i})$ is the antenna gain of the downlink RRH/RRU unit (Figure 11.1) due to the q_i activated uplink CPE transmission on the ith cell with an angle of transmission $\theta_{qi,i}$

L_{qi} represents the expected path losses of a q_i active unit on the ith cell given by 3GPP standards and measurements $L_{qi}[dB] = 85.25 + 33.48 \log R_i$

f_i is the expected interference reduction factor due to the isolation scrambling code [32], with typical values of $f_i \in \{0.2, \ldots, 0.4\}$

φ_i is a second interference reduction factor due to some optional activated radio features of interference rejection combining (IRC) [33,34], or UE (CPE) 5G advanced interference coordination [35]

According to the expected interference coordination algorithm, on each neighbor cell a MAC scheduler will attribute a number of PRBs to the active CPE units with a specific probability, depending on the cell load. Therefore, we should multiply the expected interference contribution of each ith neighbor cell on the nth PRB with the respective use probability of this nth PRB from neighbor cells $pr_{n,i}(\lambda)$. To estimate that probability a semianalytical multilayer birth–death model is proposed according to Figure 11.3. On that specific model we consider $0 \leq \lambda \leq N_{sub}$ connected CPE indoor units (serving the sink traffic of several sensors) asking for a number of PRBs to send the service with corresponding service time μ via uplink. On each CPE request, a MAC scheduler will attribute a number of PRBs with reduced probability p_k/n so that $p1 < p2 < \ldots < pk$, considering of course the fact that a MAC scheduler might simultaneously attribute k maximum consecutive resources PRBs under the 3GPP uplink restriction of $k = 2^{\alpha} \cdot 3^{\beta} \cdot 5^{\gamma}$, α, β, $\gamma \in Z$, and $1 \leq k \leq ((BW_{cell}/[180\,kHz]) - BW_{guardband})$.

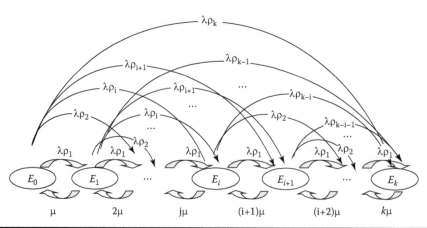

Figure 11.3 Probabilistic birth–death model for $p_{rn,i}(\lambda)$.

The probability calculation follows a recursive formula [30] as follows:

$$pr_{n,i}\left(\lambda,\mu,k\right) = \frac{1}{\left(n-1\right)\cdot\mu}\cdot\left[pr_{n,(i-1)}\left(\left(n-2\right)\cdot\mu + \lambda\cdot\sum_{j=0}^{k-n+1}\rho_j\right)\right]$$

$$-\frac{1}{\left(n-1\right)\cdot\mu}\cdot\left[\lambda\cdot\sum_{v=1}^{n-1}pr_{n,v}\cdot\rho_{n-v}\right], \quad 2\le n\le k \tag{11.3}$$

normalized under the total probability restriction $\sum_{n=1}^{k} pr_{n,i}(\lambda,\mu,k)=1$.

The expected ratio $\gamma_{RB} = SINR = \left(S_{RB}/N + I_{RB}\right)$, where $N + I_{RB} = N(1+(I_{RB}/N)) = N\cdot\beta_{I,RB}^{UL}$ and the factor $(1+(I_{RB,n}/N)) = \beta_{I,RB}^{UL}$ is known as the *interference load margin*.

Hence, $\gamma_{RB} = SINR = \left(S_{RB}/N + I_{RB}\right) = \left(S_{RB}/N\cdot\beta_{I,RB}^{UL}\right)$.

Recursive formula calculations are not easy to perform and the only fast and accurate way is by simulation over MATLAB. Indeed, a MATLAB simulation for $\beta_{I,RB}^{UL}$ provides, in the general case and for different radio link channels, the expected values shown in Figure 11.4 [30].

Simulated results in Figure 11.4 are produced under the following simulation assumptions:

- Two-branch RX diversity
- Modulation schemes: quadrature phase-shift keying (QPSK), 16-QAM, 64-QAM
- Channel models: EPA5 (pedestrian 5 km/h), EVA70 (in-car model, 70 km/h), and ETU300 (highway 300 km/h)

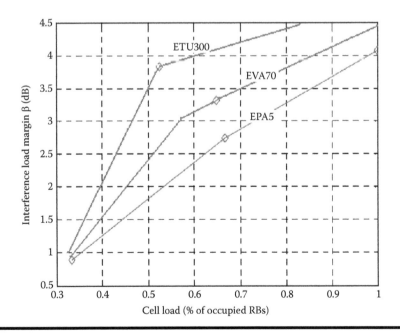

Figure 11.4   Interference load margin simulated results.

- Monte-Carlo simulation for the mobility of the q_i^{th} pieces of UE on each ith neighbor cell with $R_i = 150$ m
- $0.001[W] \le P_{q_i,i}^{UE,RB} \le P_0^{UE} = 0.2[W] = 23\text{dB}_m$ as typical values for each LTE-A outdoor unit or user handset piece of equipment, also considering power control algorithms
- $G_{q_i,i}^T\left(\theta_{q_i,i}\right) = 1$
- $G_{q_i,i}^R(\theta_{q_i,i})$ for a typical Kathrein-type antenna with a maximum gain of 18 dB$_i$
- $R = 150$ m, → coverage area $A = 0.044$ km^2, intercell distance $d = 3/2$, and $R = 225$ m

Of course, the general extended typical urban (ETU) 300 km/h highway-moving piece of UE or the extended vehicular A (EVA) 70 km/h urban user piece of equipment scenarios are useless in our dense, urban 5G sensor-based multilayer case study since the CPE pieces of equipment are motionless. However, the extended pedestrian A (EPA) 5 km/h dense urban scenario is quit close to the CPE case study, since the expected orthogonal frequency and code division multiplexing (OFDM) errors are produced due to dispersive channel multipath contributions [36].

11.3.3 Intercell Interference Auto-Coordination Proposed Algorithm

In this chapter, we would like to propose an advanced algorithm to mitigate and coordinate the expected intercell interference on 5G networks for IoT sensor–generated tumultuous traffic. We would like to prove for 5G cooperative networks as well as for relay broadband wireless sensor networks (like 5G LTE-A) that basic SINR performance could be improved if dynamic frequency allocation were included in the radio resource management (RRM) system's functionality. Indeed, such a solution might have an important role in the performance since it results in less transmission power, which is an important metric for SINR improvement as well as intercell interference reduction.

Traditional optimal implemented RRM algorithms (like the intercell interference cancellation, ICIC, radio feature [28]) with interference metric feedback reports (closed-loop algorithms) need an open-source (OSS) database–centralized processor with full knowledge of the spatial distribution profile of the network base stations. On the contrary, in 5G C-RAN virtual networks, where the central base station node (BBU controller) is centralized over the cloud and RRH/RRU clients are distributed over the entire geographical area, a centralized RRM algorithm would increase the capacity of the signaling load considerably. In this case, a decentralized RRM algorithm with random frequency allocation coordination is naturally requested. In the proposed decentralized RRM algorithm, RRH/RRUs are divided into different clusters based on cell planning topology. For the shake of simplicity, the path-loss channel model we consider is the common free-space path-loss model, which gives a more refined model than that given in the existing literature. It is easily proven then that this distributed random strategy converges to a suboptimal spectrum assignment, without any extra centralized intracluster coordination process, thus minimizing the BBU microprocessor cloud-RAN load and fronthaul optical network load, as well as saving the cloud node to the distributed RRH radio equipment's signaling capacity in the optical transport network. In other words, the algorithm converges to a local minimum of the aggregate interference of the network.

We do consider a number of three sectored 5G C-RAN remote RRH pieces of equipment with $b_i = 1, 2, \ldots, N_B$ cells neighboring each other, each of them serving u_i sensor devices (SD) in uplink. The intercell distance between two cells b_i and b_j is considered to be R_{ij} with $f_1, f_2, \ldots, f_c$ channel bands available, known as *physical resource blocks* (PRB). For simplicity, it is considered that with each u_i SD on any RRH piece of equipment, cell b_i transmits with power αP_u, where parameter α ranges $0 < \alpha < 1$ and is coordinated by the existing LTE-A power control algorithms. P_u is the maximum possible SD uplink transmitted power, restricted only by the SD hardware's capability. The distance between an SD u_i and RRH cell b_j is considered to be d_{ij} and the expected path loss on the RRH cell's receiving side due to distance is a factor of $1/d_{ij}^2$. For any random time period t, any random RRH equipment cell b_i has allocated a number of radio resources (PRB) in the subset band $S_i(t)$, $i \in (f_1, f_2, \ldots, f_c)$. This allocated band is reserved as long as a new BBU RRM decision on PRB allocation per RRU/RRH (called the PRB *channel band resource update*, CBRU) is executed. This CBRU takes place during discrete time instances $t_1, t_2, \ldots, t_3$, that are always greater than the 5G C-RAN transmission time interval (TTI) period. The CBRU period updates follow a random distribution and each RRH/RRU piece of equipment updates the allocated subset band $S_i(t)$, $i \in (f_1, f_2, \ldots, f_c)$ in an asynchronous way without any correlation to other neighbor RRH/RRU pieces of equipment, since there is no coordination with the other base stations in the network. This random procedure introduces a simple but effective performance.

The basic metric to evaluate the proposed algorithm's performance is the total mean uplink interference in the RRH/RRU cluster network. For each allocated subset band $S_i(t)$, the expected uplink interference on one RRH/RRU sector b_i by the neighbor RRH/RRU sectors b_j holding randomly allocated subset bands $S_j(t)$ at time instance t_1 is evaluated as $_{i \neq j}$

$$I_{b_i} = \sum_{i \neq j} \frac{aP_{u_j}}{d_{ij}^2} \mu\left(s_i(t_1), s_j(t_1)\right)$$

where $\mu\left(s_i(t_1), s_j(t_1)\right) = \begin{cases} 1, \text{if} & s_i(t_1) = s_j(t_1) \\ 0, \text{if} & s_i(t_1) \neq s_j(t_1) \end{cases}$ is the Kronecker delta function.

The total uplink interference in the RRH/RRU cluster network at time t_1 is calculated as

$$\bar{I}_{t_1} = \sum_{i=1}^{N_B} I_{b_i} = \sum_{i=1}^{N_B} \sum_{i \neq j} \frac{aP_{u_j}}{d_{ij}^2} \mu\left(s_i(t_1), s_j(t_1)\right)$$

The total cluster mean uplink interference in a large time period T is defined as

$$\langle I \rangle_T = \frac{1}{T} \sum_{t=t_1}^{T} \bar{I}_t = \frac{1}{T} \sum_{t=t_1}^{T} \left[\sum_{i=1}^{N_B} \sum_{i \neq j} \frac{aP_u}{d_{ij}^2} \mu\left(s_i(t), s_j(t)\right) \right]$$

The CBRU algorithm steps describing the allocation of available consecutive subset band $S_i(t)$, $i \in (f_1, f_2, \ldots, f_c)$ is the following:

1. Each RRH/RRU sector $b_i = 1, 2, \ldots, N_B$, make an independent decision on allocated the subset band $S_i(t)$ to its connected SDs based on real instant traffic load measurements.
2. Each RRH/RRU sector $b_i = 1, 2, \ldots, N_B$ on the time interval $\tau = t_i - t_{i-1}$ scans all of the available PRBs' bandwidths and finds a group of consecutive frequencies on the subset band $S_i(t)$, $i \in (f_1, f_2, \ldots, f_c)$ so that the uplink interference $\langle I \rangle_\tau$ is estimated to be the minimum possible interference. This group is allocated on the next τ instance to its SDs on a CBRU update.

$$\langle I \rangle_\tau = \frac{1}{\tau} \sum_{t=t_{i-1}}^{t_i} \bar{I}_\tau = \frac{1}{t_i - t_{i-1}} \sum_{t=t_{i-1}}^{t_i} \left[\sum_{i=1}^{N_B} \sum_{i \neq j} \frac{aP_{u_j}}{d_{ij}^2} \mu\left(s_i(\tau), s_j(\tau)\right) \right]$$

3. If it is not feasible to find a better subset group of frequencies, then the previous subset is held.

Lemma: mean uplink total interference $\langle I \rangle_T$ converges into a local minimum on a finite period of time T_c.

Proof: Uplink total mean interference $\langle I \rangle_T$ is a bounded function on zero, since

$$\langle I \rangle_T = \frac{1}{T} \sum_{t=t_1}^{T} \bar{I}_t = \frac{1}{T} \sum_{t=t_1}^{T} \left[\sum_{i=1}^{N_B} \sum_{i \neq j} \frac{aP_u}{d_{ij}^2} \mu\left(s_i(t), s_j(t)\right) \right] \geq 0, \ \forall T \in [0, \infty]$$

and equality is a rare event but not an impossible event depending on the number of simultaneously connected SD devices per RRH/RRU sector, the subset group allocated per neighbor RRH/RRU sector, as well as the expected throughput per RRH/RRU sector.

Supposing that one RRH sector b_v holds a subset S_v, $v \in (f_1, f_2, \ldots, f_v) \subseteq (f_1, f_2, \ldots, f_c)$ then the expected uplink interference on time instance t_m is defined as

$$\bar{I}_{t_m} = \sum_{k=1}^{N_B-1} I_{b_k} + I_{b_v}(v) = \sum_{k=1}^{N_B-1} \sum_{i \neq j} \frac{aP_{u_j}}{d_{ij}^2} \mu\left(s_i(t_m), s_j(t_m)\right) + \sum_{v \neq j} \frac{aP_{u_j}}{d_{vj}^2} \mu\left(s_v(t_m), s_j(t_m)\right)$$

On next time instance t_{m+1}, the CBRU update is expected and the new subset group state on the RRH/RRU sector b_v is updated to S_μ, $\mu \in (f_1, f_2, \ldots, f_\mu) \subseteq (f_1, f_2, \ldots, f_c)$. The expected interference is then defined as

$$\bar{I}_{t_{m+1}} = \sum_{k=1}^{N_B-1} I_{b_k} + I_{b_v}(\mu) = \sum_{k=1}^{N_B-1} \sum_{i \neq j} \frac{aP_u}{d_{ij}^2} \mu\left(s_i(t_{m+1}), s_j(t_{m+1})\right) + \sum_{v \neq j} \frac{aP_u}{d_{vj}^2} \mu\left(s_\mu(t_{m+1}), s_j(t_{m+1})\right)$$

According to the second step of the proposed aforementioned algorithm for a CBRU update, the newly allocated S_μ subband follows the rules of minimum interference, hence $I_{b_v}(\mu) \leq I_{b_v}(v)$ and as a result $I_{t_{m+1}} \leq I_{t_m}$, where equality is rare and holds for the cases where it is impossible to find any subband to minimize the interference. Consequently, the mean total interference in every step will be always equal to or less than the previous step's CBRU update. Hence, interference has a lower bound on zero and is also a decreasing function with a certain rate driving inevitably to an interference minimum (local or total).

Theorem: CBRU algorithm converges to a local or total interference minimum on finite update steps

Proof: We shall proceed with further analysis using a combinatorial approach. Taking into account that each CBRU update on the RRH/RRU sector allocates the maximum available number of consecutive ν PRBs out of the total available $(f_1, f_2, ..., f_c)$ to each connected SD_i, we expect to have in total k groups of allocated frequencies, $\lfloor f_c/\nu \rfloor \leq k \leq f_c$; hence, the maximum number of possible connected SDs in a cell might be $u_i = k$ on an interval $\lfloor f_c/\nu \rfloor \leq k \leq f_c$.

The number M of possible replacements of the total $f = f_c$ PRBs when m available groups of similar spectrum bands exist, and where $1 \leq f_m \leq \nu$ so that $f_1 + f_2 + \cdots + f_m = f$, is calculated from combinatorial theory to be $M = (f\,!/f_1\,!\cdot f_2\,!...f_m\,!)$.

RRH/RRU sector equipment will finally be able to select M_s combinations of PRBs out of the available number of possible replacements (always the number of simultaneously connected SDs under restriction $\lfloor f_c/\nu \rfloor \leq u_i \leq f_c$). Following the combinatorial theory for M, the selected objects out of M existing objects, the total number of available selections (CBRU subsets) is concluded from the binomial distribution:

$$C(M, M_s) = \binom{M}{M_s} = \frac{M!}{M_s!(M - M_s)!}, \quad M \geq M_s$$

Since there are, in general, N_B available RRH/RRU sectors in a network cluster with the possibility of CBRU selection repetitions, the total number of cluster selections will be

$$C(N_B M + N_B M_s - 1, N_B M_s) = \binom{N_B M + N_B M_s - 1}{N_B M_s} = \frac{(N_B M + N_B M_s - 1)!}{N_B M_s!(N_B M - 1)!}, \quad M \geq M_s$$

Finally, each of the neighbor RRH/RRU cells out of the total NB will make a selection M_s out of the total available $C(N_B M + N_B M_s - 1, N_B M_s)$ with an expected probability of $P = 1/C(N_B M + N_B M_s - 1, N_B M_s)$. The number of different possible interference values is

$$\frac{(N_B M + N_B M_s - 1)!}{N_B M_s!(N_B M - 1)!}$$

The worst-case scenario would be the selection of the same M_s out of each cell out of the total N_B. Hence, every subband PRB allocation update $S_i(t)$, $i \in (f_1, f_2, ..., f_{100})$, from one cell will randomly contribute. In a worst-case scenario, the interference reduction would be at least $1/(N_B M_s d_{ij})^2$.

There exist $(N_B M + N_B M_s - 1)!/N_B M_s!(N_B M - 1)!$ different interference values in N_B cells. Hence, the total number of interference selections will be

$$C(I) = \frac{\left(\dfrac{(N_B M + N_B M_s - 1)!}{N_B M_s!(N_B M - 1)!} + N_B - 1 \right)!}{\left(\dfrac{(N_B M + N_B M_s - 1)!}{N_B M_s!(N_B M - 1)!} \right)!(N_B - 1)!}$$

Consequently, in a worst-case scenario there would be $C(I)$ steps toward reaching a local or total minimum of interference, which are finally finite and the intercell interference would be mitigated on 5G C-RAN sectors!

11.4 SINR Considerations

Continuing our analysis and considering the second planning considerations, it is crucial to ensure the signal-to-noise ratio over the uplink receiving levels [37] so that $\gamma_{RRH}^{uplink} = \gamma_{target}^{uplink}$ on a RRH/RRU unit, otherwise several severe side effects might take place:

- Intercell Interference on neighbor RRH/RRU cells is increased if $\gamma_{RRH}^{uplink} \gg \gamma_{target}^{uplink}$.
- Intercell Interference from neighbor RRH/RRU cells to a serving cell is increased on the condition that $\gamma_{eNodeB}^{uplink} \ll \gamma_{target}^{uplink}$.
- There is a decreased expected uplink throughput if $\gamma_{RRH}^{uplink} \ll \gamma_{target}^{uplink}$ due to a lower than expected allocated number of PRBs n_{RB}.

11.4.1 Signal-to-Interference Ratio γ_{target}^{uplink} Design Restrictions

The requested uplink γ_{target}^{uplink} depends on the power ability $P_{o,target}^{UE}$ of the 5G or LTE-A outdoor CPE unit as well as the RRH/RRU sensitivity (RRH sensitivity $SE_{RRH} = P_R^{UL}\big|_{min}$). Suppose that the CPE outdoor unit transmits on power level $P_{o,target}^{UE}$ and that the receiving RRH unit receives a signal strength $\geq SE_{RRH} = P_{R,min}^{UL}$, then the RRH receiving unit will be able to successfully decode the received signal under a noisy interference channel link [38].

Receiving sensitivity SE_{RRH} is defined as the minimum receiving signal level $P_R^{UL}\big|_{min}$, depending on the requested CPE outdoor unit's transmitted power $P_{o,target}^{UE}$ and is given by the following formula:

$$P_R^{UL}\Big|_{min} = SE_{RRH} = \frac{P_{o,target}^{UE} G_o^T\left(\theta_o\right) \cdot G_o^R\left(\theta_o\right)}{L_{pathloss} L_j L_{LNA} L_f L_C} \tag{11.4}$$

where:

L_j	are the jumper losses on RRH antenna unit
L_{LNA}	is the LNA losses if used
L_f	are the waveguide (feeder) losses
L_C	are the feeder connector losses over LNA

It is worthwhile on this point to emphasize the noise and interference levels and their significance on RRH sensitivity. Indeed, following Equation 11.4 and considering Figure 11.5, it is obvious that RRH sensitivity depends on $N = N_t \cdot RB_{BW} \cdot N_f$ and also on interference $I_{RB,n}$. The ideal condition for the successful decoding of the receiving RRH unit is

$$SE_{RRH} \geq N_t \cdot RB_{BW} \cdot \left(N_f^{LNA} + \frac{\left(N_f^R L_{pathloss}^{feeder}\right) - 1}{G_{LNA}} \right) \tag{11.5}$$

Substituting Equation 11.5 with Equation 11.4 will contribute to the sufficient uplink sensitivity condition of a RRH receiving unit:

$$SE_{RRH} = \frac{P_{o,target}^{UE} G_o^T\left(\theta_o\right) \cdot G_o^R\left(\theta_o\right)}{L_{pathloss} L_j L_{LNA} L_f L_C} \geq N_t \cdot RB_{BW} \cdot \left(N_f^{LNA} + \frac{\left(N_f^R L_{pathloss}^{feeder}\right) - 1}{G_{LNA}} \right) \Rightarrow$$

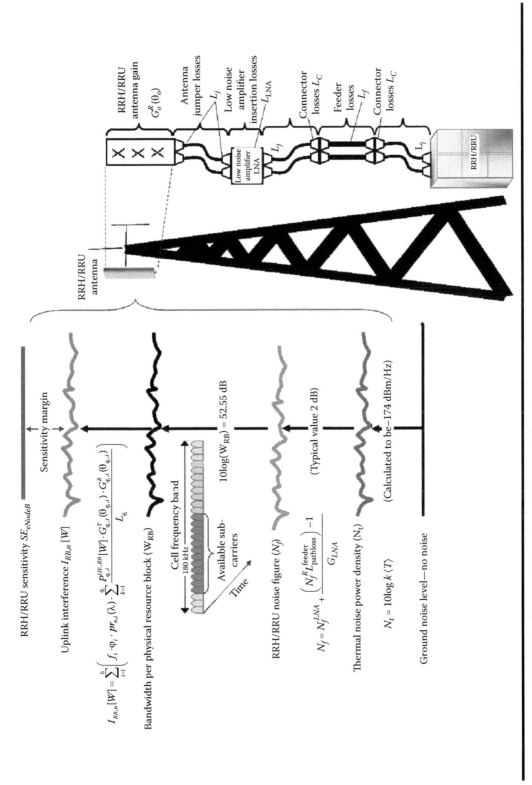

Figure 11.5 Uplink link budget analysis and sensitivity considerations.

$$P_{o,\text{target}}^{UE} \geq \frac{N_t \cdot RB_{BW} \cdot \left(N_f^{LNA} + \frac{\left(N_f^R L_{\text{pathloss}}^{\text{feeder}} \right) - 1}{G_{LNA}} \right) L_{\text{pathloss}} L_j L_{LNA} L_f L_C}{G_o^T (\theta_o) \cdot G_o^R (\theta_o)} \tag{11.6}$$

LTE-A for C-RAN has a superior power control algorithm to compensate for the adequate power for the received level of $P_{o,\text{target}}^{UE}$, however, there should be further considerations regarding some extra restrictions, since maintaining the condition in Equation 11.6 is not always feasible. This is because the CPE outdoor unit has predefined hardware restrictions on the maximum allowed transmitted power P_0^{UE}. Moreover, there is a maximum allowed uplink power threshold $P_{\max,ul}^{UE}$ posed by a RAN optimizer to mitigate intercell interference and to keep it as low as possible (an example might be the Ericsson parameter *pMaxServingCell*).

Considering these extra restrictions Equation 11.6 is rewritten as follows:

$$\left. P_R^{UL} \right|_{\min} = SE_{RRH} = \frac{\min \left(P_o^{UE}, \min \left(P_{\max,ul}^{UE}, P_{o,\text{target}}^{UE} \right) \right) G_o^T (\theta_o) \cdot G_o^R (\theta_o)}{L_{\text{pathloss}} L_j L_{LNA} L_f L_C} \tag{11.7}$$

The major problem that RAN designers might face on LTE-A C-RAN planning for IoT sensor applications is that quite often, due to the load (intercell interference in the area), an LTE-A outdoor unit might easily be saturated on uplink of the transmitted power. This means that the power control algorithm might request (under loaded conditions) the CPE outdoor unit to increase the uplink transmitted power $\left(\approx P_{o,\text{target}}^{UE} = P_{0,\text{uplink}}^{\text{req}} \right)$ *to fulfill the RRH/RRU received SINR or power level, however, the CPE outdoor unit might fail (saturates), since*

- The requested CPE outdoor unit's transmitted power $P_{o,\text{target}}^{UE} > P_{\max,ul}^{UE}$, → and hence saturates, since $\min \left(P_{\max,ul}^{UE}, P_{o,\text{target}}^{UE} \right) = P_{\max,ul}^{UE}$. That is, it is restricted from the configured parameter (i.e., the Ericsson parameter *pMaxServingCell*).
- The requested CPE outdoor unit's transmitted power $P_{o,\text{target}}^{UE} < P_{\max,ul}^{UE}$ → and hence there is enough power, since $\min \left(P_{\max,ul}^{UE}, P_{o,\text{target}}^{UE} \right) = P_{o,\text{target}}^{UE}$, but at the same time $P_o^{UE} < P_{o,\text{target}}^{UE} < P_{\max,ul}^{UE}$ → as a result fails (saturates) to respond to that power request because of hardware circuitry restrictions since $\min \left(P_o^{UE}, \min \left(P_{\max,ul}^{UE}, P_{o,\text{target}}^{UE} \right) \right) = \min \left(P_o^{UE}, P_{o,\text{target}}^{UE} \right) = P_o^{UE}$ → saturation occurs due to CPE outdoor power specifications.

Considering both previous conditions, it holds that

$$\text{Requested } \left(P_{o,\text{target}}^{UE} > P_o^{UE} \right) \cup \left(P_{o,\text{target}}^{UE} > P_{\max,ul}^{UE} \right)$$

And as a consequence always

$$SE_{eNodeB} < N_t \cdot RB_{BW} \cdot \left(N_f^{LNA} + \frac{\left(N_f^R L_{\text{pathloss}}^{\text{feeder}} \right) - 1}{G_{LNA}} \right)$$

1st Conclusion: C-RAN designers, considering the necessary CPE outdoor unit uplink connectivity, have to ensure that the previous saturation conditions should never happen!

2nd Conclusion: Considering all design restrictions as well as the RRH/RRU sensitivity conditions:

$$SE_{eNodeB} = \frac{\min\left(P_o^{UE}, \min\left(P_{\max,ul}^{UE}, P_{o,target}^{UE}\right)\right)G_o^T\left(\theta_o\right)\cdot G_o^R\left(\theta_o\right)}{L_{pathloss}L_j L_{LNA} L_f L_C} \geq$$

$$N_t \cdot RB_{BW} \cdot \left(N_f^{LNA} + \frac{\left(N_f^R L_{pathloss}^{feeder}\right)-1}{G_{LNA}}\right) \Rightarrow$$

$$\min\left(P_o^{UE}, \min\left(P_{\max,ul}^{UE}, P_{o,target}^{UE}\right)\right) \geq \frac{N_t \cdot RB_{BW} \cdot \left(N_f^{LNA} + \frac{\left(N_f^R L_{pathloss}^{feeder}\right)-1}{G_{LNA}}\right)L_{pathloss}L_j L_{LNA} L_f L_C}{G_o^T\left(\theta_o\right)\cdot G_o^R\left(\theta_o\right)} \Rightarrow$$

$$P_{o,target}^{UE} \geq \frac{N_t \cdot RB_{BW} \cdot \left(N_f^{LNA} + \frac{\left(N_f^R L_{pathloss}^{feeder}\right)-1}{G_{LNA}}\right)L_{pathloss}L_j L_{LNA} L_f L_C}{G_o^T\left(\theta_o\right)\cdot G_o^R\left(\theta_o\right)} \tag{11.8}$$

Considering strict condition for $\min\left(P_o^{UE}, \min\left(P_{\max,ul}^{UE}, P_{o,target}^{UE}\right)\right) = P_o^{UE}, \forall r \leq R$:

■ The initial setting of the maximum power $P_{\max,ul}^{UE}$ parameter configuration on every cell coverage area $r \leq R$ (i.e., Ericsson's parameter *pMaxServingCell*) shall be such that $P_{\max,ul}^{UE} \leq P_o^{UE} \rightarrow \min\left(P_{\max,ul}^{UE}, P_{o,target}^{UE}\right) \leq P_o^{UE} \ \forall r \leq R$.

■ The simultaneous power control parameter configuration, combined with maximum geographical coverage R should be such that $P_{o,target}^{UE} < P_{\max,ul}^{UE} \leq P_o^{UE} \forall r \leq R \rightarrow \min\left(P_{\max,ul}^{UE}, P_{o,target}^{UE}\right) = P_{o,target}^{UE} \ \forall r \leq R \rightarrow \min\left(P_o^{UE}, \min\left(P_{\max,ul}^{UE}, P_{o,target}^{UE}\right)\right) = P_o^{UE} \ \forall r \leq R \rightarrow$ ensuring that the condition $P_{o,target}^{UE} \ \forall r \leq R$.

A good C-RAN proposal is to use a design margin $P_{marg} \approx 3$ dB, so that any noise and interference peaks will be overdimensioned and absorbed on its initial design. In such a case:

$$SE_{eNodeB} = \frac{\min\left(P_o^{UE}, \min\left(P_{\max,ul}^{UE}, P_{o,target}^{UE}\right)\right)G_o^T\left(\theta_o\right)\cdot G_o^R\left(\theta_o\right)}{L_{pathloss}L_j L_{LNA} L_f L_C}$$

$$\geq N_t \cdot RB_{BW} \cdot \left(N_f^{LNA} + \frac{\left(N_f^R L_{pathloss}^{feeder}\right)-1}{G_{LNA}}\right) + P_{marg}$$

$$\min\left(P_o^{UE}, \min\left(P_{\max,ul}^{UE}, P_{o,target}^{UE}\right)\right)$$

$$\geq \frac{\left[N_t \cdot RB_{BW} \cdot \left(N_f^{LNA} + \frac{\left(N_f^R L_{pathloss}^{feeder}\right)-1}{G_{LNA}}\right) + P_{marg}\right]L_{pathloss}L_j L_{LNA} L_f L_C}{G_o^T\left(\theta_o\right)\cdot G_o^R\left(\theta_o\right)} \Rightarrow$$

$$\text{Power Control decision } P_{o,\text{target}}^{UE} \geq \frac{\left[N_t \cdot RB_{BW} \cdot \left(N_f^{LNA} + \frac{\left(N_f^R L_{\text{pathloss}}^{\text{feeder}} \right) - 1}{G_{LNA}} \right) + P_{\text{marg}} \right] L_{\text{pathloss}} L_j L_{LNA} L_f L_C}{G_o^T \left(\theta_o \right) \cdot G_o^R \left(\theta_o \right)}$$

(11.9)

11.4.2 CPE Cell Selection: Camping Suitability Conditions

Cell selection in idle mode (camping) is also crucial for the C-RAN CPE outdoor unit [30], since wrong cell camping will lead to RRH/RRU sensitivity condition failure! The answer is to always follow the 3GPP specifications (i.e., 3GPP TS 36.304) [38] (Figure 11.6).

According to 3GPP TS 36.304, cell camping is validated following the following recommendation:

$$S_{rxlev} = Q_{rxlevmeas} - \left(Q_{rxlev\,min} + Q_{rxlev\,min\,offset} \right) - P_{\text{compensation}} > 0$$

(11.10)

where:

$Q_{rxlevmeas}$ is the real CPE outdoor unit measured downlink RRH transmitted power over the reference signal's RS (RSRP) signal strength measurement

$Q_{rxlev\,min}$ is a configurable cell parameter broadcasted over BCCH channel on the downlink

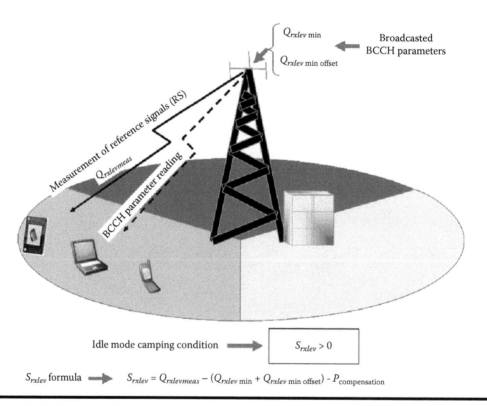

Figure 11.6   **Cell camping procedure.**

$Q_{rxlev\,min\,offset}$ is an offset configurable parameter for fine tuning purposes

$P_{compensation}$ is a power configurable parameter and according to 3GPP recommendations

$$P_{compensation} = \max\left(P_{EMAX} - P_{UMAX}, 0\right)$$

P_{EMAX} is based on 3GPP $P_{EMAX} = P_{max,ul}^{UE}$ and P_{UMAX} is, according to 3GPP, $P_{UMAX} = P_o^{UE}$

Substituting this into Equation 11.10, we could get the updated cell camping suitability condition:

$$S_{rxlev} = Q_{rxlevmeas} - \left(Q_{rxlev\,min} + Q_{rxlev\,min\,offset}\right) - \max\left(P_{max,ul}^{UE} - P_o^{UE}, 0\right) \tag{11.11}$$

Following nominal cell planning and considering the LTE-A outdoor unit cell selection to guarantee the Equation 11.9 sensitivity conditions, cell planners should always select camping parameters so that

■ In every geographical cell coverage area, the $r \leq R$ condition to be fulfilled is $\left(Q_{rxlev\,min} + Q_{rxlev\,min\,offset}\right) < S_{rxlev}\ \forall r \leq R$, so that always $S_{rxlev} > 0$.

■ In every geographical cell coverage area $r \leq R$ condition to be fulfilled is $P_{max,ul}^{UE} \leq P_o^{UE}\ \forall r \leq R$, so that always $\max\left(P_{max,ul}^{UE} - P_o^{UE}, 0\right) = 0\ \forall r \leq R\ \rightarrow\ S_{rxlev} > 0, \forall r \leq R$.

11.5 Cross-Layer Considerations

In this section, we will consider the MAC to physical cross-layer optimization with an emphasis on throughput. Integrity (throughput) is one of the major issues in a dense ad hoc sensor-based wireless networks due to its tumultuous data traffic nature. Especially in IoT networks relying on C-RAN architecture, a sensor's update and reporting functionality is randomly distributed with peaks and valleys in the traffic volume.

Following the analysis in [37], the mean transmission rate is $\langle R_{data}\rangle_{uplink} = \langle M_I\rangle / \langle T_{delay}\rangle$ and the expected mean throughput is

$$\langle T_{delay}\rangle = \frac{m_{mac}\langle M_I\rangle}{M \cdot n_{RB} \cdot r_{TTI}} T_s + \frac{M_{over}\left(\dfrac{\langle M_I\rangle}{M_{mac}} + 0.5\right)}{M \cdot n_{RB} \cdot r_{TTI}} T_s \tag{11.12}$$

$$+ \frac{\left(\dfrac{\langle M_I\rangle}{M_{mac}} + 1.5\right)M_{mac}}{M \cdot n_{RB} \cdot r_{TTI}} T_s + \langle n\rangle T_s$$

where:

$\langle M_I\rangle$ are the average IP sensor service packets for transmission

M_{mac} is the IEEE MAC transport block size created from the sensor MAC software and forwarded to the LTE-A indoor BBU for further processing

M_{over} is the overhead added when adding an IEEE sensor-based MAC transport block size into a 3GPP LTE MAC packet size on a CPE BBU

r_{TTI} is the number of 3GPP transport block size bits created from a CPE BBU, including the IEEE MAC transport block size bits with coding bits for the C-RAN LTE-A link quality channel (the size is selected from an enhanced link adaptation unit inside the 3GPP MAC software)

M is the number of spatial multiplexing if MIMO is used (a typical value for LTE-A is $M = 4$ or $M = 8$)

T_s is the subframe period of 1 ms duration

An important optimization parameter is the n_{RB} allocated number of PRBs from the C-RAN 3GPP MAC scheduler for the specific CPE outdoor unit and the RRH/RRU radio link quality [37,38]. The reader should always remember that the MAC scheduler and link adaptation software blocks are neither on the CPE outdoor unit nor on the CPE indoor unit nor on the distributed RRH/RRU units, but rather on the cloud blade servers.

The basic optimization question is how n_{RB} is estimated, or even better *how planners should reconsider the C-RAN planning to ensure the allocated max n_{RB} and consequently the expected throughput?* Future 5G C-RAN network link adaptation functionality as well as MAC scheduler functionality is not easy to study since they are never released to the public from system vendors. However, there are some simple but crucial steps and rules to be followed in order to ensure better performance and maximum capacity. Link adaptation functionality is subject to following restrictions/demands:

- *1st Demand*: The link adaptation unit manages to allocate a number of n_{RB} PRBs to the CPE-embedded BBU in order to fulfill the requested $\gamma_{RRH}^{uplink} = SINR_{target} = \gamma_{target}^{uplink}$ per sensor service. γ_{RRH}^{uplink} is the measured received signal-to-noise ratio and the demand of $\gamma_{target}^{uplink} = SE_{RRH}/N \cdot \beta_{I,RB}^{UL}$ is the requested minimum received signal-to-noise ratio so that error correction and error detection on the 3GPP HARQ MAC layer and ARQ RLC would be able to correct the corrupted packets.
- *2nd Demand*: The received uplink signal-to-noise ratio γ_{eNodeB}^{uplink} should *never* be less than γ_{target}^{uplink}. If that was the case then the CPE indoor/outdoor unit might be less than the expected!
- *3rd Demand*: The received uplink signal-to-noise ratio γ_{eNodeB}^{uplink} should *never* be more than γ_{target}^{uplink}. If that was the case then the CPE indoor/outdoor embedded unit might transmit larger MAC transport blocks and increase throughput. However, it will deprive the extra PRBs from other CPE customer units in the same cell coverage area, reducing substantially their potential throughput!

Residing on these restrictions and planning demands, optimizers shall be able to estimate the allocated n_{RB} PRBs. Consider the worst-case scenario of uplinking the maximum transmitted power $P_0^{UE} = P_{max,ul}^{UE}$ (with typical values $P_{max,ul}^{UE} = 20$ dB$_m$ και $P_0^{UE} \approx 23$ dB$_m$). Suppose that the allocated PRBs are n_{RB} and that the transmitted power per PRB is $P_{max,ul}^{UE}/n_{RB}$, then the expected uplink-received power per PRB over the distributed RRH/RRU would be

$$P_{R,RB}^{UL} = \frac{P_{max,ul}^{UE}/n_{RB} \; G_o^T(\theta_o) \cdot G_o^R(\theta_o)}{L_{pathloss}} = \frac{P_{max,ul}^{UE} G_o^T(\theta_o) \cdot G_o^R(\theta_o)}{n_{RB} \cdot L_{pathloss}}.$$

The expected uplink signal-to-noise ratio per RB is

$$\gamma_{RRH,RB}^{uplink} = \frac{P_{R,RB}^{UL}}{N + I_{RB,n}} = \frac{P_{max,ul}^{UE} G_o^T(\theta_o) \cdot G_o^R(\theta_o)}{n_{RB} \cdot L_{pathloss} \cdot N \cdot \beta_{I,RB}^{UL}} \tag{11.13}$$

Since the MAC scheduler always attempts to allocate the appropriate n_{RB} PRBs so that $\gamma_{RRH}^{uplink} = SINR_{target} = \gamma_{target}^{uplink}$, then

$$\gamma_{RRH,RB}^{uplink} = \gamma_{target}^{uplink} = \frac{\dfrac{P_{max,ul}^{UE} G_o^T(\theta_o) \cdot G_o^R(\theta_o)}{n_{RB} \cdot L_{pathloss}}}{N + I_{RB,n}} = \frac{P_{max,ul}^{UE} G_o^T(\theta_o) \cdot G_o^R(\theta_o)}{n_{RB} \cdot L_{pathloss} \cdot N \cdot \beta_{I,RB}^{UL}} \Rightarrow$$

$$\lceil n_{RB} \rceil = \frac{P_{max,ul}^{UE} \cdot G_o^R(\theta_o)}{\gamma_{target}^{uplink} \cdot L(R)_{pathloss} \cdot N \cdot \beta_{I,RB}^{UL}} \Bigg|_{R=R_{max}} \tag{11.14}$$

where γ_{target}^{uplink}, a physical layer factor depending on cell planning and network deployment, is always provided from vendor RRH/RRU equipment as a general recommendation of existing hardware sensitivity. Indeed, this is a cross-layer optimization problem for IoT throughput and traffic volume; optimizers should plan the C-RAN coverage adequately in order to maximize the received signal and minimize the interference against MAC scheduler decisions.

Considering Equation 11.12, parameter m_{mac} is the number of CPE uplinks to the C-RAN RRH/RRU unit's MAC layer retransmissions, which depends on the physical layer conditions for $\gamma_{RRH}^{uplink} = SINR_{RRH}^{uplink} \approx \gamma_{target}^{uplink} = SE_{RRH}/N \cdot \beta_{I,RB}^{UL} = f(BER_{RRH}^{uplink}) = f(p_b)$, estimated in [36] and [37] to be $m_{mac} \approx (\sum_{k=0}^{\infty}((M_{mac}+k-1)!/k!(M_{mac}-1)!)p_b^k) - 1 = M_{mac} \cdot p_b$, under the condition that $|p_b| \ll 1$.

C-RAN designers should always remember, however, that the necessary condition of $\gamma_{RRH}^{uplink} = \gamma_{target}^{uplink} = SE_{eNodeB}/N \cdot \beta_{I,RB}^{UL}$ might not always be easily fulfilled. From a network design perspective, failing to fulfill these conditions depends on [37]

- Cell coverage design $R = R_{max}$: Planners should always ensure that a CPE unit is not on the cell edge (R_{max}).
- Path loss: Always consider the sufficient cell camping conditions, that is $(Q_{rxlev\,min} + Q_{rxlev\,min\,offset}) < S_{rxlev} \cap P_{max,ul}^{UE} \le P_o^{UE}$, so that always $S_{rxlev} > 0 \,\forall r \le R$.
- The maximum CPE uplink transmitted power per PRB (with typical value 23 dBm). Planners should always ensure that the CPE outdoor unit is not too far away (path-loss scenario) so transmitted power $P_{RB}^{UE} = \min(P_o^{UE}, \min(P_{max,ul}^{UE}, P_{o,target}^{UE}))/n_{RB} = P_{max,ul}^{UE}/n_{RB}$ or $P_{o,target}^{UE}/n_{RB}$, as long as the restrictive design condition $P_{o,target}^{UE} < P_{max,ul}^{UE} \le P_o^{UE} \,\forall r \le R$ is valid to avoid uplink power saturation.

11.6 Conclusion

This chapter investigates the 5G C-RAN virtualized network's deployment, for IoT sensor traffic, based on 3GPP and 5G PPP standards and researching the related international literature. Uplink C-RAN design is always the most difficult link for planning and optimizing, affecting the IoT traffic volume and service performance. Especially for sensor networks, the expected uplink traffic is tumultuous with high-load peaks, and C-RAN designers have to consider many restrictions on RRH/RRU deployment over the network topology. This chapter investigates and studies the planning difficulties and restrictions related to interference, throughput, accessibility, and uplink connectivity, proposing solutions and rules to be followed. C-RAN planners should fulfil the proposed recommendations when optimizing 5G IoT network performance.

References

1. EU PROJECT METIS-II, 5G RAN architecture and functional design, White Paper, https://metis-ii.5g-ppp.eu/wp-content/uploads/5G-PPP-METIS-II-5G-RAN-Architecture-White-Paper.pdf.
2. EU PROJECT 5G NORMA, Functional network architecture and security requirements, https://5gnorma.5g-ppp.eu/wp-content/uploads/2016/11/5g_norma_d6-1.pdf.
3. NGMN Alliance, 5G White Paper, March 2015. https://www.ngmn.org/5g-white-paper.html.
4. C. Chen, J. Huang, W. Jueping, Y. Wu, and G. Li, Suggestions on potential solutions to C-RAN, NGMN Alliance project P-CRAN Centralized Processing Collaborative Radio Real Time Cloud Computing Clear RAN System, version 4.0, January 2013.
5. S. Louvros, and M. Paraskevas, LTE uplink delay constraints for smart grid applications, 19th IEEE International Workshop on Computer Aided Modeling and Design of Communication Links and Networks (CAMAD 2014), Special session on "Smart energy grid: theory, ICT technologies and novel business models," invited paper, Athens, 1–3 December, 2014.
6. Flex 5Gware Project: www.flex5gware.eu/.
7. 5GPPP use cases and performance evaluation models, version 1.0, http://www.5g-ppp.eu/.
8. 3GPP RP-152129, NGMN requirement metrics and deployment scenarios for 5G, December 2015.
9. 3GPP S2-153651, Study on architecture for next generation system, October 2015.
10. U. Dötsch, M. Doll, H-P. Mayer, F. Schaich, J. Segel, and P. Sehier, Quantitative analysis of split base station processing and determination of advantageous architectures for LTE, *Bell Labs Technical Journal*, Vol. 18, No. 1, pp.105–128, May 2013.
11. Ericsson Cloud RAN, https://www.ericsson.com/res/docs/whitepapers/wp-cloud-ran.pdf.
12. Cloud RAN: Reconstructing the radio network with cloud, web portal on www.huawei.com/en/news/2016/4/CloudRAN.
13. C-RAN & LTE Advanced: The road to "true 4G" & beyond, web page file: http://www.heavyreading.com/details.asp?sku_id=3090&skuitem_itemid=1517.
14. Ericsson unleashes gigabit LTE and creates hyperscale cloud RAN, https://www.ericsson.com/news/160204-ericsson-unleashes-gigabit-lte-and-creates-hyperscale-cloud-ran_244039856_c.
15. China Mobile Research Institute, C-RAN; The road towards green RAN, White Paper, version 2.5, October 2011.
16. A. Koubâa, M. Alves, M. Attia, and A. Van Nieuwenhuyse, Collision-free beacon scheduling mechanisms for IEEE 802.15.4/Zigbee cluster tree wireless sensor networks, *Proceedings of 7th International Workshop on Applications and Services in Wireless Networks (ASWN2007)*, Santander, Spain, May 2007, 1–16.
17. G. Smart, N. Deligiannis, R. Surace, V. Loscri, G. Fortino, and Y. Andreopoulos, Decentralized time-synchronized channel swapping for ad hoc wireless networks,, *IEEE Transactions on Vehicular Technology*, Vol. 65, No. 10, pp. 8538–8553, 2016.
18. A. Checko, H.L. Christiansen, Y. Yan, L. Scolari, G. Kardaras, M.S. Berger, and L. Dittmann, Cloud ran for mobile networks: A technology overview, *IEEE Communication Surveys & Tutorials*, Vol. 17, No. 1, pp.405–426, September 2014.
19. J. Rodriguez, *Fundamentals of 5G Mobile Networks*, 2015, Wiley.
20. RYSAVY Research, LTE and 5G innovation: Igniting mobile broadband, 4G Americas, file:///C:/Users/spyros/Desktop/4G_Americas_Rysavy_Research_LTE_and_5G_Innovation_white_paper.pdf, August 2015.
21. 3GPP TS 36.304 v8.6.0 Technical specification group radio access network, E-UTRA, user equipment (UE) procedures in idle mode.

22. 3GPP TS 36.101 0 technical specification group radio access network, E-UTRA, user equipment (UE) radio transmission and reception.
23. 3GPP TS 36.213 v8.8.0 technical specification group radio access network, E-UTRA, physical layer procedures.
24. S. Louvros, K. Aggelis, and A. Baltagiannis, LTE cell planning coverage algorithm optimising uplink user cell throughput, ConTEL 2011 11th International Conference on Telecommunications, IEEE sponsored (IEEE xplore data base), Graz, Austria, 15–17 June 2011.
25. S. Louvros, and M. Paraskevas, Analytical average throughput and delay estimations for LTE uplink cell edge users, *Journal of Computers and Electrical Engineering*, Elsevier, Vol. 40, No. 5, pp. 1552–1563, July 2014.
26. 3GPP, TR 36.819, Coordinated multi-point operation for LTE physical layer aspects.
27. Project CHARISMA: converged heterogeneous advanced 5G cloud-RAN architecture for intelligent and secure media access, ICT 2014: advanced 5G network infrastructure for the future Internet, http://www.charisma5g.eu/wp-content/uploads/2015/08/CHARISMA-D5.3-Standardisation-and-5GPPP-liaison-activities-Plan-v1.0.pdf
28. C. Kosta, B. Hunt, A. Ul Quddus, and R. Tafazolli, On interference avoidance through intercell interference coordination (ICIC) based on OFDMA mobile systems, *IEEE Communications Surveys and Tutorials*, Vol. 15, No. 3, December 2012.
29. J. Lee et al., Coordinated multipoint transmission and reception in LTE-advanced systems, *IEEE Communications Magazine*, Vol. 50, No. 11, November 2012, pp. 44–50.
30. S. Louvros, I. Kougias, K. Aggelis, and A. Baltagiannis, LTE planning optimization based on queueing modeling & network topology principles, *2010 International Conference on Topology and Its Applications, Topology and its Applications*. Vol. 159, No. 7, pp. 1655–2020, 2012.
31. S. Louvros, Topology dependant IP packet transmission delay on LTE networks, Anniversary *Proceedings of International Conference on Topology and Its Applications*, selected paper, Nafpaktos, 2015.
32. 3GPP Technical Report TR 36.942, E-UTRA radio frequency system scenaria.
33. Y. Sagae, Y. Ohwatari, and Y. Sano, Improved interference rejection and suppression technology in LTE release 11, *NTT DOCOMO Technical Journal*, Vol. 15, No. 2. pp. 27–30, 2013.
34. D.A. Wassie, G. Berardinelli, F.M.L. Tavares, O. Tonelli, T.B. Sorensen, and P. Mogensen, Experimental evaluation of interference rejection combining for 5G small cells, *IEEE Wireless Communications and Networking Conference* (WCNC), pp. 652–657, March 2015.
35. W. Nam, D. Bai, and J. Lee, Advanced interference management for 5G cellular networks, *IEEE Communications Magazine*, Vol. 52, No. 5, pp. 52–60, May 2014.
36. S. Louvros, and I.E. Kougias, Analysis of LTE multi-carrier signal transmission over wireless channels with operators on Heisenberg group H(R), *International Conference on Topology and Its Applications*, selected paper, Nafpaktos, 2015.
37. K. Aggelis, S. Louvros, A.C. Iossifides, A. Baltagiannis, and G. Economou, A semi-analytical macroscopic MAC layer model for LTE uplink, IEEE 5th International IFIP Conference on New Technologies, Mobility and Security, (NTMS 2012), Istanbul, Turkey, 7–10 May, 2012.
38. A. Al Masoud, G. Ashmakopoulos, S. Louvros, V. Triantafyllou, and A. Baltagiannis, Indoor LTE uplink cell planning considerations for symmetrical & unsymmetrical MIMO techniques, IEEE Wireless Telecommunications Symposium (WTS 2012), London, UK, 18–20 April, 2012.

Index